POLICE

THE CONSTITUTION AND THE COMMUNITY

*A collection of original essays
on issues raised by*
The Police and Criminal Evidence Act 1984

Edited by
JOHN BAXTER &
LAURENCE KOFFMAN

PROFESSIONAL BOOKS LIMITED
1985

Published in 1985 by
Professional Books Limited,
Milton Trading Estate, Abingdon, Oxon.
Text Preparation by SuperService, Ross-on-Wye.
Printed and bound by Biddles Limited, Guildford.

ISBN: 0 86205 105 3 Hardback
0 86205 106 1 Paperback

CONTENTS

Introduction   1

1   The Uniformed Mind   5
     Stephen Sedley

2   Safeguarding the Rights of the Citizen   11
     Laurence Koffman

3   Policing and the Rule of Law   38
     John Baxter

4   Policing Industrial Disputes   62
     Richard de Friend and Steve Uglow

5   "Bobbies", "Aliens" and Subversives: The Relationship   72
     between Community Policing and Coercive Policing
     Philip Rawlings

6   Stopping the People – Crime Control Versus Social Control   91
     Mike Brogden

7   Confession Evidence, the Police and Criminal Evidence Act   111
     and the Confait Case
     Christopher Price

8   The Police and Mental Health   118
     William Bingley

9   Policing Women   124
     Melissa Benn

10   The Police Act and the Probation Service   140
     Brian Campbell

11   Police and Race Relations   149
     Robert Reiner

12   Reasonable Force   188
     Michael Molyneux

13   Data Protection and Policing Technology   202
     Marie Staunton

14   The Police and Criminal Evidence Act and the Press   219
     John Williams

15   Crisis in Accountability   237
     Paul Boateng

16   Police Complaints Procedure: Why and For Whom?   246
     Barbara Cohen

Notes on Contributors   268

Index   270

Acknowledgements

The commissioning and editing of this set of original essays on modern policing was a genuinely collaborative process, which makes these acknowledgements much more than a mere formality. First, our thanks go naturally to all the contributors to this volume for their time, commitment and patience. We sincerely hope that each of them is pleased with the final, collective product.

The book was produced by the preparation of a camera-ready text, and for the extremely high quality of this, we wish to record our appreciation of the fine work done by Trudy West and Karen Powell of SuperService, Ross-on-Wye. We should also acknowledge their unfailing patience and kindness in advising us on technical details and for completing the work so promptly. In addition, our thanks go to Eileen Pryce and Christine Davies at Aberystwyth, not only for the preliminary typing of certain chapters, but also for the numerous letters which were necessary to put this project together. We also wish to express our gratitude to Professor John Andrews, Head of the Faculty of Law in which both editors work, for making resources available to us, without which the book would have been impossible. Furthermore we would like to acknowledge the advice and guidance given to us by Bill Hines of the Law Library at Aberystwyth.

We also wish to thank our publishers, Professional Books Ltd., for their confidence in us and their patience during the delays which were inevitable in producing a collection of this nature. In particular, we are grateful to Allison King for her enthusiasm and kindness in her handling of this project. Finally, it is with great pleasure that we place on record our thanks to our wives, Jane Baxter and Valerie Koffman, not only for their unceasing support, but also for their immense help with proof-reading, indexing and the general design of the book. The collaboration of all these people, and many others that we have not mentioned individually, have made this book both possible, and pleasurable to produce.

Introduction

In Britain there is no formal, written constitution to guarantee the rights of the citizen. We tend to take such matters on trust and pride ourselves on our liberal institutions and our temperate attitudes. This is particularly evident in the traditional relationship between the police and the public. We have attempted to strike a balance between effective police powers, for instance to investigate crime, to enter premises, to use reasonable force and to arrest suspects on the one hand, and the rights of the citizen to privacy and liberty on the other. But the recent legal and political developments in policing strategy have convinced many people, of quite diverse political viewpoints, that the balance has shifted significantly in favour of the police, authoritarianism and confrontation and away from mediation, tolerance and our more liberal traditions. The police are becoming, increasingly, politically motivated and manipulated, and they are in serious danger of losing the respect and support of the general public, without which they cannot operate effectively in dealing with crime. In recent times there has been an inexorable and alarming drift away from the concept of policing by consent of the public, towards a more coercive and belligerent style of policing.

Our criminal justice system is deceptive in appearance; outwardly it seems scrupulously fair with a rhetoric of citizens' rights and safeguards against unfair detention, interrogation and prosecution. Yet the reality is quite different. It was largely as a result of widespread disquiet about police misuse of investigative powers and the lack of safeguards for our citizens, especially the less privileged and articulate ones, that the Royal Commission on Criminal Procedure was established. Yet its specious recommendations were a triumph for the police over their civil libertarian critics. It supported an increase in coercive powers, countervailed by nothing more than token safeguards for accused persons. Thus the hectoring and scaremongering tactics of successive influential police chiefs, such as Sir Robert Mark and Sir David McNee, proved a resounding success. Their simplistic and quite misleading philosophy, that increased police powers represent more effective crime control, gained uncritical acceptance. Even worse, McNee openly admitted that the police already assumed the powers that they felt were necessary and he flaunted this unlawful behaviour in front of the timorous Royal Commissioners. His curious argument being that as extra powers were enjoyed de facto by the police, they should be formally bestowed upon them by statute to legitimise this behaviour. It is indicative of the prestige and power of the police that an admission of such unconstitutional and lawless behaviour should be accepted with equanimity in a liberal democratic society. It is ironic that any proposals for extending police accountability to elected authorities are countered by exaggerated claims of political interference with operational discretion and independence. Yet the police can openly and successfully admit to re-writing the law to suit their own requirements. In turn, the law has been formally re-written. The Police and Criminal Evidence Act 1984 has now officially provided a substantial increase in intrusive, confrontation-oriented powers and it is an indication of how our society is to be policed in the future. The new mode of policing is by coercion, and not by public consent.

If the debate about policing were merely concerned with differences of opinion about the type of powers required by the police to combat crime, it would be a relatively straightforward legal and operational issue. No one denies that the police perform a difficult and sometimes dangerous job, for which they need effective powers. Unfortunately, the problem is far more complex than the 'law and order' lobby would have us believe. The fight against criminals, 'muggers', 'hooligans' or any designated 'enemy within' is not a politically neutral issue. All law enforcement is discretionary and based on the priorities of the 43 police areas and the idiosyncrasies of their Chief Constables, who jealously guard their 'operational discretion' against any democratic accountability. This is a fundamentally important point. Investigative powers are not used by the police in an unbiased, neutral or even-handed way. On the contrary, their use reflects crude stereotyping and unchallengeable priorities given spurious respectability by the very statistics that are compiled from such policing policies. Thus the increased use of stop and search powers, granted under the new legislation, will accentuate an existing pattern of use of such provisions against ethnic minorities, the young and less privileged members of society in inner city areas. The alarming lessons of Brixton, Toxteth and Moss Side which so recently illustrated the corollary of such practices, have been foolishly ignored.

It is not being suggested that policing strategy is responsible for the deep divisions in our society, but that it is exacerbating the problem. In a recent impartial, independent report by the Policy Studies Institute, the Metropolitan Police were found guilty of overtly racist attitudes. Moreover, after the Brixton riots, the police response to the Scarman Report's strictures was to publish statistics which give a breakdown of crime, selectively and sensationally, on the basis of race. The simplistic and misleading equation of blacks with crime has been firmly embedded in the public's consciousness to serve as a justification for increased powers and renewed aggression by the police.

So far we have considered the policing of 'traditional' types of crime, but there is a much more sinister recent development; namely the deployment of the police as a political weapon by an unscrupulous Government. To facilitate this marriage of convenience, the new Tory Government in 1979 seduced the police by granting them immediate and generous pay increases. In contrast to its parsimony elsewhere, the Government has continued to view 'law and order' as a growth area; this was a clear indication of its long term strategy. The police were to play an important role in this plan, for both practical and symbolic reasons. Practically, they were necessary, for instance in emasculating picketing as an industrial weapon and mass demonstrations as a means of peaceful political protest. Indeed, the whole area of public order is now to be the subject of even more politically motivated increases in police powers. Symbolically, the use of the police in this way is most disingenuous by the Government. Police involvement can lend a misleading legality and neutrality to such policies. The Government is capitalising on the traditional image of a politically unbiassed police service enforcing the law in an even-handed manner. Critics of the police, and of their enlarged powers and duties, can now be conveniently characterised as subversive, anti-law and order or the 'enemy within' our society.

But this cunningly conceived strategy must not obscure the simple fact that those who serve in Britain's police force are now being asked to intervene in problems of a directly political nature. Even the traditional policing of our city streets is partly an exercise in dealing with disturbing levels of unemployment, especially amongst young, black and poor communities. The police are being asked to harass and disrupt peaceful protests such as those organised against the presence of American nuclear weapons in Britain. Policing methods are becoming increasingly violent in handling political demonstrations whether they be Greenham Common women, protesting students or picketing miners. The police use of wedge formations, horses, charges, 'snatch' arrests and Police Support Units are now becoming commonplace. This 'conflict-model' of policing is heavily based on experience acquired in the policing of disturbances in Northern Ireland, despite the inappropriateness of this strategy in mainland Britain. How long will it be before the callous and brutal use of the plastic bullet is witnessed in one of our cities?

Of course the major example of this distressing trend is the policing of the miners' strike in 1984-5. There is good reason to suspect that the use of the police to neutralise the most potent weapon of the miners, namely the mass picket, was planned well in advance by the Government like a military operation. It might pertinently be asked how such a strategy was possible given the supposed independence of the police. But operational independence at a local level was conveniently overlooked when, through the National Reporting Centre, the police were deployed as a type of political army against the striking miners; and the small element of democratic accountability of the police which existed prior to the dispute, was soon whittled away as the strike continued. Police forces were despatched from one area to another without the consent of local police authorities. Chief Constables were able to commit unlimited sums of ratepayers' money to such strategies. The whole operation was centrally co-ordinated by a non-accountable, unelected head of the National Reporting Centre. The criminal law was extended by the police as they went along, as individual liberties were eroded without any legal authority. Even where the police were invoking the law, often it was done in a partial, petty and vindictive manner. In all, there were nearly ten and a half thousand criminal charges relating to the miners' strike, covering a range of well over thirty types of offence. This was enough to tax the ingenuity of even the most competent and inventive criminal lawyer. In short, the handling of this bitter and unfortunate political dispute serves as a serious warning about the direction of modern policing. The British police were shown to be moving rapidly towards a non-accountable, but national force, capable of unilaterally extending its lawful powers and using its legitimate powers for overtly political ends.

Thus the traditional nature of policing in our society is undergoing considerable, even fundamental change. These developments represent nothing less than a constitutional crisis. Unfortunately, British people are unaccustomed to the use of the word 'Constitution' and, traditionally, this has inhibited the discussion of the subject in these terms. Yet questions about police accountability to the local electorate, the relationship between the police and the executive, the nature of the law making process, the complaints procedure against the police, the adequacy of safeguards to protect individual liberty and privacy, the interpretation of the 'Rule of Law' and the relationship between the police and the community in general, and minority groups in particular - are all properly described as constitutional issues of utmost significance.

Drawing on expertise from a variety of fields, this collection of essays seeks to examine these issues in detail and to acknowledge their true importance. There is no uniformity of approach taken by the different essayists, but what unites most of them is a broadly critical view of contemporary developments in policing strategy and in the laws relating to police powers. The book does of course deal with important political issues, but this should come as no surprise, since the day that liberty ceases to be a political question will truly mark the arrival of a totalitarian age.

1. THE UNIFORMED MIND

Stephen Sedley

It was indeed significant that the name of last year's symposium of the Association of Chief Police Officers and the local authorities was "Society's role in relation to law and order." As 1984 ran its symbolic course, it contained more and more poignant examples of the shift of authoritarianism from strident assertion to comfortable assumption. Today, chief constables no longer demand that we should get our priorities right: five years of radical right-wing government have got them right, and the task for those who handle power is now to get society to behave accordingly - in particular to recognise its responsibilities towards law and order.

What is turning out to characterise current thinking, although in form a far cry from Orwell's vision, is in content a series of long and determined steps along the road to a similar society. The shifts we witness almost daily in language and expression are a kind of inverted Newspeak: not the regulation of words to control reality - at least not yet - but the reflection in words of the control that is being asserted. Sir Keith Joseph's contribution to the Prime Minister's Family Policy Group, leaked amid a press furore and then quickly forgotten, was able to adopt as its premise the existence of large numbers of "irresponsible" parents, and to proceed quickly and comfortably to a consideration of the equally simple expedient of cutting off their supply of children at source. Such language is neither ill-considered nor shorthand. It is part of a political vocabulary in which words like "deprivation" and "disadvantage" are obsolescent and words like "responsibility" and "self-reliance" are in vogue.

Like every language, the Newspeak of Thatcherism has its basis in hard reality. The reality for the beneficiaries of Sir Keith Joseph's plans is a government which is systematically augmenting the economic and social causes of deprivation and penalising its victims. You cannot inflict penalties without first attributing blame - hence the need to translate "disadvantaged" into "irresponsible" before passing sentence.

The sentence for social failure is often nowadays a severe one. What is more, it is part of a long-term change in social policy which predates the Thatcher government and should give pause to those who too readily credit individuals or cliques with the power to make history. For more than a decade a lattice of social work training, policy changes, bureaucratic intervention, legislative provisions and judicial decisions has grown in breadth and intricacy to all but envelop child care. The desperate middle-class parent can generally turn to relations, friends or the au-pair when the children get too much and life seems to be falling apart; and if shortage of money is contributing to the crisis, family, friends and bank managers may help with what is often a short-term problem. The jobless working-class parent, often single, trapped in hardship, trying to live on benefit in a rent-rebated council flat, perhaps in the local authority's punishment block for arrears or upsetting neighbours, is the one who is finally going to phone social services and threaten to kill the children because it's all got too much. There is the first proof of inadequacy - the failure of self-reliance, and there too is the call for intervention - the children are at risk. By definition the clients of social services departments may be said in inverse Newspeak to be inadequate and irresponsible: if they were not, they would not be demanding help from the state.

Who can say exactly why these clients, instead of receiving the well-meaning companionship, advice and subventions of an earlier generation of social workers, now have to confess their inadequacy as the price of help and still as often as not have their children taken away for adoption? The social administrator is conscious of the lack of any funds or back-up for direct assistance; the social worker is conscious of the constant fear of another Maria Colwell case; the social administration teacher is conscious that kinship is an atavistic idea not readily compatible with social management; the politician is conscious that eugenics cannot yet safely be preached but may relatively safely be practised on the non-vocal undeserving. The legal powers designed to "protect" children provide them all with the machinery of social control. The parent is offered a rest from the children for a couple of weeks, and they are placed with a foster-family who are assured that they will be able to adopt if they later want to. From then on a cynical game is played. Sometimes the errant parent gets the children back; but as often the parent is prised away from the child, using a place of safety order as the lever, cutting down access until advice is given to mourn the child and forget it; and the process is completed by adoption by a family which not only desperately wants the child but conforms with carefully monitored canons of respectability. No need for institutions, no need for endless visits to the feckless parent, no risk of criticism from those with politically audible voices: another irresponsible parent has been removed from office, another child may grow up to be an insurance salesman instead of a burglar.

Who has willed it? Who has argued and decided that this is the right way to do things? If it is a conspiracy, it is as much one of circumstances as of individuals. It is one of the more marked examples of a widespread and long-term drift in British society.

It appears to be a constant factor in governed societies that authority has an appetite which grows with what it feeds on. Its potential power is enormous because it has the resources to persuade people that submission to its dictates is in their best interests. Formally in Britain the ring is held by a system of parliamentary democracy by which the people can be said to govern their governers. In reality authority strives and commonly manages to recreate itself constantly in its own image. Both the Police and Criminal Evidence Act 1984 and the point of our history at which it has reached the statute book may illustrate and amplify my propositions.

The Act is not a measure which is either going to improve the quality of policing or ensure a greater measure of justice in the courts. It is a step on the road to a police state, not in the propagandist sense that it is increasing police powers but in the constitutional sense that it is vesting in the police powers over which there is no political or judicial control.

Not for the first time, the measure has found itself anticipated by judicial legislation. During the Bill's passage the Judicial Committee of the House of Lords decided in effect that the power of arrest was sufficiently elastic to make an arrest lawful if its object was to induce the suspect to confess. (1) The decision is not only another judicial assault on the right of silence (though one which fades to near-insignificance beside the new statutory powers of prolonged detention): it adopts a form of reasoning which has become a prevalent aspect of judicial double standards, relating to the concept of what is "reasonable".

6

Students used until relatively recently to be taught that what is reasonable is a question for the courts. So for example a contractual provision in restraint of trade would be struck down if on the evidence the court considered it unreasonable. (2) A public policy interest was perceived, as it still is, in the elimination of barriers to free competition, even if doing so meant interfering with contracts supposedly freely entered into. The growth of administrative law in the present century has however introduced a new and artificial concept of what is "reasonable", designed to give proper scope to administrative discretions while retaining full judicial control at the boundaries. In this special sense "reasonable" means not what the adjudicating body thinks reasonable but anything which is not so capricious or contrary to the statutory purpose that no reasonable body or person could arrive at it. (3) In the context of statutory discretions and local democracy it makes sense, but in recent years it has been uprooted from its natural habitat and planted in alien soil where, like a weed, it has started to flourish. In 1976 the Employment Appeal Tribunal began to sabotage the ability of industrial tribunals, which had till then been aptly regarded as "industrial special juries", to decide that a dismissal which in their view was unreasonable was therefore unfair. It became instead the doctrine that only where an employer had acted as no reasonable employer could possibly do might an industrial tribunal intervene. (4) The following year a provision in the Education Act 1944 which had always, and rightly, been supposed to allow the Secretary of State to overturn a local authority decision which he thought unreasonable was held likewise to limit intervention to cases where he could properly consider the local decision to be positively perverse. (5) Since then we have seen the courts abdicate the control of confidentiality in child care cases to the discretion of local councillors, (6) and the criteria of lawful arrest to the discretion of individual police officers.

If this were part of a long-term trend towards decentralisation of decision-making and delegation of responsibility away from the bureaucratic centre it might deserve a cautious welcome. But there are few signs that it is. With the unhappy propensity the bench often has for increasing the suspicions of its critics, the cases in which it has decided on a hands-off policy have turned out to assist employers to the detriment of employees, to assist a local authority resisting the introduction of comprehensive education, to encourage councillors who want to use child care as a means of social control – and now to give an open cheque to the police at the expense of individual freedom.

By contrast the situations in which the law is increasingly asserting judicial control and intervention are legion. The decision that teachers at a Polytechnic can be ordered to identify their students in litigation in which the teachers themselves are uninvolved, and face penal consequences for non-compliance, (7) is one recent example of judicial interventionism, lying interestingly parallel to the new statutory provision enabling the premises of innocent third parties to be searched by the police. Both provisions come in the wake of the development in the last decade of a novel and draconic jurisdiction of the courts to sit in secret and grant an order allowing a plaintiff who complains of an interference with his copyright or trade secrets to raid an unwitting defendant for evidence. (8) The civil courts have not felt the need to wait on Parliament for licence to act: by the most tenuous appeals to precedent they have found their excuses for using the law in defence of property and to restrict personal liberty and have devised their own powers to do so.

I would argue therefore that the illiberal statute sired by the Home Office out of the Royal Commission is not simply a triumph for bureaucracy nor simply a tyrannical excursion by a right-wing government. It represents the highest point so far of a form of social policy which, in many of its essentials, transcends both the life-span and the policies of the Thatcher government. What that government has contributed to the drift of policy is articulacy and acceleration. In particular it has created the conditions in which it no longer has to pretend that it is liberalising the law. It is able openly to counterpose threats to law and order to the protective role of the police who stand today not between the god-fearing citizen and the crook (even assuming that they once did) but between the privileged and the undeserving, the home-owner and the scrounger, the white and the black, the employer and the striker.

Will it work? There is in middle England a resigned willingness to assume that the government knows best, to give it a try. After all, there is still a serious problem of violent and fraudulent crime, and the well-off are by no means the main sufferers from it. Might it not work to give the police the extra powers they want to catch criminals?

The first answer is that the extra powers the police are getting do not represent the wherewithal for better policing but for more of the same policing as before. In the hands of metropolitan police forces who regard the determination of guilt as their function and the courts as an impediment to it, an increase in the power of officers to detain, interrogate and search is simply an increase in the armoury of instruments of oppression. It is almost inevitable that for every extra conviction of a guilty individual the augmented powers will bring about convictions of innocent people.

Behind this lies a fallacy which has been propounded with increasing frequency since the period when Sir Robert Mark first abandoned the image of the police as mere mechanics servicing laws made by others and turned them into a vocal, political lobby claiming special interests and special consideration. It is that policing is a specialised function whose needs and limits its own senior officers are best equipped to determine. Constitutionally no government should have any trouble in resisting and rebutting such a claim. The problem comes when a government takes office which has no wish to resist or rebut it because the ideology of policing, now consistent, articulated and respectable, dovetails so accurately with its own.

This, I believe, is the pass we are now at in this country: we are witnessing the growth of its police forces into a separate limb of the state. Their chief officers form a tight, homogeneous and powerful association, collectively accountable to nobody, while individually their accountability is so tenuous as to be almost insignificant. Executive government has watched the process with complacency and occasional encouragement; political government has wanted either the wit to see what was happening or the will to stop it. The current upshot is the writing of a series of blank cheques in favour of the police by both Parliament and the judges - but the long-term implications are much graver. A society in which the police are able to determine citizens' rights, whether by legislative prescription or by the creation of legal free-fire zones, is not a democracy but a police state.

The second answer is that experience gives little ground for hope that once the appetite for greater powers has been appeased the job of detection and prevention will be done and the demands will cease. It should not be forgotten how Sir David McNee presented his demands to the Royal Commission: his officers, he said, were so constricted by the law as it stood that they were constantly having to break it in order to do their job. The media silence which greeted this admission - no, assertion - of lawlessness was deafening. McNee got his way: the bounds of lawful police conduct have been increased to encompass existing practices hitherto beyond the pale of the law. Will police practice now halt at its new frontiers? Why should it?

Our police forces are in the forefront of the exercise of social control in a society which is being increasingly polarised into fundamentally divergent interests. What is more, the police are not neutral in the conflicts: to acknowledge and protect property, authority, respectability is to suspect and condemn their perceived opponents, the dispossessed, the dissident, the undeserving. And the uniformed mind is not only pointed by law and training in that direction: it tends frequently to be a mind for which authority has its own special attraction, to which the helmet and the truncheon have a particular appeal. The probability is that every ordered society has this problem, but the fearsome thing is that ours is joining the ranks of those which do not regard it as a problem.

So, for example, the enormous conundrums posed for personal liberty by modern techniques of data collection and transmission are relegated to crank concerns. If you have nothing to hide, why should you have anything to fear? And if you have something to hide, don't the authorities have to be able to find out about it? Many of the arguments which are now deployed in favour of larger state powers of interrogation and surveillance would do equally good service in favour of the reintroduction of torture.

With a legal system which is itself instrumental in according more draconic powers to the police, another coming casualty is the administration of justice. We have seen in Northern Ireland how the process unfolds from the abandonment of jury trial to the trade in purchased and perjured Crown evidence. A civilised legal system cannot afford to fight fire with fire: in the attempt it will destroy the very system of justice it is setting out to defend. It is not irrelevant that one of the main sources of pressure for the abandonment or restriction of jury trials in mainland Britain is the police. Like Diplock in Northern Ireland they argue that the acquittal of criminals is not a price worth paying for the protection of the innocent, because once police thinking has been allowed to substitute its own judgment for that of the courts there is no such thing as an innocent accused. This is the very stuff of authoritarianism. It is one thing for it to be voiced privately or publicly by an interest group: it is another for it to become, as it has, the conventional wisdom of government.

To this jeremiad a balance is needed. We still have juries in mainland Britain; we can still vote for some at least of those who govern us; the people whose patriotism does not take the form of exporting capital in pursuit of percentages have traditions of unsinkability and occasional surprising resistance. It is too early to make a reliable prognosis, but the diagnosis is that the body politic has a progressive disease: prescriptions for its cure differ, and none of them will work without the patient's awareness and co-operation. At the worst it could prove fatal.

9

NOTES

1. Holgate-Mohammed v Duke [1984] A.C. 437.

2. See for example the authorities cited in Halsbury Laws of England (4th ed.) vol. 47, para. 21, no.2., from the year 1711 onwards.

3. Associated Provincial Picture Houses Ltd. v Wednesbury Corporation 1948 1 K.B. 223; Padfield v Minister of Agriculture [1968] A.C. 997.

4. Vickers Ltd v Smith [1977] I.R.L.R. 11.

5. R v Secretary of State for Education, ex parte Tameside M.B.C. [1977] A.C. 1014.

6. R v Birmingham City Council, ex parte O [1983] 1 A.C. 578.

7. Harrington v North London Polytechnic [1984] 1 W.L.R. 1293.

8. Anton Piller KG v Manufacturing Processes Ltd. [1976] Ch. 55.

2. SAFEGUARDING THE RIGHTS OF THE CITIZEN

Laurence Koffman

Introduction

It is time that the rights of citizens under our legal system were taken seriously. Our system has a considerable facade with its impressive list of theoretical "rights" for accused persons, but these "rights" are contravened as a matter of routine amid great cynicism by the police and this is accomplished with the connivance of the judiciary. It was recently stated by the highest court in the land that "it is no part of a judge's function to exercise disciplinary powers over the police or prosecution as respects the way in which evidence to be used at the trial is obtained by them." (1) It has recently been revealed that court administrators can even manipulate their rotas so as to ensure "tough" judges will hear certain cases. (2) It is remarkable that a leading group of lawyers could have expressed the opinion that in our system "fairness seems often to be thought of as something which is due to the defence only." (3) This is clearly misconceived, for what is conspicuous about our criminal justice process is its lack of practical safeguards for ensuring fairness to accused persons. This is exacerbated by the pretence that the suspect has many rights and that our system is scrupulously fair, or even too lenient. For those who study the actual workings of the criminal justice system, this is entirely specious. There is a world of difference between legal theory and police practice vis-à-vis the right of silence, access to a solicitor, rights against unlawful arrest, detention and search, and methods of interrogation. In practice, the police exceed their theoretical powers especially in relation to certain 'target' groups, lawyers are not accessible to most defendants, and the very process and atmosphere of interrogations at the police station is inimical to voluntary or reliable evidence being obtained. As Doreen McBarnet has aptly stated:

> "A wide range of prosecution evidence can be legally produced and presented, despite the rhetoric of a system geared overwhelmingly to safeguards for the accused, precisely because legal structure, legal procedure, legal rulings, not legal rhetoric, govern the legitimate practice of criminal justice, and there is quite simply a distinct gap between the substance and the ideology of the law." (4)

There are innumerable examples of this dichotomy between the theory and practice of criminal procedure and these have been well documented. It is stated, for instance (formerly in the Judges' Rules), that every person, even if in custody, is entitled to consult privately with a solicitor at any stage of an investigation. (5) This is subject inevitably to the wide exceptions that such consultation will not be permitted if it causes an unreasonable delay to the investigation or hinders the administration of justice. From the research of Baldwin and McConville and also that of Zander (6) it appears that of those suspects who ask to see a solicitor, about three-quarters of them are refused. What is more telling is that only a minority of accused persons actually ask to see a solicitor. The Royal Commission on Criminal Procedure wondered, with characteristic naivety, "why so few suspects make such a request." (7) The answer is not so hard

11

to discern. From their position of vulnerability they appreciate a reality of which a body of commissioners, or academic writers, are blissfully unaware - namely that their request to see a solicitor is generally a waste of time, as it would meet with a refusal.

A further example relates to the police interrogation of suspects. The law, according to ex-Commissioner of the Metropolitan Police, Sir David McNee, "gives virtually no assistance to police and every assistance to a suspect wishing to hide his guilt." (8) This is the theory of the law. It is therefore surprising that in practice the police place so much reliance on evidence obtained from interrogation. (9) Also, it is clear that the accused is subject to psychological coercion and pressure from which the law provides little genuine protection. In a recent study by Barry Mitchell, based on a random sample of cases heard at Worcester Crown Court, his findings emphasised the cause for disquiet about both the frequency of confessions and their reliability. (10) In over ninety per cent of the cases he looked at, there was no-one other than the suspect and the police present at the interview. Moreover, some defendants were eventually acquitted by the jury despite the "confessions" they had made, thus underlining the need for close scrutiny of the reliability of admissions of guilt. The researcher concludes:

> "There is considerable evidence to suggest that cautioning suspects has very little effect in reality. If suspects are to be given real protection against possible police malpractice and psychological pressures then they must be given legal rights. This can only be achieved if there is some way of providing independent monitoring of the interrogation. Formal police questioning is virtually inevitable, and only a small proportion of defendants enter the court room without having made a confession or damaging statement. There is now ample research evidence to raise doubts as to the reliability of some of these statements...." (11)

The purpose of this chapter is to evaluate the proposals that were made by the Royal Commission, and the recent legislation, for strengthening the safeguards for accused persons. One of the major reasons for setting up the Commission was that there was widespread concern about police officers ignoring the rules when investigating crime and interviewing suspects. Yet despite this fact, investigative powers have been substantially increased. Assurances have been given frequently by the Government, during the passage of the Police and Criminal Evidence Act 1984, that such new powers are balanced by a strengthening of safeguards for the citizen's civil liberties. We must assess the extent to which this has been achieved. First, however, it is instructive to consider the process of law reform in relation to criminal justice.

The Law Reform Process

From the arguments adduced so far it is clear that the chasm between legal rhetoric and legal practice is vast. Logically the arguments of reformers and civil libertarians (often mistakenly dismissed as "the Left", as if this in some way explains their critical stance) would appear difficult to resist. Yet for some enigmatic reason, well documented evidence, research and carefully reasoned arguments are not sufficient; it often requires 'causes célèbres' to capture the imagination of both practitioners and the general public. It is normally unwise to generalise from isolated, dramatic examples but it cannot be denied that they rally support in a most effective way. Thus the campaign for reform of criminal investigation and prosecution gathered momentum due to a spectacular miscarriage of justice in the notorious Confait case. This case, quirkishly referred to by the name of its original victim, posed searching questions about the interrogation of suspects (especially subnormal or young persons); the misuse of forensic evidence; the making of confessions in breach of the Judges' Rules; the organisation of the prosecution process; and the very nature of our constitutional law. (12)

The facts of the case, and the chain of events it unleashed, have been dealt with admirably in this volume by Christopher Price -- to whom much credit is due for securing a just conclusion to the case. There is no need to recapitulate the facts. What is important is the doubt it cast on the fairness of our criminal justice process. What confidence, if any, could we have that it was simply an isolated and unfortunate mistake? There is a tendency to dismiss cases like Confait as a rare departure from the normally high standards of British justice. Yet there is a persistent fear that discovery of the injustice was entirely fortuitous and not due to any inherent safeguards in our criminal justice system. Indeed, there are those, such as Doreen McBarnet, who contend that such miscarriages of justice arise almost inexorably as a result of a deficient process:

> "In short, conviction based on an inaccurate version of events was not an accident or freak occurrence but exactly what was aimed at in a system based on adversary investigation and advocacy. The Confait case is a telling indictment not just of individuals but of the legal system." (13)

Or, in the words of Baldwin and McConville:

> "The extraordinary feature of the Confait case was not that it happened at all but that so much of what was done came to light. It is simply a well-documented illustration of a process that overlooks, and even legitimises, misconstruction, one-sided investigation and partisan selectivity." (14)

These are fundamental and challenging criticisms of our adversary system of criminal justice and are not concerned simply with piecemeal reform. They are saying, quite simply, "never mind the minutiae of such cases, we have the basic principles wrong". Unfortunately, law reform bodies, such as the Royal Commission on Criminal Procedure, opt out of such discussion and start from the comfortable premiss that no fundamental reform of our process is to be seriously entertained. (15)

Another important feature of the Confait case was the contrast it provided to the work of the Criminal Law Revision Committee in its 11th Report, which dealt with problems of evidence. This group of eminent lawyers and judges attacked the accused's 'right of silence' and recommended that adverse inferences should, in certain circumstances, be drawn from a person's silence. Thus, whilst not constituting evidence of guilt, it would be held against a defendant. The Committee wished "to go as far in getting rid of restrictions on admissibility of evidence as is possible in the modern conditions." (16) The background to this report was the supposed problem of dealing with sophisticated and professional criminals

13

who exploited unduly lenient rules of evidence and procedure in their effort to avoid conviction. The Confait case amply demonstrated a quite different problem. Namely that inarticulate, young and inexperienced people have insufficient protection from oppressive questioning and detention; and far from relying on a 'right of silence', will even make incorrect and damaging statements about their involvement in crimes. Another vivid example of this was provided more recently by the case of Errol Madden, a 17 year old black student, who was arrested on his way home from the cinema one night, suspected of theft. After lengthy interrogation, he signed a statement admitting the theft of two model toys found in his possession. In fact, Madden had bought the toys himself and possessed a receipt! Once again, the case reveals the vulnerability of the suspect in the custody of the police, and also the undue reliance of the police on interrogation at the expense of other investigative methods.

Thus two quite distinct approaches to the law reform process are discernible. On the one hand there is the civil libertarian approach and on the other is the 'law and order' lobby, which points to the theory of the law and its supposed safeguards for the accused and which supports, inter alia, an increase in police powers of arrest, stop and search, detention and seizure of evidence. This lobby is spearheaded by the police themselves through groups such as the Association of Chief Police Oficers, the Police Federation, the Superintendents' Association and the political statements of successive Commissioners of the Metropolitan Police. (17) It has effective access to the media, as the "fight against crime" (or blatant scaremongering) always makes good copy for newspaper editors. The B.B.C., which can sometimes be so sensitive about who is permitted to deliver the Dimbleby lecture, allowed Sir Robert Mark in 1973 to make an outspoken and provocative attack on the people and procedures which, in his opinion, hampered the police in their work. According to Mark, the police are forced to operate in a framework of rules which "give every advantage to the defence" and he argued that they were outmoded when applied to "the trial of experienced criminals, using skilled legal assistance." (18)

Thus it was a major tenet of the 'law and order' lobby's philosophy (or at least its propaganda) that criminal procedure was largely concerned with hardened and professional criminals. This, of course, is a totally unwarranted assumption. Another cornerstone of their arguments was the notion that the police's viewpoint necessarily represents the "best interests of society"; that is, that they have no vested, professional interest in such reforms, but they claim extra powers merely as the mouthpiece of the general public. In so far as this relationship is ever alluded to by leading police officials, they are not reticent in backing up their assumptions with veiled threats. In his evidence to the Royal Commission on Criminal Procedure, Sir David McNee prefaced his claims for a substantial extension of police powers by stating:

> "It is, of course, a matter for society at large to determine what kind of police service it wants and what reasonable constraints must be placed, in the interests of civil liberty, on police action, but at the same time society must recognise that Utopian measures introduced to ensure excessive protection of the individual citizen lessen the chances of criminals being caught and convicted, which increases the risk of further rises in crime....we must always seek to ensure that the scales of justice are correctly balanced. If

not, other fundamental rights such as the right to live peacably (sic) in the security of one's house and the right to go about one's business un-molested, may be seriously threatened." (19)

Yet there is no empirical evidence to indicate that an increase in police coercive powers leads to a more effective control of crime. Indeed, certain powers such as extensive use of stop and search on 'reasonable suspicion', (which is often anything but 'reasonable'), can be criminogenic. Even though the search may be unwarranted it can lead to charges of assault or obstruction. But the most telling criticism of such powers is that they alienate the police still further from the community they are policing. This style of coercive policing leads to harassment of certain 'target' groups and sections of society; the less privileged, young males in inner-city areas, and especially coloured youths. The professional or experienced criminal, the cause of so much concern to the Criminal Law Revision Committee and Sir Robert Mark, is unaffected by such powers. In the wake of civil disorders like those of Brixton, Toxteth, and Moss Side, it is both inept and myopic to be introducing provisions under the Police and Criminal Evidence Act that will increase the likelihood of a recurrence of such trouble. The police need the co-operation of the public to perform their difficult tasks effectively and further coercive powers are a hindrance to gaining public support. (20)

In view of the much publicised miscarriages of justice already referred to, and the powerful arguments to support the civil libertarian critics of our criminal justice process, it is surprising that the new law substantially increases police powers. This is largely because there is no effective political support for the civil libertarian perspective. Many of the politicians who sympathise privately realise that it is not a popular 'vote-catcher'. The general public, fed on a remorseless diet of sensationalised accounts of the growing rate of violence, "mugging" and burglaries, expects to hear more belligerent noises from ambitious politicians. (21) Quite simply there are far more votes to be won by 'law and order' policies than by support for civil liberties. The latter can thus be comfortably dismissed as the rantings of extremists and intellectuals, despite the fact that such matters vitally concern the lives of everyone, and dictate the type of society in which we live. Unfortunately, even more enlightened governments than the present one have a depressing record in relation to the protection of civil liberties.

The Labour Government of the day was in error in setting up a Royal Commission on Criminal Procedure, which it probably did to stall for time after the critical findings of the Fisher Report. The Commission, under the chairmanship of Sir Cyril Philips, reported in January 1981 and its findings immediately caused controversy. There can be little doubt that the Report dealt a shattering blow to the hopes of civil libertarians, in giving the police and the 'law and order' lobby more than even they could have hoped for. In turn, the recent Police and Criminal Evidence Act has further extended the coercive powers of the police from those recommended by the Royal Commission, and some of the tenuous safeguards that were originally proposed have been omitted. (22)

How is it that the Royal Commission, whose composition was at least superficially fair, can have been so wide of the mark in its recommendations? Two major reasons spring to mind. First, the powerful police lobby has become increasingly articulate and belligerent in its demands, which have received wide publicity, of which the commissioners were well aware. The evidence of Sir David McNee to the Philips

Commission "dominated the public perception of the choices it faced". (23) It matters not that the police, to mask their insecurity at the probing of the Royal Commission, were employing something of a bluff and overstating their claims. This 'sabre-rattling' exercise was enough to unbalance a timorous body of commissioners. For resisting any of the police's demands, the Commission earned considerable praise from certain credulous writers.(24) The second major reason for the disappointing performance of the Royal Commission was its mistaking of theoretical or 'paper' safeguards for the citizen for viable, practical protection. As one critic stated, "its research was good, its logic sound, and its organisational reforms welcome. But what it lacked, both in its membership and in its proposals, was a sense of street-wisdom, and a practical appreciation of how copybook safeguards get blotted in police cells and in court-rooms". (25)   This aptly sums up the naivety of the Royal Commission and some of its supporters were guilty of the same error. One eminent supporter, Michael Zander, stated:

> "My own view....is that the report represents a major step towards significantly better safeguards for the accused. The first is the requirement throughout the report that the police keep detailed records of what transpires and why, and that the subject be given a copy. This is no trivial point". (26)

The safeguards proposed by the Commission will be analysed in the next section. The above quotation shows the intellectual confusion which pervaded the work of the commissioners and the thinking of some of its supporters. The extra coercive powers of the police, for instance, to stop and search and to detain for questioning in the police station, were to be balanced by the requirement that the police must write down an acceptable reason for deciding to use these powers.   But it is not difficult to see how this 'safeguard' will soon become a meaningless gesture as the police learn by rote some vacuous phrase that will pass muster as a genuine reason for the exercise of such powers.   The recording of such decisions, without any effective means of challenging them, will soon be reduced to a cynical formality. At worst, the greater bureaucracy will assist the police in compiling intelligence, (for example by the use of stop and search powers), on certain suspected or 'target' groups in society. It is a 'safeguard' that could back-fire on the general public. (27)

In summary, the avowed aim of the Royal Commission was to arrive at a "fundamental balance" between the community's interest in bringing offenders to justice and the civil liberties of the individual. Its composition was intended to ensure a fair and balanced approach. Yet, in the words of David Leigh:

> "Desperate for unanimity, according to its members, the liberal and radical members of the Commission started horsetrading with the police, trying to sense what compromises would satisfy them". (28)

In reality, the Royal Commission had to contend with a powerful, and increasingly politically-oriented, police lobby. Successive Commissioners of the Metropolitan Police and police professional bodies had attempted to and had succeeded in influencing public opinion and the process of law reform. Their statements also provided a useful distraction from the revelation of serious defects in our criminal investigation system, and the consistent flouting by the police of the Judges' Rules. The police may have been alarmed at the setting up of the Royal Commission, but its final Report registered the success of men like Sir Robert Mark and Sir David McNee. The claims of civil libertarians were easily brushed aside and critical comment was dismissed, even by a supposedly sympathetic commentator, as a "left-wing knee-jerk reaction". (29) The police were to be given further powers, according to the Royal Commission, and the Police and Criminal Evidence Act goes even further. The success of the police lobby is even more extraordinary in view of the flagrant abuse of existing powers that currently takes place - a fact which was openly admitted by McNee in his evidence to the Royal Commission. Thus the defeat of the civil libertarian cause was thoroughgoing. The Royal Commission's Report was claimed to be a "package" which they ought to accept as they would do no better. It was stated that the Report and the new Police and Criminal Evidence Act contain genuine safeguards for the accused. What are the proposed safeguards that are supposed to balance the extra coercive powers that have been so readily granted to the police? Moreover, which methods of protecting the citizen's civil liberties have been omitted?

Safeguards - An Introduction

We have seen how, despite the wealth of evidence in its favour, the civil libertarian cause lost valuable ground to the law and order lobby. The latter had gained acceptance for its simplistic philosophy; namely, that more coercive powers result in more effective crime control. Of course, this is to seriously confuse police powers in a quantitative sense with the quality with which they are exercised. It is to ignore the increasing rift between law enforcement officers and the community they police. The police are no longer ordinary 'citizens in uniform'; they have far-reaching and intrusive powers with which to regulate our lives through intimate body searches, road blocks, stop and search powers, to name but a few. We would thus expect to find effective safeguards to prevent the further erosion of our civil liberties.

The promised safeguards appear to be the requirement of reasonable suspicion in the exercise, for example, of stop and search powers (although no attempt is made to define this concept and it is certainly not an objective standard); (30) and the recording of decisions by the police, which might quickly become a meaningless formality. In addition, there are codes of practice for the detention, treatment and questioning of persons by the police and for the exercise of stop and search powers, but a breach of these codes by the police "shall not of itself render [them] liable to any criminal or civil proceedings". (31) There is to be an experiment with tape-recording of interrogations at certain police stations, despite the view of the Royal Commission that the time for further experiments to test feasibility is past. Rather belatedly, the Government has introduced legislation to make limited reform of the prosecution system. The idea of some form of independent prosecution service was the 'face-saver' of the Royal Commission, its one widely-acclaimed proposal. Thus it was an act of utmost bad faith that this proposal was omitted totally from the Government's original Police and Criminal Evidence Bill, which fell due to the calling of the general election, in 1983. Notable omissions from the list of desirable safeguards are an exclusionary rule of evidence to deal with unlawful police practices and the evidence thereby obtained, and a genuinely

17

independent complaints procedure against the police. (32) It is now intended to evaluate some of the major safeguards that could be used to protect the citizen's civil liberties, amongst those proposed and those omitted from the recent Act.

An Independent Prosecution System

First, a word of warning: by itself, an independent prosecution system is no safeguard against police abuse of coercive powers, either on the street or in the police station. It cannot prevent harassment of certain social or racial groups and thus it is virtually irrelevant to deteriorating police-community relations. It has not been seriously considered whether an independent prosecutor should have investigative functions; (33) and assuming that current reform proposals will have no effect on the process prior to a suspect being charged, it is difficult to understand how this innovation can seriously be described as a safeguard against police malpractices, especially in relation to stop and search and detention for questioning. At best, it is a long-stop which may prevent a few of the more overtly ill-chosen cases from proceeding to trial and promote greater consistency in prosecution policy. Also, it may have some symbolic value in breaking the monopoly of the police over criminal procedure, investigation and prosecution. For this reason, rather than its intrinsic merits as a safeguard of the accused's rights, some form of independent prosecution system has been widely canvassed. However, it is submitted that the recent Prosecution of Offences legislation will not lead to a substantial improvement in our law. To explain this assessment, it is first necessary to examine the background to the new legislation.

It is a most distinctive tradition of our criminal justice process that there is no effective separation of investigative and prosecutorial functions. In the vast majority of criminal cases both are dominated by the police. This is in stark contrast to nearly all other civilised countries. Unlike our Scottish neighbours, with their procurators fiscal, we possess no independent, legally qualified person to review evidence, direct further enquiries, decide whether to prosecute, and if so, decide upon the nature of the charge. Our prosecuting solicitors, which are now widespread, are not analogous to the independent officials of the Scottish (and other) systems. The advice of a prosecuting solicitor is not binding on the police and the relationship is merely that of solicitor and client. (34) Moreover, the solicitor is not always allowed access to all available arrest information.

Therefore our prosecution process is anomalous and unsatisfactory and its reform has been contemplated for some time. This was never envisaged as some sort of "trade-off" with the law and order lobby over increased police investigative powers. Instead it was almost universally accepted as a necessary and desirable reform per se, which would lead to enhanced efficiency and fairness in our criminal justice system. It would, moreover, enable the police to concentrate on their primary functions of preventing, detecting and investigating crime.

The Fisher Report was restricted to cases involving the Director of Public Prosecutions, as in the Confait case. His discussion was not therefore concerned with the more general question of reforming the prosecution process for all criminal cases. Nevertheless, Fisher's conclusions are of interest, despite their narrow outlook. In particular, he was impressed by the need to involve an independent, legally trained official, at an early stage, in order to evaluate the strengths and weaknesses of the prosecution case.

"A system like the Scottish would ensure that decisions to prosecute were taken by someone who had not been deeply involved in the investigation. It would ensure that every case was under continuous professional supervision from the start right up to trial. It would ensure that proper and uncommitted evaluation of the prosecution's case at an early stage would always take place, and that prosecutions would not be permitted to proceed with important issues unexamined". (35)

It is submitted that such a system would substantially reduce the chance of gross miscarriages of justice from occurring in the future. In the Confait case, according to Fisher, five distinct opportunities for a detached analysis of the prosecution case were missed, allowing weaknesses to remain unchallenged. However, it must be stressed that prosecution reform would do little to check the misuse by the police of coercive powers. It would provide no protection for black youths from repeated and demeaning searches by the police based on no greater suspicion than clumsy racial stereotyping. It would do little to prevent lengthy detention in the police station for suspects without access to legal advice. In short, the reform might prevent some more blatantly misguided prosecutions, but it would make little impact on the present system, which is more fundamentally unfair. For, as we have seen, there are two distinct perspectives on our system: first, that cases such as Confait and Madden and many others are aberrations which occur in an otherwise basically fair system. The Royal Commission tacitly accepts this approach. (36) Alternatively, there are those who maintain that such miscarriages of justice are far from uncommon and, indeed, are manifestations of a fundamentally unfair system. If this is true, prosecution reform will do little to ameliorate our criminal justice system. Notwithstanding this cautionary point, most critics would agree that there is a strong case for improving the fairness of the prosecution process.

In 1970, the British Section of the International Commission of Jurists (Justice) published its seminal criticisms of our prosecution system. (37) The report expressed particular concern about the absence of an independent prosecuting official. It recommended that decisions to prosecute, except in the most trivial cases, should not be taken by the police, but by a national prosecuting authority. These recommendations were reiterated in Justice's evidence to the Royal Commission. (38) It observed that even where the police officer is honest and conscientious he tends to become emotively involved in securing a conviction once he feels a suspect is guilty. Consequently, it is unrealistic to expect the police, whose role is central in both the investigation of the crime and the decision to prosecute, to achieve a detached and objective analysis of the case. Far from pursuing enquiries which might weaken their case, the police are apt to ignore discrepancies in the evidence. For instance, in the Confait case, in view of one of the defendants', Colin Lattimore's, unshakeable alibi for the time when the murder appeared most likely to have occurred, it was in the police's interest that the time of death should remain vague. In this way the damaging confessions of the three boys would not be revealed as entirely erroneous. Also, the police failed to provide the pathologist with all the available evidence relevant to the time of death. (39)

Another problem lies in the discretion of the police to issue an official caution as an alternative to prosecution. This is an oral warning by a senior officer that the police could bring a successful prosecution against an accused person, but that they will not do so on this occasion. It is a warning that a future crime will lead to prosecution and it is used widely in relation to young offenders and for certain crimes such as theft and minor sex offences. (40) A major problem lies in the regional variation of cautioning rates, which reveal serious inconsistencies amongst the 43 separate police areas, as cautioning practice is determined by the Chief Constable of each area. (41) For instance, until recently the Metropolitan Police, (42) Greater Manchester and Merseyside made very little use of cautioning for males over 17, and this failed to utilise cautioning as a reasonably effective way of dealing with offenders where prosecution is unnecessary or inappropriate. It is a policy which resulted in a higher use of absolute and conditional discharge in these areas. Although cautioning practice might reflect geographical differences, and even different crime patterns from one area to another, this does not excuse wide discrepancies in cautioning; much greater uniformity is required throughout the criminal justice system. In addition, limited resources should be protected, for as the Home Office Memorandum to the Royal Commission stated:

> "Cautioning will usually represent a saving for the courts....the pressures on many magistrates' courts are such that the relief afforded by diversionary procedures such as cautioning is not measurable solely in financial terms". (43)

Further disadvantages of our system are that the police are in a position to exploit their formidable power and bargain with suspects, exert pressure on counsel to take a hard line, or even resort to more overtly dishonest practices. The trial is clearly not a suitable place for uncovering irregularities in the preparation of the case or the gathering of evidence. Indeed, the courts have no real interest in this role. This needs to be achieved earlier and, as the Justice report correctly stated, some independent scrutiny of the police evidence is required before a prosecution is allowed to proceed. Thus it recommended that a totally independent Department of Public Prosecutions be created to assume responsibility for the decision to prosecute, as well as the conduct of the case. A distinctive feature of their proposal is that the Department would be at liberty to pursue further enquiries and suggest these to the police. It would not be restricted simply to receiving and accepting evidence gathered by the police. (The new Prosecution of Offences legislation does not grant such powers to the Crown Prosecutor). These recommendations attracted considerable support from a variety of sources and they constituted a well argued and practical alternative to our anomalous system, in which there is dwindling confidence.

Unfortunately these sensible proposals ran aground on the perilous rocks of political opposition, specious economic objections and inertia. The Royal Commission on Criminal Procedure supported much more modest reforms and even these were a notable omission from the Government's original Police and Criminal Evidence Bill. The then Home Secretary, William Whitelaw, insisted that "to legislate on the matter at this stage would be premature". (44) It is difficult to comprehend why that was so. Perhaps to deflect a further barrage of criticism, limited reforms have now been proposed under the Prosecution of Offences legislation; but these proposals still fall well short of Justice's recommendations.

The Royal Commission expressed some doubt whether "the application of a legal mind necessarily improves the fairness of decisions to prosecute". (45) It pointed out that prosecuting lawyers might also develop a psychological commitment to securing convictions. This is undoubtedly true and there is also some force in the Commission's observation that a complete separation between prosecutorial and investigative functions is not always possible or even desirable:

> "The two roles overlap and intertwine. This is partly because the decision to prosecute is not a single intellectual act of a single person at an identifiable moment in the pre-trial process but it is made up of a series of decisions of a widely different kind made by many people and at various stages in the process". (46)

But the Commission surely overstated the problems of separating the investigation of crime from the prosecution of suspects. Its insistence that comparisons with the Scottish system are undesirable, due to practical differences between the two systems, is also unsatisfactory.

The Royal Commission did not accept the need for fundamental changes to our system of prosecution. Instead, it argued that existing arrangements should be developed. It recommended that the police retain complete responsibility for investigating offences and for making the decisions to charge, proceed against the suspect and to caution. (47) At this point the case enters the court's jurisdiction and it is here, according to the Philips Commission, that the division of responsibilities should occur between the police and the prosecutor. The prosecutor may then decide to proceed, to modify or withdraw the charges on the information before him. The official would be called "Crown Prosecutor" and the system was to remain locally, rather than nationally, based. In defence of its cautious approach, the Report appealed in turn to the tradition and resilience of our existing institutions, the cost of more fundamental change, and the fear of upsetting the police. (48)

It is difficult to understand how such proposals, or those contained in the new legislation, would provide any substantial safeguard for accused persons. The Crown Prosecutor's independence and influence would be relevant only at a comparatively late stage in the process. The Royal Commission was over anxious about the possibility of damaging police morale by reforming the prosecution process. If the system were being run for the benefit of the police and to pander to their sensibilities then such concern might have been more apposite. In fact, the Commission's worries were misplaced, as their proposals were not likely to upset the police unduly. The Crown Prosecutor's responsibility for a case would occur only once a charge had been made. This is a critical point and it is submitted that this is too late in the process. The whole purpose of reform is to make the prosecution process genuinely independent, and impartial, and not based on police discretion and police priorities. If the original charge is unjust or misguided then lasting damage may already have been done before the prosecutor even considers the case. The Royal Commission was careful not to damage police morale, but its concern did not stretch to the status of the new Crown Prosecutor. As Tom Sargent astutely observed:

> "[T]he proposed new arrangement must surely diminish the status of the Crown Prosecutor in that it precludes him from asking intelligent and probing questions about the evidence on which the charge is based....it appears that the prosecutor will have to accept the police evidence not only as reliable, but also as constituting all the relevant evidence". (49)

If the police investigation is fair, there should be no objection to an independent prosecutor playing a more prominent role than that outlined by the Royal Commission, in evaluating the evidence before a suspect is charged. The prosecutor would then have greater confidence in the strength and fairness of the police case. These criticisms go to the root of the Commission's proposals as they illustrate that such reforms would do little to prevent serious miscarriages of justice. The changes proposed by the Commission, and more recently by the Government in its Prosecution of Offences legislation, are more concerned with the facade than the substance of prosecution reform.

Despite these important criticisms, the Royal Commission's proposals on the prosecution system gained wide acceptance; it was one of the few sections of the Report which commanded general support and did not cause fundamental differences of opinion. It is therefore ironic that the Government should have proceeded with its contentious increase in coercive police powers before attending to the problem of prosecution reform. This is especially remarkable in view of the fact that the need for the latter reform predates any movement to alter police investigative powers. Such a policy was a clear betrayal of the Royal Commission's idea of a 'fundamental balance', where an independent prosecution system was seen as a countervailing factor to giving the police further powers to stop and search, arrest and detain for questioning. The Government was probably surprised at the extent of the hostile reaction to its original Police and Criminal Evidence Bill. Criticism was so widespread that it could not be comfortably derided (and then coveniently dismissed) as the predictable complaints of 'the Left'. Some action was needed to deflect criticism, but this reform was still omitted from the recent Police and Criminal Evidence Act; instead a "dismal and mostly unnoticed White Paper" (50) was presented to Parliament in October 1983, which forms the basis of the recent Prosecution of Offences Bill. If we briefly consider the policy behind the White Paper, it will assist our understanding of the limitations of the proposed legislation.

The White Paper favoured the introduction of a national prosecution service headed by the Director of Public Prosecutions and under the general inspection of the Attorney-General. Yet there are no additional safeguards for the accused here, for the scheme promises little more than an extension of prosecuting solicitors' departments to the whole of the country. The most that is offered is that "they would not be subject to direction or influence by the police or any local body in deciding whether charges should proceed or be dropped or how a case should be conducted". (51) Yet this is no protection for the accused from misguided charges and misuse of investigative and interrogative powers. The Government was chiefly concerned with opposing any system involving an element of accountability to a local supervisory body. (52) It somehow managed to twist the meaning of the word 'independent' to mean independent of any local (elected) body, rather than independent of the police. The inference being that there is greater danger in any local or democratic control of prosecution policy, than there is in police influence over the prosecution process.

The police were suspicious of prosecution reform and, as we saw, the Royal Commission proceeded most cautiously so as not to offend them. Even so, the Police Federation expressed concern at the Commission's proposals and this is presumably what was meant by the Government when it stated that "strong reservations were expressed about whether this aspect of the Royal Commission's proposals would be workable, or consistent with the service's independence". (53) The White Paper stated baldly that its analysis had confirmed these suspicions. It is indeed unfortunate that such a sceptical approach was not directed towards some of the Royal Commission's genuinely contentious proposals in relation to an increase in police powers on the street and in the police station. Instead, the powerful police lobby (and a more than sympathetic Government) ensured that even a potential safeguard for the accused could be emasculated and misrepresented. It could also be turned to their advantage in a most disingenuous way: the idea of a nationally controlled prosecution service might assist the police in rejecting any demands for local accountability. The following statement in the Police Federation journal certainly lends support to this idea:

> "The price may however be worth paying, provided that such a Prosecution Agency was not locally accountable, but directly accountable to Law Officers of the Crown, preferably the Attorney-General. This connection would enhance the legal accountability of the police and provide a countervailing power to that of local politicians, because through the process of submitting cases to the prosecutor the police would be accountable to him for the quality of their evidence and thereby for the effectiveness of their policing". (54)

In this way, the recent legislative proposals will do little to enhance police accountability in relation to prosecution policy. Indeed, they may even be detrimental to this end, that is when they are eventually implemented. All that can be predicted with confidence is that fundamental reform of the prosecution process, which is long overdue, will not be achieved by the new legislation. The rights of suspects will not be significantly better protected under the new system than they were under the old one.

Tape-Recording Of Police Interrogations

A recurring and seemingly intractable problem is that of disputed evidence of what occurs in the course of police interviews with suspects. The difficulties surrounding the "verbals" are exacerbated by the fact that the evidence in question is often central to the prosecution case. In many cases the interview at the police station is vital and we saw earlier that there is considerable cause for concern about both the frequency of confessions and their reliability (55); relatively few defendants reach their trial without having made some form of incriminating statement. It is at this stage of the criminal justice system that accused persons are particularly vulnerable. In determining the outcome of a case, much may depend on which of two conflicting accounts are believed by a jury; that of the police officer or that of the defendant.

It is meaningless to provide safeguards for the suspect's rights elsewhere (even assuming that we do), if there is little public confidence in police 'verbals'. Such disputes as to the accuracy of police accounts of interviews are costly, time-consuming, and often unnecessary. Yet because of the crucial importance of this stage of criminal procedure, the police are hostile to any monitoring of the conduct of interviews by independent or mechanical means.

However, many critics feel that an obvious safeguard for both the suspect and the police would be the practice of tape-recording interrogations at the police station. There is nothing novel about such proposals. In 1972, the Criminal Law Revision Committee, in addition to its attack on the right of silence, favoured wider use of tape-recorders during interrogation (56); this met with considerable hostility from the police, a fact which may have been influential in the non-implementation of the Report. The Confait case also illustrated the lack of confidence in official accounts of police interviews; namely the confession of two boys to a killing they did not perpetrate. In his Report, Sir Henry Fisher acknowledged that the Confait case lends support to those who favour the introduction of tape-recording. He stated that "if the proceedings had been tape-recorded, the course of subsequent proceedings might well have been different". (57) Indeed, his inquiry might have been unnecessary.

The practical objections to tape-recording are well known; difficulties of selective recording, tampering, attempts to mislead the court, the status of unrecorded evidence, the cost, technical problems and the possible demand for transcripts. However these problems are often exaggerated and there is certainly scope for worse abuses in other areas of the criminal justice system. In support of a system of tape-recording interrogations, it is axiomatic that a mechanical record of what takes place during an interview, (which is often so critical to the outcome of the case), is better than any ex post facto account. In contrast to a written summary, it offers the precise words exchanged and also the tone of voice of the parties involved. It would save much time at the trial where such evidence is frequently contested. It might deter the police from unfair interrogations, but it would also protect them from unwarranted allegations of unfairness. In short, "if tape recorders were properly used for interviews inside police stations an enormous amount of time and money could be saved". (58)

The official response, to the overwhelming arguments in favour of its introduction, has been one of suspicion and procrastination. In 1976 the Home Office produced a report on this subject to consider the feasibility of an experiment with tape-recording. (59) Its limited approach has been strongly criticised by Pauline Morris as follows:

> "Somewhat surprisingly, the Committee nowhere specifies the purpose of the tape recording. It would seem that its Report was prepared predominantly from the viewpoint of administrative convenience, rather than as a serious attempt to consider whether tape recording would be a feasible means of protecting the interests of suspects whilst at the same time assisting in law enforcement". (60)

The Royal Commission considered the tape-recording of interviews at the police station to be feasible. But, it argued that it is neither practicable nor desirable to record the whole interview, on a cost and benefit calculation. (61) This appeared to ignore the widely held view that tape-recording could shorten trials significantly and actually save money. The Commission proposed that at the end of an interview (if there is no written statement), the officer involved should summarise orally the main points to emerge and make a written record of them. This process, and where appropriate the taking of a written statement, should be recorded on tape, with the consent and knowledge of the suspect. The suspect should be given an opportunity to comment on his treatment. (62) The Report favoured this approach as an economic and viable scheme, with a gradual introduction of tape-recording, enabling the main points of an interview to be recorded, without problems of transcription.

The disadvantages of these proposals, as a safeguard of the accused's rights, are obvious; indeed, it has been described as the introduction of "verballing by tape recorder". (63) The summary might bear little relation to what has gone earlier. Yet the suspect would be inhibited from recording his dissent or complaints. It gives virtually no insight into the tone of the interview and its conduct by the police, which after all is the main purpose of tape recording. In short, such proposals would do little to inspire confidence in the accuracy of police accounts of interrogations. Thus the recommendations of the Commission were widely seen as a pusillanimous retreat when offered a genuine opportunity to support a long overdue reform.

On the other hand, the Report's cautious approach may have been due to its anticipation of political and practical objections to full-scale tape recording. Its scheme might have hoped to lead to a gradual extension of tape-recording once initial circumspection was eroded. However, this is a most benign interpretation and it is hard to discern how such proposals would have significantly protected the rights of the accused and ensured fair interrogations at the police station. It is remarkable that, in view of the cautious approach adopted by the Royal Commission, the Government should still have omitted this reform from its original Police and Criminal Evidence Bill; especially in view of the Government's supposed "commitment to the principle of tape-recording". (64) It is surprising that the Government was so dilatory in starting its tape-recording trials, as the Royal Commission emphasised that the time to test feasibility is past. Thus the Government's recent announcement of field trials in just six police areas should elicit something less than three cheers. (65) But at least entire interviews at the police station are to be recorded, and not just the summaries.

Although there is now a statutory provision for the Home Secretary to issue a code of practice on the tape-recording of interviews with suspects at the police station, it appears that the Government is still stalling for time. (66) The "field trials", which started in the early months of 1984 in the six areas, are still an experiment and not a system. This suspicion was voiced by Christopher Price as follows:

> "I suspect that the experiment will run for a couple of years....the police will throw up their hands in horror....The Home Secretary will then consider the matter for a further two years and we will be into another decade before there is universal tape-recording". (67)

In a recent article, a member of the Steering Committee which was responsible for drafting guidelines for the field trials, explained the scope of these further tests. (68) But in reading this explanation, it is still difficult to understand why such trials are necessary, if there was a genuine commitment to the introduction of tape-recording as a safeguard against unfair interrogation at the police station. Instead, it seems that powerful police opposition and lobbying succeeded, for many years, in preventing the introduction of a reform which commands overwhelming support; now that such an innovation is almost inevitable, the tactic is to cause delay and stress the practical difficulties involved. However, it has been widely accepted that tape-recording will, when finally introduced, considerably improve the fairness of interrogations by the police. The aforementioned article states that "tape-recording will tend to outlaw oppressive questioning". (69) But there is a real danger that the police may neutralise the beneficial effects of this new safeguard.

A recent interim report of the Scottish Home Office and Health Department clearly illustrates the problem. (70) The report was concerned with the first two years of an experiment with tape-recording in Dundee and Falkirk and based on 2,149 taped interviews at police stations in these two areas. Although, superficially, the practice of recording had no profound effect upon the behaviour of suspects, it seems to have affected police behaviour to a considerable degree. In a recent important article, Michael McConville and Philip Morell (71) have assessed the impact of tape-recording on police practice in these experimental areas.

> "One immediate result, in both areas, was that the number of suspects interviewed dropped from the level obtaining in the pre-experiment period. This, according to the S.H.H.D. Report, could only be accounted for by officers omitting to interview suspects completely on tape, interviewing them elsewhere than in a police station or interviewing them in a police station but not on tape". (72)

It was also apparent that taped interviews were much shorter than they had been prior to the experiment. For instance, in Falkirk, the average length of interview fell from 39 minutes in the pre-monitoring period, to just 6 minutes after the introduction of tape-recording. In Dundee, the average duration was reduced from 25 to 10 minutes per interview. In addition, there was an increase in cases where suspects made no formal response to police questioning and fewer statements were made. However, it seems that the police now conduct 'preliminary' interrogations away from the inhibiting tape-recorder. In both experimental areas, the incidence of statements made by suspects prior to their arrival at the police station has been on the increase. For example, in Falkirk such statements went from 14 per cent (pre-experiment) to 44 per cent after tape-recording was introduced. It also seems that lengthy interrogation frequently took place before the tape-recorder was switched on; but when the interview was eventually recorded "the police abandoned their usual interrogation techniques and instead utilised a formal, rather rigid style of questioning". (73) This is the main reason why interviews have become much shorter and suspects appear to be less responsive. The results of the experiment do not, therefore, suggest that suspects can effectively rely on their right to silence, but rather that the police seek the information they require in the pre-interrogation interview with suspects. In this way the safeguard of the tape-recorder is circumvented whilst maintaining the pretence of fairness.

There are important lessons in this unfortunate turn of events which can be seen in the Scottish experience. It must not be assumed that tape-recording is, by itself, an adequate safeguard for the citizen against oppressive police interrogation. The hostility of the police to such monitoring of interviews is such that they can still evade or neutralise such a safeguard. It may well be impracticable to record the entire encounter between the police and their suspects, but it must be remembered that the formal (recorded) interview may not present the whole picture. Also, tape-recording must be introduced together with further protection of the accused's rights; it is not a panacea, but merely one of a number of measures that might help to achieve fairness in a criminal justice system that is increasingly becoming too weighted in favour of the police and the prosecution.

Exclusion Of Unfairly Obtained Evidence

In our criminal justice system there is no judicial or independent official to conduct or even supervise the questioning of suspects. From the moment of arrest and detention, the accused person is in a highly vulnerable position and it is essential that effective protection is provided against unfair treatment and interrogation. It must be emphasised that whatever safeguards exist in theory, the atmosphere at the police station will be extremely intimidating to the accused and "coercion, if not duress, is implicit in the situation". (74)

The rules governing the treatment of suspects in custody are intended to ensure that they are treated humanely, that their basic rights are observed, and that any statements made are reliable. However, once again we see a considerable disparity between legal theory and actual legal practice. Police behaviour in relation to a citizen being arrested (or detained) and questioned at the police station is still not strictly regulated. The main protection for the suspect used to be found in a variety of sources; principally it was contained in the Judges' Rules and Administrative Directions. These Rules and Directions were not, in fact, rules of law, but "a guide and a standard rather than an absolute statement of what the court will and will not admit as evidence". (75) The Royal Commission recommended that the rules be codified to achieve greater clarity and precision. Yet this was to deliberately miss the point of criticisms of our system. The main weakness of the protection given to accused persons under the Judges' Rules (and now the Codes of Practice) is that the rules can be simply disregarded with impunity by the police. There is no effective sanction against police officers for breaking the rules relating, for instance, to the right of access to legal advice and the nature of the caution to be given to an accused. Disciplinary action against officers for contravening the Judges' Rules was virtually unknown. (76)

The Confait investigation is a prime example of the lack of regard which both police and lawyers had for the Judges' Rules and Administrative Directions. (77) In that case, the three suspects were not informed orally of the rights and facilities available to them, namely to communicate by telephone with a friend or solicitor; two of the boys were questioned by the police without a parent or guardian being present. In neither case would it have caused undue delay to the interview or have been otherwise impractical. Yet the defence counsel at the trial (with one exception) made no submission that the Judge should exercise his discretion to exclude this evidence. Moreover, Sir Henry Fisher observed that police officers and lawyers were ignorant of some of the Rules and Directions and needed to make more effort to learn them. (78) This is a good indication of the esteem in which the Judges' Rules were held by the very people who were supposedly constrained by them and by those who should have scrutinised their effectiveness and safeguarded the rights of the accused.

There is nothing to suggest that the new Codes of Practice under the Police and Criminal Evidence Act will ameliorate the position. (79) If the police frequently failed to act in accordance with the Judges' Rules, it is difficult to have confidence in their adherence to the new Codes. Thus the main weakness in our law remains; that evidence which is unfairly obtained is not normally inadmissible. (80) Of course, a confession will not be admissible if it is obtained either as a result of oppression by the police or in circumstances which make it likely to be unreliable. (81) But outside these narrow restrictions, evidence can be admitted even if it is obtained by improper or unfair means. There is a judicial discretion to declare such evidence inadmissible under Section 78 of the Police and Criminal Evidence Act 1984, but when armed with similar powers in the past, judges have virtually abdicated responsibility in this area and exerted hardly any genuine control over police malpractices; and "when judges both assert that the police should discipline themselves, and yet admit evidence that has been obtained by lack of the judicially imposed discipline, the stultification of our professions becomes patent". (82)

But of much greater concern than professional inefficiency, is the lack of protection given to the accused's "rights" once in the custody of the police. At this stage in the process there is such a disparity between the interviewer and the suspect that the paucity of judicial control over unfair interrogation is unpardonable. If we acknowledge that a suspect has rights, the corollary must surely be that these rights deserve protection by the judiciary, and not depend on some misplaced belief that the police will maintain discipline and self-control amongst their own ranks. (83) Indeed it is fallacious to talk of "rights" in this context unless they are supported by certain and effective remedies.

Failure to enforce a suspect's rights by an automatic exclusion, at trial, of improperly obtained evidence, has two major deleterious consequences. First, it casts doubt on the accuracy and reliability of evidence obtained by such methods. Secondly, it condones unlawful and unfair police interrogation. The courts become a party to this unlawfulness, leading to disrespect for both the law and the judiciary and inducing cynicism on the part of the police and the general public (but for different reasons). Theoretically, the law stipulates certain standards to be observed in the conduct of investigations, yet in practice these standards can be openly disregarded by the police. The judiciary claim that this is none of their business as it is not their function to exert any disciplinary power over the police or prosecution.

The unlawful behaviour of the police is frequently advantageous to them and, thus emboldened, they are encouraged to continue their malpractices. As we saw earlier, a suspect is frequently denied access to a solicitor, in spite of the "right" of access formerly contained in Administrative Direction No. 7 (and now contained in a Code of Practice for the detention, treatment and questioning of suspects). There is still to be considerable discretion on the part of the police in deciding whether to permit access to legal advice. (84) There is, once again, little hope that misuse of this discretion will be challenged in the courts. It is most unlikely that clear guidelines will emerge to indicate when a police officer is legally justified in refusing to grant an accused person's request to consult with a solicitor. On rare occasions in the past, individual judges have made attempts to take the suspect's rights seriously. In Allen, Mackenna J., excluded statements made by the defendant after he had been refused access to a solicitor. His now famous statement contrasts starkly with the more typical attitude of his judicial colleagues:

> "[I]f the police are allowed to use in court evidence which they have obtained from suspects to whom they have wrongly denied the right of legal advice, they will be encouraged to continue this illegal practice". (85)

Despite its logic and fairness, this exclusionary approach is not normally associated with our law. The new legislation gives no cause for optimism and evidence will continue to be admissible despite the use of unfair methods to obtain it. The Royal Commission on Criminal Procedure characteristically rejected any suggestion of introducing safeguards against improper police methods that could actually have any practical significance; it naively hoped that "the civil courts may therefore prove to have a useful role to play" in enforcing the rules of conduct for the police. (86) The Commission, which was so unquestioning in its acceptance of overtly ineffective methods of controlling police malpractices, fastidiously attacked the exclusionary rule - the one genuine method of attempting to ensure fairness. Thus, the automatic exclusionary rule was emphatically rejected. (87)

Yet it is strongly submitted that our law does not give effective protection to accused persons against unfair and improper treatment in custody, as there is no machinery for enforcement of so-called "rights". This is inimical not only to the interests of an individual victim of unfair treatment, but to the criminal justice system generally, and to our constitutional law. A bolder approach, like that in the United States, is required to positively assert the rights of accused persons. (88) This approach is both logical and just. If a system confers rights upon its citizens then it has a moral duty to observe and protect them. Complaints about a guilty person being acquitted on a technicality miss the constitutional importance of safeguarding the accused's rights and inspiring confidence in the system. In other words, evidence obtained by unconscionable methods should be excluded simply because its use would be offensive. A further defence of this exclusionary approach is that it might also have a deterrent effect on the police. If the courts were to consistently adopt such an approach, we might witness the erosion of the disregard which the police quite openly express for the citizen's rights.

Naturally the adoption of a strict exclusionary rule is opposed by many and for a variety of reasons. Some argue that it would provide only minimal control over police malpractices as many defendants plead guilty or the case does not proceed to trial. However, it is worth remembering that the exclusionary rule need not be the sole method of ensuring fair treatment for accused persons; there would still be a need for contemporaneous control of police behaviour. The other main line of attack is to deny the deterrent value of the rule. The Royal Commission, on the most tenuous evidence, maintained that "the harshest criticism of the rule is that it is ineffective." (89) This will be considered below; but by analogy, if we were to adopt this argument in other areas of the criminal justice system, we should stop punishing offenders for deterrent reasons as it is not a particularly effective method of reducing crime. Another objection to the exclusionary rule is its inflexibility. (90) According to some critics, if it were introduced, its effect would be too drastic in cases where the breach was trivial or accidental. Thus vital evidence for the prosecution might be excluded on a technicality and a guilty person would go free. Yet the U.S. Department of Justice, basing its conclusions on the American experience in 13 States, recently found very little evidence of this.

A possible compromise between an automatic rule and our present position, is a formula similar to that proposed by the Australian Law Reform Commission. (91) It suggested a scheme for the automatic exclusion of any illegally obtained evidence unless the prosecution can satisfy the court that it should be allowed in the public interest; that is, because of a minor breach, or the gravity of the crime being tried, or the exigencies of the circumstances of the case. The main objection to this "reverse onus exclusionary rule" is that it would leave much to the discretion of the judge and the record of the judiciary in this area is far from encouraging.

With no genuinely independent complaints procedure against the police, and no effective remedy to enforce the 'rights' of suspected persons relating to their treatment in police custody, there is much to be said for a strict "exclusionary rule". In the United States illegally obtained evidence is inadmissible in a criminal trial. (92) However, this found no favour with the Royal Commission (as we have seen) which concluded that the United States experience gave little support to those who proposed the introduction of an exclusionary rule in this country. Yet there is some reason to doubt the rigour of the Commission's research into this important matter.

How effective is the American system of excluding illegally obtained evidence? A recent writer, Jim Driscoll, who has made a study of the American experience, is highly critical of the Royal Commission's analysis for a number of reasons. (93) First, it relied heavily on a now dated and much criticised piece of research, which is far from representative of current police practice in the United States. (94) Secondly, it distorted the empirical evidence in claiming that the exclusionary rule possesses no deterrent value in relation to police misconduct. (95) Thirdly, it argued that over here the solution to the "disciplinary principle" should reside in police supervisory and disciplinary procedures; yet it was precisely the failure of such methods of enforcement which led the U.S. Supreme Court in Mapp v Ohio to rule that both state and federal trials should adhere to the strict exclusionary rule. (96) In other words, other agencies cannot be trusted to check police malpractices. In Mapp it was stated that "the obvious futility of relegating the Fourth Amendment to the protection of other remedies has, moreover, been recognised by this Court." (97) Lastly, the Commission misinterpreted the undoubted differences between the American system and our own, with its implication that this was the sole reason for such a rule in the United States and, conversely, why it was not required here. Yet the greater involvement of the police in the prosecution process under our system may lead to an exclusionary rule being even more effective in England and Wales.

Thus, in contrast to the most superficial conclusions of the Royal Commission, it would seem that more recent research into the American experience lends support to those who favour an exclusionary evidence rule as a safeguard of the citizen's rights. As Driscoll states:

> "Although no one claims that the exclusionary rule effectively disciplines all aspects of police behaviour there is convincing evidence that it has fostered a significant and increasing improvement in the standard of police behaviour in the United States. The rule also ensures that the integrity of the judicial process is not tainted by condoning police illegality. It provides the courts with opportunities to protect civil liberties and helps to ensure that controls over police behaviour do not become illusory." (98)

Conclusion

No one would argue against the need for efficient law enforcement, and the police being equipped with the necessary powers to bring offenders to justice. Indeed, "we may take the general justifying aim of the administration of criminal justice to be that the guilty should be detected, convicted and duly sentenced." (99)   But although this may be the general purpose of the criminal justice system, it is constrained by the need for fairness, not just in the theory, but in the practice of the law. The agents of law enforcement now possess formidable powers of investigation and coercion and, as a professional body, the police are an articulate and powerful political faction. They have shown themselves capable of dictating the course of law reform, cajoling and threatening both public and politicians alike. However, it is not the purpose of this essay to deny that police officers have to perform an increasingly difficult and sometimes physically dangerous job.

The aim of this chapter has been to contrast the supposed or theoretical rights of the citizen under our system with the actual practice of the law. Here we see that the gulf is enormous: 'reasonable suspicion' means whatever the officer concerned wants it to mean; the rules relating to fair treatment and interrogation are routinely ignored with no fear of effective sanctions; there is no genuinely independent complaints procedure; there is further delay in the national introduction of tape-recording; an emphatic rejection of a strict exclusionary evidence rule; and despite a 'right of silence', few defendants reach their trial without making some form of damaging statement. Thus it seems that the rights of the citizen, under our criminal justice process, are still not taken seriously. The Royal Commission on Criminal Procedure missed a golden opportunity to do so. The Police and Criminal Evidence Act tips the scales yet further in favour of the police. This legislation is not bad law simply because it gives more powers to them, but rather, "it is bad because it gives them without providing a satisfactory independent framework for supervising and monitoring their exercise; without building them on to an acceptable bedrock of citizens' rights, and without appreciating how they will work out in practice on city streets and in police cells." (100)

NOTES

1.   Per Lord Diplock in R v. Sang [1979] 2 All E.R. 1222 at 1230 (H.L.).

2.   Sentencing in the Crown Court, Occasional Paper No.10, Centre for Criminological Research, University of Oxford.

3.   Criminal Law Revision Committee, 11th Report, 1972, Cmnd.4991, para.27.

4.   D.J. McBarnet, Conviction, 1981, p.155.

5.   Code of Practice for the Detention, Treatment and Questioning of Persons by the Police, s.6 and Annex B, Home Office, 1984.

6.   J. Baldwin and M. McConville, "Police Interrogation and the Right to See a Solicitor" [1979] Crim.L.R. 145 and M. Zander, "Access to a Solicitor in the Police Station" [1972] Crim.L.R. 342.

7.   Royal Commission on Criminal Procedure, 1981, H.M.S.O. Cmnd.8092. (Hereafter Royal Commission).

8.   Evidence of the Commissioner of the Metropolitan Police (Part I) to the Royal Commission, 1978, p.71.

9.   See J. Baldwin and M. McConville, Confessions in Crown Court Trials, Royal Commission on Criminal Procedure Research Study No.5 (1980) H.M.S.O.

10.   B. Mitchell, "Confessions and Police Interrogation of Suspects" [1983] Crim. L.R. 596 -604.

11.   Ibid., p.604.

12.   See: Report of an Inquiry by the Hon. Sir Henry Fisher into the circumstances leading to the trial of three persons on charges arising out of the death of Maxwell Confait and the fire at 27 Doggett Road, London S.E.6. H.C. Papers, Session 77-78, No.90. (Hereafter Fisher Report).

13.   D.J. McBarnet, "The Fisher Report on the Confait Case: Four Issues", Mod.L.R., Vol.41, pp.455 -63, at p.456.

14.   J. Baldwin and M. McConville, Courts, Prosecution and Conviction, p.192.

15.   Royal Commission, op.cit., supra, note 7, paras, 1.6 -1.10.

16.   Criminal Law Revision Committee, 11th Report, 1972, Cmnd.4991, para.24.

17.   For a good example of an overtly political statement, see Les Curtis' (Chairman of the Police Federation) statement in October 1984.

18. Quoted by M. Kettle in his essay in P. Hain (ed): Policing the Police, p.18.

19. Evidence of Sir David McNee, op.cit., supra, note 8, pp.3-4.

20. In particular, the extension of powers to stop and search has been described as a "recipe for racial disaster", by Geoffrey Robertson, Guardian, November 20, 1981. Also see M. McConville, "Search of Persons and Premises: New Data from London" [1983] Crim.L.R. 605, esp. 607-14.

21. This is no exaggeration of the attitude of the press to crime reporting. See J. Ditton and J. Duffy, "Bias in the Newspaper Reporting of Crime News" (1983). Brit. Jo. Criminol., Vol.23, pp.159-165.

22. Why was the Royal Commission so disastrous to the civil libertarian cause? It was "enfeebled by over-representation of amateurs and academics, its report was a meandering and compromising package taken apart at the seams by a new government more interested in the additional powers that it recommended for the police than the safeguards it suggested for the citizen." G. Robertson, Guardian, May 9th, 1983.

23. M. Kettle, New Society, January 8th, 1981, p.52.

24. Ibid, p.52: "Commissioner McNee's demands have become the focus of the whole right-wing thrust towards a more authoritarian law and order system. Many have feared that the Royal Commission would cave in to such tactics. Not only were the police the most powerful pressure group, but also other major organisations were less than wholehearted in resisting them....To a considerable and welcome degree, the Commission has stood firm on these issues."

25. See G. Robertson, loc.cit supra, note 20. Some critics were not even this charitable in their interpretation. For instance, see David Leigh, Observer, March 27, 1983.

26. M. Zander, Guardian, January 12, 1981.

27. See Louise Christian, Policing by Coercion, 1983, p.147.

28. Quoted in Louise Christian, ibid., p.13.

29. Zander, Guardian, January, 1981.

30. For a detailed discussion of this subject, see Mike Brogden's essay in this volume. Also see Royal Commission on Criminal Procedure, paras.3.24-3.25.

31. Section 67(10), Police and Criminal Evidence Act 1984.

32. This needs no further discussion here, as it is the subject of an admirable essay by Barbara Cohen in this volume.

33. The Royal Commission favoured leaving "the police with complete responsibility for investigating offences and for making the initial decision whether to bring the matter before a court." (Para.7.7).

34. In its evidence to the Commission, the Prosecuting Solicitors' Society in England and Wales stated "that even where a prosecuting solicitors' department is in existence, there is no obligation upon the police to consult their solicitors or having consulted them to follow the advice tendered....[and many had]....experience of incidents where advice that, as a matter of law, there was no case had been rejected."

35. Fisher Report, H.C. Papers, Session 77-78, No.90, para.2.44.

36. Royal Commission, op.cit., supra, note 7, paras.7.7-7.11.

37. Justice Report, 1970, "The Prosecution Process in England and Wales."

38. Justice, 1979, "Pre-Trial Criminal Procedure" (Evidence to the Royal Commission on Criminal Procedure, Part I).

39. Fisher Report, op.cit., supra, note 35, paras. 2.29-2.40.

40. Generally, see Home Office Research Unit Study No.37, Police Cautioning in England and Wales.

41. Evidence to the Royal Commission on Criminal Procedure (Memorandum No.VI), "Cautioning by the Police".

42. But, as Louise Christian observes in Policing by Coercion (p.197), Sir Kenneth Newman recently told the Metropolitan Police to require a higher standard of evidence for bringing a prosecution and he gave wider discretion to officers in deciding whether to prosecute.

43. Op.cit., supra, note 41.

44. Police and Criminal Evidence Bill, Hansard, 30th November 1982, col.159.

45. Royal Commission, op.cit., supra, note 7, para.6.28.

46. Royal Commission, ibid., para.6.31.

47. Royal Commission, ibid., para.7.7.

48. Royal Commission, ibid., paras.7.1 and 7.12.

49. T. Sargent, "The Prosecution Process", New Law Journal, March 12, 1981, p.276. This article makes particularly perceptive criticisms of the Royal Commission's proposals.

50. Jason Ditton, The Times, April 6, 1984.

51.   "An Independent Prosecution Service for England and Wales", Home Office, Cmnd. 9074, para.4.

52.   This was its objection to the Commission's modest proposals; see Royal Commission, paras. 7.22-7.37.

53.   White Paper, op.cit., supra, note 51, para.9.

54.   D.A. Waddington, "The Proper Way to Police Accountability", Police, June 1983 and quoted in Louise Christian's Policing by Coercion, p.199.

55.   For example, see B. Mitchell, loc.cit., supra, note 10.

56.   Criminal Law Revision Committee, 11th Report, 1972, Cmnd. 4991, paras.48-52. A minority of three members even supported the view that in respect of interrogations at police stations, statutory provision should be made for the compulsory use of tape-recorders at police stations in larger areas.

57.   Fisher Report, op.cit., supra, note 35, para.2.24.

58.   Mr. Edward Gardner, M.P., Hansard, November 30, 1982, col.170.

59.   "The Feasibility of an Experiment in Tape-Recording Police Interrogations", 1976, Home Office, Cmnd.6630.

60.   Pauline Morris, Police Interrogation - Review of Literature, Royal Commission on Criminal Procedure, Research Study No.3, p.34.

61.   Royal Commission on Criminal Procedure, 1981, Cmnd. 8092, para.4.26.

62.   Royal Commission, ibid para.4.27.

63.   See N.C.C.L.'s criticisms, The Times, October 23, 1982.

64.   Hansard, November 30, 1982, col.159.

65.   "The Tape-Recording of Police Interviews with Suspects: Procedural Guidance", Home Office 1983.

66.   See section 60 Police and Criminal Evidence Act 1984.

67.   Hansard, May 4, 1983, cols. 317-318.

68.   David Roberts, "Tape-Recording the Questioning of Suspects - The Field Trials Guidelines" [1984] Crim.L.R. 537. The author, the Law Society's representative on the Home Office Steering Committee, estimated that a national scheme will not emerge until after 1987.

69.   D. Roberts, ibid., p.543.

70. Scottish Home Office and Health Department, "Tape Recording of Police Interviews: Interim Report - the First 24 months", 1982. My attempts to obtain a copy of this report were blocked by the reply that it was a "confidential report and not available to the public".

71. M. McConville and P. Morrell, "Recording the Interrogation: Have the Police got it Taped?" [1983] Crim.L.R. 158. Being unable to see the Scottish Report (see note 70) personally, I found this article most valuable.

72. Ibid., p.160.

73. Ibid., pp.161–162.

74. P. Morris, op.cit., supra, note 60, p.26.

75. Home Office, Evidence to the Royal Commission on Criminal Procedure, Memorandum No.V, "The Law and Procedures Relating to the Questioning of Persons in the Investigation of Crime", para.22.

76. "When the N.C.C.L. last inquired of the Metropolitan Police how many officers had been disciplined for such conduct, the reply was 'none'". (B. Cohen in letter to Guardian, November 1st, 1982).

77. Fisher Report, H.C. Papers, Session 77-78, No.90, para.2.11.

78. Fisher Report, ibid., paras. 2.17–2.18.

79. See sections 66 and 67 of the Police and Criminal Evidence Act 1984. A police officer will face only the unlikely threat of disciplinary proceedings for breach of the Code; failure to comply with the code "shall not of itself render him liable to any criminal or civil proceedings."

80. Section 78 Police and Criminal Evidence Act 1984 states that judges can exclude unfairly obtained evidence at their discretion. The judiciary's record on this subject is not however a cause for optimism.

81. Section 76(2) Police and Criminal Evidence Act 1984.

82. Glanville Williams, Jo.Criminal Law, Criminol., and P.S. (1961), p.51.

83. For such a misguided view, see Royal Commission, para.4.127.

84. See Annex B, contained in Draft Codes of Practice, London, Home Office, 1984.

85. Allen [1977] Crim.L.R. 163; contrast Elliot [1977] Crim.L.R. 551, in which Kilner Browne J. adopts the more traditional approach. Also see Lemsatef [1977] 2 All E.R. 835.

86. Royal Commission on Criminal Procedure, 1981, Cmnd.8092, para.4.122. Generally see paras.4.117–4.130.

87.   Royal Commission, _ibid._, para.4.128.

88.   See _Miranda v. Arizona_ 384 U.S. 436 (1966), in which the defendants' appeals were allowed by the Supreme Court because their statements were improperly obtained. The case of _Gallegos v. Colorado_ 370 U.S. 49 (1962) also provides an interesting contrast to the Confait case.

89.   Royal Commission, op.cit., supra, note 86, 4.125.

90.   Yet as Driscoll points out, L.A.G. Bulletin June 1981, p.131, that in the United States "the operation of the exclusionary rule is not automatic and the Philips Commission was wrong so to describe it."

91.   Royal Commission, op.cit., supra, note 86, paras 4.128-4.129.

92.   _Mapp v. Ohio_ 367 U.S. 643 (1961).

93.   J. Driscoll, "Excluding Illegally Obtained Evidence - Can We Learn From The United States?" Legal Action Group Bulletin, June 1981, 131.

94.   Dallin Oaks, "Studying the exclusionary rule in search and seizure", 37 Ch.L. Rev. 665 (1970).

95.   See recent studies; for instance, B. Canon, "Is the exclusionary rule failing in health? Some new data and a plea against precipitous conclusion", Ky L.J. 681 (1974).

96.   See _Mapp v. Ohio_ 367 U.S. 643 (1961).

97.   _Ibid._, p.652.

98.   J. Driscoll, loc.cit., supra, note 93, p.131.

99.   A. Ashworth, "Concepts of Criminal Justice" [1979] Crim.L.R. 412.

100. G. Robertson, _Guardian_, May 9, 1983.

3. POLICING AND THE RULE OF LAW

John Baxter

When the legal historians come to consider the emergence of the Police and Criminal Evidence Act 1984 it is to be hoped that its date will not have acquired an unfortunate irony. As Stephen Sedley has observed, the prognosis is not good but not beyond hope. The legislation came at a time when policing had become a major feature of the political debate, not only because of the immediate issues surrounding the coal industry dispute, but because of the cumulative effect of a series of issues which had been emerging since the early sixties. A succession of exposures of police malpractice served to undermine, for some, the traditional confidence that comfortable Britain has in those who enforce the law. Notable among such events are the excesses of some Sheffield policemen in 1963, the Challenor case of the same year, and the events following the Confait case in 1972. The arrival of Sir Robert Mark at Scotland Yard and his determination to purge the Metropolitan Force of corruption and the inconclusive Countryman Investigation confirmed many in their suspicions that all was not well and that there was to be no quick solution. The Profumo Affair and the Poulson bankruptcy in their turn played their part in shaking confidence in the standards of those involved in government, whilst for young people the alternative lifestyles of the sixties brought about an increasing contact between young people and the police. In the forefront of this contact was the use of stop and search powers in response to the drug problem inherited from the "turn on and drop out" subculture of the sixties, police handling of demonstrations, and the use of the "sus" laws in a way which put minority racial groups at greater risk. Growing unemployment, social and environmental deprivation and policing styles were all eventually to be recognised by Lord Scarman's Inquiry into the riots of 1981 as playing their part in a growing alienation which had occurred between the police and sections of the community.

In contrast to this decline in confidence other factors were combining to place greater confidence in Authority. In particular the growing emergence of the "Law and Order" debate and the perceived "War on Crime" would concentrate public attention on police effectiveness and the apparent inability of the authorities to turn the tide of the rising crime rate. Consequently a hardening of both public and police attitudes led to an acceptance of toughened policing styles whether through the increased availability of public order hardware, through a preparedness to push legal powers to the limits of illegality, or through a toleration of outspoken chief police officers who did not see their independence as requiring silent and anonymous service outside the political arena. The consequence has therefore been to politicize the police, so that it is now commonplace to see chief officers explaining their views on criminal justice or public order before the television cameras or hear them on the radio. The police have become lobby politicians in their own right whether through the Association of Chief Police Officers or through the Police Federation, and it is difficult to disassociate these developments with the divergence of opinion which has come about between the two major political parties. The police have become associated, whether by intention or circumstances, with a political approach to the war on crime which emphasises Power rather than Liberty, and the policing of the miners' strike has only served to confirm this conclusion.

The acquisition of a political role and the power that accompanies it has led to the acquisition of greater physical, administrative and legal power. The technology of policing has come a long way since the first use of riot shields in Lewisham in August 1977. Public order hardware is only part of the story. Computerisation has led to greater data-management ability and improved response-times, and the availability of guns has led to increased fire power. Surveillance technology and force mobility and direction through airborne support are all now part of the policing facility, which can be mobilised under the name of "mutual support" to deal nationally with national problems like the riots of 1981 and the coal industry dispute of 1984-1985. All these developments have come about within an administrative structure laid down by the Police Act 1964 which in effect gives little scope for local politicians to influence the various trends in policing style while providing opportunities for chief officers and the Home Office to influence policing either in concert or by individual initiatives. Central government can give both physical and political support to the policing function whilst the local police authorities will be confined to narrow interpretations of the requirement to "secure the maintenance of an adequate and efficient force" (1) on the basis that anything more would trespass upon "operational independence". Although there is a convincing legal argument to contradict this state of affairs (2) the political facts of life have meant that police authorities who seek a greater say are condemned as seeking political control whilst those authorities who acquiesce in new policing styles in their area are seen as apolitical. Presumably the same is thought of those in central government who can encourage or condemn, and who know in the last resort their influence can take the shape of legislation which alters the balance between Power and Liberty. It is for these reasons that those who think that we have moved towards a de facto national police force might be forgiven for reaching that conclusion.

In contrast, the police view is that accountability is not accountability to persons but to the law, and through the independence of the law the citizen will find protection from abuse of power. This is a view shared by a Prime Minister whose legal training has equipped her with the language of the classical theory of the Rule of Law. The political vocabulary of Prime Minister and Home Secretary alike includes calls for the maintenance of respect for the law, support for the police and the preservation of law and order. Since this argument proceeds on the comfortable assumption that all these phrases correspond with reality in so far as the exercise of public power is concerned, and that the main problem is to make citizens comply with the law, the climate for criticism of the police is often hostile. It is almost as though criticism of the police is a denial of the Rule of Law, which although never explained to the wider public, contains all that is good and which every right-thinking member of society should be striving for. The extent of the politicians' explanation of this evocative phrase is normally left to the implication that it means that citizens must obey the law and that law observance by Government may be taken for granted. However, a closer examination of some of the developments of the past decade can prompt the conclusion that the demotion of the idea to the status of a political catch-phrase, may, in the policing environment which has come about during the past two decades, be itself a subversion of the Constitution and it is the purpose of this chapter to consider the selective application of the idea in past policing practice, and to assess whether the idea will have any meaning as a constitutional doctrine in the policing of the future.

Politics And The Rule Of Law

The law and order debate very often involves individuals talking in terms of a declining respect for the law which is in some way linked to indiscipline in schools or the family. (3) Those who support such views will call for more law in the hope of obtaining more order, but it is an oversimplification to think that such calls always amount to the maintenance of the Rule of Law. As we shall see later, this is because the Rule of Law not only refers to the existence and the observance of law but also to its quality. The central concern for observers of the police should always be the degree to which the achievement of order coincides with the standards which should be secured in a society which takes the principle of the Rule of Law as one of its fundamental philosophies. This question is not necessarily answered in terms of legality only. If, for example, the police decided that order could be established by rounding up large numbers of picketing strikers on the basis that order could best be preserved with them in prison, the action could be seen as very effective. If there was no such power then quite clearly the law has not governed the actions of the police. If there was such a power, then it can be argued that the standards for which the Rule of Law performs a shorthand function, e.g. freedom from arbitrary power, have been ignored by the legislators who gave the police such a power in the first place. Whether legal or not, such action would fall short of many people's expectations as to the quality of law. The correct course is for government to govern according to laws which meet a certain qualitative standard so that obedience to them is generally accepted and achieved. However, the last two decades have been characterised by two different types of law-breaking problems. Firstly, the continuing rise in the crime rate has made law and order a political issue, and secondly, political issues themselves have led to various forms of law breaking ranging from disruption of public inquiries through to terrorism. (4) The police have had to deal with both areas of growth in illegal activity with the consequence that the police have become involved in the political debate seeking new laws to deal with the disorder which confronts them. Unfortunately, the emotive nature of the issues has lead to a blurring of the distinctions to be drawn between the effectiveness of law and the underlying values which influence its quality. The popular usage of the phrase does not articulate these values, so that a gulf has arisen between those who campaign for effectiveness and those who do not wish to sacrifice quality. Where the danger lies is in the two approaches being seen as one and the same thing.

Some examples of this blurring of effectiveness and quality can be found in the views expressed by spokesmen for the Police Federation. When the Federation launched its campaign for the re-introduction of the death penalty in March 1982, its then Chairman, Mr James Jardine called on policemen to "go to war" on crime and condemned government for "paying lip service to the rule of law". (5) Mr Jardine's reference to the Rule of Law is here to be taken as synonymous with law and order and effectiveness since he condemned the abolition of the "sus law", and criticised the "armies of specialists" who emphasised the need for a tolerant police force rather than law enforcement. The present Chairman, Mr Les Curtis, continued this theme in a speech delivered in January 1983 when he accused the GLC Police Committee of giving support to groups, "which are working to undermine the rule of law", (6) and in a speech in October 1984 commenting on the Police Debate held at the Annual Conference of the Labour Party he said,

"The petrol bombers, the looters and burners were praised, as defenders of their communities, from a jack-booted police army of occupation...."

He also expressed concern as to how the police could operate under a Labour Government in the light of the party's attitude to the coal industry dispute,

"The police service deeply, bitterly, and fearfully resents the Labour Party's verdict on the police. We are fearful, because we wonder how it will be possible to serve the people of this country, in some future crisis of this nature, if the party in power adopts a policy of blaming the police, and forbidding them, incredibly, to intervene to restore law and order, if the lawbreakers happen to be engaged in an industrial dispute!"

The Police Review saw the dangers of this continued intervention into a polarising debate and in an editorial suggested that the time had come for the Police Federation to seek its Parliamentary Adviser (currently Mr Eldon Griffiths, Conservative)from the more neutral ground of the Alliance benches. (7) This suggestion was not taken up and it is left to the observer of the debate to try and separate the rhetoric from the reality. One thing seems to be quite clear, the police feel that they are threatened by disruptive elements whose criticisms have unacceptable motives and that,

"....only the Police and, on track record, a minority of the legal profession, will speak for law and order in the enforcement sense. On the other side will be ranged the big guns of every minority group and sociological agency – many with doubtful motives – propounding the theory of a violent and unfeeling Police Service whose only aim is to inconvenience, or convict, as many innocent persons as possible". (8)

It may be observed that the emphasis here is "law and order in the enforcement sense" and this may be contrasted with law and order in the qualitative sense which is better described by the phrase Rule of Law. The enforcement sense has dominated the police contribution to the debate and the danger of casting the debate in the language of the war on crime is that those who seek to articulate the qualitative sense are also perceived as enemies. But it is perfectly possible to be critical of the police, desire law and order and seek a less selective application of the values implied by an acceptance of the Rule of Law, without being a subversive or a member of the enemy within. That there are those who think the contrary is perhaps shown in the allegations that officers of the NCCL have in the past had their telephones tapped (9) and in the way police critics have been invested with unspecified sinister motives. There is however a more innocent explanation of the criticism which the police as an institution has attracted during the past two decades, and that is that the police themselves have not sufficiently recognised that the original principles underlying the Rule of Law were directed towards the exercise of public power and that as well as having a duty to enforce the law it is incumbent upon them to obey the law in carrying out their work. The problem of ensuring the proper exercise of public power is an enduring and complicated one and it is no answer to ignore the difficulties. In order to understand those difficulties it is necessary to go back to first principles.

The Principles Of The Rule Of Law:

Ordinary Law In Ordinary Courts

In all the debate surrounding the policing issues culminating in the Police and Criminal Evidence Act 1984 there was little reference to the origins of the notion of the Rule of Law. No one seems to have related its origins in that often cited, but little appreciated, document, Magna Carta, 1215, which placed even the Sovereign under the law, and still less did anyone draw the attention of the public to the writings of Professor A.V. Dicey who in 1885 attempted to explain what English lawyers understood by the phrase. (10) Even before we start to consider what Dicey understood the phrase to mean there is some doubt as to whether this is a worthwhile exercise. Professor De Smith, in his student textbook, refers to Dicey's "....idiosyncratic ideas ....rooted in Whiggish libertarianism...." (11) and concludes that they no longer merit detailed analysis. A phrase so often used by politicians and policemen merits little more than half a page. Nevertheless, the prominence of the phrase in the policing debate does not permit the consignment of Dicey's views to the constitutional attic.

That the Rule of Law involves more than mere obedience by citizens to laws created by those with power should be obvious from the great lengths which Dicey went to in setting out what he saw as the three meanings of the phrase. In essence he re-iterates the principles of Magna Carta Articles 39 and 40, but he takes the matter further by setting certain standards for the content of the law which government is to be subject to. In his first meaning he states that punishment can only result from a distinct breach of the law which has been established in the ordinary legal manner before the ordinary courts. Such a system which has this idea of "due process" is distinguishable from systems of government which are "based on the exercise by persons in authority of wide, arbitrary, or discretionary powers of constraint." (12) It can be seen here that Dicey is concerned not only with the arrangement of the legal system which ensures that it is courts and not officials who decide whether or not to penalise a citizen, but with the nature of the powers wielded on behalf of the state. As a generalisation this meaning has its limitations as it does not deal directly with wide powers conferred by law but by implication this is also a mischief which Dicey sees as being inconsistent with the Rule of Law. Arbitrary or discretionary powers are undesirable whether derived from law or from force of arms, since in the end it amounts to the same thing and it is this characteristic which will distinguish a Rule of Law system from those which are not. Even if we make allowance for the way 20th Century government in Britain has had to make use of discretion in order to meet certain public objectives, the lesson of this particular Victorian moral for today's politicians and policemen is that powers which are based on discretion always require close scrutiny in their creation and exercise in order to control their extent. It is therefore perfectly respectable, if we accept this tradition, to question the granting and exercise of discretionary powers and it has been the task of Administrative Law, only emerging towards the end of Dicey's career, to perform this function in the context of administrative bodies and tribunals. Dicey's principal safeguard in ensuring that developments going counter to the Rule of Law did not come about, was his great faith in the representative principle. Although Parliament was subject to no higher law and could pass laws in conflict with the Rule of Law, the representative principle would operate to confine it within acceptable limits and so the achievement of the Rule of Law will be dependent upon the views of the prevailing majority in Parliament. (13) Although it is now necessary to recognise that Parliament should be aware of the United Kingdom's obligations under the European Convention on Human Rights, in the first instance the balance between confined power and discretionary power can be altered by Parliament, and the choice which had to be made in the context of police powers was whether order was worth purchasing through the granting of more discretion.

It is at this point that we find the first non-subversive criticism of the 1984 Act. At several places new powers are given which will be dependent upon a police officer forming a view. This might be whether he has reasonable grounds for suspecting that a person is in possession of stolen goods or prohibited articles, whether an offence is a serious arrestable offence, whether a name or address given by an offender is sufficiently reliable to make an arrest unnecessary or whether it is practicable to make a particular record at a particular time, or appropriate to allow a person in custody to have his presence notified to some third party or to allow access to a solicitor. (14) The fear which should be prompted by the Dicey tradition is whether these discretions are capable of sufficient control so that police practice does not lapse into convenient short cuts which for the most part go unchallenged. It will be seen later that this has happened with certain police practices in the past. That police powers are discretionary has been confirmed in the case of Mohammed-Holgate v. Duke (1984) (15) where it was held that the power of arrest was an executive discretion and would have to be exercised in accordance with the well established principle of administrative law set out in Associated Provincial Picture Houses v. Wednesbury Corporation (1948) (16) that discretions are to be exercised reasonably i.e. irrelevant factors are not to be taken into account and the exercise must not be tainted by bad faith. However, the exercise of police discretion has not been seen as an obvious category of administrative law, and in the light of the few cases there have been the courts are reluctant to intervene since to do so is seen as encroaching upon operational freedom. (17) Nevertheless, it may be that in view of the new mixture of rules brought about by the 1984 Act a new phase of controlling police discretion may start. In the past a challenge to the exercise of police power could come in the form of an action for assault, false imprisonment or trespass, sometimes with a choice of either criminal or civil proceedings, or through an application for Habeas Corpus. All of these have their limitations in that the initiative has to be taken by the individual and the practice of the courts with regard to Habeas Corpus of adjourning applications for 24 hours has limited its usefulness. Other challenges may come in the form of a defence in criminal proceedings such as prosecutions under Sec 51 of the Police Act 1964 for assault or obstruction of an officer in the execution of his duty. Other opportunities may come in the form of a claim that evidence is inadmissible. This diverse collection of possible controls has not however prevented abuses of the stop and search powers or the imposition of road blocks nor indeed breaches of the Judges Rules, and it remains to be seen whether the addition of a new mixture of rules will add to the existing armoury. Police power is now declared in case law, statute law and the various Codes of Practice provided for under the 1984 Act. Although a breach of the Codes cannot give rise to any criminal or civil proceedings they may be taken into account where it appears to the court that the matter is relevant to any question to be determined, and the officer will be liable to disciplinary proceedings provided this is not precluded by the double jeopardy rule, i.e. where a police officer has been acquitted or convicted of a criminal offence and the disciplinary offence is substantially the same. (18)   The other route for the aggrieved citizen is to avoid court proceedings and make a complaint under the Complaints Procedure. As is discussed elsewhere in this collection this also has its limitations and much will depend on the degree of credibility it can acquire in the absence of independent investigations.

It can be seen from this brief survey that making the constable accountable to the law may be possible but there are many difficulties to be overcome in the form of proof, securing the right legal advice, as well as risking costs at the end of the day. The main disadvantage is that they all take the form of post mortem action and are a poor substitute for meticulous law observance on the part of the police, and it would be a dangerous state of affairs if the risk of such action were regarded by the police as one of the inevitable overheads of the system. It is no answer for the police to say that should the citizen feel the police have invoked a dubious power or have acted in the absence of even dubious authority, that the citizen can always challenge the power in the courts. (19)   To do so fails to recognise that the police have the greater advantage in the legal system which arises not only from their resources but from their status as both law enforcer and law observer. This raises issues connected with Dicey's second meaning.

Equality Before The Law

Dicey's second meaning was associated with his first. Whilst officials were not to have wide, arbitrary or discretionary powers neither were they to be beyond the range of the courts "....every man, whatever be his rank or condition, is subject to the ordinary law of the realm and amenable to the jurisdiction of the ordinary tribunals." (20)   We have seen above how this can come about but achieving the principle of equality before the law is not easy. It should mean that where a police officer breaks the rules there should be just as much vigour in dealing with him as there would be for other citizens. There is of course an argument which would suggest even greater vigour than usual should be applied in that a police officer has been entrusted with special powers and status and in departing from that trust should expect severe treatment. Such was the view expressed by Mr Justice Cantley in sentencing Sarah Tisdall for breach of the Official Secrets Act "It is very important that people put in a position of trust....should not flout their obligation." (21)   Furthermore, since the police response to demands for a greater degree of accountability to police authorities is always met with the answer that the police are accountable to the law, (22) then there is still further justification for exacting requirements from the police when it comes to observing rules. In any one year a diligent reader of the newspapers will come across many examples where police officers have been prosecuted for criminal activity, but these should not be seen as the only form of rule-breaking which take place in the police community. Nor should it be assumed that bringing officers before the courts is without its problems. Loyalty to colleagues and the force have to be overcome. As an editorial in Police Review noted,

> "The satisfaction that normally comes from a successful prosecution can never be experienced when the defendant is a police officer.

Giving evidence against an officer with whom you have never worked, have never seen before, is stressful enough. Prosecuting someone whose family knows your family, who has paraded for duty with you, eaten the same canteen meals, and dodged the same sergeant, is a special kind of trauma." (23)

The editorial went on to comment that there was nothing remarkable to the layman in reports that one police officer has prosecuted another, but perhaps it is somewhat remarkable that we expect the police to investigate wrongdoing among their own ranks. They are certainly here being given equal treatment with other citizens in that they are investigated by the police but there the equality ends since the policeman investigating the citizen is automatically apart from the broader community by virtue of his membership of a close and interdependent group, and we would certainly find it unacceptable if an offence committed by a citizen were investigated by his workmates. There are two sides to this problem, firstly the question of whether internal mechanisms are enough and secondly, and just as important, whether they are convincing to the general public. As usual, Justice should be demonstrated to be done and the police are not the only professional group to have difficulty convincing their critics that they are effective in maintaining standards. It is because of these human difficulties that the complaints system has featured so much in the debate surrounding the 1984 Act, but it is ironic that such a process sounds very much like the special procedures for special people which Dicey is warning of in his first two meanings of the Rule of Law. Granted, they are in addition to the ordinary processes but if confidence in this aspect of police work is not restored then independent investigation proposals will be difficult to resist. The revelations of the PSI report and the preparation of a code of ethics for the Metropolitan Force announced by the Commissioner in 1983 may be one way forward along with the wide range of training programmes that are being developed. Past practice and the special status of the police officer means that there are no short term solutions, and the way the police use their new powers will have a great influence on the success of these initiatives.

Whilst the PSI report found that the Metropolitan Force had lost the confidence of a large number of white youths and that there was a dangerous lack of confidence in the police on the part of London's black youth, Londoners as a whole were satisfied with the policing service. (24) This no doubt reflects an inevitable satisfaction with the police on the part of the general public who have very little to do with the police and who are regularly cast in a favourable light by the media. In this context the police have a considerable advantage over their critics in that their successes and their difficulties can at times be given considerable publicity which will show how they are in the frontline in the war on crime. The recent appearance of the BBC Television programme, Crime Watch UK, is just one way in which the police have been able to present a favourable image through well-chosen officers and through graphic illustrations of the kind of criminal and crimes they have to deal with. Despite a standard warning at the end of the programme that violent crime is a comparatively rare occurrence it is difficult to leave the programme without feeling that it cannot do anything to reduce irrational fears which might lead many viewers to have an indulgent attitude towards the police. It is also hard to avoid drawing comparisons with the scenes of RAF Operations rooms so beloved of post-war film makers in which the progress of the enemy is plotted. The backdrop of typists and telephonists is a powerful image and must be regarded by the police, not only as an important method of gaining public involvement in the investigation of crime, but as a very effective method of gaining and maintaining public sympathy. Other more specific coverage of police work has also become a feature in news programmes so that when a major investigation has been completed, such as the drugs conspiracy case, Operation Julie, or the Yorkshire Ripper Case with the conviction of the culprits, a full documentary account of the police investigation is presented. Sometimes media coverage can misfire as with the Police documentary on the work of the Thames Valley Constabulary, or with the press conference announcing the arrest of the Yorkshire Ripper where the emotions of victory seem to have negatived the presumption of innocence; but even these lapses can add credibility to the broader public perception since the police can be seen to be fallible and in some cases prepared to show themselves to the public, "warts and all".

Even without this modern form of real-time police coverage the hazards of the policing job will inevitably give rise to events which will command public sympathy. Each week will produce examples of the policing task carried out well and illustrations of the dangers through events like the Harrods Bombing and the murder of Yvonne Fletcher outside the Libyan Embassy. Police survivors of road accidents, stabbings, shootings and blindings are an unfortunate fact of the police occupation as are the occasional multiple tragedies like the drowning of the police officers at Blackpool in a seafront rescue. The combined effect of media coverage can therefore be seen as a danger in that it could blind many to the faults of the police and make criticism a disloyal if not distasteful activity. If an indulgent attitude is thus created then events like Confait, the Stephen Waldorf shooting and pistol whipping and the excesses of policing styles in industrial disputes, will be made that much easier to regard as aberrations which disclose little cause for concern. A legal system which claims to achieve equality before the law must not allow itself to be selectively used and the climate of opinion within which policing takes place recognised as one of the factors which can undermine the translation of rhetoric into reality.

The power of the press is not only recognisable in its reporting of police work but in the way the police could use the press, through a public relations function in constabularies, which seeks to present the police and the news it generates in a way which is conducive to the policing function. It has been recognised that "the public" is no longer accessible to the police because of what may be described as the privatisation of society,

> "The cynic could argue quite persuasively that the best police endeavours to recapture personal contact by returning officers to the beat may already be doomed. For the public is no longer available. Instead, leafing through the Sun, glued to the television screen, tuned on to local radio for a daily diet of action news and comment, the man in the street of yesterday has been transformed into the armchair pundit of today, vicariously involved in the drama of global affairs from his ringside seat provided by the media, ready to question, challenge and heckle on cue." (25)

Consumers of the police function are seen as being capable of influence either for or against the police and accordingly the objective of police public relations work is to "win the hearts and minds of the public", whether through evening classes to educate the public about the role of the police in society or through the maintenance of particular crimes in the public eye. This is part and parcel of the response by the police to the criticism that they have attracted in recent years and although public relations is only now becoming a more recognisable police resource it is one which has considerable potential for a disproportionate response to the criticism levelled at the police. If this occurs then an inequality in the ability to communicate with the public may arise and the distinction between education and propaganda may be difficult to draw. Once police officers changed from silent servants to outspoken critics then it was only a matter of time before consideration was given to the way the police view should be presented. and we have probably started to leave the age of the embarrassing impromptu statement by a police spokesman. It was perhaps apt that 1984 saw Sir Kenneth Newman named "Communicator of the Year" by the British Association of Industrial Editors. In his acceptance Sir Kenneth stressed the importance of communication skills which required admission of error where criticism was justified and robust rebuttal where it was not and undertook to make, "....every effort, wherever and however possible, to give due publicity to the courage and dedication, the warmth and patience, demonstrated by Metropolitan police officers." (26) This emerging trend is now well-established and is a reaction to the "perceived big guns of every minority group and sociological agency...." which the Superintendents Association felt were ranged against them in the policing debate. (27) It is likely that the use of the press by the police, if it secures greater prominence in the minds of our privatised citizens, than the views of the critics, will emphasise an inequality in the debate and make criticism of post 1984 policing more difficult to place before a public which has never been entirely sure of its rights and which will no doubt be left to become aware of the extent of the new police powers as a result of its own efforts, criminal or otherwise.

If the police acquire a superiority in communication resources then this will complete a collection of advantages that the police have over the public. A similar inequality is the ability of the police to speak with authority as to what they think the law is at any given time. They are able to take the initiative and should they be challenged they have all the resources of a public authority available to them which of course includes an institutional rather than a personal liability for the expenses of litigation. The police may also be said to receive an invisible subsidy through the ignorance of the public,

> "It is impossible to argue that a person should not know his legal rights, but it must be admitted that the police have benefited in the past from some ignorance on the part of the public generally." (28)

This ignorance is perhaps an indictment of our education system as well as the information environment within which ordinary people exist. The oversimplification of procedures which filters through media phrases such as "helping with enquiries", "detained for questioning", and the frequent absence from news reports of the grounds upon which people have been arrested, do not encourage a "due process" frame of mind. On occasions there may be good reasons for restricting information but it is difficult to see what reasons there are for not emphasising civil liberties and police powers in our education system other than they are seen as irrelevant, or are taken for granted or perhaps even seen as socially counterproductive. In contrast, other attempts at emphasising rights may be seen as very desirable such as the need to make people aware of their rights as consumers which runs in many towns to the extent of having publicly funded advice centres for shoppers. Indeed it is likely that citizens' rights may be crowded out by the moves to make "better consumers" of our citizens. In its publication, "A Better Class of Consumer" (29) the National Consumer Council urged greater emphasis on teaching young people their role as consumers in society, not only as shoppers, but as consumers of public services, and in recent years the Law Society has been in the process of preparing teaching programmes for schools intended to bring the pupils' attention to the working of the law and its relevance to them as citizens. It remains to be seen what balance will be struck between the narrower view of consumers as shoppers or clients, and the broader approach which emphasises individual liberty. A possible difficulty with the teaching of civil liberties to school children, if it ever comes about, may be along the same lines as has been experienced with the teaching of Peace Studies in that the substantive subject is not easily separated from politics, and that allegations of bias from both sides of the debate are likely when the distinction between Law and Order and the Rule of Law reflects the absence of consensus on the relationship of effectiveness to Liberty. According to one researcher the legal education that our young citizens receive at present emphasises the duty of obedience to the law with a consequent ignorance of civil liberties and in particular the law of arrest. (30)

Since an informed citizen is probably the best check on an abuse of power at source it is perhaps time that the attention of legislators was shifted from post-mortem controls like the complaints procedure to a general deterrent against abuse of power in the form of an informed public. For the moment the legislation has avoided a general exclusionary rule for improperly obtained evidence, but should the 1984 Act fail to deliver the purported package of the Royal Commission which was to strike the right balance between powers and safeguards, then this may in the end have to be the way the police are kept within the rules. If a practitioner knows that the use of short cuts will disqualify him from the game then the temptation to pursue them will be considerably reduced. Likewise, if the policeman knows that he will not be able to rely on the passive ignorance of his suspect, then there is an improved chance that the policing function will operate in an atmosphere of mutual respect; where the citizen knows his rights, and where the policeman recognises the limits of his powers. The difficulty of course lies in the quitting of bad habits and old suspicions and this is something which, if possible at all, will take time to achieve.

Further difficulties of equality generally may be cited which contribute to the special status of the police. In recent years the pay of police officers has been increased so that with overtime and housing allowances they are now very much better off than many of the people they police and there is a danger that the already institutional separation from the community will be magnified by this economic advantage. Political decisions have brought this about which are consistent with the policy of a government which wishes to be seen doing something about Law and Order. On the other hand resources are not limitless and decisions will have to be made as to how policing priorities are to be arranged. With chief police officers claiming operational independence it is inevitable that decisions will not always be seen as neutral so that the mutual aid of the Coal Industry dispute will lead the police directly into the political arena, irrespective of whether they have been encouraged by the support of central government. If a well-paid and powerful group such as the police are seen to be socially and politically partisan then the chances of those affected by such policing developments seeing the police as having the same standing before the law as themselves become greatly reduced. Indeed, equality of treatment under the law is unlikely to be achievable whilst economic problems prevail. Even before the government is able to consider action on the recommendations of the Royal Commission on Legal services that there should be a nationwide network of Legal Advice Centres, (31) the Law Centres that do exist experience continual problems of funding and workload whilst even the well established Citizens Advice Bureaux find themselves affected by the consequences of rate-capping, and with the long-running Coal Industry Dispute (1984/5) the ability to give citizens equal protection under the law is severly strained. As a visitor to the Thames Valley Constabulary observed,

> "It was quite a revelation to see just how much the miners' strike is straining police resources - especially in the holiday season. On the evening of our visit there were only four constables 'on the beat' (either on foot or in cars) in the whole city of Oxford sub-division, - so few that half our visiting group of six had to go off to Cowley so that we could each be allocated to a car." (32)

The expectation of equality before the law can only be achieved through expenditure which is and more controlled by central government. The degree of commitment to equality before the law can be gauged by the investment government is prepared to make towards this end. The Police and Criminal Evidence Act 1984 has been justified as necessary to tackle the rising crime rate but it should also be justifiable through an attempt to improve safeguards for the innocent. It was the failure of existing provisions which triggered the reform process, and at the beginning of a "new police" era it may be that such considerations will have come in a poor second in view of the peculiar environment created by policing a society under stress.

A Judge-Made Constitution

Of Dicey's three understandings of the Rule of Law his last is probably the most unsatisfactory to the modern observer of constitutional trends since he bases his favourable view of judge-made constitutions on the generalisation that grand declarations of rights are worthless unless those who create the declarations also provide remedies by which those rights can be secured. Furthermore, he was of the opinion that such declarations could be easily suspended whilst the liberties guaranteed by the ordinary law of England could not be taken away without "a thorough revolution in the institutions and manners of the nation." (33) Where Dicey's error lies is in the failure to realise that such a change in institutions and manners can come about more gradually so that the overall erosion of liberties is almost imperceptible in its advance and that the judges can be party to this process just as much as the legislators and those who exercise lawless power. Indeed, it is perhaps ironic that English law as it now stands in effect suspends, for the purpose of litigation in our domestic courts, the rights of citizens which are declared in the European Convention on Human

49

Rights. Parliament has played its part in this by failing to pass incorporating legislation and the judges have been unable to depart from the bonds of Parliamentary Sovereignty. (34) The consequence has therefore been a gradual legislative intervention into matters of civil liberty with the courts more often than not filling in the gaps in the law in a way which favoured the state rather than the individual. But this is only part of a constitutional drift since there are areas of law where the courts have not been asked to intervene because of the difficulty of equality discussed above. The relevance of this third sense of the Rule of Law to the present discussion is that the way the 1984 Act is operated will be conditioned in the first place by the style of policing which invokes it and in the second, by the degree and nature of the courts' role in supervising its operation. Although the courts will be working within a new mixture of rules the past performance of the courts as a medium for protecting liberty may give some indication of the possible extent of this future supervision. It can also give some indication of how the police have regarded past rules and show how practices will have to be changed.

Most of the parts of the 1984 Act which apply to the investigative process and the relationship between suspect and police officer have been areas of law which have involved varying degrees of abuse by the police and a less than protective attitude by the courts. In some cases the courts have been little used whilst in others their decisions have often been indulgent towards police power. The treatment and questioning of suspects under the Judges Rules became a matter of admissibility with the emphasis being on the voluntary nature of confessions. Subsidiary issues such as access to a solicitor would not be the basis for disciplinary action by the courts through excluding evidence unless the breaches involved the voluntariness of the confession. (35) The Judges Rules were still being disregarded by the police in 1984. (36)

The rules on search and seizure of evidence in the absence of a warrant were extended on the basis of reasonableness as spelled out by Lord Denning in Ghani v. Jones (1970) (37) and subsequently in Garfinkel v. Metropolitan Police Commissioner (1972) (38). Leigh, whilst recognising the disadvantages of an exclusionary rule and the need for legislation observed that, "There is something repellent in dicta which, purporting to uphold the rules relating to the freedom of the individual, nonetheless appear to connive at trespass and overbearing conduct by police officers." (39) The exclusionary rule as incorporated in the 1984 Act is confined to cases where the prosecution fail to show the absence of oppression or circumstances rendering the confession unreliable. In addition there is a discretion to exclude unfairly obtained evidence. (40) There is therefore still scope for the courts to be stricter with the police or to continue the approach discernible before the Act.

Even where search warrants would be appropriate there would seem to be a grey area where consent to searches is relied upon so that the judicial process is not the automatic check which it might at first be thought to be. Lidstone found that over four fifths of searches carried out in three police areas during a six week period were conducted without a magistrate's warrant with the majority of searches being justified on the basis of consent. Even where the warrant is issued there is doubt as to whether the magistrates do anything more than ratify an operational decision of the police. (41) Indeed, the Royal Commission on Criminal Procedure reached (42) the conclusion that for road checks such a warrant would amount to no more than that, yet they were happy to see the magistrate's warrant continue for the search of premises.

As Mike Brogden has shown elsewhere in this collection, stop and search has not been based on "due process". Even policemen now admit to their failings in this respect. Les Curtis has said that, of the thousands of people he had stopped and searched whilst an officer on the beat, 50% of the stops would be questionable, but that to do otherwise would have been against the interests of law enforcement. (43) The draft Code of Practice published by the Home Office states,

> "Statistics on the use to date of powers of stop and search indicate that in most cases no such article was found, and there is strong evidence that on many occasions these powers have been used where reasonable grounds to suspect the individual concerned of having the article in question on him did not in fact exist." (44)

The reason why there is so little litigation can be partly explained by the nature of the power in that it should not usually involve any prolonged detention and in many cases the victims will have no doubt provided resentful co-operation on the basis that this involves less risk of further complications like prosecution for obstruction or assault of the officer. The new powers have attempted to state more clearly the duties of an officer on making a search but the uncertainties of the law relating to the definition of an offensive weapon consisting of prima facie innocent articles have been continued. A possibility which the Royal Commission anticipated but which it regarded as a matter to be left to reform of that specific law rather than to deny the police a power of enforcement. (45) The Royal Commission also felt it would not be possible to state a precise formula as to what amounted to "reasonable suspicion" for the purposes of a search (46) and this has been left to the Code of Practice in Annex B which emphasises the objective requirement of the concept, the dangers of stereotyping and the requirement of suspicion for stop and search powers being no less than that required to make an arrest for the substantive offence. The new rules therefore incorporate what in theory should have been happening anyway. The requirements of giving the officer's name and station to the suspect and of informing him of the object of and grounds for the search are more demanding than the only lately recognised requirement to tell a suspect the reason for a search (47) but the main omission is that evidence obtained in breach of these requirements will not automatically make any evidence so obtained inadmissible and it is unlikely that a court would find it unfair under the Act. (48) There is therefore no street level penalty and the purported safeguard of records being available for up to a year after the search (49) may well make overall observation of the system possible but it is difficult to see how such records will help an aggrieved suspect unless a police officer is foolish enough to record an obviously improper motive for the search. These requirements might be of assistance to suspects who, having resisted what they regarded as an unlawful search, have been prosecuted for obstructing or assaulting an officer in the execution of his duty since the provisions are worded in a mandatory form and therefore a failure to comply, before starting the search, would take the officer outside his duty. The officer must take reasonable steps to achieve the communication and therefore unreasonable steps could have a similar effect. If there is an emerging trend in the courts to broaden the meaning of wilful obstruction for the purpose of such prosecutions then these provisions could be of the utmost importance to defendants. (50)

The associated power to set up road checks by comparison does not impose any duty on the operational officer to give reasons for the road check and vehicles may be stopped according to any criteria once the setting up of the check has been authorised. (51)   It is an interesting historical coincidence that the two most publicised applications of road blocks, as opposed to checks, have come to the fore prior to the coming into force of the Act. The stopping of miners on the way to pickets has shown how de facto powers can be taken leaving the matter to be sorted out later in the courts, the purpose by that time having been achieved, leaving individuals charged with obstruction of an officer to probe the limits of the law through the medium of his defence. Quite clearly many unlawful stops and re-directions have occurred (52) and the next step will be, if past practice is anything to go by, for the police to ask for the authority to make such stops legal since they were plainly effective. Similarly the road blocks which have been mounted near the Molesworth Air base and which are anticipated by the Chief Constable's plans to issue passes to local residents, (53) will be added to the legislative agenda of those in the forefront of the law and order campaign which has already characterised the eighties.   Commenting on these developments a Guardian editorial said,

> "the miners' strike has provided meaty examples of the police's appropriation of control over freedom of movement. In spite of a court ruling which said that road blocks against pickets were only justifiable where an imminent breach of the peace was anticipated, there has been a standing police "intercept" policy on the roads of the working coalfields. The police have consistently turned back anyone whom they considered might be a picket (and have arrested them for obstruction if they have tried to continue)....next time you go to Molesworth, don't worry. Its only a simple administrative convenience for law enforcement. Ordinary people are grateful that these controls are in force. Its only the civil liberties lobby who are kicking up a fuss." (54)

Even a well established mechanism such as arrest has not been without its problems and the courts have shown themselves to be lacking in overseeing the process. It is true that where a person takes civil action for false imprisonment substantial sums can be recovered. For example, in 1982 two cases against the Metropolitan Police Force resulted in damages of £12,000 and £4,250 (55), but there is an area of police practice which is not so spectacular, but which nevertheless shows a preparedness to put effectiveness before legality. Prior to the 1984 Act the law on arrest could be found in several sources, basically, in the definition of "arrestable offences", in the list of statutes which conferred powers of arrest for specific offences, and in common law powers such as arrest for breach of the peace. To some extent then it could be excusable for officers not to carry round all the intricacies of this long list in their heads although we expect London taxi drivers to perform the mammoth task of memorising the map of London. Occasionally cases will reach the courts which show that a power has been invoked where none existed, but it can be seen that where it does not have a bearing on the proof of an offence the courts will be little concerned.

In the case of R. v. Brown (1977) (56) where it was alleged that the wrongful arrest might taint a prosecution under the breathalyser law the Court of Appeal caused great consternation for some (57) in that the court seemed to be saying that there was a period of detention permitted which allowed constables to decide whether an arrest was appropriate. One report makes clear however that detention for questioning in the absence of an arrest is illegal (58) but it is an interesting case since the police officers concerned appear from the facts to have had a power of arrest anyway, but which no one seems to have invoked. The case arose out of policemen wishing to stop someone due to the nature of his driving although they had not at that stage reached a suspicion of a particular offence. Mr Brown was pursued and eventually stopped his car, double parked, and ran off. Responding to the chase one of the police officers stopped Mr Brown with a rugby tackle. At that stage no lawful arrest had been executed since the officer did not suspect an offence until he smelt alcohol on Mr Brown's breath after taking him back to the police vehicle. He refused to give a specimen of breath and was arrested. The argument was therefore whether this arrest could be lawful since he was already under arrest. It does not appear to have occurred to the officers, and is not mentioned in the case, that as soon as Mr Brown left his car double parked, with the door open, that they could have arrested him for obstruction of the highway. (59) The level of knowledge about powers of arrest seems to have been poor with general suspicion and immediate action conditioning the officer's actions and is a good example of acting first and then trying to sort out the legality of the action at a later stage. This combined with a variation in the reports and a lack of precision in language showed that even the simplest of questions on arrest can become confused.

At least there seems to have been grounds for arrest in Mr Brown's obstruction of the highway, but in cases of obstruction of a police officer there is no such power. Such a categorical statement has however failed to affect police practice since arrests for this kind of obstruction have been regular occurrences. The history of this abuse of power is a good example of how habits replace lawful authority. According to some reports the arrests of miners refusing to turn back at police road blocks have been carried out on this basis and they might also be expected in the demonstrations at Molesworth and similar events. (60)

The section which creates the offence is Sec. 51 of the Police Act 1964 which also provides the offences of assaulting an officer, resisting arrest, as well as the offence of wilfully obstructing an officer. The section says nothing of a power of arrest but some conduct anticipated by the section will give rise to independent grounds for arrest such as where the conduct comes within the power to arrest for a breach of the peace or where there is violence of a nature bringing the conduct within the definition of an "arrestable offence." (61) The 1964 provision re-enacted similar earlier provisions and therefore brought with it the case of Gelberg v. Miller (1961) (62) which is clear authority for the contention that by itself Sec. 51 creates no power of arrest. There are however several cases which proceed on the assumption that there is such a power. In Rice v. Connelly (1966) (63) it was held that remaining silent when asked by a constable for a name and address did not amount to the obstruction offence, yet the facts reveal that Mr Rice had been arrested for the Sec. 51 offence. The case was concerned with the meaning of "wilful" for the purposes of the offence and so the legality of the arrest was not relevant. Nevertheless, in the absence of an expression of disapproval of the arrest, the court loses the opportunity to remind constables of the limitations to their power. Respectability is given to the police action by Lord Chief Justice Parker's observation that, "....the police at the time and throughout were acting in accordance with their duties." (64)   Since Mr Rice does not seem to have been violent he should have merely been told that he would be reported but if a name and address is not available this is rather frustrating for the operational policeman whose only route to a prosecution lies down an illegal path.

Had it been alleged that Mr Rice's conduct was, or caused a breach of the peace to be apprehended, then the decision in Duncan v. Jones (1936) (65) could be relied upon since there the offender seems to have been arrested because the obstruction of the officer arose while the constable was carrying out his duty to prevent an apprehended breach of the peace. Even here there should be some reluctance to describe the case as one authorising arrest for obstruction of an officer, but an arrest for breach of the peace followed by a prosecution under Sec. 51. If that is the case then a lawful arrest can only be secured by giving the correct reason for the arrest i.e., apprehended breach of the peace. It is probably in these cases that we find the origins of the unreliable folk memory which leads policemen to think they have such a power. The blurring of the two powers prevents distinctions being made so that cases can give the impression that to tell a person that he is being arrested for obstruction of an officer constitutes a lawful arrest.   Since the wrong reason is being given and the true reason may not be obvious to the arrested person, the arrest is unlawful according to long established principle. (66) In Piddington v. Bates (1960) (67) a picket was told that he could not proceed to the back entrance of premises since the constable considered that a breach of the peace would be likely if the number of pickets was increased from two to three. The Old Street stipendiary found that this was reasonable and therefore in refusing to turn back, the defendant had obstructed the officer, but it is not clear what reason for the arrest was given. In a case in 1979, a recorder, having referred to the Piddington case, thought that the safe procedure would be to ask such a person to move and then, upon a refusal, to arrest on the basis of obstructing an officer. (68) The case of Tynan v. Balmer (1966) (69) is a case of such an arrest where there was no breach of the peace. The Case Stated which arose from the prosecution for obstruction of an officer says that the strike was well managed and entirely lacking in disturbance but nevertheless the leader of the picket was arrested for obstructing the officer in refusing to stop his members walking round in circles in front of the entrance to their place of work. The judgement is silent as to the legality of the police action although Sec. 121 of the Highways Act and the offence of obstruction of the highway was recognised in so far as it showed that the constable in seeking to remove the obstruction was acting within his duty. It was a pity he did not invoke the power of arrest provided for in that section. (70)

Another explanation for the purported power perhaps lies in the failure of Moriarty's Police Law to recognise the distinctions involved since this standard work on Police Law can be found asserting a common law power of a constable to arrest anyone who assaults or obstructs him in the execution of his duty. Such a statement persists between the 15th edition in 1959 through to the 23rd edition in 1976 and takes no account of the Gelberg decision back in 1961. By the 24th Edition in 1981 the statement of the law takes into account the case of Wershof v. Metropolitan Police Commissioner which had been decided in 1978. (71)   In that case a newly qualified solicitor had been called to the family jewellers where a police officer was trying to take away a ring which he believed to be stolen property without giving a receipt. Mr Wershof insisted on a receipt and was eventually arrested for obstructing an officer with a consequent amount of man-handling whilst being taken into custody. It was held in later civil proceedings that there was no power of arrest for obstruction of an officer except where the conduct gave rise to an apprehended breach of the peace which was not the case here. Unfortunately the wording of the case could still lead officers to think that where there is such an apprehension that the reason for the arrest should be based on obstruction whereas the correct reason should be that of the common law justification for breach of the peace. Whether or not this is the explanation for subsequent cases the idea of arrest for obstructing an officer persists and the criminal courts do not see fit to point out the error of officers who seem to adhere to the incorrect statement of the law which survived for so long in Moriarty. In Ashton v. Merseyside Police in 1981 (72) a young man was arrested and prosecuted for the offence because he had reminded his girlfriend that she was entitled to remain silent in the face of police questioning although the court felt that this conduct did not come within the meaning of "wilful obstruction" for the purpose of the offence. No mention is made of there being any apprehended breach of the peace nor is any comment passed on the illegality of the arrest. In Marsh v. Arscott in 1982 the Times Law Report attributed the following comment to Lord Donaldson: "In appropriate circumstances the police might arrest a person for obstructing or assaulting a police officer in the execution of his duty, for breach of the peace, or for common assault...." (73) although another report has Lord Donaldson making no such statement. (74) Since the former report is the more likely to be read this is an unfortunate divergence in reporting. Two other cases seem to be recognising this non-existent power and inaccurate practice of arresting for obstruction when only breach of the peace should be cited. In Hills v. Ellis in 1983 (75) a football fan witnessed a fight and saw a police officer arrest an innocent party. In trying to draw this to the attention of the arresting officer the defendant was arrested for obstructing an officer. Although the Justices in their Case Stated said that the defendant's intervention had been in an "excited and agitated fashion" there is no suggestion that it caused the arresting officer to apprehend a breach of the peace and even if it did he does not seem to have mentioned this when making his arrest. A similar case followed in 1984 in Lewis v. Cox. (76) Here two football fans had been drinking and one was arrested for being drunk and disorderly and put in a police van. His friend opened the rear door of the van to try and find out where the police were taking the prisoner. On doing this a police officer warned that the friend would be arrested for obstruction if he opened the door again. The door was opened again and the arrest followed. Again no mention is made of the illegality of such an arrest and a conviction for "wilful obstruction of an officer in the execution of his duty" was upheld.

These cases show that the courts have not been eager to point out the extent of police powers when it is a matter of deciding upon questions of law for the purposes of substantive offences. It may of course be said that such people, having been convicted, have little to complain about, but this of course relegates procedure and legal entitlement to a subordinate level after expedience and avoids the question of whether only guilty people find themselves being arrested in such a way. It also raises the question of whether this "power" will survive the passing of the Act of 1984. Since it will be just as questionable in 1985 as it was back in 1961 there is no compelling reason to think that it will not, and it is a good example of how de facto power operates with the courts choosing to ignore the niceties of the law. Following past events, should any condemnation of this practice ever be voiced which the police institution regards as a serious challenge, calls to make such a practice legal should be expected. In the meantime the requirements for arrest in the 1984 Act should be viewed with the knowledge that the police have managed to invent a power of their own despite legal authority to the contrary since 1961.

The new powers of stop and search and arrest may give rise to difficulties associated with the matters just discussed. Since the combined effect of these reforms is an extension of powers then it is likely that more people will find themselves objecting to the exercise of police power and therefore being arrested for obstruction. For this to be brought about legally under the Act it must be shown that one of the general conditions of arrest is available under Sec. 25 and it is here that we find a new discretion for the police to exercise. If the cases seen above are considered against the new provisions then an officer seeking to make such an arrest must think that the service of a summons is impracticable or inappropriate because of the offender's name or address being unknown or unreliable, or because there is a reasonable belief that the arrest is necessary to prevent physical injury, loss or damge to property, an offence against public decency or an obstruction of the highway. In other words, there will probably be many cases in which one of these subsidiary requirements will be present so that the police will have acquired a legal power to make an arrest for the offence. On the other hand there is also scope for further high handed action or expedient practice which will no doubt pass without comment before the courts.

The offence of obstruction is only one non-arrestable offence which combined with a general condition may lead to a person being taken into custody. If for example a minor litter offence or bye-law offence is committed and an officer is able to identify a relevant general condition, then an arrest can follow. If a constable wishes to bring about custody for the purpose of gaining a confession then it would seem that the decision in Mohammed-Holgate cited earlier (77) will be no bar to such an ulterior motive, and the officer who wishes to depart from the rules by making a false allegation of a minor offence or of the presence of a general condition may well prove difficult to control given the problems of inequality discussed above and the disinclination of courts to condemn procedural irregularity.

Furthermore, there is a risk that the new powers, if combined with an insensitive style of policing which places the emphasis on effectiveness rather than legality, will add to the friction between the police and certain communities. The Law Society in its memorandum commenting on the Police and Criminal Evidence Bill said, "....it is not difficult to imagine situations following the grant of this wide new power, in which certain police officers might be tempted to harass members of this community....". (78)

In the passing of the Police and Criminal Evidence Act we have seen the Parliamentary process amending our Constitution in a particular way so that whatever might be said of safeguards, in the end the police have more power. The Constitution for what it is worth has had a different tradition in the past which gave power begrudgingly to the policeman or other public official. The time has long since past when our Consitution could be described as judge-made since it is now Parliament, or more correctly, a

Parliamentary majority which will call the tune. It is that majority which will decide whether or not to allow British judges to apply the provisions of the European Convention on Human Rights in our domestic courts and it is that majority which will have to listen to the next wave of demands for more public power. The trend seems to show that Parliament may not be able to resist such calls. In the meantime Parliament's latest constitutional amendment will come into force and how far the extent of the new constitution will be determined by operational policemen and judges remains to be seen. The past performance of both groups should give rise to some scepticism on the part of those concerned with constitutional matters and perhaps prompt some questions about the Constitution we have inherited. We are not a nation of Constitutionalists because in modern terms we don't really have one. Instead we have a diffuse system far removed from the apprehension of the ordinary citizen which is easily reduced to a system of law in which the requirements of the citizen to obey dominates all else to the exclusion of quality. The Rule of Law could perhaps at one time be seen as a convenient description of all those attributes which were self-evident to Victorians like Dicey, but today there seems little agreement as to what is self-evident in our Constitution. Selective constitutional blindness and sometimes ignorance, have all afflicted those who have advocated "effectiveness" for our policing system. In the years toward 2000 it will not only be the people who need some education in constitutional matters but also our policemen and politicians. If that is a subversive object, then so be it, but others might see it as seeking to achieve the Rule of Law in preference to the more simplistic and dangerous concept of Law and Order.

NOTES

1. Sec 4 (1) Police Act 1964.

2. Richard Clayton and Hugh Tomlinson, "Bad History and Dubious Law", 134 NLJ 880.

3. For example, Eldon Griffiths in TV AM interview 13.3.85 and Margaret Thatcher, House of Commons 14.3.85 in response to rioting at Luton Football ground.

4. See Why is Britain becoming Harder to Govern? Edited by Anthony King.

5. Guardian 18.3.82.

6. Times 14.3.83.

7. Full text of speech and editorial Police Reveiw 12.10.84.

8. Written Evidence of Police Superintendent's Association of England and Wales, p.1 para 5.

9. "20/20 Vision", MI5's Official Secrets, Channel 4, 8.3.85.

10. Introduction to the Law of the Constitution, A.V. Dicey. First published 1885.

11. Constitutional and Administrative Law, 4th Edition at p. 30.

12. Op cit p. 188.

13. Op cit Chpt 13.

14. See Sections 1, 116, 25, 3, 56 and 58 respectively of Police and Criminal Evidence Act 1984.

15. [1984] 1 All ER 1054.

16. [1948] 1 KB 223.

17. See R v. Metropolitan Police Commissioner, ex parte Blackburn [1968] 2 QB 118.

18. Sec 104 Police and Criminal Evidence Act 1984.

19. Such was the reaction of a spokesman for the Kent Constabulary with regard to the stopping of miners at the Dartford Tunnel.

20. Dicey, op cit p. 193.

21. As reported in the Guardian 24.3.84.

22. See for example "Answerable to the law alone", Robert Bartlett, Police Reveiw 23.11.84.

23.   30.11.84.

24.   Police and People in London: Policy Studies Institute: See Vol 1. pp 316 - 327.

25.   "The Consistent Hard Sell," Roger Busby, press officer for Devon and Cornwall Constabulary, Police Review 23.3.84.

26.   Reported in Police Review 2.3.84.

27.   Op cit note 8.

28.   Ibid at p.3 para 12.

29.   Published March 1983.

30.   See Ignorance of the Law, G. Vorhaus, Hillingdon Legal Resources Centre 1984.

31.   Royal Commission on Legal Services Cmnd. 7648.

32.   Observation of a Church of England Vicar reported in his parish magazine.

33.   Op cit at p.201 but see pp 195 to 202.

34.   Contrast Entick v. Carrington (1765) 19 State Tr. 1029 with Malone v. Commissioner of Police of the Metropolis (No.2) 2 All ER 620.

35.   See Commissioners of Customs and Excise v. Harz and Power [1967] 1 AC 760, R. v. Prager (1972) 1 WLR 260 and R. v. Sang [1979] 2 All ER 1222.

36.   See survey conducted of 31 Camden Solicitors reported in Legal Action September 1984.

37.   (1970) 1 QB 693.

38.   (1972) Crim. L. Rev. 44.

39.   L.H. Leigh, Police Powers in England and Wales at p. 196. See also Reynolds v. Commissioner of Police for the Metropolis [1984] 3 All ER 649.

40.   Secs 76 to 78.

41.   K.W. Lidstone, "Magistrates, the police and search warrants", (1984) Crim. L. Rev. 449.

42.   Cmnd 8092 para 3.33.

43.   Stated in an interview with John Edinow in The Police Bill: A fair Cop? : Radio 4 UK: 28.4.83: author's transcript. Les Curtis, Chairman of the Police Federation.

44. Draft Code of Practice for the Exercise by Police Officers to Stop and Search : Second Draft : January 1985, Note for Guidance 1B.

45. Op cit para 3.21.

46. Ibid para 3.25.

47. Pedro v. Diss [1981] 2 All ER 59.

48. The operation of Sec 78 will make an interesting study when cases start coming before the courts.

49. Sec 3.

50. See "The Offence of Obstruction" (1) Obstructing the Constable and (2) Obstructing Freedom by T. Gibbons and K.W. Lidstone respectively (1983) Crim.L.R. pp 21 and 29.

51. Sec 4.

52 See "Stopping the Miners", R. East and P.A. Thomas 135 NLJ 63.

53. Announced early March 1983 and reported in Guardian 6.3.83.

54. 6.3.84.

55. The cases of Reynolds (1982) Crim. L.R. 600 CA (award of damages by a jury) and Smith (1982) CLY 899: See also the case of Mr Millington, Times 28th May 1983 who was awarded £800 for unlawful detention for 12 hours longer than was necessary.

56. [1977] Crim L.R. 291.

57. See Zander (1977) NLJ 352 and 359 and Lidstone [1978] Crim L.R. 333 and Telling, p.321.

58. (1976) 64 Cr App Rep 231.

59. Sec 121 Highways Act 1959 now replaced by Sec 137 Highways Act 1980.

60. See Guardian editorial 6.3.84 and "Picket Courts", S. Gregson-Murray, Legal Action, August 1984: According to the Guardian editorial 185,000 people were turned back during the first six months of the strike. See also note (52) above.

61. Sec Criminal Law Act 1967 now replaced by Sec 24 of the 1984 Act.

62. [1961] 1 WLR 153 and see also the annotation to the section in Curent Law Statutes.

63. [1966] 2 QB 414.

64.   Ibid at p. 419.

65.   [1963] 1KB 218.

66.   Christie v. Leachinsky [1947] AC 573.

67.   [1960] 3 All ER 660.

68.   R. v. Podger [1979] Crim L.R. 525 (Bristol Crown Court).

69.   [1966] 2 WLR 1181.

70.   The reference in the report to Sec 151 must be a mistake since that section deals with the erection of bridges.

71.   [1978] 3 All ER 540 and see Moriarty's Police Law, 23rd Edition at p. 17 (Mr Wershof was awarded £1000 damages).

72.   [1981] CLY 2096.

73.   The Times 3.3.82.

74.   (1982) 75 Cr. App 211.

75.   [1983] 2 WLR 234.

76.   [1984] 3 WLR 875.

77.   Op cit note 15 above.

78.   Memorandum by the Society's Standing Committee on Criminal Law: Powers of Arrest and Detention, January 1984.

4. POLICING INDUSTRIAL DISPUTES

Richard de Friend and Steve Uglow

Introduction

Policing was a major issue in the experience of all those who were directly or indirectly involved in the miners' strike of 1984-85. For the strikers themselves, their families and neighbours, in mining villages and communities throughout the country, a massive police presence dominated their everyday lives and was a physical symbol of the government's determination to beat the strike. For the NUM, the police operation posed fundamental tactical and strategic problems since, as in 1972 and 1974, the union relied on picketing to bring out working miners, to dissuade striking miners from returning and to stop the import of coal and oil. (1)

For the political, media and academic commentators, discussion of the strike, rightly described as a 'landmark in the political and economic development of post-war Britain', (2) centred on the the manner in which it was policed, obscuring other equally important issues.

Most comment has tried to assess the effect that the police operation had on the strike's eventual outcome and the implications that this holds for a trade union movement faced with a government that sees industrial disputes as a form of civil war and strikers as the 'enemy within.' But here the concern is not with the significance of the police for the strike but the significance of the strike for the police. Does it improve our understanding of the nature and role of policing and in particular of the basis of its legitimacy in comtemporary Britain?

It can be argued that the police operation conflicted with the traditional model of 'legitimate policing'. Yet at the same time, it was an operation with many precedents in the history of policing industrial disputes and reflected recent trends within British policing.

The Legitimacy Of Policing

The effectiveness of any agency, public or private, depends on the material resources, including labour, that it is able to command. This is one measure of the agency's power. But it gives little indication of an agency's authority which is crucial to its ability to carry out day-to-day functions on a continuing and unproblematic basis. For the police, this is encapsulated in the phrase 'policing by consent' - consent and authority derive from their actions and decisions being seen as legitimate.

Legitimacy, for government agencies in liberal capitalist societies, is resolved by the 'rule of law', albeit in varying degrees. The exercise of power, in their actions and the making of decisions, must conform and be seen to conform with the law. This idea of 'rule of law' is of particular importance in establishing the legitimacy of police action. The functions and methods of policing are peculiarly sensitive within terms of liberal constitutional theory, resting as it does on a closely scrutinised relationship between the individual and the state. While other agencies, particularly those responsible for the provision of goods or services, have different criteria on which they can be assessed - namely whether those goods or services are being provided efficiently and effectively (3) - such a clear definition of functions or objectives does not exist for the police. Finally 'rule of law' is central to the police because policing is not merely based on law but is integral to and representative of the law itself.

But police functions and powers are only to a certain extent specified in law - police decisions, as with other agencies, are inevitably discretionary. (4) For these to be legitimated under the 'rule of law' requires that they conform, not to any identifiable statutory provision, but to a set of broad standards that recent jurisprudence has characterised under the notion of 'fairness'. This is clearly indeterminate but represents the underlying standard of procedural or formal justice which is contained in the idea of 'rule of law' itself. It has certain institutional and operational consequences for legitimating police action.

Firstly it implies independence for the command structure. Policy, those discretionary actions and decisions, should be determined by and accountable to the law, rather than to any political process. The police should be immunised from external influences or control.

Secondly it requires that police action be taken on the basis of legally defensible criteria - whether these are decisions about the broad operational guidelines to be followed or whether it is a particular decision to prosecute an individual. What constitutes such criteria is difficult to specify but would generally include sensitivity to the rights of individuals and indifference to the racial, political or ethnic character of those affected by the decisions.

Finally policing in the abstract is open-ended - there are no limits or constraints implied in the work itself. But liberal constitutional theory and the 'rule of law' would impose such constraints, chief of which would be that police intervention should be 'reactive'. In other words police action should only occur on the basis of a reasonable belief that a breach of the law or the peace has occurred or is imminent.

However much these ideas accord or have accorded with the reality of police practices, it is the model of legitimate policing proposed by not only lawyers and the civil liberties lobby but also by the police themselves. (5) It is also the model insisted upon by those who seek to counter demands for greater democratic accountability by stressing accountability under the law.

Policing The Strike

How far did the operation mounted during the miners' strike conflict with with model of 'policing under law'? That it was more than a normal response to an abnormal situation can be seen in the way that the operation was managed and funded and the tactics that were employed.

From the start, there was a unique level of central management and funding of the operation, stemming from the government's view that the strike had to be seen to be defeated and that any measures taken to achieve this were, in Nigel Lawson's phrase, a 'good investment'.

The management was largely in the hands of the National Reporting Centre (6) which was integral to and relied upon existing inter-force 'mutual aid' which was given statutory basis in the 1964 Police Act. (7) This had been considerably improved over the last decade by the establishment of Police Support Units (PSUs). (8)

The NRC's role, on one hand, has been claimed to be nothing more than a central agency for the processing of information and, acting on this, for co-ordinating the movement of men and material around the country. The opposite view sees it as an operational command centre for what was a national police force. Martin Kettle argues that though such claims might be doubted, there is evidence that it did perform 'executive' functions for the operation as a whole - indeed, the operation would not have been possible without the Centre. The consistency of the tactics employed suggests a level of co-ordination and control that went beyond mutual aid.

Whereas the structure of the command system and the political influence over it remain matters for speculation, the tactics adopted by the police have been extensively documented. (9) On the picket lines themselves, the police pursued two separate but related aims - the first was to achieve physical control over the pickets in order to prevent those pickets from stopping men going into work. The second was to establish the police presence at each picket line as the sole source of decision and authority.

The former aim was largely achieved through force of numbers and equipment with carefully planned deployment on a grand scale. The police were rarely outnumbered and were well-equipped with riot control and communications equipment. They enforced spatial separation between those picketing and those going into work, corralling pickets behind a 2 or 3 deep line of officers. This became increasingly heavy as the transport bringing miners to work drew near and passed by, with concerted pushing against the picket line and the occasional frontal assault or snatch squad.

To judge from our own experience in Kent and Warwickshire, the police did establish themselves as the decision-makers, with the senior officer determining whether any NUM member was able to stand at the colliery gate, or to talk to those going into work, where the pickets were allowed to stand or indeed what they were able to shout as working miners passed by. These decisions seemed at any given moment less a response to a particular situation that the police were facing and more an application of a pre-established plan for the management of picket lines. As Scraton puts it,

> "On the picket lines, the police remain the sole agency of decision. The interpretations, definitions and restriction imposed on the strikers by police officers are political decisions which combine operational policy with discretionary practice." (10)

This argument that the police operation was based upon a predetermined plan aimed mainly at neutralising the pickets receives support less from the manner in which the picket lines were policed than from the related actions over road blocks and in those communities which had working miners within them. The road blocks were designed to prevent prospective pickets from entering working areas - in particular Nottinghamshire. Equally the saturation policing of villages was apparently aimed at harassing the pickets in those communities and facilitating the 'back-to-work' movement.

The objective underlying these tactics of the police operation has been obscured by a number of factors. Debate has been dominated by the very scale of the exercise, the manner in which it was managed and funded, the variety of tactics adopted and the legal, political and civil liberties issues that have been thrown up by it. More importantly the police and government saw the strike as entailing breaches of the criminal law on an organised and mass scale and therefore the police had to respond to this.

Any account of the aims of the police operation depends on what view is taken about the degree of integration there was between the government, the NCB and the police over the counter-strike measures in general. This is affected by whether the Tory government are seen as having planned the strike and the response to it, with the objective of breaking one of the last remaining sources of labour indiscipline. (11) But whatever standpoint is adopted, few doubt that the consistent aim of the police throughout the strike was to render picketing as ineffective as possible. This is hardly surprising since the mass picket was the main reason behind the success of the 1972 and 1974 strikes. It was also clear that the NUM again intended to rely heavily upon this tactic.

There is circumstantial evidence that the neutralisation of pickets was the major goal. This is shown by the variations in the level of police activity throughout the strike. Coulter, Miller and Walker (12) show that in the first three months, the operation was directed exclusively at preventing pickets from entering or remaining in 'working areas'. The next three months which culminated in the 'Battle of Orgreave' saw police deployed at power stations, steel works and ports as the NUM shifted its attention to the importation and use of coal and oil.

In the final six months, police activity was in the striking heartland - Yorkshire, Scotland, South Wales and Kent - to support those miners who were seeking to break the strike. Such activity though, throughout the strike, involved the deployment of men and material in a manner which was grossly disproportionate, in many cases, to any picketing that was taking place. Indeed it was often pre-emptive, (13) in advance of such picketing and justified by the police themselves in terms of a 'right to work'. (14)

The contrast between this police operation and the suggested model of 'legitimate policing' could not be starker - the independence and autonomy of chief constables came under attack· as there was direct pressure from the Prime Minister (15) and the Home Secretary to adopt particular strategies and tactics; the traditional neutrality of the police disappeared as they overtly supported one side in an industrial dispute; finally, though there were instances of reactive policing on the picket lines, the structure of the conflict was shaped by a pre-determined, co-ordinated strategy with the consistent aim of neutralising the union's main weapon.

Policing Industrial Relations

The history of trade unionism and the law encompasses the events of 1984 with ease. It has been a continual saga of the legislature and judiciary criminalising industrial action. The police have continued this tradition, though on a scale and with an intensity that is unprecedented. But the police have been used against strikers from the earliest periods of the 'New Police',

> In 1837, some 38 policemen were absent from London for the purpose of suppressing anti -Poor Law riots in Yorkshire, Essex and the West Country. During Chartist disturbances of 1839, detachments of the Metropolitan Police were sent to Loughborough, Mansfield, Monmouth, Bury, Bedlington and Cockermouth....(16)

£10,000 was voted to defray the costs of the officers engaged in the anti-Chartist campaign. (17)

> In the period, 1883-94, the Liverpool Head Constable sent detachments to defend the Caernarvonshire quarries against strikers,

crossed the city boundary to deal with a seamen's strike in Bootle and the Mersey to terminate a Cheshire saltworkers' strike, into St Helens to support an employer against his workforce, to Trafalgar Square for a political demonstration and to Lancaster for a racecourse dispute. (18)

This period was that of the Great Depression with job losses, workers being forced to accept pay cuts as well as being put onto piece work rates instead of being paid on a daily basis. In this crisis of profitability, there were the stirrings of the New Unionism and the police were omnipresent to suppress signs of working class organisation.

Violence was habitually used by the police against strikers, as illustrated by Tom Mann's account of the 1911 dock strike.

If the worst and most ferocious brutes in the world had been on the scene, they would not have displayed such brutality as the Liverpool City Police, and their imported men....such a scene of brutal butchery was never witnessed in Liverpool before. Defenceless men and women, several of whom were infirm and many of whom were aged, were deliberately knocked down by heavy blows from the truncheons of powerful men, and even as the crowd fled from this onslaught, the police still continued to batter away at them....(19)

Ironically a few years later the Liverpool police found themselves facing the violence of the state when troops and tanks were brought in to disperse police strikers in 1919, protesting against the barring of the police from union activity. (20)

A classic example of police actions against dissent was seen with the National Unemployed Workers' Movement, set up in 1921 'as a militant organisation to campaign on behalf of the unemployed'. (21) From the start it was linked to the Communist Party of Great Britain and naturally attracted police attention. They infiltrated the movement so effectively that they had first-hand information about the deliberation of the higher councils of the union. (22) Meetings were broken up when it was sought to hold them outside labour exchanges. The Hunger March of 1932 was heavily policed for its entire journey and culminated in the police seizing the petition (of over one million signatures) that the March wished to present to Parliament. The union HQ was raided and the leaders were prosecuted on charges ranging from sedition to breach of the peace. They were given heavy prison sentences.

Such tactics have exemplified police policy towards unions over the past 150 years. This was not surprising in the context of the membership of the old Watch Committees who paid the wages and controlled the policy of their police. This direct class control of the police no longer exists but is mediated through the state and made legitimate through the 'rule of law'. But police still treat collective dissent, whether political or industrial, as illegitimate if not illegal. Governments are not unnaturally apprehensive of the effects of collective protest and the police are the means to contain those effects, by invalidating the protest or neutralising the striker.

Examples involving the miners are not difficult to find. In Durham in the General Strike there are accounts of the police informing pickets that '.... the Law did not allow pickets to stop Motor Traffic. (23) The same pickets, especially those perceived as the leaders, the 'disaffected', the 'communist agitators', find themselves arrested and then imprisoned or heavily fined by compliant benches of magistrates on the exaggerated and uncorroborated evidence of the police.

The strategy of escorting 'working' miners to work has its precedents. A famous photograph of 1929 shows three men being escorted by 75 police through the hostile stares of villagers in the Garw Valley. (24) A further parallel with 1984 can be seen in Nottinghamshire in 1937 where the once powerful Nottingham Miners' Association had to call on the national Miners' Federation of Great Britain to help in the struggle against 'Spencerism' - the setting up of puppet 'company' unions. This struggle for union recognition centred on Harworth Colliery where the time-honoured tactics of the police were again in evidence, protecting 'working' miners by inundatory policing of small mining communities. The resultant hostility led to a major public protest against the police, as a result of which 11 miners and one miner's wife received prison sentences. (25)

Sometimes the use of the law and the police backfires - in 1941, 4000 miners at Betteshanger in Kent went on strike. Using wartime regulations, the government sought to prosecute 1000 faceworkers - 3 leaders were imprisoned and the rest fined on a day when Canterbury Court resembled a grand picnic as charabancs brought miners and their families out for the day. Within days the government were forced to back down, release those imprisoned and silently take no action to recover the fines. (26) The lesson of those events was evident 5 years later when similar action was urged against the dockers and the Attorney-General, Sir Hartley Shawcross said:

> "You might as well try to bring down a rocket bomb with a peashooter as to try to stop a strike by the process of the criminal law. The way to stop strikes is not by a policeman but by a conciliation officer, not by the assize courts but by the arbitration tribunals."

The 1984 coal strike has witnessed the resurgence of the use of the criminal justice system against industrial dissent - mass policing outside colliery gates, police invasions of mining villages, (27) convoys escorting handfuls of working miners, charges with shield, truncheons, horse and Range Rover, thousands of arrests (28) often on spurious charges, the abuse of bail conditions, heavy sentences for minor offences by magistrates, the allegations of the exclusion of Labour JPs from benches trying miners and the systematic abuse of their powers by the police (29) who have sought to impose curfews, set up arbitrary roadblocks and tell housekeepers who can and who cannot lodge in their houses.

Policing Modern Britain

Since 1964 there have been major changes in the organisation, techniques, training and equipment of the police that make the operation against the miners less of a departure from the proposed model than might be supposed. The independence of local forces from central government is still significant but so is Home Office influence. (30) Though the appointment of a Chief Constable is still nominally in the hands of the Local Police Authority, they can only choose from a short list of candidates drawn up by the Home Office. The national and regional co-ordination of forces is encouraged by the Home Office through the Inspectors of Constabulary. This reached a peak with the development of the National

Reporting Centre in 1972. Whatever its role, the police are capable of being mobilised on a national basis with immediate links between central government and Chief Constables. The local and democratic participation is very limited, even over the financial accountability of the local force. (31)

The British police have traditionally been constrained in their ability to use force. But since 1964 the government have been more directly involved in the control of the police who have been reorganised into more efficient units for the use of force. The impetus for this has often been laid at the door of international terrorism, though Britain has suffered remarkably little from such action. The recipients of the contemporary 'new policing' are British citizens. (32)

The first aspect of this reshaping has been the development of para-military units within local forces. These are maintained on a permanent footing, such as the Special Patrol Groups or Tactical Firearms Units. Secondly we have seen more emphasis on the training, not just of the specialists, but also of the ordinary constable. Ten per cent of the force is now trained in riot control techniques. Though such officers are normally on divisional duties, as Police Support Units, they can be mobilised and rushed to any part of the country, co-ordinated through the National Reporting Centre. Such potential for mass police presence escalates the possibilities for confrontations between protestors or strikers and the police.

The third aspect of this reshaping process has been the expansion of the arsenal of the British police. From the unarmed constable in The Blue Lamp, we have arrived at the stage where the police can call upon handguns, shotguns, rifles, sub-machine guns, rubber bullets, water cannon and CS gas. This has often occurred without the knowledge or consent of the local police authority concerned.

Traditional limits on policing -- the command structure, the capacity to mobilise, the lack of training and the restraints on the use of force -- meant that public order policing tended towards low visibility, persuasion and negotiation, the management of situations through consensus rather than through intervention. But the changes considered above have changed the police into a force so that the state is able to contemplate a successful confrontation with industrial or political dissenters. It is hard to avoid the conclusion that the objectives pursued by the police in such situations are not policing objectives but goals of the government. (33)

Conclusions

Policing the coal strike was not an abnormal operation in police history. But the scope and intensity of the exercise were wholly unprecedented. However even these are a logical outcome of the changes in organisation, training and equipment which have been taking place over the past twenty years. The police are now in a position to deal with the political and industrial dissent which is the predictable result of the structural unemployment in Britain in the last quarter of the 20th century.

It has been argued that the model of police legitimacy founded on the liberal consensus and 'rule of law' has never been the reality of everyday policing but its importance has been more ideological - as a model it strengthened beliefs in a 'policed society' and confirmed assumptions about the constitutional relationship between citizen and state. In accomplishing this, ideas about policing have had a role in obscuring the nature of class relationships in capitalist society.

But for a year Britain has been dominated by the image and the reality of a quasi-national police force, centrally controlled, pursuing the political objectives of government in a pre-emptive and co-ordinated manner. This must undermine the criteria on which the police base the legitimacy of their actions - that is, under 'rule of law' notions. It may also have the effect of diminishing the value of the police as a political symbol, representative of the law in liberal constitutional theory.

We should now expect the police to seek legitimation in other ways - there may be an increasing reliance on their instrumental qualities. In other words, they will present themselves as effective in providing services or reaching objectives, as is the case with other public agencies. Local forces have already introduced 'policing by objectives' schemes which designate particular targets to be achieved within a time limit. Police action and decision-making would be judged by its effectiveness and efficiency in reaching the objective and not by its conformity with the law.

Such efficiency/effectiveness criteria has no place within the liberal model which is less concerned with the ends of policing than with the manner in which policing is carried out. The resulting 'inefficiency' of the police has been a major safeguard in the relationship between the citizen and the state, placing significant limits on the state's capacity to intervene into private lives. The move away from 'rule of law' ideals implied in the management of the coal strike operation and the move towards managerialist attitudes in policing might still prove to be one of the most significant and costly consequences of the strike.

NOTES

1. Scraton P.: 'From Saltley Gates to Orgreave: A History of the Policing of Recent Industrial Disputes' in Fine R. and Miller R. (eds.) Policing the Miners' Strike (1985) (London).

   Beynon H.: 'Introduction' in Beynon H. (ed.) : Digging Deeper (1985) (London).

2. Beynon: op.cit.

3. Corresponding to Weberian 'substantive rationality'.

4. Davis K.C.: Police Discretion (1975) (St. Paul).

5. Metropolitan Police: The Principles of Policing and Guidance for Professional Behaviour (1985) (London).

6. Kettle M.: 'The National Reporting Centre and the 1984 Miners' Strike' in Fine and Miller (eds.) : op.cit. p.23.

7. Police Act 1964 s.14(3).

8. State Research: 'Policing the Eighties' Bulletin 19 at p.146.

9. Coulter J., Miller S. and Walker M.: State of Siege (1984) (London)

   National Council for Civil Liberties: Civil Liberties and the Miners' Dispute (1984) (London).

10. Scraton: op.cit. p.159.

11. Beynon H. and McMylor P.: 'Decisive Power: The New Tory State Against the Miners' in Beynon (ed.): op.cit. p.29 especially the discussion of the Ridley Report at p.34.

12. Coulter, Miller and Walker: op.cit.

13. de Friend R. and Grigg-Spall I.: 'Out of Court' The Guardian 4/4/84.

14. For example, Charles Mc Lachlan, Chief Constable of Nottinghamshire and chairman of ACPO 1984/85 made this argument on several occasions.

15. McIlroy J.: 'Police and Pickets' in Fine and Miller (eds.): op.cit. p.101 at 105.

16. Brogden M.: 'All Police is Conning Bastards' (Paper delivered at the British Sociological Association, University of Warwick, 1979).

17. Report of Metropolitan Police Commissioner (1839) Parl. Papers XXX1 at 702 on the role of the police in the Chartist period, see Mather F.: Public Order in the Time of the Chartists (1959) (Manchester).

18. Brogden M.: op.cit.

19. Coates K.: Tom Mann's Memoirs (1967) p.220 (cited in Brogden: supra).

20. Judge A. and Reynolds G.: The Night the Police Went on Strike (1968) (London).

21. Stevenson J. and Cook C.: The Slump pp.161-175 and ch.12.

22. Police spies date from the earliest years of the Metropolitan Police. William Popay's infiltration of the National Political Union was one of the earliest - Bunyan T.: The Political Police In Britain p.63.

23. Williamson B.: Class, Culture and Community (1982) (London).

24. Page Arnot R.: The Miners (Years of Struggle) (1961) (New York) p.497.

25. Page Arnot R.: The Miners (In Crisis and War) (1961) (New York) ch.5.

26. Jackson R.M.: Enforcing the Law (1967) (London) Appendix.

27. For an account of the police raid on Armthorpe, see the Guardian 3rd December 1984 p.15.

28. The statistics are reported in the Guardian 4th March 1985. They include 275 charges under s.7 Conspiracy and Protection of Property Act 1875, 'watching and besetting'.

29. Coulter, Miller and Walker: op.cit.

30. Brogden M.: The Police: Accountability and Control.
    Baldwin R. and Kinsey R.: Police Powers and Politics (1982) (London) ch.4.

31. See comments by Peter Wright, Chief Constable of South Yorkshire in Police Review 18th January 1985 at p.109.

32. Manwaring-White S.: The Policing Revolution (1983) (London) State Research: op.cit.

33. Beynon and McMylor: op.cit. p.43 '....state power, accumulated over a period of dealing with the relative strength of organised labour has united with the determined control of the Tory Party and the transactions and prejudices of class in a concerted assault upon the collectivity of labour. The scale and power of the assault is quite awesome.'
    See Edgar D.: 'Bitter Harvest' New Socialist Sept./Oct. 1983 p.19.

5. "BOBBIES", "ALIENS" AND SUBVERSIVES: THE RELATIONSHIP BETWEEN COMMUNITY POLICING AND COERCIVE POLICING

Philip Rawlings

"Round [our] way....they've now got community policing. You're walking along the street, a police van pulls up, a squad of coppers leap out, pin you to the ground and tell you the time". (Alexei Sayle) (2)

"The stresses and strains which four million unemployed could bring on our society may require any government to have at its disposal a very hard and repressive police machine". (John Alderson) (3)

The most difficult question in policing, and the least asked, is, what are the police expected to do? To a large extent the police have been left to formulate their own objectives and to define their own strategies, yet even within the force there is often no clear statement of aims despite an increasing enthusiasm amongst senior officers to make public statements on policing. In this paper I will seek through a critical review of strategies to uncover the ends, or at least the concerns which guide the police in their decisions on those strategies.

The strategies of the police are their answers to problems which they regard as relevant and important. The first step is to identify the causes of a problem. By doing this discussion about solutions becomes restricted to certain "relevant" issues, others being dismissed as irrelevant. So the identification of the causes of a problem is curiously reassuring since it provides an interpretation of the problem which gives it meaning and so provides the hope of a solution. Within policing the problems of rising crime, falling detection rates and the riots of 1981 have led to two analyses of the essential underlying causes. In both the "blame" is located not within the police, but within society. In the first interpretation the essential cause is identified as social disintegration which led to a collapse in respect for, and deference to, authority as symbolised by the police. According to this analysis since the problem lay in a lack of community, the solution was to reconstitute the community around a morality defined by the police. The other analysis saw the essential cause as a "disruptive alien presence" which has diluted the moral purity of British society and which must, therefore, be controlled.

Alderson And The Golden Age

John Alderson represents the most developed example of the view that the essential cause of the policing crisis lies in general social disintegration. By the use of an image of a golden age in which there was good order and minimal crime Alderson presents the causes of the problem and its solution allegorically: simply compare the two societies, discover the differences and in them lie both the causes and the solution. The question of whether or not the golden age actually existed is of little importance to Alderson, its function is simply to provide a backdrop against which his view can be presented as objective fact.

In his book 'Policing Freedom' Alderson quotes A.H. Halsey for the image of the golden age,

> "Working class districts, including those where incomes were very low, and housing amenities poorly provided, were also areas of domestic peace and neighbourly trust of a standard which we do not know today. People never thought of locking their houses if they went out during the day, and theft would have been a cause for amazement". (4)

It was an age, according to Alderson, when people respected and obeyed rather than questioned authority, and this was symbolised by deference to the police which Alderson refers to as policing by consent.

This golden age passed away some time ago, although exactly when is unclear. The reasons for this lie within society and the changes it has undergone; changes that have resulted in a collapse of the community spirit that welded people together in common cause and its replacement by individual self-interest. Today's society is, according to Alderson, pluralist and mobile; it has been created by rapid industrialisation and characterised by immigrant communities with alien cultures; it has provided increased prosperity and reduced individual responsibility; its mass education has not only taught children their rights, but also how to insist upon them; its parents have lost control of their children. In essence, he mysteriously asserts, there has been an "excess of liberty". (5)

If society has changed, the police, according to Alderson, have not, they have steadfastly clung to the old values. On this point Sir Robert Mark was even more forthright,

> "The police are....very much on their own in attempting to preserve order in an increasingly turbulent society in which Socialist philosophy has changed from raising the standards of the poor and deprived to reducing the standards of the wealthy, the skilled and the deserving to the lowest common denominators". (6)

This analysis of the causes of the policing problem makes criticism of the police largely irrelevant; on the other hand it opens up society to examination and to reorganisation by the police according to the standards which they espouse as the true, traditional values.

Apart from his rather simplistic process of subtraction – taking one age from another in order to find the causes of and solutions to contemporary problems – Alderson's analysis is based on the assumption that the community has moved away from its traditional position of respect for, and active co-operation with, the police and this has made policing more difficult. This amounts to an assertion that the relationship between the police and the community in the past was largely unproblematic. This is a view which has been challenged by Mike Brogden who has shown that in certain sections of society police-community relations have always been strained and have regularly exploded into violent confrontation, so that rather than policing by active popular consent, policing has been, at most, by passive acquiescence. (7)

The "Disruptive Alien Presence"

This viewpoint also raises a comparison between today and "the past", although here the golden age is generally implicit since this analysis tends to steer away from theoretical rationalisation. However, as with Alderson's analysis, "the past" acts to show that the policing problem is new and its causes lie in the importation of new habits which have destroyed traditional values. These destructive habits are identified with a "disruptive alien presence": brown, but more especially black people. These people provide an instant social problem in their failure to fit in with "British" society. Superintendant Roach of the Community Relations Branch recently wrote,

> "The general difficulty of identifying the police with the community was most sharply seen in relations between black and Asian immigrant groups and the almost exclusively white Metropolitan Police....Although the immigrants came largely from Commonwealth countries, their cultural background and social structure differed significantly from the indigenous community and they did not readily recognise or accept the traditional English way of policing". (8)

The problem lies not with the police, but with the failure of cultural outsiders, "immigrants", to fit in: it is society and not the police that has shifted its position.

Although the whole of the black and brown population is, therefore, seen as a problem, it is the black youth who are seen as the most disruptive section. The police feel that these youths have broken the tradition of deference which symbolised the authority of the police. One officer in the Metropolitan Police told a Home Office researcher that the "voice of authority doesn't mean anything to them", and another said,".... West Indians....just don't like authority". (9)

Certain crimes are regarded as symptomatic of this collapse in traditional values. "Mugging" and rioting become crimes which are frightening on an individual level and also subversive to the 'British' way of life. These crimes are represented as revealing a cultural divide between black and white which has resulted in the devaluation of 'British' society. This divide is presented most powerfully by the image of black 'muggers' only attacking helpless white people, with both 'mugger' and victim representing not only an individual incident, but also the wider issues of a society defenceless in the face of the violent outsider. By this means the policing problem is not merely, or even chiefly about individual crime, it becomes a problem of a "disruptive alien presence" which is deliberately attacking 'traditional' – in other words, white – society.

The link between 'mugging' and black people was forged in two ways. (10) The sudden appearance of the term 'mugging' in 1972 (11) seemed to cut the crime off from its long history as street robbery; here was a new, un-British activity of a particularly frightening kind, something imported by aliens. Statistics were later used to substantiate the link. Twice in 1981 the government had claimed that it was not possible to collect criminal statistics based on the ethnic origin of the offender "as the identity of the offender is often not known". (12) Despite this, in the following year figures were published by the Metropolitan Police with the approval of the Home Secretary. The publication was allegedly prompted by "public demand", although this seems to have consisted of requests from two Conservative M.P.s, Harvey Proctor and Nicholas Winterton. (13) The difficulty of collecting such figures was ignored, as were the problems about defining exactly what 'mugging' meant. There was no caveat to the implicit conclusion that criminality was due to skin colour, nor was there a satisfactory explanation for picking out certain crimes committed in a certain area. There was no suggestion that high black crime might be related to high unemployment, poor housing, poverty, discrimination and so forth.

To reinforce this image of 'mugging' as a crime which separates the 'alien' from 'British' society, the colour of the victim has been brought onto the stage. Alan Clark, the Conservative M.P., incensed by William Pitt, the Liberal M.P., who had referred to racialist attacks on black and brown people, retorted

> "Is he not aware that the blacks never mug their own race but only elderly and defenceless white people?" (14)

This battery of images which had been deployed around 'mugging' was neatly summed up by Judge Gwynn Morris at the trial in 1975 of five black youths for 'muggings' in Brixton and Clapham,

> "Within memory these areas were peaceful, safe and agreeable to live in. But the immigrant resettlement which has occurred over the past 25 years has radically transformed that environment. Those concerned with the maintenance of law and order are confronted with immense difficulties. This case has highlighted and underlined the perils which confront honest, innocent and hardworking, unaccompanied women who are in the street after nightfall. I notice that not a single West Indian woman was attacked". (15)

The 1981 riots, despite the involvement of white youths, were used to emphasise the frightening nature of black street crime, once again it was presented as an 'alien' activity. The rioters used molotov cocktails not petrol bombs. (16) Margaret Thatcher - suffering from a convenient lapse of memory - remarked that even during the depression of the thirties people had not rioted. (17) The Conservative M.P., John Stokes went even further when he referred to the riots as "without precedent for 200 years....something sinister in our long national history...." (18) The implicit conclusion was that the differences between the eighteenth century or the nineteen-thirties and today lay in the 'alien' presence. (19)

The riots were linked both to crime against white people and to 'mugging'. The Daily Mail in its coverage of the riots included a story headed "Woman raped as she tries to flee the riots". The story's first paragraph recorded how,

> "A WHITE woman was raped by a black youth as she prepared to flee from the Brixton riots, Scotland Yard said last night". (20)

Once again the dual function of the imagery: individual crime by black people on white, and symbolism of the defenceless white woman as representing the old society being violated by the 'aliens'. But it was 'mugging' that was most consistently presented as the motivation for the riots, especially in Brixton. Since the immediate precursor of the Brixton riots had been Operation Swamp which was supposedly a campaign against 'mugging', the rioters were labelled by the Police Federation as muggers aggrieved at the successes of the police. (21) Similarly despite being critical of police tactics in Brixton, Scarman concluded that criticism of the S.P.G., who had been involved in various alleged campaigns against mugging, was founded upon the group's successes. (22)

The police emerge once again as the sole defenders of traditional values in a society which has somehow lost its way. Scarman in his report wrote that the police

> "stood between our society and a total collapse of law and order in the streets of an important part of the capital". (23)

The division is between "our society" and those who threaten it, the muggers, the rioters, the 'disruptive alien presence'.

It is this image of the police as the last line of defence that underpinned the law and order campaigns of the Police Federation. The 1982 campaign to reintroduce hanging had little to do with murder – which was actually decreasing at the time – it was a dramatic presentation of increasing violent crime and its threat to society which could only be diverted by the most drastic of measures, and by association it carried with it an image of an embattled police force needing not criticism but support. Hence, Jim Jardine, then the President of the Federation, rather than speaking of issues such as the likely effect that hanging would have on murder and violent crime, spoke of the need to wage 'war' on crime. (24) The imagery of a society under attack with the police as its last line of defence.

Both Alderson's analysis and that characterised by the idea of the 'disruptive alien presence' exhibit important areas of agreement. For both, the problem of crime and the genesis of criminogenic conditions lies in the community's loss of traditional moral values. The police are regarded as the sole repositories of these values, and, therefore, their function is seen as stretching beyond simple law enforcement into the rediscovery, reinterpretation and restoration of these values. In order to achieve this task the police must be independent of the defective community, so autonomy becomes an essential part of policing the community.

On the other hand, the two analyses also have important areas of disagreement. For Alderson the central task is to reconstitute a moral community which can then be used against criminals: the mobilisation of the 'good' against the 'bad'. He sees policing, therefore,

> "not only....as a matter of controlling the bad but includes activating the good". (25)

The idea of policing problems being rooted in a 'disruptive alien presence' takes the view that the 'good' elements of society are largely unproblematic; here the principal task is the identification of the 'bad'. Against Alderson's concern with the disintegration of the community is posed the view that the 'bad' in fact form a particularly cohesive community. However, this difference becomes more apparent than real, since the tendency of Alderson's solution is, as I will show, to concentrate on deviant communities.

Alderson And Communal Policing

Alderson refers to his solution as 'communal policing' in an attempt to mark it off from those community policing schemes which simply involve putting more officers onto the beat. For him "Communal policing has little or nothing to do with the enforcement of the law but is concerned in dealing with social disorganisation leading to crime, thereby serving the common good". (26)

Immediately one of the principal features of policing, law enforcement, is put to one side,

> "Law enforcement in communities should be the province only of the police and other enforcement agencies...." (27)

This is, of course, because the cause of the policing problem lies in the community not the police.

He seeks to establish the local community through either recreating or creating afresh a community spirit. Each community "must have its own identity, however tenuous, or its identity must be created". (28) It is clear that these communities become important only as they become problematic, because Alderson's strategy requires the police to concentrate on areas where there is a crime problem. The police analyse "crime and other social phenomena" - housing, employment, planning, youth, social services and probation - in order to discover the local causes of crime. (29) These "other social phenomena" are given an identity by their causal connection with crime, so that, for instance, unemployment is not a problem so long as the unemployed stay at home.

It is on these terms that the agencies whose primary task is to deal with these phenomena are drawn into policing. Meetings are held at which the analysis is presented to the community for comment, although the main form of consultation is with a committee of "community leaders", by which is meant persons prominent in local organisations. (30)

At all points the police take the leading role as moral guardians. For instance, in schools, according to Sir Jack Smart, leader of Wakefield Council, speaking at a recent police conference,

> "there is scope for liaison between police and teachers to identify those standards of social and moral behaviour and those examples of 'good citizenship' that are fundamental to our way of life". (31)

This leadership is presented by Alderson as quite natural because the community is constituted around crime over which, in the final analysis, police as law enforcers must have control. (32) Consequently, a community is being constructed around issues and values over which it ultimately has little or no control. Alderson firmly rejects the idea of the community being allowed anything more than a consultative role, (33) it has no right to direct the police, nor are the police accountable to the community since this would destroy their autonomy which is regarded as vital in protecting the police against deviant elements in the community. After all it is the community which has gone astray. Indeed, even consultation is severely restricted by the superior importance laid on law enforcement by Alderson. He regards consultation as applicable to those crimes in which the general public occasionally indulge, but not to crimes committed by those "who have taken a conscious decision to operate beyond the law", these are for the police supported by the community. (34) How the distinction is to be made is left to the imagination. Such consultation as is allowed is, to a large extent, going to be reliant upon the police for information and for their willingness to enter into discussions. Furthermore, his strategy is geared more to talking to the articulate, the 'community leaders', than to those on the street.

So, despite its name, communal policing centres upon the notion of a police penetration of the community rather than the community's penetration of the policing function.

Communal policing is also potentially dangerous to the police. Since its aims are to reconstruct society around certain values and objectives it inevitably raises the question of who is to decide those values and objectives. For Alderson it is the police. As I have shown, he gives the community a very limited role. What Alderson fails to recognise, but it seems that other senior officers have recognised, is that his strategy might actually work to increase the challenge to police autonomy. Communal policing invites the community to define crime, and hence direct policing and limit autonomy. Indeed the most serious challenge would be if the community did not regard the reduction of crime as the most important objective, and asserted, for instance, that unemployment was in itself of more importance than any crime for which it might be blamed. Alderson rather simplistically assumes that there would be no real problem in achieving an agreement to the values and objectives which he espouses, thereby ignoring the possibility that if there was no such agreement the police would be forced to enter the political arena even more overtly, so undermining one of the bases of their claim to autonomy, namely their apolitical nature. He fails to recognise that his appeal to traditional values and his assumption of consensus is not apolitical and unproblematic, it is the very stuff of politics and debate.

Controlling The Streets

In the strategy based upon the notion of a 'disruptive alien presence' the crimes which are regarded as symptomatic of this 'presence' and the destruction of traditional values which it causes are street crimes; therefore, the essential issue becomes one of controlling the streets. Sir Kenneth Newman called this "a higher objective". (35) The policing of the 1981 riots was dominated by criticism of the police in St. Paul's the previous year who had withdrawn from the area. One officer commented

"Nobody rules the streets of London, Brixton, or even Railton Road, except the Metropolitan Police". (36)

The extreme violence of both crowd and police in the final bout of rioting in Liverpool 8 in 1981 seems to have been provoked by police desire to revenge earlier defeats, as Kenneth Oxford, the Chief Constable, said,

> "To put it crudely the people have spat in my face". (37)

The violent confrontation is, however, a fairly rare aspect of the exercise of control. Indeed it is an indication that control has failed. More common is the control symbolised by the recognition of police authority through the deferential behaviour of street people when stopped by a police officer. The identification through stereotyping of black youths as disruptive elements provides a target for this theatre of control, indeed it is not simply the image of black people as muggers which provides this stereotype, but also the police view that black people reject the deferential role.

Stop and search is therefore an important part of policing. To the accusation that it involves harassment, the reply is simply to point out that control can only be achieved through harassment. Inspector Basil Griffiths, at the Police Federation Conference in 1982, said,

> "in every urban area there's a large minority of people who are not fit to salvage. The only way in which the police can protect society is quite frankly by harassing these people". (38)

This sweeping of the streets is most clearly directed at the black people, as one officer remarked, "Whenever you see two blacks hanging about on a street-corner, you know they're up to no good". (39) McNee, then the Commissioner of the Metropolitan Police, in defending the S.P.G. and the use of the "Sus" laws, told a black reporter, "If you keep off the streets and behave yourself you won't have the S.P.G. to worry about". (40)

The apogee of this theatre of the police was Operation Swamp '81 and the S.P.G. raids that preceded it. These have virtually no meaning if seen simply as crime prevention or detection exercises, since, as Scarman recognised, they were inevitably very short-term, (41) and anyway mugging is not particularly suited to detection through such a highly visible police presence. The raids are only explicable in terms of control and theatre. The police saw them in terms of subjugating the community: the officer in charge of one such raid said, when asked why he had not consulted with the official local consultative committee beforehand,

> "No good general ever declares his forces in a prelude to any kind of attack". (42)

The local community do not simply submit, reaction can be expected and so the police have to judge their actions carefully to prevent a loss of control, which would amount to a failure. Operation Swamp did provoke a violent reaction in the form of the Brixton riots, but more commonly the counter-theatre consists of non-violent murmurings of discontent or symbolic actions. In 1983 when strip searches were conducted in the street by Brixton police:

79

"The word got around and people began dropping their trousers when police approached them, hoping to cause enough embarrassment to prevent the search". (43)

This non-violent, as much as the violent, confrontation creates a spiralling of tension, a criminalisation of black youth and the fulfilment of the stereotype of a 'disruptive alien presence'. (44)

From the police viewpoint this concentration on the issue of control achieves five things. It brings to the forefront, and hence emphasises, an image of violence which presents the streets as dangerous places to go onto and society's traditional values as being under attack. It legitimises not only the use of coercion by the police against the street people, who are regarded as responsible for this violent society, but also an extension of police powers. It diverts attention from the apparent deficiencies of the police who, on the evidence of criminal statistics, are increasingly unable to fulfil their role as crime fighters: the main issue is no longer crime, but something far less tangible. By paring down the problem to a 'disruptive alien presence' policing becomes simply a task of identification and harassment of whole sections of the community rather than the singling out of certain persons who have committed crimes. Finally, by identifying deviance with the community and promising repression of that deviance it rejects any significant form of accountability, for to make the police accountable to that community would be absurd.

Inevitably the corollary of selecting black people as targets for control necessarily means that crimes against black people, specifically attacks by white racialists, tend to be ignored. Many communities feel that the police ignore complaints, or deny any racialist motive, or even harass the victim. (45)

Policing After The Riots

The riots of 1981 led to significant developments in policing. Ironically although the riots were a reaction against coercive policing tactics, such as Operation Swamp '81, they actually enabled the development of coercion. By 1982 the Metropolitan Police had reorganised their riot tactics by the creation of full-time Instant Response Units, later called District Support Units. (46) Nationally, police forces expanded their Police Support Units, squads of officers were taken from ordinary duties for public order work. In addition, police forces now hold stocks of riot shields, water cannon, C.S. gas and 20,000 plastic bullets. Increasing numbers of officers are trained in firearms, and these are issued more frequently. (47) The use of computers has enabled the systematisation of criminal intelligence, which includes information on persons who are neither accused nor suspected of crimes. (48) In tandem with these and other developments of physical powers, there has been an increase in the police's legal powers, for instance through the Police and Criminal Evidence Act.

Within the Metropolitan Police this expansion of coercive capability mirrors the cult of aggression amongst rank and file officers noticed by the Policy Studies Institute in their study of the force. The P.S.I. found that whilst it was rare for officers to experience actual violence, the idea of violence was very much a part of rank and file ideology, "we find that the idea of violence is often central to the conceptions that police officers have of their work. This is partly because the central meaning of the job for most officers is the exercise of authority, and force (rather than knowledge or understanding) is for them the main <u>symbol</u> of authority and power, even if they actually impose their authority in other ways. Also it is because many police officers see violence as a source of excitement and glamour...." (49)

A second development in policing since the riots has been in the strengthening of police autonomy through centralisation. Increasingly policing has become centralised through the creation of the National Reporting Centre which organises the movement of police officers between different areas to deal with public order incidents and industrial disputes. There have also been the moves towards national computer link-ups and the centralisation of information at the Police National Computer Unit in Hendon. (50) Albert Lougharne, Chief Constable of Lancashire, said recently, "In days of widespread unrest and protest, of terrorist violence and the like, when every force may be under great pressure, a lack of cohesive command could become a serious, perhaps crippling weakness." (51)

On the other hand, complete centralisation is not welcomed since this might threaten police autonomy by making them an easier target for central government control. So James Anderton has suggested that the existing 43 forces be reduced to 10 regional forces. This would not make the police easily identifiable with a single, local community, nor with central government. (52)

Community Policing And Coercion

It is not surprising to find that Alderson's communal policing strategy found no favour with the Association of Chief Police Officers (53) since, despite his rejection of accountability to the local community, his plan involved decentralisation and a closer identification of the police with the local community which would tend to encourage demands for effective participation in police decision-making. Indeed senior officers have shown in a number of ways their general lack of commitment to community policing. Where officers have been returned to the beat the tendency appears to have been not to use mature officers. (54) Rural police stations have been closed.

Among the rank and file beat officers are generally regarded as of rather low status, "hobby bobbies", efficiency still being measured through arrests. (55) The Police Federation has also been scathing about community policing, criticising Newman's creation in London of neighbourhood watch schemes as "sensitive policing", despite their being far less than Alderson advocates, and at their 1982 conference one officer said that Scarman's report and the riots had led to timid policing which abrogated the police's responsibility to the majority of people. (56) Both senior officers and the rank and file have shown something less than enthusiasm for any form of consultation which might challenge the police forces' control over decisions on policing. Alan Goodison of the Association of Chief Police Officers has been decidedly cautious about consultative committees, (57) and Jim Jardine of the Police Federation said in 1982 that:

"Genuine consultation is all to the good, providing the people you consult with are on the same side and there is goodwill and a willingness in maintaining the rule of law." (58)

Consultation becomes more a means of legitimizing police strategies and tactics than the seeking of any genuine input from the community.

The most tangible evidence of the lack of commitment has been the generally poor response to the Home Office circular (59) issued in the wake of Scarman's report which directed all Chief Constables to set up community policing schemes involving consultation. In the end it was necessary to make such schemes obligatory in the Police and Criminal Evidence Act, albeit in rather vague terms. (60) Just as significant were the resignations of Alderson and Webb. Both had pioneered community policing schemes and both had received much acclamation after the riots from senior officers, politicians and Scarman. Within a short time both had left the force disillusioned at the lack of commitment amongst senior officers to community policing. (61)

This is not to say that community policing schemes were not initiated; not to take some action on this front, even if only to put officers onto the beat, would have laid the police open to much wider criticism, especially the forces which experienced rioting. However, these were much less than Alderson's strategy. They tended either to put officers on the beat or to be neighbourhood watch schemes. The neighbourhood watch schemes were started in South Wales (62) and spread, most notably by Newman, to London. On his appointment Newman announced that more officers would be put on the beat and consultative committees would be created all over London. (63) But the emphasis in these schemes is very much on crime prevention through watching neighbours' property or guarding your own and through the passing on of information to the police, rather than on effective involvement of the community in taking policing decisions. Furthermore, in tandem with these schemes Newman also initiated targetting in which the police start not with a crime, but with a suspect who is kept under surveillance by an Area Intelligence Unit. (64) Implicit in this tactic is the idea that there is a criminal class which is easily identifiable and quite separate from the rest of society. Since this idea has no real basis in fact targetting inevitably means widespread surveillance of certain areas and people based on stereotypes: in other words, a tactic which will naturally tend to a deepening harassment of inner city areas and of street people. Newman's appointment does not seem to have changed the stereotype. Although he criticised the ethnic breakdown of criminal statistics, he has still released statistics on request by M.P.s, and it will come as no surprise that such requests were forthcoming. (65)

Targetting links in with Newman's neighbourhood watch schemes since it seems that for senior officers one of the few advantages of community policing has been its use in gathering the sort of low level intelligence needed for targetting. The gathering of this sort of information has, however, bewildered the rank-and-file more than the public. On a scheme in South Wales, The Police Review reported

"The people in South Wales have been encouraged to report even seemingly trivial incidents. To them a strange car going up a cul-de-sac is worth noting. While that may be the view of the higher echelons it is difficult to persuade those at the grass roots of the force - those that have to take all the 'trivial' phone calls - that it is a worthwhile exercise". (66)

Commander Alex Marnoch on his appointment to the Lambeth district in 1983 declared that it was his intention to set up a Community Involvement Unit which would work in youth clubs "to spot 'potential troublemakers' and prevent their slipping into crime". (67)

Growing Politicisation

One constant theme in policing has been the autonomy of the police. It is regarded by the police as a crucial part of both community and control policing. The riots and the election of a Greater London Council committed to making the Metropolitan Police effectively accountable to them added fuel to the debate on autonomy. In order to justify police autonomy some senior officers have moved more deeply into the political arena by seeking to shift the focus from the police and onto a threat of subversion to the constitution. This move is merely an extension of many of the themes already noted in my discussion of the idea of the traditional society under attack. In 1982 during a row with his police authority in Manchester over his handling of the Moss-Side riots and his strike-breaking at Lawrence Scott where police helped remove machinery from a factory, Anderton said,

> "A quiet revolution is taking place around us and the prize is political power to be wielded against the most cherished elements of the establishment, including the monarchy. It is as much the duty of the police to guard against this as it is to guard against crime. I sense and see in our midst an enemy more dangerous, insidious, and ruthless than any faced since the Second World War.
> I firmly believe there is a long-term political strategy to destroy the proven structure of the police and turn them into an exclusive agency of a one-party state. I am also convinced that the British police service is now a prime target for subversion and demoralization". (68)

In other words, any one who criticises the police or seeks more accountability is a subversive who seeks to destroy the constitution. This was merely one such pronouncement in a long series. In a television interview in 1979 Anderton said that in the future the primary concern of the police would not be what he called "basic crime", it would be subversion. (69) More recently he has linked the miners' strike to this subversion by referring to the picketing as "terrorism without the bullet and the bomb". (70) Newman has added to this mix in his Annual Report for 1982 where he talked of "extremist activists" who criticised the police and caused antagonism amongst "a minority of the young and alienated sections of the community" thereby creating "a destabilising influence and a threat to public order". (71)

These allegations of subversion mean that to allow accountability to an elected body would make the police the tool of any extremist party which might gain control of that body. Although Anderton acknowledged that the police were involved in politics, he added, these were "politics with a small p". He wrote:

> "There are serious attempts now being made to undermine the independence, impartiality and the authority of the British police service. I honestly believe we are now witnessing the domination of the police service as a necessary prerequisite of the creation in this country of a society based on Marxist-Communist principles. The current concern over policing being expressed by certain political factions has got precious little to do with better community participation in police affairs, or the improvement of democracy - rather it is the first conscious step manifesting itself towards the political control of the police, without which the dream of a totalitarian, one-party state in this country cannot be realized". (72)

The irony of this is, of course, that Anderton and Newman praise and claim to be protecting representative democracy whilst at the same time denying that it applies to them. Furthermore, it seems that the growing politicisation of the police has started to create concern amongst the rank and file who are no longer able to see themselves as apolitical. Their disorientation surfaced most clearly during the miners' strike. An editorial in the 'Police Review' attacked the government for failing to resolve the strike and for leaving the police to wonder "whether it is being used to preserve law and order or to implement government policy". (73) The same questions might easily be fired at the senior police officers.

Conclusion

There is, then, no single accepted strategy for policing. There is, on the one hand, what has been called the 'soft' approach of community policing, and, on the other hand, the 'hard' approach of controlling the streets. To add to the confusion advocates of these different approaches seem to swop positions easily. So, for instance, Superintendent Roach's comments on the problems posed for the police by "black and Asian immigrant groups" are presented within the 'soft' context of the Community Relations Branch, and Alderson puts crime-fighting uppermost in his 'soft' strategy.

This disagreement, or apparent disagreement, between the advocates of 'soft' and 'hard' policing occurs as much within the police as without. The Police Federation, for instance, which represents the lower ranks, sees the police officer as essentially a crime-fighter, so it espouses 'hard' policing and is critical of 'soft' policing on the grounds that the police are dealing, or should be dealing, with criminals and there is no point in consulting them. Senior officers, on the other hand, have tended to adopt a rhetoric of 'soft' policing since the Scarman report in 1981: publicly they support efforts towards better community relations through community policing. However, in practice their commitment to 'soft' policing is less certain. Indeed, their strategies are chiefly guided by the desire to strengthen the autonomy of the police and to propagate an image of the police as defenders not of the state but of society as a whole.

The difficulty the senior officers have faced in achieving their aims has been that despite an expanding police force there has been an increase in crime and a decrease in the clear-up rate, which tends to suggest that a large and more powerful police force actually does little to protect society from crime. In response to this has been developed the idea that recent changes within society have caused the increase in crime, changes which demand further increases in the police's powers, be this by reorganising the community around the police in order to re-establish the supremacy of the police, or by giving the police extra physical and legal power which de facto would re-establish police supremacy.

Alderson's 'soft' policing has generally found little favour within the police force since it might tend to make the police subsidiary to the community; instead the police have favoured greater coercion. This has been justified by the use of 'folk devils' (74) - the 'disruptive alien presence' - who commit particularly frightening crimes and who can, therefore, be shown to threaten what is left of the 'traditional' moral values. Policing, thereby, has a target which reassures those frightened by the image of the folk devil. Policing is also made easier since the folk devil is identifiable by means of a stereotype rather than through the rather uncertain connection of a particular criminal incident to a particular person. Furthermore, police autonomy is enhanced since the 'good' members of society are regarded as peripheral and as having a purely supporting role to the police who are protecting them against the folk devils who threaten nothing short of the collapse of the 'traditional' society. This also fits the image of crime-fighters which the police have of themselves.

Still, the problem of the post-riots period for the police has been the growing attack on their autonomy, for not only has police autonomy been seen as increasingly unacceptable in a country based upon the ideology of representative democracy, but also the riots highlighted the discriminatory nature of policing based on the 'disruptive alien presence' idea. In part this has been met by an extension of the 'disruptive alien presence' idea - rioting as an alien habit - and in part by the adoption of the rhetoric of community policing, but just as interesting has been the use of the riots to divert attention even further from crime-fighting as an objective of policing and to build up the image of the police as moral guardians of society. This is, of course, merely a development from the role of the police presented in both the ideas of communal policing and 'the disruptive alien presence'. Indeed the links between those who wish to subvert society and the 'disruptive aliens' was made most explicit by senior officers during the riots of 1981 who propounded the view that roving white anarchists had organised the rioting.

Demonstrating that the major policing problem is subversion of the "constitution", a subversion which would necessarily start with the police, justifies wider powers and a larger police force, it would mean less need for crime-fighting success and enable the police's critics to be dismissed as part of the subversion, and, most importantly, it would reinforce the need for the police to be independent of outside influence. However, at this point it starts to become less easy for the rank-and-file to understand the objectives of policing; the target is no longer easy to identify. This creates doubts: doubts about the relevance of collecting low-level intelligence; doubts about whether their role in the miners' strike was more to do with enforcing a particular government policy than with fighting crime.

Even so, both rank and file and senior officers see the public relations value in community policing. It is not a question of the police having to make a choice between two different styles. Community policing has an important part to play in the legitimation of coercive policing, it is a mobilisation of the support of the 'silent' majority around increases in the powers and autonomy of the police.

NOTES

(1)   I wish to thank Karel Williams for his help on this paper. He did much to decode the original draft and give it something like a structure; more importantly he gave encouragement.

(2)   Quoted in M. Kettle and L. Hodges, Uprising! The police, the people and the riots in Britain's cities, London 1982, p.241.

(3)   J. Alderson, 'Policing for the future' 90 Police Review no. 4649 (19 March 1982) p. 526-529 at 527.

(4)   J. Alderson, Policing Freedom. A Commentary on the Dilemmas of Policing in Western Democracies, Plymouth 1979, p.46-47.

(5)   J. Alderson (1979), op.cit., p.123-124, 176-177, 187-190.

(6)   Quoted in P. Hain, Political Trials in Britain, London 1984, p.61.

(7)   M. Brogden, "All Police is Conning Bastards" - Policing and the Problem of Consent' in B. Fryer, A Hunt, D. McBarnett & B. Moorhouse (eds.) Law, State and Society, London 1981, p.202-228.

(8)   Superintendent L. Roach, 'The Metropolitan Police Community Relations Branch', Police Studies no. 3 (Sept. 1978), p.17-23, at p.18.

(9)   P. Southgate, Police Probationer Training in Race Relations, Home Office, Research and Planning Unit, Paper 8, London 1982, p.6.

(10) The classic study of 'mugging' is, of course, S. Hall, C. Critcher, T. Jefferson, J. Clarke, B. Roberts, Policing the Crisis: Mugging, the State, and Law and Order, London 1978.

(11) Hall et al, op cit., p.3-9.

(12) Parliamentary Debates: Commons vol. 3(1980-81), Written Answers, 14 Apr. 1981, c. 84; vol. 13 (1981-82), 27 Nov. 1981, c.478.

(13) Parliamentary Debates: Commons vol.18 (1981–82), Written Answers, 18 Feb. 1982, c. 189; vol. 19 (1981–82), Written Answers, 8 Mar. 1982, c. 78–81; vol. 20 (1981–82), Written Answers, 15 March 1982, c. 14.

(14) Parliamentary Debates: Commons vol.13 (1981–82), 26 Nov. 1981, c. 1040.

(15) Hall et al, op.cit., p.333.

(16) Eldon Griffiths, Parliamentary Debates: Commons, vol. 3 (1980–81), 13 Apr. 1981, c.25.

(17) The Birmingham Post 14 April 1981.

(18) Parliamentary Debates: Commons, vol. 3 (1980–81), 13 Apr. 1981, c.29.

(19) Following the Brixton riots, Harvey Proctor, M.P., asked if the government would end immigration from the "New Commonwealth" and "encourage repatriation": Parliamentary Debates; Commons vol. 3 (1980–81), 13 Apr. 1981, c.27.

(20) Daily Mail 14 April 1981.

(21) Kettle & Hodges, op.cit., p.185.

(22) Lord Scarman, The Brixton Disorder 10-12 April 1981: Report of an Inquiry By the Rt. Hon. the Lord Scarman, O.B.E., cmnd. 8427, London 1981, para. 5.53.

(23) Scarman, op.cit., para. 4.98.

(24) Guardian, 18 March 1982. Soon afterwards, Eldon Griffiths, M.P. and spokesperson for the Police Federation, compared policing operations to the taskforce in the Falklands War: Guardian, 21 May 1982.

(25) Alderson (1979), op.cit., p.38.

(26) Alderson, 'Policing Freedom – The Challenge of the Eighties', 13 Cambrian Law Review (1982) p.5–13, at p.9.

(27) Alderson (1979), op.cit., p.48.

(28) Alderson (1982), op.cit., p.9.

(29) Alderson (1979), op.cit., p.193.

(30) Alderson (1979), op.cit., p.193–194.

(31) 93 Police Review no. 4754 (30 Mar. 1984), p.625. See also, Parliamentary Debates: Commons, vol. 60 (1983–84), 17 May 1984, c. 494–5.

(32)   Alderson (1982), op.cit., p.9; Alderson (1979), op.cit., p.201.

(33)   Alderson (1982), op.cit., p.9-10 & p.12; Alderson (1979), op.cit., p.194.

(34)   Alderson (1979), op.cit., p.182.

(35)   Times, 24 March 1982.

(36)   Daily Mirror, 13 April 1981.

(37)   Kettle & Hodges, op.cit., p.173.

(38)   Guardian, 22 October 1982.

(39)   D. Leigh & P. Lashmar, 'Are Our Police Still Wonderful?' Observer, 15 November 1981.

(40)   Guardian, 18 June 1979; see also, D. J. Smith & J. Gray, Police and People in London: IV The police in action, Policy Studies Institute, London 1983, p.129.

(41)   Scarman, op.cit., para. 4.78.

(42)   Quoted in Report of the Working Party on Community/Police Relations in Lambeth, London 1981, p.6.

(43)   Guardian, 27 April 1983.

(44)   Report of the Working Party, op.cit., p.15-17, p.8.

(45)   Kettle & Hodges, op.cit., p.68-75.

(46)   Report of the Commissioner of Police of the Metropolis for the year 1983, cmnd. 9268, p.120, p.33.

(47)   Policing London: The Policing Aspects of Lord Scarman's Report on The Brixton Disorders, Greater London Council, London 1982, p.13-14. Figures for plastic bullets, Jeremy Corbyn, Parliamentary Debates: Commons, vol. 59 (1983-84), 11 May 1984, c. 1252. On firearms, see chapter by Michael Molyneux in this volume.

(48)   Guardian 22 March 1982; Jeremy Corbyn, Parliamentary Debates: Commons, vol. 59 (1983-84), 11 May 1984, c. 1253.

(49)   Smith & Gray, op.cit., p.87.

(50)   92 Police Review no. 4671 (18 May 1984), p.977.

(51)   Hain, op.cit., p.55.

(52)   Hain, op.cit., p.55-56.

(53) Hain, op.cit., p.56.

(54) J. Mervyn Jones & J.T. Winkler, 'Beyond the Beat: The Facts about Policing in a Riotous City' 9 Journal of Law and Society no. 1 (Summer 1982), p.103-114.

(55) Ibid.

(56) Guardian, 22 October 1982; Times, 19 May 1982.

(57) Times, 11 February 1981.

(58) Guardian, 18 March 1982.

(59) Times, 17 June 1982.

(60) Section 106.

(61) On Webb, see J. Brown, Policing by Multi-Racial Consent: The Harmondsworth Experience, London 1982. On the resignations, see Kettle & Hodges, op.cit., p.237-239.

(62) D. Pead, 'Community Watch: A baby with teething problems', 91 Police Review no. 4714 (17 June 1983), p.1140-1141.

(63) Times, 2 October 1982.

(64) Times, 25 January 1983; L. Christian, Policing by Coercion, London 1983, p.141; Leon Brittain, Parliamentary Debates: Commons vol.59 (1983-84), 11 May 1984, c. 1207-8.

(65) Times, 2 October 1982; Times, 24 March 1983; Parliamentary Debates: Commons, vol.39 (1982-83), Written Answers, 22 March 1983, c. 366-70; vol.40 (1982-83), Written Answers, 28 March 1983, c. 3-5.

(66) Pead, op.cit., p.1141; see also, Eldon Griffiths' comments in 'The Police and the public' 6 Poly Law Review no.2 (Spring 1981) p.3-19. at p.6.

(67) Guardian, 15 February 1983.

(68) Hain, op.cit., p.37.

(69) Leigh & Lashmar, op.cit., p.15; Guardian, 20 October 1980.

(70) 92 Police Review no. 4768 (6 July 1984), p.1299.

(71) Report of the Commissioner of Police of the Metropolis for the year 1982 cmnd. 8928.

(72) Hain, op.cit., p.37-38.

(73)   92 Police Review no.4770 (20 July 1984), editorial.

(74)   Stanley Cohen, Folk Devils and Moral Panics : The Creation of the Mods and Rockers, London 1972.

6. STOPPING THE PEOPLE –
CRIME CONTROL VERSUS SOCIAL CONTROL

Mike Brogden

"The practise of aggressive patrol becomes petty and mean even though good people may devise it and good people carry it out". (George Kelling, U.S. Police Foundation)

Introduction

The stop provisions of the Police and Criminal Evidence Act are clear and succinct. They empower a police officer, in uniform, to stop and search any person or vehicle which he or she may reasonably suspect of carrying an offensive weapon or possessing a prohibited item. Subject to certain safeguards, police officers are permitted to use their discretion in accosting members of the public on the street and asserting specified rights of search and accusation.

Within the rhetoric of legal syntax, the powers are self-evidently rational and considered. Justified in the preceding exposition as fulfilling the police requirements in the "war against crime", in practice, the stop-and-search clauses of the Act follow logically and directly from the spirit of a peculiar policing system in which traditionally no institutional distinction has been made between arresting and prosecuting functions. Given that synthesis of processes within what is formally the law enforcement agency, what could be more natural than extending that juxtaposition, stripped of its juridical garb, to the domain of the beat constable? The stop-and-search powers authoritatively endow the patrol officer with the structural capacity to confront, to inquisitorially interrogate, and to dispose (either back to the street or to the degradation of the court-room process) of those persons, that he or she regards as suspect.

Stop-and-search powers legitimise at street level the same institutional convergence that marks out the police institution in England and Wales. To appreciate the hidden rationale for the embodiment in law of stop-and-search practices, one must pay some attention to both that arrest-prosecution relation and further, to the overall legal context of the extended power. The orthodox civil libertarian critique, because it dissects the Act section by section, fails sometimes to be conscious of the significance of the totality of the legal structure in which the powers are embedded.

This chapter has two aims. The initial intention is to demonstrate that the stop-and-search power can justifiably be rejected by those orthodox critics who hold the same idealistic model of law and of law enforcement as do the proponents of the powers. Within that idealistic model are two major components – a belief that the practice of English criminal law occurs within a framework of due process, and secondly, that the primary function of the law enforcement agency is one of crime control. Stop-and-search powers have conventionally been challenged as undesirable because they appear to deviate from the larger model of an adversarial system of due process. They have been denied value because all the vast body of empirical evidence suggests that few changes in police powers are likely to have any significant impact on the level of reported crime. Ipso facto, as the orthodox critics have it, the powers are aberrant within the legal system and they are patently of little value, damaging civil rights without any positive gain. These and subsidiary related arguments provide the bulk of the idealistic rejection of the powers. As such, they have considerable weight.

Nevertheless, they are mistaken - not in their detail but in their fundamental assumptions. The second intention of the chapter is to suggest that the justification for the stop-and-search power can be combated more effectively by contextualising that legal innovation within the overall development of the system of legal control in England and Wales. Conventional refutations of the stop-and-search power, which deal with it without reference to context and to history fail to arrive at the real kernel of the problem - that the stop-and-search power is in fact symmetrical with the overall practice of law enforcement and of judicial disposition in England and Wales. The power is contiguous with the evolution of street legislation. It fits neatly within the totality of a legal system increasingly characterised by a denial of adversarial due process.

The Royal Commission And The Act

While the underlying premise for the inclusion of the stop-and-search sections of the Act, was indubitably that of enhancing police powers in relation to crime, that argument was wrapped by the Royal Commission on Criminal Procedure within a presentation package of legal coherence. As the Report pointed out, stop-and-search powers at that time were either confined to the implementation of legislation against specific activities, or were restricted to particular locations. There appeared to be a certain illogicality about that present situation, flaws which should be remedied through legal reform.

Powers to stop-and-search persons and vehicles already existed in English law but they were largely confined to particular offence categories - ranging from the Misuse of Drugs Act 1971 (s.23 (2)) to the Protection of Birds Act 1967 (s.11). Some dozen separate purposive pieces of legislation enacted during the previous fifteen years had contained clauses empowering police officers to stop-and-search a person in the street or in a vehicle "....where there are reasonable grounds for suspecting that a person is committing, or has committed, an offence under the Act, and that evidence of the commission of the offence is to be found on that person or any vehicle or article which he may have with him". (Badgers Act 1973, s.10). In addition, there were separate powers to stop persons (such as section 4 of the Conservation of Seals Act 1970) which were not linked with powers of search.

To the majority of members of the Royal Commission, these separate items of legislation were messy and disorderly. The heterogeneous collection of assorted stop-and-search regulations required some tidying up. A new Police Bill was the obvious place to standardise such powers.

Secondly, under municipal legislation, stop-and-seach powers had been recognised in certain localities since Victorian times. To the members of the Commission, it was anomalous that the police of towns and cities such as Liverpool, Birmingham, and Burnley should have possessed stop-and-search powers since the nineteenth century but that other forces should have had to make do without. If they existed in one police area, it was logical that they should be universally available. In arguing for such an extension, the members of the Commission were aware that similar powers had been granted to the Scottish police under the Criminal Justice (Scotland) Act, 1981.

This principle of consistency became the guiding logic portrayed to Parliament for the subsequent development of the Police and Criminal Evidence Bill, and the succeeding Act.

Section 1 of the Act therefore extends to universal application what had previously been discrete or local legislation. Police officers, in or out of uniform, are given the power to search both persons and relevant vehicles if they have reasonable suspicion that the person in question is carrying either an offensive weapon, (i.e. anything designed, adapted or intended for causing injury) or a prohibited article (items for use in burglary, in theft, in stealing motor vehicles, or for obtaining property by deception).

The following sections, 2 and 3, specify certain conditions that should be satisfied in relation to the use of that power. A detailed record is to be retained in the local police station and made available to the person searched on request. In particular, Sections 2(8) and 2(9) permit the officer to reasonably delay the suspect and to require the removal of only specified items of outer clothing. Section 4 provides for the setting up of road checks to ascertain whether a vehicle is carrying an offender or suspect where a senior officer believes that a serious arrestable offence has been committed, or is intended, and the suspect is, or is about to be, in the area.

A further qualification to the arbitrary use of the powers is included in Section 5(2) which states the requirement for records of the stops to be provided in the chief officer's annual report. Finally, to meet the consistency requirements of the Royal Commission, Section 7 abolishes the existing powers of stop-and-search in the Vagrancy Act Section 8 and in the various local legislation, superseding them with the new consolidated powers.

In sum, the Act represents both a universal application of the local stop-and-search powers and an extension of the grounds on which those powers can be applied. Justification lies primarily in the various memoranda from the police institution (1), where the power is depicted as essential to police strategies in combating crime. It follows the Royal Commission route in including particular safeguards against abuse.

The Orthodox Critique:
Reasonable Suspicion – The Gap Between Rhetoric And Practice

Assaults on the extension of police powers have been many and varied. The powers enshrined in the Police and Criminal Evidence Act have been assailed by liberal critics variously as unworkable, too vague, unnecessary, and as harmful to more important policing objectives.

In the first place, opponents have argued that the concept of "reasonable suspicion", with its traditional formulation in English law is too imprecise. The test of this reasonableness is that the officer must be able to justify the search not by reference to intuition, hint or subjective suspicion but in terms of objective facts in the light of which his or her action appears reasonable (Polyvios 1983).

But such objective facts are rarely evident in practice. In Willis' study of stop-and-search practices for the Home Office, in London and Luton, police officers found it extremely difficult to explain their reasons for stopping someone in the street (Willis 1983). For her police officer respondents, the primary reason for "stopping" was in relation to "movements" – a term on whose meaning they were unable to agree. In over half the cases studied, police officers had only a vague intuition about the reasons for the stop. Prejudice about such factors as race and age inevitably influence those judgements. Indeed, officers were often unsure about the statutory power under which the stops were conducted. In effect, the cloak of reasonable suspicion encourages officers "....to stop, question,

and search any young man carrying a bag on the street at night...".
(N.C.C.L. 1983 p.8). Mere appearance is the ground for many if not most
searches. The courts have traditionally failed to check the indiscriminate
abuse of the notion of reasonable suspicion as the grounds for a search.

As Lambert says: "Let there be no doubt that their special statutory
powers, combined with an increased readiness on the part of the courts to
allow non-statutory stops, give the police wide and persuasive authority to
carry out on-the-street detentions.... the statistics suggest that large
numbers of presumably innocent people are being caught in the net of law
enforcement....The recent cases suggest that their vigilance is wavering"
(1974, p.478). Abuse of the concept of reasonable suspicion by police
officers is not curtailed by the courts who regularly fail to question police
officers' resort to that legitimation.

In the study of policing practices by the Policy Studies Institute for the
Metropolitan Police, no such reasonable suspicion was said to exist in some
one-third of all cases observed. That report commented

> "....this criterion does not act as an effective constraint on police
> officers ....it is clear from the way police officers talk about stops
> that the question of what their legal powers may be does not enter
> into their decision making, except in the case of rare individuals.
> Officers considered the chance of getting a 'result' but this was
> often unconnected with any concept of reasonable suspicion" (Smith
> 1983, p.185)

Further,

> "....a substantial number of stops are made, if not randomly, at any
> rate without there being a specific reason for making them, or one
> that would give grounds for reasonable suspicion". (ibid, p.98)

In that study, officers were asked to indicate which of several stated
reasons was the nearest to their own justification for the stops conducted.
Nearly half (47%) indicated that the stop occurred because someone was
perceived "running, hurrying or loitering", one-in-seven for being rowdy or
drunk, and just over one-in-twenty (7%) for having an unconventional
appearance. In only one-in-ten cases had an offence been seen or
acknowledged as a reason for the use of the power.

The minority contribution to the Royal Commission on Criminal
Procedure expressed this view vocally. To earlier commentators such as
Barbara Wootton, Bernard Williams, and Michael Schofield, what
conventionally happens under the guise of reasonable suspicion (particularly
under the Misuse of Drugs Act) is that searches take place on mere
intuition, and often on the basis of factors like dress, hair style, and
personal appearance.

The condition of "reasonable suspicion" as the justification for invoking
the stop power, is in practice highly permissive. Like the notions of
"helping with enquiries", "obstruction", "resisting arrest", reasonable
suspicion remains in practice a euphemism. It offers vast discretionary
powers to a police officer seeking to control or structure a particular
encounter while not being bound by the niceties of a precise charge and
the safeguards of due process.

Safeguards And Reasonable Suspicion

If the stop-and-search power is unlikely to be well articulated in practice then logically the Act's safeguards are equally open to difficulties. The requirement in Section 3 of the Act (which requires records to be kept) paradoxically meets similar problems. The Royal Commission had argued that a written report would deter officers from abusing those powers.

However, the critics claim that given the vague practical requirements of reasonable suspicion and the inability of police officers to articulate specific reasons for resorting to the power then two consequences would follow in relation to the proposed safeguards. Either the stops would not be recorded or some inventiveness would be required in justifying the action on paper. In either case, some fudging of the issue would occur. The Policy Studies Institute's reservations on the safeguards issue illustrate these points.

> According to the Institute, the safeguards would not have a "....radical effect on police practice....because of the great difficulty in arriving at a watertight definition of police powers....and because the consequences for individual officers, where they were shown to have exceeded their powers in stopping and searching people or vehicles, would probably not be very serious". (Smith, 1983, p.345)

The very imprecision of the reasonable suspicion concept does not exactly lend itself to clarity in formal presentation on paper. In practice, senior officers, so that Report claims, will recognise the impossibility of transferring subjective intuition to paper and will find the powers almost impossible to regulate. The recently introduced Metropolitan Police code of practice (Guardian, 8th May, 1984) represents, in part, the recognition of the intractability of the problem of monitoring and recording. But, like the other well-known code governing police practice, the Judges Rules, constraining interrogation procedures, it seems as likely to be honoured in the breach as in the practice.

The evidence that officers are often unable to articulate the rationale for a stop, permits an analogy to be drawn with the practice of "verballing" in court. Officers will have to exercise a degree of imagination in transcribing suspicions from intuition to paper. According to the National Council For Civil Liberties,

> "....such inventiveness detracts from the legal and moral status of the police officer, will undermine the credibility of the..... legislation, and lead to further disrespect for the law in general". (1983, p.9)

In any case, the creation of records to safeguard against abuses of the stop-and-search powers assumes that effective police supervision and internal accountability are available. However, the present evidence is that in many cases quality first line supervision is not present (Smith, 1983). Certainly, Willis recounts no evidence of stop-and-searches being monitored by senior officers.

Finally, the concept of reasonable suspicion, as the justification for a stop-and-search, contains one major drawback for a citizen in search of redress. It is difficult, if not impossible, to obtain compensation for its misuse. According to the Royal Commission on Police Powers, 1929

"...any form of restraint by a police officer....or indeed, by anyone, is, in law an imprisonment, and if the police officer has acted wrongfully an action for wrongful imprisonment will be taken." A citizen unlawfully arrested can formally claim legal redress. However, being held under the stop-and-search power does not provide the same level of protection. There is little practical opportunity for the typical defendant to challenge police evidence of reasonable grounds for suspicion. He or she is unlikely to be granted Legal Aid because that resource is only available where damages are likely to be recovered, to justify the costs of proceeding. Most stops do not involve such damages and therefore challenges to police actions would have to be self-financed.

Further, as Demuth has argued, in the analysis of cases arising from the old Vagrancy Act provision (which utilised a similar notion of suspicion), in court it was nigh-impossible to challenge police statements of the grounds for suspicion. Where, as in those 'sus' cases, the court found in favour of the accused, the judgement was not based on an assessment of the police version of cause (which in practice remained largely inviolate) but because witnesses attested to the character of the accused (Demuth, 1978). The notion of reasonable suspicion, when pronounced by a police officer, is normally impossible to refute. Professional challenge, when available, has made little impact.

The Legal Critique - Confusion, Irrelevance, And Harm

Within the orthodox response, several other apparent legal defects have been noted. Critics have claimed that the extended powers are unnecessary, given the existing powers of arrest. Others have pointed to the potential misuse of the powers, and their irrelevance to the police function.

Legalists have argued that reliance on the concept of reasonable suspicion suggests some confusion with similar powers of arrest. Common law recognises no power apart from arrest, either to restrain an individual or to detain him or her for questioning. There is no legally recognised intermediate state between unfettered liberty and arrest, and therefore any form of restraint must be justified as an arrest, with the possible exception of certain very minor forms of compulsion. The stop-and-search power may be illusory and unnecessary since it is now generally accepted that there is a right to search arrested persons either immediately on arrest or later in custody. The police do not have to detain and search since they can arrest and search (Glanville Williams, 1960).

The minority contributors to the Royal Commission reiterated this theme, arguing that the existing stop-and-search powers should be repealed and replaced by customary powers of arrest and consequential search. This substitution would have two effects. It would simplify and rationalise the law. It would clarify and suitably restrict police powers.

The Final Report of the Royal Commission, in denying the substance of this argument, failed to give weight to the fact than an identical criterion of reasonable suspicion is available both for arrest and for stop-and-search. Either stop-and-search should require a lesser criterion or arrest a greater one. (In practice, the police constantly adopt a lesser standard for stop-and-search than for arrest). Further, stop-and-search powers add nothing to the ordinary powers of search after arrest. The advantages of the extra power (as formally conferred by the stop) are illusory, based on the erroneous assumption that the police are "....empowered to search anyone whose behaviour is at all out of the usual, even though they have no solid grounds for suspicion" (Glanville Williams, 1960, p.606).

It is generally assumed by the police that the statutory powers of stop-and-search can be resorted to on grounds which are insufficient to justify an arrest. From that perspective, under the stop-and-search provisions, the suspicion that the officer holds need not be as specific but can be of a much more general nature than in the case of an arrest. But the action, whether of stop-and-search or of an arrest, may have similar parameters. In Willis' words, "....a search is always a search, and however cursory, involves an infringement of the individual's liberty" (1983, p.24).

If it is true that qualitatively different standards operate in practice, then the implications for the nature of stop-and-search are serious and undermine the legal construction of that power. What in fact happens, is that the power becomes so weak in its requirements vis-a-vis the requirement for arrest, that the stop-and-searches occur on mere suspicion, occasionally on a random basis (Polyvios 1983). (2)

This paradox, the lack of distinction between the concepts of reasonable suspicion in the cases of a stop-and-search and of an arrest in English law, is heightened when contrasted with the situation in the United States. Under Terry v. Ohio, the police in the U.S.A. only have the power to stop an individual who is reasonably suspected of committing or being about to commit a crime. They may then proceed to a frisk (not a search) if they have reasonable apprehension that he is armed and dangerous. This is a limited search for weapons, and the standard of reasonable suspicion is less than that for a full arrest, but this is because the imposition represented by the stop it authorises is considerably less than is the case of a full arrest (Polyvios 1983).

The Royal Commission assumed that the use of arrest powers in all situations where a constable has reasonable suspicion, would be detrimental to the public. But this ignored the fact that arrest allows for the constitution of the formal legal process in which ideally, due process ensures appropriate safeguards against which the notion of reasonable suspicion can be tested (Christian 1983). These potential safeguards within the adversarial system of English justice are notably absent from a process that may conclude before the gateway of the courts - through search and temporary detention on the street.

In many cases, where the stop-and-search powers are likely to be required, there may already exist sufficient authority. For example, Willis has argued that football supporters suspected of carrying provocative items into football grounds may be controlled under the football clubs' rights to prevent entry, or within other of the private regulations of the local club. Most such recreational locations, from night-clubs to fairgrounds, have similarly restrictive powers. Secondly, as the N.C.C.L. points out, in its memorandum to the Select Committee, there are alternative powers in particular cases. For example, under Section 25 of the Theft Act 1968, police officers have the power to stop-and-search someone suspected of "....going equipped".

Indeed, the existing powers of arrest may be quite adequate to deal with all reasonable circumstances. Theft, burglary, deception, and going equipped to steal, are all arrestable offences. Arrest without warrant is possible for carrying an offensive weapon if the police officer cannot find the suspect's address or (under the Prevention of Crime Act 1953, s.1) to prevent a crime in which an offensive weapon might be used. (Christian 1983). If a person is behaving in a threatening way, then he or she can already be arrested under the Public Order Act, s.5.

Irrespective of the validity of the propositions that the power is legally redundant, that its use lowers the threshold for detention, there are additional civil libertarian objections.

Particular opposition has been expressed to the vagueness of the concepts of "offensive weapons" and of "articles for use in theft." (N.C.C.L.1983). Such an expanded use of the stop-and-search powers allows a greater degree of discretion and hence of possible abuse. Many perfectly innocent objects can be deemed to be offensive weapons "the power ...could therefore amount to a requirement that people on the streets ...justify to the police the possession of any item in their pockets" (Christian 1983, p.20). In the campaign against the 'sus' clause, Demuth cited various otherwise unobjectionable items that had at different times been construed as weapons by a patrolling constable. Similarly, the Haldane Society in its evidence to the Royal Commission illustrated how personal possessions such as penknives had been branded as offensive weapons in court. In the late seventies, it was common for police officers to strip youths arriving at seaside towns of various items of apparel - belts, braces, and shoe laces, on the assumption that they were liable to be used as offensive weapons.

Similarly, the stop-and-search provisions are vague in their definition of equipment available for assistance in the course of theft. The Haldane Society Report suggests that such objects may include screwdrivers, spanners "....keys, a credit card, any piece of plastic, car tools, or work tools" (1981, p.20). The function of a particular object may owe more to the interpretation of the patrolling police officer than to any intrinsic qualities.

In other words, the objection is that the powers are of far too general a nature. The powers of stop-and-search are transmuted by the Act from powers aimed at specific individuals and categories of behaviour to general classes of events or of objects. The extension of the powers to include offensive weapons and articles which the police officer believes might be used for theft purposes, ensures more discretion, more potential abuse, lowers the threshold over which "reasonable suspicion" can be invoked, and represents an enhancement of the legal territory not limited by the adversarial safeguards of due process. The subjective whims of the patrol officer, it is argued, become the determining factor in the implementation of street law.

Discriminatory Practice

This de facto reliance on the subjectivity of the police officer on the street, and its contribution to marginalizing particular social groups, has been the target for major critique. Several studies have demonstrated that factors of age, race and time, have provided the parameters of reasonable suspicion as the real basis for the exercise of powers under local legislation and under the Misuse of Drugs Act.

The most recent study only confirms the partiality built into the reasonable suspicion criterion (Vorhaus 1984). In the outer London district of Hillingdon, Vorhaus found that a large proportion of the young people stopped on the streets believed that they were selected by patrolling police officers because of their ethnic identity or because of their style of dress. She argued that chance factors alone could not explain (other things being equal) why the juveniles at the school nearest to the local police station were stopped at a higher rate than were others. Proximity to that station and convenience, rather than any objective notion of reasonable suspicion appeared to be significant as the precipitating factors. But race is the normal correlate.

While Tuck and Southgate (1981) in Manchester, failed to find evidence of the stop practices being related to ethnic appearance, the majority of such studies have produced contrary results. Both the important Willis study (1983) and the smaller McConville analysis of stop-and-searches in Notting Hill (1983) echoed Ann Brogden's (1981) results from Liverpool. In the two former studies, young blacks were twice as likely to be stopped as were white youths. The Policy Studies Institute found that young blacks were similarly twice as likely to be subject to stops and stop-and-searches as were whites. For young West Indians, the probability of being stopped in a single year is more than one-in-two. Willis found that despite this higher rate, the arrests resulting from such stops of young blacks were no more common than for whites, suggesting that power had been invoked as a form of harassment rather than on the basis of objective evidence. (Operation Swamp, with its pejorative title and involving large scale stop-and-search operations which immediately preceded the Brixton riots, was only the manifest demonstration of the racial factor underlying the operation of the stop-and-searches on the city streets).

The same studies also revealed the correlation between the age factor and the use of the power. In Tuck and Southgate, one-in-three males aged 16-35 years reported being stopped in the previous year. McConville, Willis, and Ann Brogden noted similar evidence. Being the wrong age, or the wrong colour, in the wrong place at the wrong time, are the real criteria for the implementation of the reasonable suspicion mandate.

Police officers patrolling the city streets, particularly during the twilight hours, are programmed by the force instructions to suspect particular groups and strata as potential or actual criminals. On the basis of linked data drawn from the reported criminal statistics, junior officers are instructed to expect deviance from stereotyped minorities carrying goods during the evening hours "....reasonable suspicion might arise from the nature of the property, the time, the place, the circumstances or the suspicious behaviour of the person or his associates". (Met. Instructions Para.13.29 - quoted in N.C.C.L., 1983). When this programming is influenced at patrol level by the type of racist ideology also documented by the P.S.I. study, the result is legalised discrimination.

Stops-And-Searches As A Necessary Weapon Against Crime

The major social science critique of the power has been in connection with its supposed utility in the rhetorical "war against-crime". A key theme in the police institution's argument in favour of the stop-and-searches, was that extension was required as a means of preventing and controlling crime. This viewpoint was given credibility at more exalted level. It was expressed strongly in the Royal Commission on Criminal Procedure (1981 p.27) and by Lord Scarman, in the report on the Brixton Riot, who bluntly added his own claim : "The power, I am convinced, is necessary to combat street crime" (1981 p.113). Even the authoritative Leigh (1981), who had previously taken a more detached view of police powers (1975), supported the argument that the power was essential in relation to crime.

In fact, the Conservative M.P. for Westminster North, John Wheeler, writing in Police Review, seems to have more evidence on his side, in expressing reservations: "Regrettably, it is hard to show that there will be a pay-off in the reduction of crime for this modest extension of police powers" (1983, p.2109). The critics have focussed on three aspects of this question of effectiveness in relation to crime. Stop-and-searches do not prevent crime. They create unnecessary offences, and in John Wheeler's words, "the principal casualty is likely to be a worsening of police community relations" (ibid). Stop-and-searches alienate that section of the public whose consent is essential to police activity in relation to crime.

A major problem in assessing the effectiveness of the stop-and-searches relates to the accuracy of the data. In its support for the enhanced power, the Home Office had quoted the Scottish precedent, (where stop-and-search powers had been included in the Criminal Justice (Scotland) Act). In Scotland, a high proportion (one-in-four) of stop-and-searches had apparently led to a charge of possessing an offensive weapon. However, given the Home Office claim that there had been little more than a thousand such stops in the whole of Scotland for that year, the inference to be drawn is not of the effectiveness of the stop-and-search power but rather one of under-recording. For example, the Policy Studies Institute reckoned that some million stops occurred in London in one year. Scotland, with half the population, could be expected to have a proportionate figure, certainly not the miserly one suggested by the Home Office.

In other words, many of the claims of the effectiveness of the stop-and-search powers in relation to crime have grossly underestimated the number actually conducted. In Willis' study, uniformed beat officers said they recorded less than a third of stops. Particularly susceptible to non-recording are those occasions when an individual is stopped without being searched (McConville 1983). Any evidence about the relative effectiveness of the stop-and-search powers must therefore be qualified by the assumption that the "real" rate is substantially larger than the recorded rate.

In the Operation Swamp police invasion of Brixton streets, 943 stops were recorded, resulting in 118 arrests and a smaller number of actual charges (75). Data quoted by Christian for the Camden area of London for 1979-1982 give a rough 12:1 stop-arrest ratio (1983). Rates in Liverpool for the six month period preceding the Toxteth riots varied (according to sub-division) from 17:1 to 43:1. The Policy Studies Institute found that only 8% of the recorded stops in the Metropolitan Police District led to arrests, and only 2% in Luton and Watford. In Oxford, Steer (in a study for the Royal Commission on Criminal Procedure) had found that only 2½% of all crimes cleared up arose from the use of stop powers. Only one-in-twenty of indictable offenders had been detected initially through the use of recorded stop-and-search powers. Willis noted that, an average of 12% of stops resulted in arrests at two London police stations, compared with an average of 3% in Watford and Luton.

Further, even where an operational decision has been made to increase the numbers of stops in a particular area, any effect on street crime may be transient. Lord Scarman's account of the Brixton riots, supports the research evidence documented by Boydstun in the U.S.A. (1975). While a high commitment to stop-and-search may temporarily reduce the number of reported offences in a district, once operations are over, reported crime seems to revert to its previous level. Further, it may be that the only effect of such operations is to displace street crime into other areas.

Not only do the powers have a small effect on the level of reported crime, but many of the crimes recorded may be constituted by the encounter itself. A high proportion of the incidents resulting in charges are precipitated by the conflictual interaction between patrol officer and citizen on the street.

The use of the stop-and-search powers may create incidents where none would otherwise have occurred (Brogden, 1982). Charges such as obstruction, assault on the police, and so on, may well flow directly from the stop. As Scarman acknowledged, a criminal offence may be the by-product of the encounter rather than its precursor. But the same offence may be used to justify the stop. Recording of stop-and-searches is subject to a process of legitimation.

The power has a particular utility for police officers striving to improve their arrest record. It eases the problem of "getting a result". Indeed, resort to the power may be a function of apparent inefficiency in other aspects of police work. Trawling the streets under omnibus stop-and-search powers may be the last refuge of an incompetent policing agency. Willis' comment lends some support to this view "....arrests from stops make up a substantial proportion ...of all relevant arrests made. This result is more likely to be due to the greater importance of stops in the clear-up of offences in London than to the particular effectiveness of stop-and-search there. It follows that the removal of existing powers of stop-and-search would greatly reduce the number of arrests for certain offences (particularly the less serious)...." (1983, p.23).

Stop-and-search powers create unnecessary work for beat officers, work that may occasionally result in a statistical success, as measured by the artificial clear-up rate. Benefits that accrue may sometimes serve organisational purposes but there is little pay-off for the public or for the wider context of police community relations. In any case, "whatever the deterrent impact of stop-and-search tactics, they run a risk of upsetting relations between the police and the public when they are practised extensively...." (Clarke & Hough 1984).

It is this latter question that has been the bedrock of the orthodox academic opposition. For policing to be effective against criminal behaviour, it requires consent from that section of the community which is most able to provide it with relevant information.

Policing And Consent

The ideological rendering of the theme of policing by consent is central to policing in Britain. Though the foundations of that consent are much shakier than previously recognised (Brogden 1982), in the specific context of crime, public support for police action is self-evidently important.

The debate over the stop-and-search powers raises two questions about this question of consent, one reflecting on the peculiar character of the interaction between citizen and police officer, the other more generally defining the relation between marginalized sections of the community and the police institution as a whole.

The Royal Commission, in recommending the extension of the stop-and-search powers, ignored the ability of the police to search a person on the street with his or her approval as an alternative to the extension of the powers. Bluntly, less antagonism is generated when searches are requested rather than required. "If the police are going to arrest someone but that person is able to avoid arrest by submitting voluntarily to a search and proving their innocence, the chances are that they will consent voluntarily to a search" (Christian 1983 p.29). If there were no stop-and-search power, the burden would be on the police officer, to persuade the citizen of the utility of the search. Blanket powers assume a coercive rather than a consensual relationship from the outset. The stop-and-search power structures the relationship within a negative framework. Co-operation with the officer is most likely to follow from the assumption of social consent not of legal coercion.

However, the major critique in relation to the question of public consent is at the general rather than at the individual level. The P.S.I. Report makes the point clearly. If the police are to receive help in investigating serious crimes, this will not happen if citizens are harassed through the use of the stop-and-search power. Willis argues similarly that "without a secure base of community support (consent), the use of powers of this kind, however extensively circumscribed, rapidly becomes hazardous and ineffective...."(1983, p.21). The public are alienated by such police tactics. In McConville's work, three-quarters of those stopped expressed hostility towards the police. To that writer, the "....vast majority (of stops) are un-productive on any measure". 1983, p.613). In Vorhaus's 1984 study, being stopped was correlated with anti-police attitudes. She claimed that any "positive" work with young people carried out by the local Police Juvenile Bureau was negated by the use of the power.

The police depend upon public consent. That support is threatened by the use of powers which, while they may generate a level of arrests for non-serious cases, may result in a lack of co-operation over more serious criminal activity.

> "The problem is that the ....power tends to be used on selective groups....Selective enforcement of this kind leads to alienation: groups mistrust the police because of what they see as harassment, the police mistrust those groups because they believe them to be suspicious, hostile or outsiders. The whole process then becomes self-reinforcing...." (McConville, 1983 p.614).

The P.S.I. Report argued that the practice of stopping ran the serious risk of causing offence to innocent persons both because most people stopped are innocent and because they are unhappy about the way police handle the incident in a substantial minority of cases. Although in that study the majority of those stopped reacted positively to police questioning, "....the relationship was more often judged to be poor when the person stopped was young or black" (Smith 1983, p.186). In the one U.S. study noted, reactions to the police became more noticeably hostile when the frequency of stopping increased (Boydstun 1975) - although there is some evidence that this hostility was diminished when the grounds for the stop were explained.

Kelling, a major figure in the work of the United States Police Foundation and hardly the most radical critic of policing style and organisation, has emphasised the dysfunctional effects of such practices as the stop-and-search. To that researcher, considerable support for policing exists, even amongst minority communities. But that support is threatened by police discretion and techniques that view the combination of age and minority group membership as a potential "crime problem" and one that must be thwarted:

> "The technique of aggressive patrol consists primarily in the use of traffic and pedestrian laws for purposes other than those for which they were intended. Because it is not applied randomly in a community but rather is targeted and directed at youthful male minorities, the strategy quickly evolves to include illegal frisks, illegal searches of cars, and illegal arrests....In so doing, they

102

generate more serious problems, the consequences of young male minorities who at best feign compliance with these practices or at worst riot in rebellion. Because these aggressive preventive patrol strategies are not randomly applied to a community but are directed and targeted at male minority youths, they not only fail and are unjust but squander and jeopardize the goodwill that police have developed in minority communities. The result has been the worst of all possible worlds." (1983. pp.165-6).

Stop powers are symptomatic of a particular policing style (as epitomized by Operation Swamp) in which police officers, without specific leads to identifiable crimes, seek to trawl potential offenders from a reservoir of suspects on the street. The result of such procedures is to institutionalise the legal inferiority of particular social groups, as marked out by the ascriptive credentials of age, race, and location in the inner city or on the delapidated housing estate. Such surveillance operations and fishing trips to the urban reservoir are the antithesis of the alternative styles of community policing.

The Twin Assumptions Of The Orthodox Critique

However, the conventional criticisms of the extension of the stop-and-search powers by the Police and Criminal Evidence Act make two primary and contestable assumptions. The legal critique takes it as unquestioned that the ideal model of English law, from which the stop-and-search powers are construed as deviating, is one of due process. Secondly, the majority of critics assume that the primary function of the British police is one of crime-fighting and are sceptical of the value of the extended powers to that activity.

A more substantive critique must take issue with each of these assumptions. Only by locating the analysis within the overall structure of the present arrest and prosecution process and historically within the development of municipal law and law enforcement can one provide a more effective appraisal of the stop powers.

From Adversarial Aberration To Inquisitorial Substance

Critics of the legalistic construction of the stop-and-search power have assumed that it has aberrational qualities, that it differs markedly from other forms of police powers. Like the now-abolished Suspected Persons Loitering ('sus') charge, the stop-and-search power appears to deviate from the ideal due process model of English law, with its adversarial safeguards for the accused and its presumption of innocence.

According to the authoritative Dicey (1952, p.208), the adversarial due process system of English justice requires as a fundamental safeguard against wrongful action that an actual offence has been committed before sanctions can be imposed. No restraint on the individual is permissible prior to the initiation of the action embodying the offence. Further, for the accused to be convicted, there must be an independent investigation of the circumstances of the act not into the intentions of the presumed offender. In Packer's words "....each of the successive stages (of the due process model) is designed to present formidable impediments to carrying the accused any further along in the process". Filters at each of the stages of the due process model, protect the citizen faced with legal visitation by the authority of the state.

However, this idealistic model of the legal process has come in for substantial rebuke in recent years. On one hand, it has been argued that the practice of law in the courts is dramatically different from the utopianism of law-in-the-books - the ideal of due process. The practical problems of dealing with large numbers of defendants results in many short cuts being taken and legal safeguards not being implemented. On the other, it has been claimed forcefully (notably by McBarnet, 1981, and in a collection of essays by Shering, 1982) that the "....very structure of legal rules and procedures allows and even facilitates the erosion of the rights of defendants...." (McConville and Baldwin p.17). The magistracy and judiciary it is claimed, will accept interpretations of events from police officers which they would disallow if put forward by defendants. The permissive essence of much English law contains sufficient ambiguities and contradictions to ensure a built-in bias against the defendant. It is the law itself, not the exigencies of practice, that disrupts the idealism of due process.

McConville and Baldwin have usefully distinguished between these critical perspectives in relation to the processes of arrest and prosecution. "Aberrational injustice", they say, "....arises as a result of mistakes or errors of judgement. They are incorrect outcomes of a sound system, a system which is framed to avoid such results." The alternative, "systemic injustice", develops "....not from human error but from the fundamental weakness within the system itself" (1981 p.17).

The orthodox legal critics of the stop-and-search power view the legislation as aberrational. The power conflicts, it is postulated, with the adversarial model of due process, primarily because it places the onus on the citizen to justify the possession of particular items. Presumed guilt replaces presumed innocence. Inquisition replaces accusation in the encounter between police officer and citizen on the street. Once possession has been established, the burden of proof actually shifts to the defendant to show that the article in his or her possession was for purposes other than for burglary or theft (Theft Act, 1968 s.25). Parallels have been drawn between the stop-and-search power and the 'sus' charges and the same arguments about inquisitorial justice raised (Brogden 1981, Willis 1983).

The question that arises therefore is whether the stop-and-search power, like the previous 'sus law', because of its inquisitorial nature, is open to abuse by ill-disposed police officers. Or whether the total system of petty law enforcement on the street, when viewed within its totality, is structured (with the stop-and-search power as only one component of that structure) to achieve the protection of the state against the citizen, not as formally portrayed in due process, the protection of the citizen from the state's potential abuses.

The case of Errol Madden, a young black Londoner, for example, can be interpreted either way. That citizen was persuaded by two police officers to confess to the theft of his own toy cars (items for which he had a receipt in his possession at the time of arrest) after being stopped and searched in the street. The orthodox critics would say that the inducement to a false confession must necessarily relate to the way ill-disposed police officers took advantage of a deviant power - that of stop-and-search. Bad and unusual law permitted harassed police officers to break the rules.

The alternative perspective would explain the incident in a different way. It is not that the police were slapdash in enquiry nor that individual officers developed a psychological commitment to prosecution that blunted their judgement. "Rather it is the way that the responsibility for prosecution in English law by the police, requires that the police officers build up the strongest possible case against the defendant through obtaining the best available evidence, evidence that must be compiled in the least time-consuming and most efficient way". Confessions are the best way of effecting that process. "Police work, therefore, is heavily geared towards obtaining admissions from suspects." (McConville and Baldwin 1981 p.192). The structure of the overall process, not psychology or bad law, determine the outcome.

Stop-and-search powers are not isolated peculiar aspects of street control but rather are a component of an overall system which is structured to disadvantage the suspect, not adversarially impede police action. The reason for extending stop-and-search powers nationally is not to add an extra legal measure to the police armoury, but rather to incorporate within the legal form practices already conducted by local police. Law follows police practice, not policing practice following in the steps of legal innovation.

The detail of the non-recording of stops illustrates this argument. In those municipalities whose police forces did not possess stop-and-search powers prior to the Police and Criminal Evidence Act, it seems self-evident that police officers have somehow managed to exercise sufficient controls in the street. (3) It is difficult to believe that the practices of the Greater Manchester Police (where there has been no previous stop-and-search power) in accosting on the street have been much different traditionally than those of the West Midlands Police (where the power has existed in Birmingham since the Victorian age). The lack of a formal stop-and-search power does not mean that stops only occurred in those few towns and cities which possessed that particular authority. Indeed, the expressed opposition of a number of police officers to the legislation embodying the stop-and-search powers has in part been based upon the fallacious belief (if precedent is anything to go by) that the requirement to record and justify the searches on paper, will restrict existing practices of street patrol. The new legislation is seen in part as an encumbrance, hindering the forms of street action that are necessitated by the particular position and requirements of the police within the English system of prosecution.

In other words, the civil liberties' opposition to the stop-and-search power in presenting that statute as aberrational, is partly misconceived. It fails to recognise the significance of the unity of the prosecutorial and arrest system, a system which differs markedly from the idealistic picture of due process and of its assumed safeguards for the accused.

The defects within the orthodox legal critique are not however encompassed by the preceding remarks. There is a case to be made that the due process model is in any case only a facade. A rather different picture emerges when other realities of that system are acknowledged. The norm may not be that of adversarial due process but one of inquisition.

For example, a high proportion of juvenile and traffic offences are determined outside the formal safeguards of due process. Some forty-five per cent of juveniles accused of offences in England and Wales are cautioned, a process in which the police officer is both accuser, effective judge, and dispositional agent. With the introduction of "instant fines" enforceable by traffic wardens as well as by police officers, the mundane regulatory context of traffic control has witnessed a diminution in due process.

In Magistrates Courts, where some ninety per cent of defendants are persuaded not to contest the charges, a guilty plea system, largely devoid of accusatorial safeguards, has come into being. In the higher courts, plea bargaining is rife (Baldwin and McConville 1977, 1981). In a range of so-called "white-collar" or "corporate" crimes, decisions are made through a process of negotiation which have little relationship to the requirements of the adversarial system. All these procedures and practices are permitted by the formal rules.

If the spirit of a legal system can be adduced from a quantitative accounting of the cases considered, then the image of due process in England and Wales is a flimsy one. The stop-and-search power, far from being an aberration, is a consistent representation of the body of justice in England and Wales. A criticism limited to the specificity of this provision has the danger of distracting attention from the larger threat to the rights of the citizen.

Policing As Social Control

The second major orthodox criticism of the stop-and-search powers has been a refutation of the notion that the powers are necessary to combat crime. The view has been expressed forcefully and repetitively that stop-and-searches and support for the police by minority and youthful groups are antithetical.

But this approach, like the central legal critique, makes a major misapprehension and one that the proponents of the expansion of powers have failed also to concede. The history of street powers such as stop-and-search, when recounted, demonstrates that the traditional practices of law enforcement on the streets have had very little connection with crime per se and a great deal to do with the social control of the urban populace. When Christian suggests that "....trade unionists and political activists could find the powers of stop-and-search used to control or prevent political protests or pickets" (1983, p. 3), she indicates not a haphazard by-product of legal expansion but rather the inevitable political dimension to the historical development of police power in the urban context.

In a recent local study (Brogden 1984), the origin of the conjoined and easily confused stop-and-search and 'sus' powers have been traced back to their mediaeval origins. In Liverpool, the development of the powers has been continuous since the thirteenth century. That history is an account of street law as a developing instrument of social control not one of incremental measures against crime.

In that city, the first published street powers appear in the municipal records during the reign of Henry III. The local halberds were formally required to "....keep in order the unruly". No specification of rights or safeguards was apparent in that omnibus mandate to control the street populace. However during the sixteenth century a series of proclamations began to demarcate the object of suspicion - the "suspectid person", and "....any maner of beggers or vacabond or eny evill disposed person" (Proclamations 42,55, 1541) (who are to be driven from the streets) from the respectable citizens. Edicts were pronounced to juridically define those citizens who were allowed to be abroad after dusk and those others who were not - "....not any suspectid personne nor persons after nyne of the clocke shall not walke, but rest and kepe they theyr hoostes houssies, uppon payne of imprisonment...." (Proclamation 13, 1542). The early police function was to control particular strata, rural migrants and the growing urban poor. Municipal street powers were simply enabling devices to legitimise that social control.

In the early eighteenth century, some sixty Watchmen were appointed to patrol the town with the major objective of apprehending "....all night-walkers and all disorderly persons". Police work was increasingly delegated from one class to the incorporated members of a lower class, with street powers that were both inquisitorial and undifferentiated in their omnibus character. Summary, sweeping powers of stopping and arresting suspected persons continued to be the defining feature of law enforcement in the city into the nineteenth century, but a degree of selectivity appeared as legal discourse started to distinguish between the roughs and the respectables, the suspects and the non-suspects. Thus the Commissioners' Instructions to the Watch, in 1817:

> "You are to apprehend all night-walkers, rogues, vagabonds, and other disorderly persons disturbing the public....you must be very circumspect....and not wantonly or inconsiderately apprehend persons of a different description.."

And the priorities of police work were re-affirmed - "....the good order of the streets, secondly, for the safety of the persons of the inhabitants, and thirdly, for the security of property...." (Instructions to the Night Watch, 1834).

With the advent of the New Police in 1836, spokesmen from the new police institution demanded the same detailed street powers that had been obtained in London through the lobbying of the Metropolitan Commissioners, (and establishing a precedent that Metropolitan Commissioner McNee was to follow in the plea for enhancement of the stop-and-search powers in relation to the present Act), and that had been embodied in the Metropolitan Police Act 1839 (Brogden 1982). The new Liverpool Improvement Act 1842 specified the major inquisitorial street control measures of the City Police in section 276 (the arrest of all "....loose, idle, or disorderly persons") and section 278 (stop-and-search powers on the River Mersey and on the City streets). On behalf of the local ruling merchant class and its law enforcement surrogates, the 'sus' charge and the stop-and-search power, the legal keys to controlling the lower strata, which had originally been expounded seven hundred years earlier to prevent rural incursions into the township, were transformed into statutory constructs, allowing legal domination of the classes occupying the thoroughfares and rookeries of the mercantile city.

The legal rhetoric of "good cause" and "reasonable suspicion" concealed the reality of the social differentiation conveyed in the Head Constable's instructions to his men:

> "....watching vigilantly the movements of all suspicious persons who pass through his beat.... If it be at an untimely hour, or if they fail to assign a proper reason for being in a place, he is to arrest them....showing bad characters that they are known and watched by him....their habits will point them out without further ado....For the purposes of seeing whether his suspicions are well-founded, he may....stop any person carrying goods which he suspects to have been stolen, he may also examine the person and detain him...."
> (Instructions to the Liverpool City Police, 1878, p.9)

And later, the 1911 Instructions reinforce the priority of 'sus' charges and stop-and-search powers to the mundane everyday street-sweeping work of the beat constable.

With the passing of the Liverpool Corporation Act 1921, the police had come into possession of a substantial social control armoury. Section 314 spelled out the centrality of the 'sus' provision and Section 514 underlined the importance of the precipitating stop-and-search power. Together with bye-laws governing almost every possible activity by the street people, from the suppression of nuisances to the licensing of pedlars, statutes on betting and gaming, on street obstructions, on inebriation, on prostitution, on begging, and on unlawful possession, the Liverpool City Police was equipped with a vast array of permissive street powers. Social control of the city streets through inquisitorial process, not crime control through due process, stands out as the defining feature of police work as laid down by the Corporation Act.

The most recent legislation, the County of Merseyside Act, 1980, re-affirmed the stop-and-search power:

> "A police constable may within the county....search any person (vessel or vehicle) who may reasonably be suspected of having in his possession, or conveying in any manner anything stolen or unlawfully obtained...."

before being repealed and superseded by the Police and Criminal Evidence Act 1984.

Stop-and-search powers, originally devised within the omnibus powers of the ruling class in the township of Liverpool during the reign of Henry III, used initially to clear the feudal and mediaeval towns of hungry, landless peasants, later reified to control the urban lower classes of the nineteenth century, as they engaged in transactions and recreation on the mercantile city's streets, was to be justified in the wake of the Toxteth riots of 1981, as a major device for containing the street population - now marked as suspect by the characteristics of race and age, rather than by rural origin - of the 1980s.

Unravelling the history of street powers demonstrates that social control of particular, troublesome, populations, not crime control, has always been the primary feature of the legal mandate of the city police in England and Wales. The stop-and-search power symbolises not a new discrete weapon in the rhetorical "war against crime" but simply one component of the totality of the legal controls by which lower classes and minority groups are and were suppressed. Orthodox criticisms of the stop-and-search power which do not recognise the historical continuity of such legal authority, and its wider social control relationship, are restricted to the shadows of the argument, not to the substance.

Stopping The Police

The failure of the civil libertarian criticisms to dent the armour of the Police and Criminal Evidence Act has little to do with the merits of their case. Exposing successive flaws in the argument for the extension of the stop-and-search power may win the debate but patently it has not affected the outcome. Moral virtue doubtless lies in the hearts of those who regard the power as a deviation from adversarial due process. Statistical denials of the utility of the power in clearing-up crime may give rise to academic satisfaction. But with the commencement of the Act, citizens will be successfully legally harassed under the new power throughout the length and breadth of the country.

In the short-run, of course, the failure of that opposition has much to do with the arithmetic of Parliamentary majorities. No reasoned case, documenting the legal inconsistencies of proposed street powers, and their potential danger to the citizen, could have much effect on a Government which in a variety of other matters - from enforced redundancies to the promotion of queue-jumping in access to health care - has trodden over the rights of ordinary people.

But in the long-term, an appreciation of the wider context of the argument, together with the detailing of the civil rights' case, may have a different impetus. Opposition to the legalisation and extension of the powers of stop-and-search cannot be dissociated from a critique of the use of law as one device, amongst others, by which a particular form of unequal society is maintained, a society in which the function of law is to protect the state against the people not the people from the depredations of the state. The debate over the stop-and-search power, in particular, and over the Police and Criminal Evidence Act more generally, must be complemented by a recognition of the totality of the system of law enforcement as experienced, and of the historical continuity of legally sanctified class practices.

REFERENCES

Baldwin,J. & McConville,M. (1977). Negotiated Justice, London.
Boydstun,J.E. et al (1975). San Diego Field Interrogation: Final Report, Foundation, Washington.
Brogden,A. (1981). "'Sus' is dead but what about 'Sas'?", New Community,IX,,1,
Brogden,M.(1982). The Police: Autonomy and Consent, Academic Press, London.
Brogden,M. (1984), "From Henry III to Liverpool 8", International Journal of the Sociology of Law, 12.
Christian,L. (1983). Policing by Coercion, Greater London Council, London.
Clarke, & Hough,M. (1984). Crime and Police Effectiveness, Home Office Research Study No.79, H.M.S.O., London.
Demuth,C. (1978). "Sus" - a report on the Vagrancy Act, 1824, Runnymede Trust, London.
Dicey,A.V. (1952). Introduction to the Study of the Laws of the Constitution, Macmillan, London.
Haldane Society of Socialist Lawyers, (1981). The Police, the Law, and the People, London.
Kelling,G. (1983). "On the accomplishments of the police". In Control in the Police Organisation (M.Punch ed.), M.I.T. Press, London.
Lambert,J.L. (1974). "Police powers of stop-and-search", New Law Journal, Vol. 124, pp.476-8.
McBarnet,D. (1981). Conviction, Macmillan, London, 1981.
McConville,M. & Baldwin,J. (1981). Courts, Prosecution, and Convictions, Clarendon Press, Oxford.
McConville,M. "Search of persons and premises" [1983] Criminal Law Review, 605-614.
National Council for Civil Liberties. (1983). Briefing on the Police and Criminal Evidence Bill, London.
Polyvios,P. (1983). Search and Seizure, Duckworth, London.
Shearing,C.(1981). Organisational Police Deviance, Butterworths, Toronto.
Smith,D.J. (1983). The Police and the People in London, IV, A Survey of Police Officers, Policy Studies Institute, London.

Tuck,M. & Southgate,P. (1981). Ethnic Minorities, Crime, and Policing. Home Office Research Study No.80, H.M.S.O., London.

Vorhaus,G. (1984). Police in the Classroom, Hillingdon Legal Resource Centre, Hayes.

Williams, Glanville. "Statutory powers of search and arrest on the grounds of unlawful possession" [1960] Crim. L.R. 598.

Willis,C. (1983). "The use, effectiveness, and impact of police stop-and-search powers", Home Office Research and Planning Unit Paper 15, H.M.S.O., London.

NOTES

1. See for example, Written Evidence of the Commissioner of Police of the Metropolis to the Royal Commission on Criminal Procedure, London, 1978.

2. There is a useful, if brief, discussion of the differences in the application of the concept of reasonable suspicion in the Policy Studies Institute account of London police practices (Smith 1984, p.231).

3. Police officers, when dealing with relatively minor events, use the law as a back-up resource tool, rather than recognising it as a constraint. Stop-and-search powers, as with other permissive street legislation, are only likely to be articulated when a rare challenge is made to the officer's authority. Given the lack of knowledge of the law by the typical recipient of that authority, lack of formal legal powers has never been a major burden to police officers on the street.

7. CONFESSION EVIDENCE, THE POLICE AND CRIMINAL EVIDENCE ACT AND THE CONFAIT CASE

Christopher Price

First a caveat; I am neither a practising nor an academic lawyer; such legal expertise as I have picked up has come from listening to trials, socialising with lawyers and reading books. My interest in confessions stems from my involvement in the Confait case, (1) in which three youths, one 18 and mentally retarded, another 16 and very disturbed and another 14 and of Turkish-Cypriot origin, confessed in some detail to a killing and an arson in 1972, were convicted, spent three years in custody and were finally exonerated and compensated 7 years later. (It is unusual for a murder case to have become known by the name of its victim. It would be more appropriate for this celebrated miscarriage of justice to be known by the names of the policemen who investigated it, the doctors who got their expert evidence wrong or the judge and the lawyers who allowed justice to miscarry in court. But since the 'Confait case' shorthand has achieved widespread currency, I continue to use it - with apologies to the relatives of Maxwell Confait who continue to live in Lewisham and would, I know, prefer the whole saga to go under some label other than that of their family name).

A very brief summary of my involvement. While canvassing for election to Parliament in 1974, I met the mother of one of the wrongly convicted young men, and when elected successfully lobbied for a referral of the case to the Court of Appeal, which, under the then Sir Leslie Scarman, quashed the convictions. A unique enquiry then took place, under the chairmanship of Sir Henry Fisher, a former judge, who made some useful recommendations for reform of interrogation procedures, (1) but came to the wrong conclusions on the facts, virtually reconvicting two out of the three young men. Partly as a result of Fisher's report, a Royal Commission on Criminal Procedure (2) was set up, the recommendations of which were substantially incorporated into two Police and Criminal Evidence Bills, during the first of which (while still an MP) I served on the Standing Committee and the second of which became an Act in November 1984. Meanwhile, in 1979, evidence had come to light which revealed Confait's true murderer (together with a friend who witnessed the act) and led to the complete exoneration of the three young men. Two years later Confait's murderer committed suicide, and a number of other individuals, who had feared to speak in the meantime, revealed further facts about exactly what happened.

As a result of this involvement over the past decade I have tried to address two questions with particular reference to this case. First, why is it that the authorities fail to recognise a false confession - especially when other evidence makes it inherently unlikely that the confession could accord with what actually happened? Second, why do people - normal, healthy adults as well as children and the mentally impaired - confess to crimes of which they are innocent? False confessions are often thought to be an isolated phenomenon - a vagary which the law has to tolerate because it does not understand. Not so; from long before Confait through to 1984 when a British airman, stationed in Cyprus, confessed under pressure from the military police to spying, false confessions have been common. It is the exposure of the phenomenon and discussion of what to do about it that is new.

First, why the propensity among the police, the professions, the judiciary, lawyers and (less often) juries to be taken in by so many false confessions? I have come to the conclusion that it is something to do with the compelling nature, as evidence, of the confession document. It mesmerises; it looks plausible. To those brought up with certain sets of experience, habits and assumptions it is almost impossible to believe that such a document has no foundation. To illustrate: whenever I asked a non-lawyer to compare the confession document of Ronnie Leighton (typed by the police) with his first letter home from Wormwood Scrubs still denying the murder (written by him) the reaction was immediate. They felt Ronnie had been conned by the police into a confession and was telling the truth when he wrote home to his mother from custody. (Both documents are reproduced in The Confait Confessions.) (3) But to many lawyers, doctors and other professionals to whom I showed the documents, Ronnie was telling the truth in his 'confession' and lying in his letter home from the Scrubs. I had alighted on what was - to me - a curious psychological chasm.

Some indications of this professional tunnel vision. None of the three defence solicitors thought it necessary to call evidence from independent forensic pathologists. They relied on the prosecution expert, Professor Cameron, whose evidence was not clear at the trial and was changed at a later appeal. Why such an omission? A subconscious assumption of guilt? Neither the prosecution counsel (Mr Richard Du Cann QC) nor the DPP official who authorised the prosecution seriously tested the authenticity of the confessions before proceeding. Why? They wanted a conviction too much? I don't think so. Rather, the weight of the signed confessions was so impressive that other commonsense evidence paled into insignificance. The judge (the late Mr Justice Chapman) never put this 'improbability' (Scarman's word) of the confessions properly before the jury. From his point of view all signed confessions weighed ponderous, and other evidence about their implausibility in the Confait case remained 'imponderable' (his word). Some lawyers have since told me that it was 'jolly bad luck' for the young men concerned. I don't believe it was luck; rather, a subconscious assumption of guilt among the professionals, associated with the whole formal paraphernalia of presenting confessions in court, prejudiced the case from the start.

A further illustration. Had Hercule Poirot or Lord Peter Wimsey been investigating the Confait case, they would have picked up in a flash the improbability of the confession evidence compared with the solidity of other evidence which was there, but not even noticed. A small example. There were extensive police photographs of the scene of the crime; there was also extensive anecdotal evidence available about the habits of Maxwell Confait. Quite apart from his sexual proclivities, he was a 'record' freak. He had - and everyone knew he had - a superb collection of records. In the 'scene of the crime' photographs there is a record player, but not a single record; there is also on one of the photographs, for everyone to see, lying on the floor, a small triangular core, which had fallen out of the last 45 record, when Confait's real murderer decided to remove everything that might contain a fingerprint and drop the lot in a Sussex reservoir. No one - not the police, the defence counsel, the judge, the jury (or me, for that matter) - noticed this simple clue. Why? Partly because they were not pop music enthusiasts - but mostly because, rather than concentrate on the real evidence at the scene of the crime, they were all fixated by the fairy tale evidence in the confessions - the 'flex', with which the young men said they had strangled Confait (no flex was ever used - Confait was strangled with his own women's tights)and the 'keys' which one of the defendants was meant to have thrown away (there never were any keys). So one tiny piece of 'hard' evidence - that Confait's records had disappeared and the young men could not possibly have disposed of them - was never canvassed.

Much of the problem, then, is a psycho-legal one. Because lawyers, unlike the generality of humankind, have to put a particularly high value on the sanctity of words and their meanings, and because they have seldom had any experience of being placed in an oppressive atmosphere, they can't really understand how or why people make false confessions. So though they are suspicious of 'verbals' - they all realise some policemen lie on oath from time to time - they treat suggestions that written confessions can sometimes be quite unreliable very much more sceptically. This was borne in on me when, after the initial Scarman quashing of the Confait verdicts but before the Fisher enquiry had started, my lawyer friends in the House of Commons who had been following the case would come and tell me that while one of the defendants, Colin Lattimore, may have made a false confession because he was mentally retarded, the other two were undoubtedly guilty. So I wasn't unduly surprised when, over a year later, Sir Henry Fisher came to exactly this conclusion. Neither Fisher, nor my lawyer friends, could cope with the idea that a written confession, especially one confirmed in seemingly voluntary statements made with the parents present, could be wholly flawed.

I put this point during the Committee stage of the Police and Criminal Evidence Bill to Patrick Mayhew, then Minister of State at the Home Office. He did not deny the force of it, but countered with the argument that juries were becoming more sceptical:

> "The hon. Member for Lewisham West (Mr Price) was a little pessimistic when, drawing naturally enough on his experience of the Confait case, he spoke of everyone connected with the criminal justice system and the criminal trial tending to be mesmerised by a piece of paper, the written statement of confession....However, in some ways it is regrettable that - particularly in London - it is much harder now than even a few years ago for the prosecution to secure a conviction on the basis of a confession statement alone.... Each of us has his own idea why this development has occurred. I believe that the greater part of the explanation lies in the increasing scepticism by juries about the circumstances in which confessions are taken. (4)

Patrick Mayhew may have been right about the increasing scepticism of London juries; but there would have been fewer miscarriages in the past if the professionals had been as sceptical of written confessions then as juries are becoming now.

It may be that Fisher had another reason for his reluctance to believe that the Confait confessions were erroneous, a reason which I suspect he shared with many of his legal colleagues. This was a belief that police evidence is generally trustworthy and although that of the senior officer - Detective Chief Superintendent Alan Jones - might have been unreliable, (5) it was unlikely to be the case with any of the other officers involved. Accordingly, during the Fisher Inquiry, the counsel for the young men did not try to substantiate the (perhaps plausible) allegations of mild assault in the police station, not because he did not necessarily believe them, but because repeating them might have triggered off the natural tendency of Sir Henry's judicial mind to recoil with horror at such allegations being made against respectable policemen. So a tortuous process was begun of trying to prove that confessions which bore no relationship to reality came about through mild, almost unconscious, police suggestions. Without the solid evidence to prove this fantasy quality of the confessions (which came later) (6) this proved a vain task. The solid legal confines of Sir Henry's mental processes, which blocked off that quality of imaginative insight which the ancient Greeks called enopsis, forced him to the conclusion that the police must, at any rate, have been partly right.

Why do people make and sign false confessions? The most common cause is undoubtedly hope of reward or fear of the consequences of not doing so - either of which two circumstances ought to have in the past ruled out such confessions as evidence - according to para. 6 of the preamble to the Judges' Rules. (7) But such exclusion is a rare occurrence (8) since it involves the word of a defendant against that of a policeman and is almost always impossible to prove. Some false confessions are the result of violent threats, substantial bribes or actual bodily harm; but it has already been established that the threat or bribe can be quite gentle. Especially with children, the desire to go home, especially when penned in a strange environment, can be so all-enveloping that they will sign anything to escape. They suffer from that other classical Greek emotion - to which even Odysseus was ever prone and ready to engage in any degree of perfidy to assuage - 'nostalgia', an 'aching to go home'.

Moreover in many communities the police stand in such a powerful position vis-à-vis ordinary folk, that the threat of victimisation stands as a stark reality whether the police hint at it or not. Even more powerful than fear of penalty or hope of reward, is the human desire to 'say what is wanted' - to please authority. That this characteristic is very much more widespread than most people realise was demonstrated by Barry Irving and Linden Hilgendorf in the research studies they carried out for the Royal Commission on Criminal Procedure and in particular by their description of the 'Milgram' experiments in the U.S. (9) Normal mature adults were instructed by a 'teacher' to apply electric shocks of increasing severity to a 'learner', whom they could see throughout as in acute pain from these shocks. (The 'learner' was, in reality acting.) Such was the natural desire to cooperate with authority that, although some were hesitant as the 'shocks' escalated, no one refused to continue pressing the button. Of all the mass of evidence cited, this is the most chilling proof of this human propensity to do and say as your 'policeman-teacher' tells you to.

What, finally, of the safeguards which the Police and Criminal Evidence Act has purported to introduce? The Act substitutes the new test of 'reliability' for the old one of 'voluntariness'. Most of my legal friends are sceptical as to whether it will result in judges excluding any more confessions than they do at the moment; and I shall reserve judgement for a few years until we see how it operates. Fisher (1) recommended a limited absolute exclusionary rule - for uncorroborated confessions of children, of the mentally retarded, or of anyone whose confession was either not tape-recorded or was obtained in breach of the Judges' Rules. But the Royal Commission set its face against a strategy of 'exclusion' for controlling police conduct, as did the government in legislation. I continue to believe that the government was wrong and that Sir Henry Fisher - in this instance at any rate - was right.

Some see an independent prosecuting system - which the government have now promised us - as a safeguard. I am deeply sceptical. The recent BBC series of programmes, Rough Justice, has discovered miscarriages due to unreliable confessions in Scotland (where an independent prosecuting system operates) as well as in England. In Confait, there was an independent prosecutor, the DPP, and he proved to be absolutely no safeguard whatsoever. Indeed, as I have already suggested, there can be a tendency for some lawyers to be more police-minded than the police. To the extent that an independent prosecuting system will persuade detectives to get on with the job of detecting, and dissuade them from forcing confessions out of unwilling suspects, simply to lift their personal 'charge tally', it could prove valuable. But in itself, it does not represent very much protection against abuse.

The most encouraging safeguard on the horizon is the commendable determination of the government to press ahead with the current two-year experiment in tape-recording, and eventually extend it to the whole of England and Wales. The experiment is being conducted in two divisions of the Metropolitan Police - Holborn and Croydon - and four other local authorities - Leicester, South Tyneside, Winchester and Wirral. It has already led to an interesting ruling by Mr Justice Otten, during a rape case in Croydon in June 1984, to the effect that the tapes rather than a transcript of them are the 'best evidence'; and that if a jury want to reconsider them during their deliberations, they should not demand a transcript, but come back into court to hear the actual tapes. (10) This goes some way to meet the 'mesmeric' dangers of the signed confession. In the Croydon case, the defendant had first denied rape on tape, and then in a second taped interview, admitted it. The jury heard both tapes and acquitted him. There was the same pattern in the police transcript of the Confait confessions - first a denial, then admissions. But hearing words spoken is an experience quite different from reading them on a piece of paper. Had the Confait interviews been taped, I have little doubt that the case would never have come to trial.

It is possible, however, that the Confait confessions would not even have been taped in Croydon today. Tape recordings and their use in court are currently following procedural guidelines drawn up by the Home Office. (11) I find one of these guidelines extraordinary. This states that an interview with a child, a mentally handicapped person or someone else 'at risk' need not be tape recorded. One of the grounds for this exception is that a tape recording might 'frighten' such a suspect. I am sure it is put there in good faith, on the grounds that an independent person, who has to be present at such interviews, is a better safeguard than a tape recorder. I'm not so sure. A completely independent person, a Turkish Cypriot interpreter (in addition to four of the parents) was present when the Confait defendants were making their statements (though not during the interviews); such an adult presence proved no protection. Now it is possible for juries to listen to nuances of tone in police interviews, it is essential that such evidence should always be available to them. I hope that tape recording of interviews - and one day video recording - will soon become the norm; and that if the police try to rely on confessions where it has not taken place, courts will draw appropriate conclusions.

As an incurable optimist, I am hopeful that the publicity given to the Confait case, the discussions of the Police Bill over the past two years, the recent series of BBC Rough Justice programmes and the apparent police acceptance of tape recording of interviews will cut the number of miscarriages of justice that take place as a result of police pressure -

whether of the heavy or mild variety. It ought also to lead to a more professional attitude towards criminal investigation by the police. A final ironic story of the Confait saga to illustrate my point. Only months before Maxwell Confait's murder, Confait had been sharing a cell in prison with the man who eventually killed him. A single phone call to the prison department would have provided the police with a very plausible suspect, who already had a record of violence. Instead, they decided to go in hard for a confession, and the whole thing went disastrously wrong. The hope now must be that the new reliability test, the code of conduct associated with the Police Act, an independent prosecuting system and tape recording in all police stations will encourage the police to think more and bully less. It is only sad that it will have taken so many miscarriages of justice and so much pressure over so many years to achieve it.

NOTES

1. For those unfamiliar with the case, the most comprehensive accounts are in The Confait Confessions; Christopher Price and Jonathan Caplan; Marion Boyars; 1976: Report of an Inquiry by the Hon. Sir Henry Fisher into the circumstances leading to the conviction of three persons on charges arising out of the death of Maxwell Confait and the fire at 27 Doggett Road, London SE6; HMSO HC 90 1977.

2. Report of the Royal Commission on Criminal Procedure; HMSO Cmnd 8092.

3. Op. cit. pp. 96 and 131.

4. 8 March 1983, col 1157.

5. The Fisher Report, op.cit. supra, note 1, paras. 5.31 - 5.36.

6. In 1980, an accumulation of new statements taken by the late Det. Supt. George and Inspector Ellison of the Metropolitan Police, opened up the possibility that Confait had been murdered at least two days before the fire at Doggett Road. The final conclusive evidence came from Professor Alan Usher, Professor of Forensic Pathology at Sheffield University. Without knowing that they were anything to do with the Confait case, Professor Usher examined microscope slides made from Confait's lung, aorta, heart, spleen, kidney and liver (taken from material preserved, since immediately after the post mortem following his death) and was asked for an estimate of the period between death and post mortem. Usher's estimate was 'between two to four days'. This confirmed other evidence - particularly that of abdominal discoloration revealed in the Fisher enquiry - which also pointed to a substantial period of time between the death and the fire. Fisher describes the discoloration as a 'puzzle'. The real puzzle is why the microscopic slides were never looked at before 1979 - either by the defence, the prosecution, two subsequent police investigations or the Fisher enquiry team.

7. 'It is a fundamental condition of the admissibility of evidence against any person....that it shall be voluntary in the sense that it

has not been obtained from him by fear of prejudice or hope of advantage, exercised or held out by a person in authority, or by oppression.' The rules are printed in full in Royal Commission on Criminal Procedure; The Investigation and Prosecution of Criminal Offences in England and Wales - The Law and Procedure; HMSO Cmnd. 8092-1; 1981; pp.151-161.

8.   One case of exclusion which was a direct result of the changes occasioned by the Confait case, took place in 1978; a mentally retarded man, who was accused of murdering Michelle Booth by throwing her off a train near Reading and had confessed to the offence, was discharged when the judge excluded his confession, since it had been obtained in breach of the Judges' Rules.

9.   Royal Commission on Criminal Procedure; Police Interrogation, The Psychological Approach; Research Studies 1 and 2; HMSO 1980; pp.37-9. A subsequent study which casts doubt on police ability to recognise the proper weight of evidence given by the mentally retarded, can be found in Police Interviewing of the Mentally Handicapped; Bryan Tully and David Cahill; The Police Foundation; 1984.

10.   Report in Sunday Times; 1st July 1984.

11.   The Tape Recording of Police Interviews with Suspects October 1983; Home Office, London SW1.

8. THE POLICE AND MENTAL HEALTH

William Bingley

In 1974 the Metropolitan Police declined a request from MIND to study why the police power to remove a mentally disordered person to a place of safety under the 1959 Mental Health Act was apparently used to a much greater degree in London than elsewhere in England and Wales. (1) They declined on the ground that there was no problem to examine. Eleven years later a very senior police officer in the same force was heard to remark that coping with people with mental health problems was the biggest challenge facing the police service.

The Police and Criminal Evidence Act in shifting attention to pre-trial procedure has itself nothing to say about people suffering from mental illness. It is significant (maybe more symbolically than practically) and appropriate (in view of the fact that the Confait case was one of the principal reasons for the Royal Commission on Criminal Procedure) that the Act itself mentions mentally handicapped people and provides special protection for them in court when they are charged on the basis of a confession statement obtained in the absence of an independent third party. This at least is a recognition that the criminal justice system has failed in the past and has failed spectacularly in some cases to protect at least one vulnerable group. Although it would be inappropriate to describe mentally handicapped people as having a mental health problem, it is consistent when considering the police and their dealings with people vulnerable because of mental health problems to include those who are vulnerable because of mental handicap. Although the Act itself does not mention mental illness, the Codes of Practice made under the Act do so extensively and the fifth edition (Home Office, January 1985) offers considerable protection to both mentally ill and mentally handicapped people. The provisions relate primarily to suspects in police custody and they centre on rights during questioning, which are dealt with elsewhere in this book. This wider protection represents amongst other things a growing awareness that the police as an agency do cope with a wide range of people with mental health problems or who have a mental handicap.

Barrie Irving and Linden Hilgendorf (2) in their studies for the Royal Commission on Criminal Procedure examine police interview tactics. In their field studies they estimated that 25% of their subjects exhibited some kind of identifiable mental abnormality. The abnormalities included drug-induced abnormalities, mental handicap and mental illness. At the other end of the justice process a study by Dell (3) indicated that there are a substantial number of people with mental abnormalities in prison and the vulnerability of many of them was highlighted 12 years ago by Brandon and Davies' much quoted remarks that they were struck by how many of those whose convictions had been quashed or who had been pardoned after conviction on their own evidence were "inadequate". All the evidence points to the fact that the justice process and in particular the police spend a substantial amount of time dealing with mentally vulnerable people. What is harder to ascertain is how much of police time is spent in this way, are they any good at it and what improvements could be made?

Police officers come across mentally vulnerable people in many different situations and they have a range of responses available. They may consider that a possible offender is mentally disordered and thus have to decide if they should use mental health powers as an alternative to arrest and prosecution. In more serious cases it appears that the police will sometimes prefer to charge a mentally disordered suspect because they regard the courts as having a greater range of therapeutic options than they have. They will also encounter mentally vulnerable people as victims of crime, as witnesses and, in the context of interrogation, as suspects. They are quite often involved in conveying absconding compulsorily detained patients back to hospital, attending with "approved social workers" at mental health emergencies where there is a possible compulsory admission to hospital and it is apparent that the police are frequently the first agency called in where a family member appears to become suddenly and dramatically mentally disordered. Apart from the miscarriages of justice that have arisen from false confession statements made by mentally handicapped people, it is the police power to detain people under section 136 of the Mental Health Act 1983 that has caused the most controversy.

This power entitles a police officer to remove to a "place of safety" any person whom he finds in a place "to which the public have access" and who appears to be suffering from a mental disorder (and this includes mental handicap) and is in immediate need of care and control. Such action can only be taken in the interests of the person concerned or for the protection of others. A place of safety can include a hospital, a police station, local authority accommodation and any other property where the owner is willing to let it be regarded as such. Once the person is at the "place of safety" he may be detained for up to 72 hours for the purpose of being examined by a doctor and social worker and for making any necessary arrangements for his treatment or care. The police officer is thus put in the curious position of, as essentially a layman, being able to make a judgement about an individual's mental state and then to compulsorily admit that person to "a place of safety". The legal complexities of this power are not appropriately explored here. Section 136 does, however, lie at the centre of what could be termed police psychiatric referrals and our understanding, or rather lack of understanding, of it illustrates the extent of police involvement in mental health cases generally.

Of all the compulsory admission sections of the 1959 and 1983 Mental Health Acts the power to detain under section 136 is the only one that has more or less consistently increased in use over the last few years. 1,598 in 1979, 1,885 in 1980, 1,907 in 1981 and 1,883 in 1982. (5) What is perhaps more surprising for a compulsory power whose use is on the increase is that the published figures only refer to those cases where an individual is admitted to hospital under section 136. Those people who are taken to a police station as a "place of safety" under section 136 but who are, for instance, subsequently released, charged with an offence or admitted to hospital under another compulsory admission section of the Mental Health Act, go entirely unrecorded in Central Government statistics. Police standing orders on how section 136 should be implemented vary. In London it used to be generally the case that an individual would be taken to a police station but almost immediately on to a hospital where an assessment would be made. (6) The individual would be admitted to hospital under section 136 and therefore appeared in Government statistics. Other forces regard the police station as a "place of safety" and any assessment would be made there. (7) Where this is the case the figure for section 136 hospital admissions gives no indication at all of police activity in this field. In 1981 there were 28 admissions under section 136 to hospitals in the West Midlands. (5) Twigg, on the basis of a case study in one Birmingham police division, speculated that "it was possible" that in the City of Birmingham there were approximately 560 arrests per year under section 136. (8) The inaccuracy of the published figures casts into doubt the conclusions frequently drawn from the apparent preponderance of section 136 admissions to hospital in the four Thames Regional Health Authority regions.

In 1964 they accounted for 88% of all section 136 admissions (6) and in 1982 the equivalent figure was 86%. As we have already seen, the multiplicity of disposal alternatives available to the police when confronted by somebody who appears to be mentally disordered underlines the fact that current published figures give little idea of police involvement in mental health cases. The only thing that seems certain is that their activity, even in the Thames Regional Health Authority areas, is far higher than the statistics indicate.

One of the factors that influences the level of police involvement in mental health cases is how effectively other agencies in the field operate. in particular social service availability seems a crucial determinant. One study indicated there was a tendency for section 136 to be used between 1.00 a.m. and 9.00 a.m. on weekdays, presumably when out-of-hours social services were not available. (9) Kent police recorded a 9.7% increase when "out-of-hours" social work cover was withdrawn from the county at the end of 1979. (10) Many practitioners, however, would allege that in fact most section 136s occur during weekdays when it proves difficult to get social workers out. At night and at weekends a special emergency duty team operated by most local authorities ensures an easy availability of social workers. It is difficult to ascertain from the rather sparse and sometimes elderly research what sort of people get detained under the section. Official figures indicate that just under half are women. (11) One study indicates a slight preponderance of schizophrenics, frequently single men of younger age with a liability to aggressive acts. (9) Another study remarked on how many were known or discovered by the police to be ex-patients. (12) he police seemed reluctant to put someone into hospital without medical advice. This evidence is used to lend credence to the supposition that the section is utilised principally in inner city areas on single rootless people who in the words of one researcher "the psychiatric services have obviously failed to keep in contact with". (9) There are many allegations and some evidence that section 136 (along with other Mental Health Act emergency admission sections) is used disproportionately on black and ethnic minority communities. (13)

Although this section is drawn very widely and there have been no procedural safeguards whatever (the Codes of Practice under the Police and Criminal Evidence Act, whatever the arguments about their effectiveness, provide a welcome clarification of some basic rights for section 136 detainees), two important, if again rather elderly studies, found that the police did not abuse their power. (6) (12) These two studies also indicated that where the police were deciding between criminal proceedings or some other disposal, the two most important factors were the nature of the offence and police knowledge of the offender's history. One found that a much higher proportion of prosecuted offenders had committed offences against property than had the unprosecuted. What studies there are indicate that approximately 25% of those admitted to hospital under section 136 stay for less than a week and that approximately 60% are in for less than four weeks. (12) Once the person has been detained by police then the police officers involved have to arrange for a decision about what is to happen to the individual to be taken by the appropriate senior officer and in cases of mental health disposal to start interacting with the mental health services. Little study has been made of how this crucial process takes place. Many police officers appear to resent, in "psychiatric emergencies", having to contact a social worker rather than go to a psychiatrist direct. (7) In other areas resentment is felt about hospitals not agreeing to take people who are obviously "mad" and also at the long delays in processing cases.

In an unpublished Metropolitan Police survey of cases in 1977 considered by the police to require urgent medical attention where delay had occurred, reference is made to delays of between 4 and 50 hours before admission to hospital could be made. However, it was found that the average wait in a police cell was $2\frac{1}{2}$ hours with $1\frac{1}{2}$ hours to deliver the patient to hospital. However, three officers were required for each journey which indicates the manpower that can be employed in this activity.

Speculation on how this particular section is used and on police involvement in all aspects of mental health can be endless. What does seem to be clear is that mental health problems and vulnerability because of mental illness and mental handicap are a major part of the policeman's lot. It is significant that in their study of police interviewing Tully and Cahill found that although a quarter of their 30 mentally handicapped and 15 control or "normal" subjects reported having been spoken to by police in the course of investigations into their possible misbehaviour, 15% of the mentally handicapped subjects reported other "street encounters" with a police officer while the control subjects reported none. (14) This seems to indicate that the police are significant in the lives of many mentally handicapped people at least. How good are the police in coping? In the words of the 1967 U.S. President's Commission on Law Enforcement Task Force Report "the police officer should be provided with a basis for understanding the various forms of behaviour with which he must deal, and the trainee must acquire information and understanding concerning human relations". (15) Although available studies indicate a general satisfaction with the police operation of section 136, it must be pointed out that police training in mental health issues has been more or less non-existent. Many police officers appear to have little understanding of the difference between mental illness and mental handicap let alone anything more sophisticated and in a sense, as this is the average level of understanding of most of the population, it is not surprising. What is becoming clearer is that with the realisation by many police officers of the amount of their work that includes a mental health aspect the need for training is seen as becoming more pressing. At senior levels of the force the notion of an omnicompetent police officer, which many would argue has made it difficult for police officers to admit to their imperfections, is breaking down (16), making it easier for outsiders to help in providing appropriate training and expertise.

As far as the police and mental health is concerned the picture is unclear, apart from the fact that mental health problems take up a significant proportion of police time. But it is not just the mental health problems of their customers that concern the police. Awareness is growing of the problem of stress within the police itself (17) and the issue has been raised in Parliament. (18) Aggregate this with a growing interest in "special care questioning" of those in possession of precariously remembered testimony, in particular mentally ill and mentally handicapped people, an increasing knowledge of how police officers cope with "psychiatric referrals" (19) and an escalating awareness of the need for appropriate training and it is certain that mental health will be occupying a far more important place in the police task in the future.

NOTES

1.   Gostin, L. (1975) A Human Condition, vol. 1, page 31, MIND.

2.   Irving, B. and Hilgendorf, L. (1980) Police Interrogation: The Psychological Approach, Royal Commission on Criminal Procedure Research Study No. 1, HMSO, London.

3.   Dell, S. (1971) Silent in Court, G. Bell & Sons.

4.   Brandon, R. and Davies, C. (1973) Wrongful Imprisonment, Allen & Unwin.

5.   Hansard, H.C. Written Answer, 24.1.84., col. 550.

6.   Walker, N.D. and McCabe, S. (1973) Crime and Insanity in England: vol. 2: New Solutions and New Problems (Edinburgh: Edinburgh University Press).

7.   Hardwick, L. (1984) Talking to the Police, Bulletin of the Royal College of Psychiatrists, page 111.

8.   Twigg, S. (1982) M. Phil. Thesis, Birmingham University, unpublished.

9.   Callaher, M.J. and Copeland, J.R.M. (1972) "Compulsory Psychiatric Admissions by the Police: A Study of the Use of Section 136" 12 Med. Sci. and L. 220.

10.   Letter from Kent Police to author, 24.9.82.

11.   Hansard. H.C. Written Answer, 24.1.84., col. 551.

12.   Rollin, H.R. (1969) The Mentally Abnormal Offender and the Law (Oxford: Pergamon).

13.   Littlewood, R. and Lipsedge, M. (1981) Aliens and Alienists - Ethnic Minorities and Psychiatry. Penguin.

14.   Tully, B. and Cahill, D. (1984) Police Interviewing of the Mentally Handicapped, The Police Foundation.

15.   Bull, R. and Horncastle, P. (1983) An Evaluation of the Metropolitan Police Recruit Training and Human Awareness Training, The Police Foundation.

16.   Irving, Barrie (1983) Psychology and Policing: Past and Present, The Police Foundation.

17.   Cooper, C.L., Davidson, M.J. et al (1982) Stress in the Police Service, Journal of Occupational Medicine, 24, 30-36.

18.   Hansard, H.C. Written Answer, col. 855, 14.1.85.

19.   MIND is currently undertaking a major research project into the use of section 136 and allied issues in the Greater London area.

9. POLICING WOMEN

Melissa Benn

The recent debate on the Left on policing has often focussed on the 'problem' of the riots, and politically and economically marginalised male youth, black and white. (1) In short, the policing of certain areas of the inner city. But there is an unspoken set of assumptions underlying the competing arguments in this debate, one of these being that the police are chiefly a problem for young men. But while recognising the seriousness, and implications of the issue of men's policing of men, the debate has ignored the policing of women's lives.

So what is women's experience of the police? And what sort of police force do women want? When we look closely at these two questions we find a challenge to both conservative and radical arguments about policing, and women's involvement and oppression by the state.

Women come into contact with the police in a wide range of circumstances - we cannot simplify this contact. But it seems to me that one important way that women have experienced policing is as 'victims' of a particular kind - women who are objects of male violence or exploitation (through rape, domestic violence or prostitution) and who seek the protection or the retribution of the state. For these women's experience of the police, mediated by their gender, class and race, is at best unsatisfactory, at worst, frightening.

In so many areas of their lives (work, domestic work, child care) women's experience is privatised and isolated. So too is their experience of policing, an isolation augmented by a police force saturated by traditional assumptions about, and attitudes towards, women. As the recent Policy Studies Institute report illustrated so vividly, this traditionalism - misogyny even - is strengthened by the exclusive and isolated culture that the police inhabit. (2) But it is precisely because women are fragmented and isolated, and always have been, that their experience of the police, in rape or domestic violence cases, for example, has not been a visible, viable or political issue for large sections of the Left.

More recently, however, women are increasingly coming into collective contact in a number of ways with the police, and experiencing the coercive nature of modern policing. First, through political action like the demonstrations at Greenham Common and other nuclear bases, or in mixed actions like the protest at the South African embassy in London, Stop the City demonstrations etc. Secondly, through industrial disputes like the recent miners' strike, and privatisation battles at certain London hospitals. Thirdly, in response to the Police and Criminal Evidence Act which has mobilised women as women, for example in the women's or lesbian campaign against the Police Act.

And finally, the development of the women's movement in the last decade and a half has led to the organisation and action of many groups around issues of male violence and control - rape crisis centres, women's aid centres, prostitute women's groups - which are collectively challenging police methods and tactics.

124

Melissa Benn

'Call Her An Outright Liar' - Police Investigations Of Rape

A woman wishing to bring a rape charge must go through a police procedure that reflects an inherent, and inherited misogyny.   As Susan Edwards shows in 'Female Sexuality and the Law' the characterisation of female complainants as malicious or lying or hysterical has its roots in centuries of English legal practice and medical theories (3).   Whether a woman had a 'past' or was a virgin, male 'experts' declared her testimony unbelievable.   And the old notion that a woman must display extensive signs of force, and her own resistance, still persists today.

Underlying it all is a male distrust and fear of women - a belief that women use their sex as a weapon.   The fact that by its very definition rape is about men using their sex as a weapon is often lost.   Quite unlike any other kind of assault case, the "victim" of a rape is put on trial along with her alleged aggressor (4).   The police play an important role in this process.

Women's knowledge of police procedure, and the court process, often discourages them from reporting the crime at all.   Figures from organisations like Women Against Rape and London Rape Crisis Centre show that a very low percentage of raped women do report the crime - about one in four. (5)   And in 'The Facts of Rape', Barbara Toner, says that only women "who are raped in the most dramatic of circumstances" go to the police. (6)   Fear of, at best not being believed, at worst, humiliated, haunt every woman.   A friend of mine said to me the other day "What hope would I, as a lesbian, have of ever being believed if I was raped.   I would never report it".   Neither would I.   Neither would most of the women I know.   Why?

As there is very little corroboration in most rape cases, the man's defence is usually based on the alleged consent of the woman.   Police officers acknowledge that this gives their questioning an edge of interrogation.   They will argue, officially, that as the court procedure is so hard for a woman, her story must stand up.   But does this account for this kind of "unofficial" advice to police officers on how to question women?

> "If a woman walks into a police station and complains of rape with no such signs of violence she must be closely interrogated. Allow her to make a statement to a policewoman and then drive a horse and cart through it. It is always advisable if there is any doubt about the truthfulness of her allegations to call her an outright liar. It is very difficult for a person to put on genuine indignation who has been called a liar to her face. Watch out for the girl who is pregnant, or late getting home at night; such persons are notorious for alleging rape or indecent assault. Do not give her sympathy. If she is not lying, after the interrogator has upset her by accusing her of it, then at least the truth is certified and the genuine complaint made by her can be properly investigated. The good interrogator is very rarely loved by his subject....It should be remembered that as drops of water dripping on the stone will gradually wear it away, so interrogation will achieve results". (7)

The media mêlée that followed the showing of the BBC television 'Police' programme in January 1982 when a woman alleging rape was bullied, harassed and threatened, forced the issue briefly into public consciousness. It came at the same time as an outrageous legal judgment on a woman's culpability for violence committed against her. (8) A Guardian reviewer expressed outraged liberal sentiment when he reviewed the programme the next day:

> "It was not the language, even the unmitigated toughness that shocked....it was the low key brutality of the questions....how many times had she had sex, when was the last time, did she menstruate properly, had she had psychiatric treatment – this seemed not to bother her as much as simply not being believed" (9).

Such unnecessary probing of a woman's past – of her sexual, social and psychological or even biological history – is not official police practice. But then neither is speculation in the canteen afterwards about how police officers "would have liked to have committed the offence themselves" (10).

Questioning is followed by medical examination by a police doctor. The experience of being internally examined by a man after the violence of rape is unbearable to most women. They would far prefer a woman, as the experience of this raped woman shows:

> "Weakly I asked for a woman gynaecologist. There was only a male on the ward that morning. I dreaded what was ahead of me and continued to cry. I couldn't look at him (the male gynaecologist), I felt like a zombie when he spoke to me. He was gentle but I didn't respond. After what seemed like hours I was helped onto the couch – I dread this, the last thing I wanted was for a man to look at me". (11) And police doctors are not always gentle or sympathetic, even when female (12). Here are some 'hints' given to police doctors on what to look out for when examining a woman complainant:

> "The method of undressing should be noted: is the woman a shy or retiring child, or is she a professional stripper? General appearance and demeanour of the victim should be noted including eccentricity of dress and use of cosmetics" (13).

The constant assessment of the woman as a woman – searches for displays of 'proper' female behaviour – is an essential element of police behaviour. And it pursues the woman into the court room. Suzanne Adler, a sociologist, attended 50 rape cases at the Old Bailey during 1978-9. She was monitoring changes in court room practice since the implementation of the Sexual Offences Act 1976, but found that, despite changes in the law, in the majority of cases judges still allowed questioning on the woman's past sexual and social history. Thus, the only kind of woman to 'escape harassment' by the court was the woman whose case conformed to a stereotype "the explosive encounter between 2 strangers....the offender being a dangerous psychopath". The woman had to be the "ideal victim" – sexually inexperienced, or at least respectable. "Virginity virtually guaranteed a conviction". (14)

The work of organisations like the Rape Crisis Centres and Women Against Rape have done much to challenge and change public and police attitudes and practice. So has media exposure: the 'Police' programme was very bad publicity indeed. But how much has changed in reality?

In March 1983, as a result of public pressure, the Home Office issued a circular suggesting 'guidelines' for rape investigations.

The Circular emphasises the need for women to be treated with "tact and understanding"; early medical examination in a "proper clinical environment"; notes the preference of some women for a female doctor; questioning to be done by a trained officer, and consideration given to the presence of a female police officer; a friend of the woman to be allowed to be present; questions about a woman's previous sexual history to be asked with tact and sympathy and advice that she need not answer; women to be informed of local counselling services; police chiefs to consider specially trained rape squads. (15)

But several women's groups, including the Rape Crisis Centres, the GLC Violence Against Women working group and the Royal College of Nursing did not think the guidelines, even if implemented, went far enough. Some of their suggested changes were:

- medical examination should not take place in the police station
- women should have the right of examination by a woman doctor
- specific training for police questioning, in consultation with Rape Crisis Centre groups, to be given
- women should not be questioned about their jobs, as strippers and prostitutes may have their cases taken less seriously
- rape in marriage be recognised

Personal Matters – Domestic Violence And The Police

'Never interfere in husband and wife disputes" was one of the "rules" we were taught, the theory being that she would always change her mind, and probably turn against you to boot; besides "she quite enjoyed it really' (16).

If a treatment of a woman alleging rape is characterised by disbelief and distrust, attitudes to women who have been beaten up are characterised by an absence of response, a sort of shrugging of the shoulders. And, as with rape, police attitudes are rooted in a history of patriarchal assumptions about women, men and marriage. Some individual officers are sympathetic, but the police as a whole reflect traditional attitudes to marriage and women – allied to, and exaggerated by, an isolated and predominantly male force. The PSI report showed that the police regard domestic violence work as 'rubbish work' because it does not include the element of conflict which 'proper' police work should. (17)

The police attitude to domestic violence is crudely this: they see it as taking place within an essentially private, if not sacrosanct realm, the family. Allied to this, is a belief in the superior power of the male within this realm. And the right to inflict violence – but not serious violence – is still one of the perks conceded to men within the home, a hangover from the time in English law when men had 'couverture' (complete ownership) of wife and family. (18)

Police chiefs have expressed this approach quite openly.

> "Whereas it is a general principle of police practice not to intervene in a situation which existed or had existed between husband or wife in the course of which the wife had suffered some personal attack, any assault upon a wife by her husband which amounted to physical injury of a serious nature is a criminal offence which it is the duty of the police to follow up and prosecute" (19).

But do they? In their comparative study of domestic violence in Britain and North America, Dobash and Dobash show that the police rarely bring a criminal prosecution for assault on a woman. American studies have shown a high rate (80%) of arrest and prosecution for minor offences such as public drunkeness, verbal abuse, but a negligible rate (8%) for violence inside the home. (20) The Home Office here say they do not keep figures on arrest and prosecution for domestic violence cases separate from general assault figures.

127

Traditionally domestic violence has been dealt with in the civil rather than criminal courts. And although more effective civil remedies have been open to women since the Domestic Violence and Matrimonial Proceedings Act 1976 and the Domestic Proceedings and Magistrates' Courts Act 1978, which both provide for police powers to arrest a man if he breaks a court order, they are radically different from criminal prosecutions. But even when, in civil cases, a man breaches an injunction, judges remain reluctant to imprison him. One woman barrister, experienced in family law, told me: "Judges only commit a husband to prison when the breach is particularly gross - for example, where an injunction is granted in the morning and the husband severely beats his wife up in the afternoon. But the normal procedure for a first, or even second, breach is a stern telling off by the judge".

So what do the police do when called out? First of all, do they come at all? Dobash and Dobash argue that family violence is low down on police priorities, especially when resources and police power are stretched (21). This attitude has recently been confirmed by Sir Kenneth Newman's desire to re-categorise 'domestic disputes' - a euphemism for wife battering - along with "stranded people, lost property, and stray animals" as tasks to be handed over to other agencies to release the police for "crime prevention", "detection and community policing", "real crime work" (22). Yet domestic disputes account for a large percentage of calls to the police.

Once called out the police make their assessment of the situation on the basis of a number of factors. These include seriousness of the assault, availability of witnesses, perceived character and attitudes of the man and woman and previous domestic history of the couple, wishes of the woman and the likely effect of prosecution on the domestic situation. Many of these factors are highly subjective and are bound to be affected by police pride and prejudice. The police are more likely to act when they are dealing with violence between a black man and white woman, or will more easily dismiss the fears of a black woman than a white woman. A study, based on a questionnaire to over a hundred women who lived in refuges, soon to be published by Women's Aid Federation England, shows that most of the women questioned were highly dissatisfied with police action - or non-action (23). Lack of police, or official action, was one of the main reasons for the establishment of women's aid refuges. There are now over a hundred.

This woman's experience of the police is "classic":

> "Once they gave me a telling off for phoning the police. A sergeant walks in and he says 'What's the trouble?' I says, 'He's been battering me and that. He assaulted me.' Police officer: 'What do you want me to do?' I says 'I don't know what you can do. Surely you can do something?' Then the police officer says 'Look you can't come phoning us every time your husband decides to hit you' " (24).

If the man stays cool and calm during the police visit, they are more likely to believe him (if he denies the assault) or be sympathetic to him (if he justifies it on grounds of being "nagged" or in some way pushed to the limit). But if he is awkward himself, the police may find this an affront to their male authority, and arrest him (25).

The police could make all the difference to a beaten woman. They are the only source of help, certainly the only 24 hour service. They also represent a possible countervailing authority to the husband or lover. They can help a woman with advice, follow up and sympathy. A recent tragedy highlights the failure of the police to do this. On March 8th 1984 Krishna Sharma was found hanged in the Southall house of relatives where she and her husband had been staying. She had suffered 8 years of violence from her husband. The night before, in desperation, she had rung the police for help. The next morning she was found hanged. At the inquest it emerged that the only place the police had referred her to was a Citizens Advice Bureau that had been closed for the last 8 years. (26)

Prostitution And The Police

In law, it is women, and not men, who are arrested for offences connected with prostitution - under Section 1 of the Street Offences Act - although consideration is now being given to introducing a crime of kerbcrawling. (27) As with earlier Acts of Parliament - the Contagious Diseases Act of the 1860's and the Defence of the Realm Act introduced at the beginning of the First World War - prostitution is controlled through the control of women. Women are still deemed responsible for the act of sex with men, and its aftermath. They are selling and paying for it too. Offences under Section 1 of the Sexual Offences Act are no longer punishable by imprisonment. Fines are now the norm. But failure to pay a fine - and many women cannot afford such regular financial penalties - can lead to imprisonment.

Harassment, linked to a kind of understanding between police and prostitutes about the operation of an inoperable law, characterises police behaviour to prostitute women. A special report, commissioned by the London Borough of Camden's Women's Committee, in December 1982, on prostitution in the Argyle Square area, provides a microcosmic account of police behaviour. It shows: first, that the police arrest women on an informal rota basis - and that the women accept this - but that the police can arbitrarily change the rules of the 'game', for example by picking a woman out from among a group. (28) Obviously prostitutes have no control over police action and reaction. Second, the civil liberties of many of the women are effectively denied after arrest. They are rarely cautioned during the arrest and charging procedure, a breach of the Judges' Rules; the women are occasionally searched without proper legal grounds, and regularly threatened with the withholding of bail, illegally. While these are routine breaches of the rules, as far as the police are concerned, the report concluded that they amounted to a "breach of the women's civil liberties". (29) Many prostitutes plead "guilty" to the offences they are charged with, even when technically, and with legal assistance, they would be found not guilty.

In this report, and others by local borough women's committees, the women, particularly black women, complained of routine harassment by the police. (30) The Camden report found, in contrast, that the police leave pimps, ponces and hotel owners in the area alone, with very few investigations or arrests of men involved in prostitution. (31) Prostitute women also receive little or no protection from the police regarding violence from other men - the single greatest risk of their job. And this was a finding echoed by other non-prostitute women in the area, when questioned on police protection against male violence. It is a complaint echoed by women everywhere.

"Couldn't They See It Was Because I Was Black?" Racism And The Police

"Racialist language and racial prejudice were prominent and pervasive.. many individual officers and also whole groups were pre-occupied with ethnic differences" (32)

"Hostile comments about black people are occasionally related to a race theory or to neo-fascist politics" (33)

Racist talk, racist jokes, racist graffiti on toilet walls, senior officers "orchestrating a session of absurd racialist talk with a large group of police constables in the canteen" (34)   The PSI report showed up what black people in this country have known about the police for a long time. And while we have known that black male youth, through the now abandoned 'sus' laws, the policing of the 'riots', and differential arrest rates, have been harassed by the police, what about the specific, and often ignored experience, of black women and the police?

Some black women were directly involved in the 'riots' of 1981/2. In an article "Revolutionary Anger" in Spare Rib, a woman from Liverpool 8 wrote that several black women and girls had been beaten up during the disturbances. Another woman from Brixton wrote:

> "I think that the effect of the 'riots' made black women more at risk from the police and from other white men, while pressure from black men has increased. The "riots" have been mainly a male war, with women, mainly black, left to do the cleaning-up afterwards: the women are the ones to face police harassment when homes are "searched": it's women, the mums, who bear the brunt of worry finding the money to foot the bill for the kid's fine by the court. At present, white women get stopped by the police to be asked if they're all right. Black women get treated with hostility and suspicion." (35)

Black women experience the same double oppression from the police as they do from society at large; hostility to them for their blackness, distrust and sexual abuse targeted at their femaleness - or lack of it, in police eyes. Recent research on women and the criminal justice system has shown up the myth of 'police chivalry' to women, and the particular differences in approach to black and white women. Black women are stigmatised as "aggressive" by the police, less feminine, less like women should be. (36)

Whatever the situation black women find themselves in with the police, they are likely to be singled out for special treatment. Amanda Hassan, a Guyanese feminist, active in CND, wrote recently of an 'action' at Greenham:

> I was holding onto the fence along with some other women (all white) and from nowhere a big burly policeman gave me a chop on my arms and sent me reeling into the mud. None of the other women who were also holding onto the fence got this treatment. When I commented on this, a woman said "Well you're only picked on because you're so short". (I'm under five foot) Couldn't they see it was because I was black?" (37)

Police priorities are another indication of racism - the high priority given to searching out "illegal immigrants". This, and the failure to protect communities from racist attacks, have particularly affected Asian women. Afia Begum's case is the most notorious recent example - its fame partly accounted for by the extraordinary mobilisation of Asian women - the Sari Squad - in her defence. Afia Begum was planning to come to Britain to join her husband but he was killed in a fire in East London only months before she arrived. She was allowed into Britain only temporarily, in June 1982, to sort out his affairs. Many of her relatives, including her elderly father, live in this country, and her mother is applying to come here too. Yet a deportation order was made in September 1982 and Afia, and her three year old daughter, went into hiding for over a year. The police mounted an intensive search for her, culminating in a dawn raid on her 'hideout' - she was directly put on a plane back to Bangladesh. Gerald Kaufman, Labour's shadow Home Secretary, said of the police search for Afia: "For over a year, they have been hunting Afia Begum with an intensity more suited to a search for a mass murderer". (38) Members of the Sari Squad were also victims of police harassment. In August 1983 supporters of the campaign to stop Afia's deportation chained themselves to the railings of the Home Secretary's house. Four were kept in police cells overnight, strip searched and subjected to insulting treatment - kept half naked in view of the police desk. (39)

"No End Of 'Tarts' & 'Slags'" - Women And Political Action: Some Examples

The politics of Greenham Common have irrevocably changed the political landscape. For these women, stepping outside traditional structures (the Labour movement, pressure groups like CND) has put them in an isolated and vulnerable position vis-à-vis the police. Perhaps women can demand protection from the police under penalty of conformism - to ideas of proper, right or "female" behaviour. Greenham women have forfeited this protection, although afforded another more sporadic kind of protection through press presence and publicity. The police approach to Greenham, and other camps and actions, has been ambivalent. Some chief officers have said that they recognise the 'different' nature of the law breaking going on in the peace movement. Mr Wynn Jones, Chief Constable of the Thames Valley, in charge of the Greenham operation, told the Guardian: "We have been very conscious that these are ordinary law abiding women who believe passionately in their cause....demonstrating because of their deeply held political convictions. I do not think the circumstances justify the full sanctions of the criminal law". (40)

Yet policing has become a major issue in itself for the women at the nuclear bases. There have been a huge number of arrests for trivial offences (1,775 between September 1981 - March 1984), bail conditions and bind-overs imposed, dawn raids for evictions and spurious 'searches'. Many women have been injured, some severely, in police action, and there have been several recorded incidents of sexual harassment and assault, in addition to strip-searching and photographing by the police. (41)

131

One example of routine policing of the peace women was recently recounted to me, as follows. Some women were waiting outside a London police station, for some friends who had been arrested in an action in Central London. One woman told me "A group of policemen approached the police station. One of them came up to me and said "Would you move over the other side of the road?" "Yes" I said immediately, getting up. He grabbed my arm and said sneeringly "You don't want to move. You want to be arrested, be with your friends, don't you?" And I was arrested for 'wilful obstruction', kept in a cell for six hours. All the time we were there the police kept taking the piss out of us, calling us 'smellies', and crowding into the charge room to see us. We said "with all the crime in London, don't you have better things to do?"

And the police have been conspiciously absent when women at Greenham Common have been attacked by vigilante style groups who have thrown stones, set fire to the women's tents and even thrown maggots over the women. (42)

One of the most significant developments of the recent mining dispute has been the active participation of women in the organisation of the strike, and in front line resistance to the police on picket lines. It has changed the women's attitude to themselves, to the miners they support, but most importantly to the police. More and more women have done picket duty often succeeding in adopting a less confrontational approach. Women from Oakland colliery in Gwent have said "Would we see violence like at Orgreave if it was all women? Get all the men out and let us women in and see what happens. On a picketline at Port Talbot we turned four lorries away. We used persuasion – and asked them to respect the picket line. It was lovely". (43)

Many of the police on duty at the pits are drafted in from the Metropolitan Police; their approach is radically different. One of the clearest descriptions so far has been in this letter to the Guardian from a woman who had picketed outside Calverton colliery in Nottinghamshire.

"Having surrounded us, the police started to tighten the circle, pushing us into smaller and smaller spaces; quite a few women panicked; they were arrested. "Why me?" yelled one young miner's wife as she was being dragged away "I've fancied you all evening", the arresting officer told her. Another woman was told by a police officer: "Call yourself a woman. I wouldn't even piss on you".

"The women were dragged to the police van with a brutality quite out of proportion to their size or any resistance they were offering. One in her mid-forties who offered no resistance was dragged by two officers, one with his arm around her throat. "Let her walk", said one officer "No, let's drag her", said the other. They did drag her, downwards, so that her knees and the tops of her feet (in open sandals) were all battered and grazed. She blacked out and had to be taken to hospital".

"All the time the police taunted us with jibes about Arthur Scargill, about the massive overtime they were being paid – this to families who have been living below the official breadline for four months now and with provocations such as, "Go on, hit me then", chin agressively thrust forward, and no end of "Tarts and Slags". (44)

Pictures of all the women were taken with a polaroid. Those who refused had their head yanked up. Women were refused access to a toilet and were offered a milk bottle instead. They were locked in wire cages in a tall windowless van for up to two hours. They were refused the right to make a phone call at the police station; denied the right to a solicitor, and taunted continually.

In another political action, the continuous picketing by anti-apartheid groups outside South Africa house, the police have brought a number of public order charges (obstruction/use of threatening behaviour) against the protestors, many of them women. In June 1983, three women were strip searched and photographed against their will.

Lesbians And The Police

Although there are no sanctions of the criminal law against lesbians, as there are against male homosexuals, it is becoming increasingly clear that the police are more hostile to lesbian women than 'straight' women. Lesbians have reported being singled out at Greenham Common, or at demonstrations, "they swooped in and picked off the lesbians. They definitely went for the lesbians". (45) The police have also raided lesbian and gay venues, abusing both men and women.

Lesbians are very unlikely to report crimes against them and are more likely to be abused by the police if known to be gay. A new project currently underway is researching into lesbian experience of the police. (46)

Frozen Faces And Insults: Women In The Police

Women, like the few black officers there are in the police force, are isolated through low numbers, and the overwhelming cult of a white masculine culture, heavy drinking, racism and sexism.

Many of the earliest policewomen were middle or upper class suffragettes, hooked on the excitement of law breaking. Public sympathy was not always with them for this reason. In 1915 "the average Cockney seems at present to resent their presence in the streets. The suffragettes are to blame for this in large measure, for in the public mind the 'Copperettes' as the girls are called have come to be associated, quite erroneously, no doubt, with the women who used to break windows and shout 'Votes for Women' in Parliament Square". (47) But it was a militant feminism which often informed these women's choice of work, a dislike for the double standards of the time. Early women police were in voluntary patrols - the first paid professional women police were taken on by the Metropolitan Police in 1918 on an 'experimental' basis. Their main job was to police other women and the 'vice' associated with women - areas of prostitution, railway stations where women were 'lured' into the white slave trade and large munition sites during the First World War.

During both the First and Second World War, official recruitment increased dramatically, followed by post-war backlashes against women's employment. It was in these periods that arguments against women as police officers were most vociferously expressed, arguments still expressed openly by certain police chiefs and police spokesmen.

Biographies and accounts of the early policewomen document the overt hostility these women had to endure - from policemen, senior officers and the public. There is continual reference to the "petty spite", "hostility and insults", and "years of insults, frozen faces and icy indifference" from their colleagues. (48)

Even after women were accepted into the force as paid professionals, their tasks and functions were rigidly separated from the men's. Women were given the social work side of police work - dealing with juvenile crime, sexual offences, problem families, children and prostitution. But following the equality laws of the mid 1970's (and in the case of the Metropolitan police anticipating them) women officers were 'integrated' into the force. Women are now paid the same as the men and theoretically, do the same work. But do they?

For a start, the number of women in the force is strictly kept down; the national average is now 9.2%. Some forces have higher percentages. The Metropolitan police operates an unofficial (and illegal) bar on women's recruitment - it has a ceiling of 10%. And women do not have easy access to training or promotion. One of the reasons for this is rigid sex stereotyping of women in the force. In December 1983 WPC Wendy de Launay brought a case against the Metropolitan Police. She had been taken off duty in the traffic division, where she had been driving a police car with a male colleague, and was transferred to foot patrol because her senior officer suspected that she and her male partner might be tempted into an affair "although you are not having an affair now I think that within a year you would be having a relationship and I will not let that happen". (49) Although both Ms De Launay and the male officer she worked with were experienced car drivers only Ms De Launay was moved from her job. The industrial tribunal found the Metropolitan Police guilty of sex discrimination.

The PSI report shows that generally women police officers, in sharp contrast to their male colleagues, believe they are discriminated against.

"In informal conversations most of them say that policemen are prejudiced against them, that they greatly over emphasise the importance of physical strength in the job....that women are effectively excluded from some of the more interesting kinds of work and that the men will not accept them as full members of the working group or as colleagues on an equal basis". (50)

In an interview with me in City Limits, one ex-policewomen gave a more forceful description of the demoralisation of women police officers:

"At every turn you're expected as a WPC to make the tea and wash up. That's what you're 'good for'. WPC's are called 'plonks' - good for nothings. You get chipped away, you have to take all the insults, all the wind-ups. If you ever hit back it gets worse. Every time you come on the radio you're mimicked and insulted. I resented being called a 'fucking cunt'". (51)

Women police officers clearly have a less aggressive approach to policing - they occasion far fewer complaints from the public than the men do, and it is generally agreed, have a different way of approaching their job overall. (52) They are less infatuated by confrontation, which they see as a fault or weakness - rather than a strength. But it is difficult to gauge whether more women police, like more black police, would have a beneficial, if superficial, effect on policing.

"A Threat No Woman Should Ignore - The Police And Criminal Evidence Act"

"A hideous nightmare? No, a fact of life this year if major new police powers are approved. And it's happening not in a South American dictatorship but in good old fair-minded Britain. A reminder 1984 is really here with a vengeance". (53)

The New Statesman? New Socialist? No, Woman's Own which, in a highly critical article, set out the major clauses of the Police and Criminal Evidence Bill, as it then was, and its implications for women. For the Act does have particular implications for women, as women, which it is important to recognise, separate from the general effects of the legislation. Briefly, these include:

- the regularisation of intimate body searches, the physical examination of a person's body orifices, which are degrading to both searcher and searched. Recent experience of Republican women prisoners in Armagh prison has shown the distress, humiliation, and abuses resulting from the practice. The BMA has said that doctors will not do these searches without the person's consent; in practice they may then be carried out, on women, by a policewoman.

- the extension of stop and search powers. A police officer may "on reasonable suspicion" search any person or vehicle. It may be that being in areas with a high crime rate at a certain time will make such searches more likely. This is likely to affect those women already most vulnerable to the police - black women, lesbians, prostitutes. Road blocks can also be set up and may have a similar impact.

- extension of powers to search premises, particularly the power to seize evidence from homes of innocent third parties. This right of entry may be particularly distressing when, for example, a husband is away and the woman speaks little or no English.

- certain categories of confidential information are given special status under the Act. These provisions do not extend to the seizure of research or campaigning material held by women's centres which is not held in confidence.

- lack of provision for women detained for up to 96 hours regarding arrangements for their dependent children, or older or disabled relatives.

Taking Women Seriously

The phenomenon of women organising as women around policing is a relatively new one - but it is growing. More and more is being written about the police by women, and more and more women are organising to press for change, for a different kind of police force. The first ever conference on women and the police was held early in 1984, and there are many groups, working parties, and organisations looking at the issue.

What women do not want is clear. They do not want a sexist, racist, abusive, violent, confrontational police force. Nor do women want to be made "responsible" in police eyes for crimes that have been committed against them - be it rape, domestic violence, or other forms of sexual harassment, such as happen to women continuously. More and more studies are showing that women cannot rely on the police to "protect" them from male violence, and therefore do not seek their help.

In Leeds, some feminists interviewed a group of women living in a small area and asked them for details of witnessed crime (to other women) and crime to self. They found that of the crime women had observed or experienced overall only 12% of these were reported to the police - a staggeringly small percentage. As the report's authors said "the vast majority of women do not think that the police in practice are either able or willing to protect them". (54) They also concluded that women are much more likely than the police to perceive violence to themselves as serious, and that the police do not interfere in any serious way with male violence to women.

A study in the London borough of Wandsworth had very similar findings in a smaller survey of 60 women, aged from 16 to 85; 17 were black and 5 were Asian. Three-quarters of the women interviewed who described incidents of male violence, (kerb crawling, propositioning in a public place, sexual harassment), did not report them to the police. The Wandsworth Study also noted the "patronising paternalism" of the police - the long list of do's and don'ts handed out to women, carrying with them an implication of female guilt. Women were told 'not to get upset, not to get things out of proportion, not to go out alone, not to go out at night, to avoid 'dangerous areas', not to put themselves at risk." References were made to women being 'provocative', and they discounted experiences which terrorise women as 'trivial'. (55)

Many women are living, and have come to accept that they are living, in a state of siege. It is quite accepted by men and women alike that women, routinely do not, for example:

-   go out after dark alone
-   do not go for walks in the park during the day on their own
-   do not go into pubs on their own
-   do not use certain forms of public transport, even during the day on their own.

Women's lives are restricted in numerous ways by an often unconscious fear of men and their violence toward women.

So what kind of police force do women want? Firstly, we need a police force which takes women's fears seriously, and acts upon them. If, as it is now recognised, racial harassment is widespread and the police have been negligent in acting against it, why has there been no shocked or widespread recognition that women experience just such a failure of protection?

But secondly, it is vital to emphasise that women's perceived lack of policing is not a call for more policing of the same kind. As in the pornography debate, women need to discuss and carve out for themselves a position distinct from the right wing "law and order" lobby - but one which still recognises that men are a problem for women, whether in the streets, home or the police force. What we need is a radical change in the nature of policing, and not just the extent of it. For example, we need less reactive police, concentrated on high technology vehicles and equipment, and more preventative policing - more foot patrols perhaps?

But it is also clear that there are certain groups of women who could not, even if they wished, demand protection from the police; black women, lesbian women, prostitute women. Because the police, as they are now, are inherently biased and prejudiced, racist and sexist, and harass these women in many of the circumstances in which they come into contact with them.

To see the changes we need to envisage wider changes in policing – a more representative police force, accountable, responsive and responsible, such as the Left has demanded. But, so far, women's demands have not locked into these debates. And I would argue that this is because of the Left's failure to take women's experience of both male violence and the State seriously. If the debate on accountability and public control of the police is to have any meaning for women, there must be more than a token nod to women's experience. The emergence of radical local authorities, women's committees and police committees, with their genuine attempts to take the views and experiences of all women into account has been a step in the right direction. Local authority policing policy is beginning to reflect female and black experience. Male academics, intellectuals and politicians should take note.

NOTES

(1)   See, for example, John Lea and Jock Young (eds), What is to be done about Law and Order?: Crisis in the Eighties, Penguin 1984.

(2)   The Policy Studies Institute report on the Metropolitan Police, 1984.

(3)   See, Susan Edwards, "The Routine Management of a Rape Allegation", Female Sexuality and the Law, Martin Robertson 1981.

(4)   See Melissa Benn, Anna Coote and Tess Gill, The Rape Controversy, NCCL pamphlet 1983.

(5)   Ibid. p.8. See also forthcoming study from Women Against Rape.

(6)   Barbara Toner, The Facts of Rape, Arrow 1982 p.151.

(7)   Quoted in London Rape Crisis Centre, Rape, Police and Forensic Procedure, no date.

(8)   This was the case, heard in January 1982, when Judge Bertram Richards declared the complainant in a rape case "guilty of a great deal of contributory negligence" in taking a lift from the defendant. The man was subsequently convicted and fined for the offence.

(9)   Television review by Peter Fiddick, in the Guardian, January 19, 1982.

(10)   PSI report Vol IV, P.92.

(11)   "A quiet stroll into terror", The Guardian, July 20, 1984.

(12)   Barbara Toner, The Facts of Rape, p. 176.

(13)   Quoted in London Rape Crisis Centre; Rape, Police and Forensic Procedure.

(14)   Benn, Coote and Gill, The Rape Controversy, p.19.

(15)   Home Office Circular 25/ 1983 March 1983.

(16)   Joan Lock, The British Policewoman: Her Story, Robert Hale, 179, p.192.

(17)   GLC Police Committee Bulletin, Policing London, Issue 11, p.43.

(18)   Rebecca Emerson Dobash and Russell Dobash, Violence Against Wives: A Case Against the Patriarchy, Open Books, 1980 p.208.

(19)   Evidence from the Metropolitan Police to the Select Committee on Violence in Marriage 1975.

(20)   Dobash and Dobash, Violence Against Wives, p.208.

(21)   Ibid. p.211.

(22)   The Times, October 4, 1983.

(23)   To be published by the Women's Aid Federation England, Available from 374 Grays Inn Road, London, WC1.

(24)   Dobash and Dobash, Violence Against Wives, p.213.

(25)   Ibid. p.214.

(26)   GLC Police Committee Bulletin, Policing London, Issue 13.

(27)   In August 1984, the Criminal Law Revision Committee came out in favour of introducing a criminal offence relating to kerbcrawling.

(28)   Report to Camden Council, Policing Women in the Argyle Square Area, December 1983, p.3-4.

(29)   Ibid. p.8-9.

(30)   Report to Islington Council, report on research regarding the establishment of a specialist unit to co-ordinate services to prostitute women, 1984, p.13.

(31)   Report to Camden Council, p.14.

(32)   PSI report, Vol IV, p.109.

(33)   Ibid. p.114.

(34)   Ibid. p.124.

(35)   "Revolutionary Anger", Spare Rib 110, p.18.

(36)   Elaine Player, "Women and the Criminal Justice System", Seminar given to the Howard League for Penal Reform, 1984. To be published.

(37)   Amanda Hassan "A Black Woman in the Peace Movement", Spare Rib 142, Special Issue "Peace Not Quiet", p.7.

(38)   Gerald Kaufman speaking in the House of Commons debate, reported in the Guardian, May 4, 1984.

(39)   Cited in Cathie Lloyd; Women, Public Order and the Police Bill, discussion paper from the Cities of London and Westminster Public Order Research Group, July 1984, p.2.

(40)   The Guardian, December 14, 1982.

(41)   See Duncan Campbell, New Statesman, November 18, 1983.

(42)   See City Limits, October 7-13, 1983.

(43)   Beatrix Campbell, "The Other Miner's Strike", New Statesman, July 27, 1984.

(44)   The Guardian, July 13, 1984.

(45)   GLC Women's Committee Bulletin, Lesbian Issue, June 1984, Issue 17, p.28.

(46)   The Gay London Police Monitoring Group has recently appointed a lesbian worker to look into lesbian experiences of the police.

(47)   Joan Lock, The British Policewoman, p.68.

(48)   See Lillian Wyles, A Woman at Scotland Yard, Faber 1951.

(49)   The Guardian, December 21, 1983.

(50)   PSI Report, Vol IV, p.93.

(51)   Melissa Benn "A Policewoman's Lot", City Limits, September 23-29 1983, p.10.

(52)   Ben Whitaker, The Police in Society, Eyre Methuen, 1982, p.119.

(53)   Women's Own, March 17, 1984.

(54)   Jalna Hanmer and Sheila Saunders, Well Founded Fear: A Community Study of Violence to Women, Hutchinson, (Explorations in Feminism series), 1984, p.48-61.

(55)   Wandsworth Policing Campaign, Violence Against Women: Women Speak Out, 1984.

10. THE POLICE ACT AND THE PROBATION SERVICE

Brian Campbell

If it is true that the treatment of its criminals is a measure of a civilised society, then it is also true that any significant changes in that treatment must be considered in the context of the total criminal justice process. Both the police and the Probation Service are part of the public response to, and public control of, criminal deviance. It is not that the probation officer's aims are always the same as those of the policeman. On the contrary, as Davies (1) points out, the two jobs are often in tension with each other. Nevertheless, as parts of the criminal justice system they may be seen as complementary. Indeed to press Davies further, his concept of the role of the social worker as the "maintenance mechanic" (2) of society may equally well be claimed for the police's function in society. Both are often charged with exercising a controlling function and equally both often lay claim to a caring role for society. It will be my contention in this chapter that any major change in the nature of operation of one of the component parts of the criminal justice system will have inevitable consequences for the workings of other parts of the same system. This type of effect has been well documented by Jordan (3) in relation to the changes which were brought about within the total welfare system by the partial shift of public assistance responsibilities from the DHSS to Social Services Departments following the Children and Young Persons' Act 1963. It will be my further contention that not only will interference within the system have consequences for its other component parts, but also that attitudes from outside the system, which will bring about such changes, will also affect the whole of the system and the operation of its component parts.

That is, that the system itself will always reflect the cultural, political, social and economic contexts within which it is set. If Ian Gough (4) is right in his contention that the characteristic of post-war British governments, both Labour and Conservative, up to the advent of Thatcherism was one of consensus politics, then it will be no great surprise to find some reflection of this in the legislation affecting the criminal justice system. Whatever the problems of organisation and delivery in post-Seebohm social work and whatever the difficulties in relationship with central government so ably delineated by Fitzgerald et al, (5) there was still a recognition of an essential validity and legitimacy for a social work role by the community at large. The advent of Thatcherism marked a fundamental ideological shift neatly encapsulated by Gough (6) in the term "authoritarian populism". The outworkings of this ideological shift are not hard to detect either in the general field, with its avowed espousal of Victorian social policy, or more specifically in relation to the criminal justice system itself. The introduction of the "short sharp shock" regime in certain detention centres and its extension throughout that system despite all the evidence as to its lack of success was a piece of ideological obscurantism which beggars belief. The ruthless manipulation of the criminal justice system as witnessed in the Clive Ponting and Sarah Tisdall secrets trials, and the policing of the miners' strike only form a few of the most obvious demonstrations of the texture of the backcloth into which more recent measures such as the Police and Criminal Evidence Act are woven, and against which their implications must be evaluated.

The climate within which any new legislation will operate becomes singularly important when one considers its likely effects and implications for the criminal justice system as a whole. It has been noted (7) that the new Act sets police powers at "the highest common denominator (i.e. necessary to catch the most elusive and heinous criminal) rather than at the level of the greatest support and consent from the public". Now any inspection of the raw material processed by the criminal justice system will reveal that it does not fall into this category but rather that most processed deviancy is transient rather than continual, casual rather than purposive and peripheral rather than pathological and that among this group there is a heavy bias toward one social class, age group and gender and even this small core of persistent deviants has been likened to a "stage army" of misfits, and those on the margins of society, who constitute a nuisance rather than a threat. Amid a climate of "authoritarian populism", any new legislation which adopts the test of "reasonable suspicion" in relation to "stop and search", must stand every chance of widening the net for this vulnerable group.

Indeed as Piliavin and Briar (8) long ago demonstrated the crime of "contempt of police" has in practice already emerged. With the passing of this Act, it has taken one step nearer to being formalized in the written criminal law to take its place alongside the crime of contempt of court. In the present atmosphere to hold an alternative point of view or to question authority is to invite legal invocation. The extension of the power of arrest to minor and hitherto non-arrestable offences, with the wide discretion this confers at street level, provides a further potential weapon for pro-active police operations which may involve an attack on particular racial groups, on particular moral sub-cultures or indeed on any expression of non-conformity.

It has been claimed with some justification that there are measures within this piece of legislation that are to be applauded. The internal morality of the law demands that there be rules, and that they be made known. Acting by known rule is a precondition for any meaningful appraisal of the justice of law, for as Professor Fuller points out, (9): "It is the virtue of a legal order conscientiously constructed and administered that it exposes to public scrutiny the rules by which it acts". Thus by extending lawful powers to match those exercised de facto by the police this Act could be said to contribute to greater public exposure of the rules by which the police act. Indeed it is possible to imagine that the measures in this Act, had they been introduced in a different political climate, say by a Labour Government, would have been heralded as a great step forward in the realm of police accountability. Notwithstanding this, it is hard not to see the wide discretionary powers of arrest given in this new legislation as the elevation of crime control to a position where it is valued more than the principle of accountability to the rule of law. Jerome Skolnick (10) recognised "that the conduct of police may be related in a fundamental way to the character and goals of the institution itself - the duties police are called upon to perform, associated with the assumptions of the system of legal justice - and that it may not be men who are good or bad, so much as the premises and design of the system in which they find themselves". He further points out that "whenever rules of constraint are ambiguous they strengthen the very conduct they are intended to restrain. Thus the policeman already committed to a conception of law as an instrument of order rather than an end in itself is likely to utilize the ambiguity of the rules of restraint as a justification for testing or even violating them. By such a process the practical ambiguity of the rule of law may serve to undermine its salience as a value". (11)

In a piece of legislation stemming from a government whose chief ministers continually mouth the misleading "law and order" cliche it is not unlikely that such consequences will follow. The reification of "law and order" may therefore subordinate the ideal of legality to the ideal of conformity. Such a situation invites stereotyping. The maxim "let the punishment fit the crime" is replaced by the maxim "let the punishment fit the man". So that if the pressures that make for crime remain unabated or increase, whilst the armoury of control is expanded, the only software around - people - become more vulnerable. Whilst it has been "seriously doubted whether the benefit in being able to proceed with the prosecution of a handful of minor offenders outweighs the risk to individual liberty and to police/public relations which over-vigorous exercise of these new powers might well generate", (12) it will not be so much the general public, as particularly vulnerable groups who bear the brunt of such changes. Among such highly select minorities will be the traditional clients of social work. Although a remit which social work has often claimed for itself is to enhance, compensate and make equal individuals who otherwise would suffer intolerable neglect or persecution without agents of redress to work with them and for them. Nevertheless, the probation service cannot avoid the fact that its place is also that of an integral functional component of the criminal justice system and to claim anything else would be simply fraudulent idealism. The problem then for probation/social work is how far it is determined by the relationship it has to other key components of the criminal justice system from which it cannot break free and how loudly that system must resound with the social, economic, and political climate which forms the context within which it operates. It is an appreciation of such relationships and contexts and their interactions that must be taken into account in any evaluation of the Police and Criminal Evidence Act.

Ohlin and Remington point out that "there is inadequate awareness of the fact that the administration of criminal justice is a single total process and that therefore changing one important aspect may require substantial reorientation of the entire system". (13) The bare body of the criminal justice system has always been clothed in a curious set of garments, some of which blend, some of which clash, but whose overall purpose has been to provide, with varying degrees of success, a basic clothing function of preserving decency and dignity rather than any attempt at sartorial elegance. Such garments come from a complex wardrobe of overlapping and sometimes conflicting ideologies. Much attention has been focussed on the part of the criminal justice system where these dynamics are most obvious, that is the court hearing. Pat Carlen (14) has vividly illustrated one analysis of the process in action: "there are so many vested interests in the court - police, probation officers, magistrates, solicitors, social workers. It is a matter of them all fighting over one carcass". Such analyses serve to remind us that at the very best the parameters in which the component parts of the criminal justice system can co-operate and maintain their individual ideals and integrity may be very narrow indeed.

The very nature of the process, with its simplistic and stylized distribution of roles, can so easily and subtly provoke the alliances and strategies for maintaining credibility that Carlen exposes, so that at its least culpable, the process can so easily become, in Fogel's words, "the justice of administration rather than the administration of justice". If these dangers occur at the point of the system where the component parts are most visibly interacting, what will be the interactive effects for the criminal justice system as a whole of operations carried out within the more secluded sphere of an individual agency's functioning? It seems to me that we do not have to look very far for illustrations of what these effects might be. It has been understood by criminologists for fifty years that the chief result of the introduction of additional non-custodial measures has not been to reduce the numbers in custody but rather to share out differently those who would already have received non-custodial sentences.

It is in this context, of a reduction in the use of custody, that the recent demands by the Home Secretary for local statements of objectives from the Probation Service, (coupled with his stated commitment to the use of special requirements in probation orders as the new model for probation practice), seem to have been embraced by Chief Officers of Probation with almost indecent haste. This has occurred despite the plainest of warnings by Andrew Rutherford (15) that "the role of the Probation Service in holding persons convicted of serious offences in the community has to be considered in the context of the total criminal justice process", and in the light of "the relentless expansionist course set for the prison system". Rutherford reiterates Austin and Krisberg's conclusion that "alternatives to incarceration have been introduced for the espoused purpose of altering the nets of criminal justice. Organisational research, however, suggests that the reform strategies are frequently distorted, shifting from their original purposes and producing unintended and undesirable consequences. The evidence indicates that alternatives have created:-

1. Wider nets, in the sense that reforms have increased the proportion of persons whose behaviour is regulated and controlled by the state.

2. Stronger nets, in that reforms have augmented the state's capacity to control citizens through an intensification of its powers of intervention.

3. Different nets, through the transfer of jurisdictional authority from one agency to another, or the creation of new control systems. (The Uninet Promise of Alternatives to Incarceration, Crime and Delinquency 1982 p.377)".

Such a readiness by the Association of Chief Officers of Probation to capitulate professional insights to political pressures must inevitably lead to a repetition of these phenomena. Not only does this seem to be a perfect example of the naivety of individual agency myopia but it provides yet another demonstration of the general climate and philosophy surrounding the passing of the Police and Criminal Evidence Act. Such myopia wilfully denies the existence of an interactive system of criminal justice or any obvious common goal.

However such myopia begins to look more like schizophrenia when one considers the areas in which inter-agency co-operation is actively being promoted. Government circulars on intermediate treatment and crime prevention, Scarman-type liaison committees, all seem to emerge from or are consistent with the philosophy of "pro-active policing". Indeed the very term "pro-active" has become the buzz word in certain probation services at the present time. For the past two years the Staffordshire Police have run, throughout the month of August, a SPACE Scheme (Staffordshire Police Authority Community Enterprise). This has taken the form of a massive youth activities programme which has been heavily dependent on local authority facilities and expertise, and the expertise and facilities of the county's Youth Service. It has been claimed to result in a massive reduction in juvenile crime. The true cost of this enterprise has, to my knowledge, never been made public, but at a time when local authorities' education committees and youth services are being faced with financial cuts and resource starvation and even the Chief Constable himself is unwilling to meet community demands for policing without additional resources, it is perplexing to many to account for such a concentration of the community's resources within one month of the year. But what is of far greater concern is the implication that such spectacular events have for the day-in, day-out, year-in, year-out under-resourced, under-staffed performance of real youth and community work and crime prevention.

If we look at examples of more specific inter-agency co-operation, there are the juvenile liaison meetings which meet to discuss the possible diversion of juvenile offenders from the criminal justice process. Though why this is only relevant to juveniles and not to other specially vulnerable groups, such as old age pensioners, the mentally ill and the mentally handicapped is baffling. It has often been noted that what is significant about all these measures, whether general or specific, is that they are directed and controlled by the police, and whilst one would not wish to deny the motivation or commitment of individual police officers, the centring of control in one such agency gives a potential for the transformation of a variety of social agencies (each with its own balancing philosophy to contribute) into a single, simplistic authoritarian philosophy of society. The implications for theory and training in our education services, our youth services and the social work services are unimaginable, to say nothing of the effects for social and penal policy. What we are seeing is no less than a transformation of our society and a blunt denial of decades of theory and practice.

If we return to a consideration of the criminal justice system, the Police and Criminal Evidence Act has been seen as a response to the exercise of "industrial deviance" by the police which was often claimed to be necessary in order to be able to investigate criminal offences effectively. It has been claimed that this Act grasps the nettle in that it recognises the problems of effective policing whilst at the same time offsets the dangers of increased police powers by strengthening the safeguards for suspects. Assuming that the Act is effective in this respect, it seems likely that one of its effects will be to increase industrial deviance elsewhere in the system. It has become fashionable to view the criminal justice system as a "balloon" or a "hydraulic system" so that displacement in one part may well lead to expansion in another. Pearson (16) draws attention to this phenomenon in social work, as demonstrated by a "widespread acceptance of rule breaking among social workers 'as part of the job'." He then lists a number of examples of industrial deviance and partly accounts for it because, in their education programmes, social workers are "introduced to the critical concepts of social science and to a 'professional vision' of an alternative system of welfare which transcends the shortcomings of the welfare state". He further claims that it is "industrial deviance which helps them to secure the objectives for which they are led to believe they are trained and paid". Now if this phenomenon should become evident in the criminal justice system, as Pearson already claims it to be, then it is highly likely that the legitimization of what were hitherto "industrially deviant" practices by the police will result, by displacement, in an increase in "industrial deviance" in the Probation Service and for the very same reasons to which Pearson attributes industrial deviance in social work at the present: that is because of the critical concepts of social science and a professional vision "of an alternative system which transcends the shortcomings of the present system and thus to secure the objectives for which they are led to believe they are trained and paid".

Now clearly there are limits to the acceptability of industrial deviance in any situation, both from the point of view of integrity and from the fact that there must come a point when such activity ceases to have any recognisable relationship with social work and becomes purely political action, which by definition cannot be social work in any form that it is recognised at the present time. Davies points out that "it is a fundamental precept of the idea that social work is socially sanctioned (that is to say created by, paid by and allowed to operate under the aegis of the existing regime). That its employees, as social workers, acknowledge a broad acceptance of the legitimacy of the government....the social worker may disagree with the government as a voter; he may campaign against it as a citizen; he may rise in revolt against it as an insurrectionist or freedom fighter....the social worker may do all of these things but in doing them, I cling to the view that he is not practising social work". (17) However, Davies also recognises that, "social work is not and can never be wholly apolitical because its practice depends on the state regime respecting the basic rights of all citizens. Political battles may have to be fought – and won – in order to defend the climate within which social work can be practised". (18)

That practice implies an acceptance of the fundamental nature of social work. Olive Stevenson holds that "those who commit themselves to social work contribute to the sensitisation of our society". (19) It has been recognised, even by those prepared to be critical of the role of orthodox social work, that running throughout its history is a continuous thread of "quiet" or "subdued" radicalism. (20) Pearson points out that since "social work operates at the intersection of what is 'personal' and what is 'political', (21) it is involved in 'moral hustling' which defends the weak and gives them a voice against the powerful". (22) Social work must always interrogate the system of which it is part. Social work in general or social work within the criminal justice system can never be a neutral, "technical" activity. It is to the everlasting shame of the Association of Chief Officers of Probation that it was left to the Directors of Social Work to take the stand implied in their recent policy statement "Children Still in Trouble". (23) Notwithstanding all this, social work is not, and ought not, to be equated with political agitation, still less with the practice of industrial deviance. It is for these reasons that the Police and Criminal Evidence Act, in the present political climate, poses such a fundamental threat to the very existence of anything that could be legitimately claimed to be social work in the criminal justice system.

If the Police and Criminal Evidence Act poses a threat to the internal dynamics of the criminal justice system, and the political commitment to safeguard and further the welfare of all citizens is missing from government policy, then the dangers are there for all to see. The very existence of the Probation Service is threatened because the practice of probation will become impossible. Probation Officers themselves will be divided, as Davies points out, with some setting up in rebellion against a repressive State, and others aligning themselves with the oppressors of the individuals, and so denying their basic social work identity. On the other hand the State will begin to attack its social work services because of the way in which social workers draw society's attention to the rights and needs of oppressed minorities. (24)   Already the current demands for "activity packages" threaten to make traditional probation practice unrecognisable. A probation officer has recently been threatened with dismissal for refusing to recommend a particular type of sentence to a court in line with his superiors' views of government policy. This has led one very well known commentator on the criminal justice system to state that "the probation officer should not be an instrument of government policy but an officer of the court capable of giving courageous opinions". (25)   Herein lies the challenge. It is time for probation officers openly to acknowledge not only the limitations of their task but its crucial importance to the survival of a compassionate democracy.

NOTES

1.   The Essential Social Worker, p.207. Martin Davies, 1981.

2.   Ibid. p.137.

3.   Poor Parents, p. 93. Bill Jordan, 1974.

4.   The Crisis of the British Welfare State, p. 10. Ian Gough, 1981.

5.   "Social Work, Community Work and Society" Open University Course D.E.206.

6.   Op. cit. p. 10.

7.   Policing by Coercion, Louise Christian, 1983.

8.   "Police Encounters with Juveniles", Irving Piliavin and Scott Briar p. 206-214 American Journal of Sociology, 70 (1964).

9.   The Morality of Law p. 157-158, Professor Lon L. Fuller 1964.

10.   Justice Without Trial, p. 5, Jerome Skolnick, 1966.

11.   Ibid. p. 12.

12.   "Police Powers and the Citizen" p. 93, John Baldwin and Roger Leng, Howard Journal Vol.23 No.2 June 1984.

13.   "Sentencing Structure; its Effect upon Systems for the Administration of Criminal Justice", L.E. Ohlin and F.J. Remington, p. 496, Law and Contemporary Problems, 23.

14.   "Magistrates Courts: a game theoretic analysis", Pat Carlen, Sociological Review 23, May 1975.

15.   Address to the Association of Chief Probation Officers Conference, September 1984.

16.   The Deviant Imagination, p. 136, G. Pearson, 1975.

17.   Op. cit. p. 140.

18.   Ibid. p. 210.

19.   "Editorial", Brit.Jol. Social Work, Vol 4 No.1, 1974, p.2.

20.   "Thieves and Communities in Radical and Traditional Social Work", David Webb Brit. Jol. Social Work (1981) 11, p. 143-158.

21.   Op. cit. p. 141.

22.   Ibid. p. 136.

23.   March 1985.

24.   Op. cit. p. 141.

25.   Brian Harris, Ed Justice of the Peace, reported to a Sentencing Conference, April 1985, at Manchester University.

11. POLICE AND RACE RELATIONS

Robert Reiner

'Policing a multi-racial society is putting the fabric of our policing philosophy under greater stress than at any time since the years immediately after the Metropolitan Police was established in 1829.' Sir David McNee, Guardian, 25 September 1979.
'Since the late 1960's, a sort of war of attrition has been going on between the police and black people.' Stuart Hall: 'Drifting Into a Law and Order Society', Cobden Trust Human Rights Day Lecture 1979, p.13.

. . . .

The now vast literature on police-black relations in Britain is a depressing chorus of unheeded prophecies of doom. Complaints about police harassment of black people stretch back at least as far as the end of the Second World War (1), and become a regular, ever-increasing flood by the late 1960's. Joe Hunte's 1966 pamphlet 'Nigger Hunting in England?' prefigures all the issues which were to become the sources of controversy in the 70's: police raids on black clubs, stereotyping of blacks as suspected offenders, racist abuse, and inadequate police protection against attack.(2) Speaking in the spring, not of 1981, but 1971, Margaret Simey predicted: 'The coloured community is fed up with being hounded....It could lead to civil war in the city.' (3) Her warning was not wrong - just ten years early. This sort of hostility surrounding relations between police and ethnic minorities is paralleled in other countries, most obviously the US, as was evident in the 1960s ghetto conflagrations which became an obvious point of comparison in discussions of the 1981 English counterparts. (4) All societies with significant ethnic tensions place the police, as the most visible, concrete embodiment of the dominant group's power, at the heart of the conflict. This is evident, for example, in Lee's discussion of police relations with blacks, Asians and native Americans in Canada (5), Banton's discussion of police relations with the Turkish and other minorities in West Berlin (6), Punch's documentation of the mutual hostility of police and Surinamers in his study of Amsterdam (7), Australian and New Zealand conflicts with aboriginals, and Edmond-Smith's account of how for the French Police 'socially and politically deprived, the migrant worker is an obvious victim for police excesses.' (9) The re-occurrence of similar patterns of complaint and conflict in a variety of social contexts certainly implies that (as the evidence to be examined confirms) police-minority relations are not so much a problem of individual attitudes or prejudices as one with structural roots in the role of the police and the position of minorities.
This paper will examine the literature and research evidence concerning police-black relations primarily in Britain, but drawing also on the vast American material on the issue. Despite the obvious differences in the historical and social contexts of policing and the position of minorities, the American research is illuminating on the pattern and sources of police-black conflict. The paper will be divided into three main sections, which will examine in turn the history of racial conflict with the police, the nature of black complaints and the causes célèbres which exemplify them, and the implications of sociological research on the police. Finally, there will be some discussion of reform initiatives, and the implications of the Police Act for race relations.

A. Racial Conflicts And The Police

The history of race riots in both Britain and the US falls into two clearly differentiated phases. Before the 1960's American ghetto riots, fighting was between white and black citizens (usually stemming from white racial attacks on blacks), with the police intervening in an ineffective and often partisan way. In the American urban disturbances of the 60's, and the recent British conflicts, police-black relations usually provided both the immediate spark and an underlying cause of the troubles. As Stephen Fenton has summarised the difference with respect to America: 'In the (1919) Chicago (riot commission) report, the distrust between police and black people is seen as an exacerbating factor, and as a factor which made it harder for police to quell the riot once started; in the 1967 riots police-community relations are seen as an underlying cause and triggering factor in a high percentage of the disturbances'. (10)   The earlier pattern in America is typified by the 1917 East St. Louis, 1919 Chicago and 1943 Detroit race riots. (11) (The 1935 Harlem riot is exceptional in this period and prefigures later developments. It was sparked by the arrest of a 16 year old black boy by a patrolman, which gave rise to a false rumour that he had been beaten). The trigger in East St. Louis 1917 was a car which drove through a black area shooting wildly into houses, Chicago 1919 was sparked off by an incident in which a young black swimmer 'strayed' on to a 'white' beach and was drowned in ensuing scuffles, and Detroit 1943 resulted from fights about the use of recreational facilities.

In all these instances the police intervened at best ineffectively to protect blacks from white mobs, or even supported their attacks. The conclusions of the 1918 Special Committee of Congress which investigated the East St. Louis Riots are typical: 'The testimony of every witness who was free to tell the truth agreed in condemnation of the police for failure to even halfway do their duty....The organisation broke down completely; and so great was the indifference of the few policemen who remained on duty that the conclusion is inevitable that they shared the lust of the mob for negro blood, and encouraged the rioters by their conduct, which was sympathetic when it was not cowardly.' (12)

The pattern of early British race riots is similar: white attacks on blacks precipitating widespread disorder, with police intervention at best half-hearted, at worst openly partisan. 'The race riots of May and June 1919 were tiny pogroms in ports where blacks (mainly West Indians) had settled during the first world war, or were lodging until they could get ships home. The wartime labour shortage had sucked black labour into the British home economy, and into the merchant marine especially. First in Limehouse; then in Newport, Liverpool, Cardiff, Tyneside and Glasgow; then in East London again (Poplar and Canning Town) black sailors were attacked by large crowds.' (13)   Other examples of this basic pattern are the 1911 racial attacks on the Chinese community in Cardiff, and the 1948 Liverpool clashes following attacks on a black cafe and a hostel by white crowds. (14)

The ineffectiveness and bias of the police intervention is indicated by Richmond's contemporary study of the 1948 Liverpool violence: 'The police took action which they thought would bring the disturbances to a close as quickly as possible - which, in their view, meant removing the coloured minority, rather than attempting to arrest the body of irresponsible whites who were involved.' (15)   The police intervention was a significant factor in accentuating the disorders, and specifically the fighting between police and black crowds, which the press seized upon in a classic instance of blaming the original victims. Joshua, Wallace and Booth argue that 'the unneutral behaviour of the police "legitimated" and "reinforced" the actions of the white crowds'. (16) Waskow's comments on the American riots apply to the British examples: 'The police partiality had different effects upon whites and Negroes, but in both communities, encouraged violence. To whites, unneutral behaviour by the police meant that it was "open season" on Negroes, and that the usual protections offered by the law were temporarily in abeyance. To Negroes, the police one-sidedness meant that their only defence was self-defence, since the law would not come to their protection.' (17)

The 1958 race riots in Nottingham and Notting Hill (and Dudley in 1962) in some ways fit into the earlier pattern, being essentially cases of white mobs attacking blacks. But certain aspects anticipate later developments, notably the involvement of white teenagers and (in Nottingham and Notting Hill) a fascist political element. These characteristics prefigure the growth of individualised white racist attacks after the late 1960s, and the conflicts surrounding anti-racist demonstrations against the National Front (as in Lewisham 1977, and Southall 1979 and 1981). The 1958 riots also occur in the context of the growing politicisation of the immigration issue, so that state policy, not just individual racist attitudes, was at the heart of the conflict.

The major difference apparent in most of the post-1960s examples of collective racial violence in both the US and Britain is the centrality of policing as both a background condition and the immediate trigger. The 1968 Kerner Commission Report on Civil Disorders found that: 'Some 40% of the prior incidents involved allegedly abusive or discriminatory police actions. Most of the police incidents began routinely....Police actions were also identified as the final (precipitating) incident preceding 12 of the 24 (1967) disturbances.' (18) It concluded: 'Almost invariably the incident that ignites disorder arises from police action. Harlem, Watts, Newark and Detroit - all the major outbursts of recent years - were precipitated by arrests of Negroes by white police for minor offences. But the police were not merely the spark. In discharge of their obligation to maintain order and insure public safety in the disruptive conditions of ghetto life, they are inevitably involved in sharper and more frequent conflicts with ghetto residents than with the residents of other areas. Thus to many Negroes police have come to symbolise white power, white racism and white repression. And the fact is that many police do reflect and express these white attitudes.' (19) The only major post-1960s American race riot, Miami 1980, was also triggered by a policing incident (the trial and acquittal of some white police officers for killing a black suspect), and was 'preceded by an unusually long succession of alleged police abuses and failures of the criminal justice system.' (20) But in other respects Miami seems to have been an exceptional occurrence. There was an element of inter-ethnic conflict (killing of and attacks on white and Cuban citizens by blacks) which were absent from the 60s events, and the triggering episodes 'were precisely the sort that, since the 1960s, many (American) police forces had learned to avoid.' (21)

The English disorders of 1980 and 1981 are comparable to the 60s American ones in the prevalence of policing as both a triggering incident and background cause of tension, and the absence of inter-ethnic conflict. (Indeed the involvement of white youth in some clashes with the police led several commentators to deny the racial element in them). Bristol 1980, Brixton April 1981 and July 1981, and Toxteth 1981 were all precipitated by the kinds of routine police intervention in minor offences which were the precipitants of the 60s American riots. They were also expressions of the long process of gathering tension between blacks and the police, as will be documented in the next two sections. Whereas in earlier racial conflicts policing problems may have accentuated the violence, in 1980-81 they were the core issue.

B. Black Complaints Against The Police

Since Joe Hunte's 1966 pamphlet 'Nigger Hunting in England?' there have appeared a steady stream of publications cataloguing a shocking volume of allegations of police misconduct with regard to blacks and Asians. (22) The complaints can be broadly divided into two groups: allegations of over-heavy policing of suspected black offences, and of under-policing of black victimisation, particularly in cases of racist attack. The Metropolitan Police issued a response to the allegations in Pulle's 1973 report, although since then they have not commented on these sorts of criticism with regard to specific cases. One police reviewer said of Humphry's book 'each of the cases he describes could have been written about from a police point of view and seen in a different light.' (23) While this is probably true of many of the more recent volumes too, Lord Scarman was surely right when he commented with respect to the similar allegations made to his inquiry: 'the weight of criticism and complaint against the police is so considerable that it alone must give grave cause for concern.' (24)

In this section I will give examples of the kinds of police abuse about which black complaints have been most common. The question of their extent and sources will be considered in the next section which examines the sociological research on the police.

(a)   Allegations of over-heavy policing

The basic theme implied by the evidence assembled in the Institute of Race Relations' submission to the Royal Commission on Criminal Procedure, Police Against Black People (and the similar documents cited in footnote 22) is of harassment, discrimination and other abuse of police powers in relation to blacks. Essentially we can distinguish five kinds of cases:

(i)   Discrimination In The Use Of Police Powers

Numerous cases are cited of apparently arbitrary use of powers of stop and search, or arrest, particularly with regard to the notorious 'sus' charge. (s.4 of the 1824 Vagrancy Act, repealed in 1981, but replaced by the Criminal Attempts Act which is widely feared to be a practical equivalent). I will quote just one example from Clare Demuth's study of 'Sus' for the Runnymede Trust, which also illustrates many of the other kinds of abuse which are often alleged:

'Case 10: Proven: Appeal Allowed:

Four black youths were doing their Saturday morning shopping in Upton Park. They had just come out of Woolworths when they were stopped by a group of plain clothed policemen. One of them allegedly said he had seen the boys 'operating' the Saturday before. They were taken to Forest Gate police station, put in separate cells, stripped, searched and later questioned, photographed and had their fingerprints taken. They were charged with 'sus' - jostling people in bus and shop queues and putting their hands in shopping baskets. They denied the charges.

In court the police were not sure whether one of the potential victims was black or white, could not describe the bag and disagreed over which hand she was holding it in. They failed to identify one of the defendants - one of them said that his choice was a 'guess' as 'all blacks look the same to me.' The police also disagreed over whether or not the defendants had been stripped. There were no independent witnesses. But the manager of Woolworths gave evidence that the boys were not hanging around the tills, as alleged by the police. They were convicted.

They appealed and the conviction was quashed because of discrepancies in the police evidence.'
(November 1976) p.23.

(ii)   Saturation Policing Of Black Areas

The classic illustration of this complaint is the process leading to the 1981 Brixton disorders. In the mid and late 1970s several major police operations, involving the Special Patrol Group, were launched in Brixton. 'In 1978, 120 officers, more than half the total SPG strength, were brought into the area because of the supposed "high crime" rate. Over 1000 people were stopped and 430 arrested. 40% of the latter were black, although black people were only 20% of the population in the area.' (25)

Such tactics were the background to the establishment in March 1979 by the local Lambeth council of an independent enquiry into police-community relations. The immediate trigger for this was what Lord Scarman referred to as the 'Sheepskin Saga', when three staff members of the Council for Community Relations in Lambeth were arrested, 'largely because it seemed that the only link between those who were wanted and those who were arrested was that they wore sheepskin coats.' (26) The Lambeth enquiry 'described the police in Lambeth as an army of occupation....intimidating and harassing working class people in Lambeth and black people in particular.' (27) The saturation policy tactics of which it complained continued unabated, culminating in the notorious 'Swamp 81' - 'an unfortunate name', as Scarman said - which was arranged to run between Monday 6 April and Saturday 11 April, with its expressed purpose being 'to flood identified areas on "L" District to detect and arrest burglars and robbers....success will depend on a concentrated effort of "stops", based on powers of surveillance and suspicion.' (28) The incidents which sparked the rioting on the Friday and Saturday of that week were examples of the kinds of intervention encouraged by these instructions. (29)

(iii)   Heavy Policing Of Black Social And Political Institutions

Police harassment of key institutions of black social life is a major theme of complaints going back to Hunte's 1966 pamphlet, and beyond.(30) An example is the long saga of the Mangrove restaurant in Notting Hill, which has been raided many times since 1969, often by large groups of police. (31) The heavy policing of the annual Notting Hill Carnival has been another regular source of complaint, referred to by the Carnival Development Committee as 'an insult....an unnecessary army of policemen which instilled fear in the revellers.' (32)

The events leading to the disturbances in Bristol 1980 are another instance of how this sort of routine policing can erupt into mass conflict. The incident which precipitated the disorder was a raid on the Black and White Cafe, the Bristol equivalent of the Mangrove, on 2 April 1980. The Black and White, like the Mangrove and similar black meeting places in other cities, had been raided many times before. On this occasion it was entered by 39 policemen with search warrants for drugs and illegal alcohol. (33)

Heavy policing has not been directed only at black social institutions. Political demonstrations against racist organisations, or protesting against racist attacks, have frequently been policed in a manner which implied at any rate a de facto partisanship, whatever official police intentions might have been. The heavy police presence protecting the National Front election meeting in Southall in April 1979, which led to severe violent clashes (including the killing of Blair Peach almost certainly by an SPG Officer) is the most obvious example. (Earlier instances of a similar kind were Red Lion Square in 1974 and Lewisham 1977). (34)

(iv) Complaints Of Police Abuse

In addition to complaints of discrimination and harassment is the catalogue of allegations of verbal and/or physical abuse during the processing of black suspects on the street and in the station. I shall quote just two short examples from the long list in the Institute of Race Relations' evidence to the Royal Commission on Criminal Procedure (op.cit., pp.32-3):

'In 1976 T., a West Indian youth, was walking home from a party when a police officer called out, "Come here sunshine". He said, "My name's not sunshine", and was punched in the kidneys. His injuries were verified by a police surgeon.' (Open letter to the Home Secretary from T. Anderson, United Black Women's Action Group, Tottenham; CARF, no.4, 1978).

'In 1978 in Birmingham police waiting outside a black youth club are said to have pounced on a youth who, with his friends, was running for a bus. Police grabbed hold of them and flung them in a police van; one of the boys was severely beaten in the van itself, at one point losing consciousness. They were charged with disorderly conduct.' (Testimony to All Faiths for One Race, cited in 'Talking Blues', 1978).

(v) Blaming The Victim: Complaints About The Police Reaction To Black Self-Protection

Complaints about police neglect of racial attacks are a long-standing grievance, and will be discussed in section (b) below. But there are related complaints of police treatment of black victims as the aggressor. Several such cases are cited in 'Blood on the Streets', a 1978 Report by Bethnal Green and Stepney Trades Council. The following is characteristic of many cases it cites:

'13 May 1976. A 38-year-old Bengalee man living on the Bow Bridge Estate, Bow, was assaulted by three youths armed with clubs. The incident occurred at around 10.30 pm on the estate. The victim received bruises. In addition the attack was witnessed by several people living on the estate. The victim's wife telephoned the Police and subsequently the offenders appeared in court the following day and pleaded guilty.

The victim of the attack says in the report made to us during our investigations that following the trial of the culprits he was subject to Police harassment which eventually led to his leaving the estate to squat in premises in Ellen Street, E.1.

The victim tells us that the culprits had made statements to the Police which led to the victim's arrest. The Bengalee was charged with possessing offensive weapons including a broom and a hammer after a Police search was made of his home. The Bengalee was eventually acquitted after he appealed to a Crown court.'

Several examples of collective disorder have arisen from police clashes with Black or Asian protests about racial attacks. The July 1981 Southall riot is a striking example. It arose when some 300 skinheads attended an 'Oi' concert in Southall, where Asian youth had become militant over the issue of racist violence since the infamous 1976 murder of Gurdip Singh Chaggar, and the 1979 clashes around the NF election meeting. Following some incidents when skinheads abused an Asian woman, and smashed windows, hundreds of Asian youth gathered round the pub where the concert was going on. The police who formed a cordon around the pub received many injuries from both sides, but there were also numerous civilian casualties. (35)

Another example of mass conflict arising from the racial attacks issue is the March 1981 Black People's Day of Action, protesting about police handling of the tragic Deptford fire, in which 13 young blacks died at a party. The Policy Studies Institute study of 'Police and People in London' was able to examine the police handling of the investigation, and the arrangements for the demonstration on both sides. They concluded that the police investigation was in substance probably as thorough as possible, and certainly treated with high priority. However, the police were insufficiently sensitive to the way the fire aroused deep feelings of fear and persecution amongst black people (in this the police share culpability with the media and the government). Even if the outcome had been the same, the researchers suggest 'it is hard to see that there was any need for the police to resist or publicly play down the suggestion that the fire might have been a racialist attack'. (36) The mass demonstration on 2 March was attended by 10-15,000 people. 'Although the march was largely peaceful, there were significant clashes between demonstrators and the police, and at least 28 arrests were made'. (37) One of these arrests was of a PSI researcher, Stephen Small. The report states categorically that 'there was no valid reason for the researcher to be arrested and charged with obstructing the police officer in the execution of his duty....What this demonstrates is that someone who is present at a scene of some disorder during a demonstration is in danger of being arrested and charged with an offence regardless of his personal behaviour or intentions'. (38) The study also documents verbal abuse of the researcher, and the denial of some rights such as a telephone call.

(b)   Under-Policing Of Racial Attacks

As the previous section indicated, complaints about a lack of adequate police response to racial attacks have been mounted for years. (40) In 1981, however, as a response to continued pressure from the Commission for Racial Equality, the Board of Deputies of British Jews, and the Joint Committee Against Racialism, the Home Secretary undertook an important study of racial attacks. (41) This documented the disturbing extent and rate of increase of attacks with a racial motive. They estimated that about 7,000 incidents occur per year in which there is a strong or some indication of a racial motive. (42)   Blacks (51.2 per 100,000) and especially Asians (69.7 per 100,000) are disproportionately likely to be victimised as compared to whites (1.4 per 100,000). (43)   The attack reports contained in the files of the Home Office Research Unit, the Commission for Racial Equality, the Board of Deputies for British Jews, and the Runnymede Trust, had increased since 1977, with an especially sharp rise since 1980. (44)   The Home Office study did not find a tendency for police to neglect the racist motives of attacks, a finding at odds with the complaints documented in the previous literature. It recommended better monitoring at local level of information about racial attacks, better training so that police would develop 'a greater sensitivity towards the phenomenon of racial attacks', and more liaison, so that police could explain the problems of legal evidence to community leaders. The Home Office report rejected the idea of specialised police units, as suggested by the JCAR and the CRE.

A year after the Home Office Report, the Runnymede Trust published a study which found that racial attacks continued at a disturbing level, with 108 London cases reported in the press between 17 July 1980 and 17 July 1981. (45) It found evidence of organised racist involvement in many cases.   Despite the Home Office study complaints about police indifference- or reluctance to perceive racial motives continued.   Paul Gordon also points to the continuation of this problem, citing the trial of the Bradford 12 in 1982.   The 12 black youths, who had made petrol bombs, were charged in 1981 with conspiracy to cause grievous bodily harm and to damage property.   They were acquitted by the jury which accepted that the bombs had been prepared for the purpose of communal self-defence. During the trial it emerged that the police officers involved in the investigation claimed no knowledge of racial attacks in the area, or the Home Office Report which had documented these. (46)

More recently, however, there are some hopeful indications of an awakened concern about the problem of racial attacks, in line with the Home Office's report.   Southall, for example, has been singled out by the Commissioner, Sir Kenneth Newman, for a pilot project to curb racial attacks. (47)   The cornerstone of this is that officers are now instructed to use the victim's perception of an attack as the basis of its assessment as racial.   Racial attacks are investigated exclusively by CID, but the uniform branch are also instructed to regard all such incidents as especially serious, and to involve supervisory officers immediately. Home Beat and Community Involvement Officers follow up by visits to the homes of victims, and there is close liaison on the issue with the Community Relations Council.   It is too early for any rigorous assessment of the impact of the project on either the incidence of attacks or the communal sense of security.   But at least it signifies a greater commitment to dealing with the problem.

The impossibility of such a redirection of police policy in this area has been argued in an important recent article by Jefferson and Grimshaw. (48)   They claim that special attention to racial attacks contradicts the ideology of impartial law enforcement which is the 'essential cornerstone of any state claiming democratic legitimacy....Thus, for example, the notion that some offences within particular offence categories affecting particular groups of victims should be selected out for special attention – some assaults on black victims, for example – would represent a movement far beyond what we might call the inevitably selective practice of impartial law enforcement'. (49)   Effective policy-making in relation to the problem of racial attacks, or indeed any other aspect of policing, would, they argue, require a perspective of socialist justice to redress other inequalities in the social relations of groups, not the more limited notion of democratic justice based on equal rights for individuals. Without taking on the wider issues raised by Jefferson and Grimshaw, it seems that the particular problem of inadequate policing of racial attacks is not an apt illustration for their case. The complaints about police handling of racial attacks do not amount to a demand for special attention, but for equal attention, which is compatible with either a democratic or socialist conception of justice. As the Home Office study found: 'The ethnic minorities said that what they sought from the police was not in any sense preferential treatment, but treatment equal to that which they considered was received by members of the majority community who were the victims of criminal offences'. (50) There is nothing in the existing philosophy of policing which precludes better handling of racial attacks.

Having documented the nature of black complaints about policing, I shall turn to a consideration of the sociological research on the police in order to pinpoint the extent and sources of police discrimination or abuse of racial minorities.

C. Sociological Research On Police And Race Relations

The extent of police-black conflict in Britain and the US in the last 20 years has stimulated a growing research industry on police-black attitudes and the use of police discretion in relation to blacks. The similarity in the pattern of findings in studies in both countries is really quite striking, the most apparent difference being the far higher levels of violence in the US.

1. American Research Findings

(a)   Discrimination In Police Practices

(i)   Street Practices

The evidence suggests unequivocally that the police stop and question young, low-income, ethnic minority males more frequently than any other group. The major study of 'field interrogation' found that 100% of people stopped were male, 66% black or Mexican American, and almost $\frac{2}{3}$ juveniles. (51) The likelihood of black males being stopped is out of proportion to their representation either in the population or among those arrested, according to a 1973 Dallas study. (52) Blacks who were stopped were more likely than whites to be 'innocent.' (53) Once stopped, blacks are more likely to be searched and interrogated. (54)

(ii)   Arrest

The original reports of the major observational study of American police behaviour, the massive Black-Reiss research for the 1967 Presidential Commission on Law Enforcement and Administration of Justice, (55) concluded that contrary to 'some ideological conceptions of police work..... No evidence exists to show that the police discriminate on the basis on race. The police arrest blacks at a comparatively high rate, but the difference between the races appears to result primarily from the greater rate at which blacks show disrespect for police. The behavioural difference thus lies with the citizen participants, not the police.' (Emphasis in original). (56) Similarly the Black-Reiss study found that black juveniles were more likely to be arrested (controlling for seriousness of offence) because encounters involving them were more frequently attended by (usually black) complainants who demanded arrest. (57)   Both findings were later replicated in another large-scale observational study, by Lundman, Sykes and Clark.   The Black-Reiss data do not, however, show whether 'disrespect' preceded or followed from arrest.   The later study did consider this, and suggested that in about half the cases where suspects showed disrespect this could have been a consequence of the police officer's behaviour, rather than the cause of it.   (58)   The later study also showed that while 'disrespect' accounted for the disproportionate arrest rate for blacks, it did not do so for native-Americans. Finally, a recent re-analysis of the Black-Reiss data shows that although black arrests are more often attended by complainants demanding arrest, when this is controlled for, blacks are still arrested more often than whites. (60)

The overall conclusion seems to be that while blacks (and other minorities) are arrested disproportionately even controlling for legal factors like seriousness of offence, much, but not all, of the difference is explicable by interactional or situational factors like suspects' disrespect or complainants' preferences.

(iii)   Police Abuse

(a)   Verbal Abuse

The National Advisory Commission on Civil Disorders found that 20% of blacks interviewed in a large-scale survey reported disrespectful or insulting language used by police officers, compared to only 9% of whites. (61) The Black-Reiss observational data showed, however, that while police officers 'openly ridiculed or belittled' citizens in 5% of encounters, they 'did not treat Negroes uncivilly more often than whites.' (62)   Skolnick noted, by contrast, that 'when one observes police in the routine performance of their duties, one hears all the usual derisive terms referring to Negroes and a few others besides.'   He cites a departmental directive banning use of a vast array of derogatory racial terms, implying that these were regularly used. (63)

(b)   Physical Abuse

The Black-Reiss study found that 'the rate of excessive force for all white citizens in encounters with the police is twice that for Negro citizens', and that 41.9 per 1000 white suspects experienced undue use of force compared to 22.6 per 1000 black suspects. (64)   They concluded 'that white suspects are more liable to be treated improperly by the police than Negro suspects are'.

The evidence on police use of deadly force, which became the hottest political issue in the law enforcement field in the 1970s, suggests the opposite conclusion.   During the 1970s an annual average of 300 citizens were killed by police, with a black death rate nine times greater than for whites.   Between 1960-68 51% of the people killed by police were black (while blacks are only 10% of the U.S. population). (65)   The police refute the apparent racial discrimination in these figures by pointing out the counter-threat posed to police by blacks.   Of 1,573 persons identified as killers of police 1969-78, 49% were black.   There is clearly a vicious cycle of hostility involved, with the omnipresence of guns a key factor. But close analysis of shootings by American police suggests a strong element of racial discrimination over and above what can be explained by the criminality or danger to the police offered by blacks. For example, University of California sociologist Marshall Meyer has studied shootings by the Los Angeles police for their Police Commission. (66) He found that 55% of all persons shot by police 1974-8 (and 50% of those killed) were black, although blacks constitute only 18% of the LA population and 36% of persons arrested. A greater proportion of blacks than whites were fired on for failing to obey an officer, for 'making furtive gestures', or turned out to be unarmed. The percentage of officers disciplined for 'out of policy' shootings of blacks was lower than for whites. (However, it should be noted that since some notorious shooting incidents in 1977 policy and training have been tightened, with a significant drop in police shootings).

Some studies have suggested that the proportion of black deadly force victims matches the proportion of those arrested for serious offences who are black, implying that the police are not more likely to shoot blacks other things being equal. (67) The bulk of the research shows, however, that the police do shoot blacks disproportionately, although this is complexly related to other situational variables like arrest. (68)

(iv) Police And Black Politics

The harassment, or even liquidation of militant, and even reformist, black organisations and leaders by American police forces, from redneck Southern sheriffs all the way up to the FBI has been well-documented. J. Edgar Hoover once called Martin Luther King 'the most dangerous man in America', and King was a key target of an official FBI COINTELPRO (Counterintelligence Programme) directed at all supposed 'black hate-type' groups. King was bugged continuously and information about his extra-marital (and 'inter-racial') sexual activities was used to smear and blackmail him. (69) Black nationalist groups were the subject of even dirtier tricks.

A small but interesting example of the systematic nature of this harassment is given by an enterprising 1971 experiment conducted by some California State College students in Los Angeles. 15 students with exemplary driving records and cars with no defective equipment agreed to attach Black Panther stickers to the rear bumper of their vehicles. The students were blacks, whites and Chicanos in equal numbers. They agreed to drive as carefully as possible, and had a budget of $500. The study had to be stopped within 17 days because the fines on 33 petty traffic citations had exhausted the research fund. (70)

(b) Police And Black Attitudes

A large number of American studies demonstrate police suspiciousness, hostility and prejudice towards blacks (and vice versa). It is usually argued that this is a reflection of the racism of American culture generally, and especially the social groups from which most police are drawn (lower-middle or working-class with no more than high school education). The first sociological study of American police by Westley in 1951 asked 50 policemen what they thought of Negroes. 38 had an unfavourable opinion, 22 judging that Negroes were biologically inferior. 60% thought Negro crime resulted from a taint of their racial character: they were 'lazy, irresponsible by nature', 'born criminals, love crime', 'mentally undeveloped' etc. (71) Skolnick, in his classic study of a Californian police force in the early 60s found that 'a negative attitude toward Negroes was a norm among the police studied', although 'it is likely that the attitudes of policemen toward Negroes are not significantly different from those of most comparable whites such as skilled workingmen and white-collar workers'. (72) The Black-Reiss study which claimed to find no evidence of discriminating police behaviour did find that 'over three fourths of the policemen express prejudice against Negroes.' (73) A study of police attitudes to minorities conducted in the late 60s by Bayley and Mendelsohn concluded: 'Are policemen prejudiced? The answer is yes, but only slightly more so than the community as a whole. Policemen reflect the dominant attitudes of the majority people towards minorities.' (74)

White American police have also been prominent in political opposition to the civil rights movement and in support for far-right political organisations with a racist character. In the early 40s, Myrdal in 'An American Dilemma' claimed that the police were a main basis of support for the Ku Klux Klan. More recently, police organisations have waged numerous political campaigns against liberal city administrations, most notably in their referendum campaign against the New York City Civilian Review Board in 1966, when they successfully capitalised upon white fears of black crime. (75) The liberal police chief of Atlanta, Herbert Jenkins, called the police union 'not a union at all but in fact a thinly veiled cover for Klan membership.' Black politicians attracted particular ire. During the ghetto riots in Cleveland in 1968, the black mayor Stokes was subject to a stream of vilification on police radios: 'This came in response to a report of a heart-attack case within the cordoned area: "White or nigger? Send the Mayor's Committee"....When the police dispatcher requested cars to respond to a fire call, an anonymous voice suggested that Mayor Stokes "go piss on it". Responses to other calls included: "Fuck that nigger Mayor".' (76) The other side of the coin is the unanimous finding of countless surveys of black opinion that (as the 1967 Presidential Commission on Law Enforcement put it) 'Negroes are substantially more hostile to the police than whites'. The complaints were not only about police abuse of blacks – 'Negroes also feel strongly about the need for police protection. This is not surprising, since a much greater proportion of Negroes than whites are the victims, as well as perpetrators of crime.' (77)

This is confirmed in a more recent National Crime Survey. Blacks were half as likely to rate police performance as 'good' than whites (24% compared to 47%), and twice as likely to rate it as 'poor' (19% compared to 9%). (78) But the main ways in which blacks thought police performance should be improved were the same as whites. The major complaint was of inadequate police protection: 18% of blacks wanted more policemen altogether, another 25% wanted more police of certain kinds, or at a certain place, another 11% wanted them to concentrate on serious crime, and 20% wanted them to be more responsive or prompt. Only 4% complained of discrimination, and 12% of discourtesy or poor community relations. (79) The black demand for more, not less, police is no surprise in view of the higher victimisation rates of blacks than whites. Altogether by the late 1970s it seems that a clear majority of black Americans had a positive image of the police, and complained of too little policing. On the other hand a larger minority than among whites are critical of the police. 'The heart of the police-community relations problem involves one segment of the black community. Patterns of police interaction with the black community are complex and do not affect all segments of the community in the same way.' (80) Hostility is concentrated among those low-income or unemployed young black males who are the special targets of heavy policing, while amongst other sections of the black community fear of criminal victimisation is linked with more favourable attitudes to the police.' James Baldwin's famous characterisation of the police in the ghetto as 'an occupying soldier in a bitterly hostile country' (81) is no longer as true as it was. Nevertheless the conditions of ghetto life are such that police-black contacts will be frequently conflicting and hostile. The 1969 National Commission on the Causes and Preventions of Violence in a study of Philadelphia found that 50% of black males had been arrested by the age of 18 (disregarding traffic violations), compared to 20% of white males, but 'these differences in urban violent crime rates are not, in fact, racial; they are primarily a result of conditions of life in the ghetto slum.' (82)

2. British Research Findings

Systematic research on the British police remains much less common than in the United Sates, despite a veritable explosion of it in recent years. But what there is suggests very similar patterns of police attitudes and practices as in the US, the obvious exception being the comparative absence of the deadly force issue.

(a) Police Attitudes

There is no survey data on the attitudes of the British police towards ethnic minorities. But all the major studies of the British police do indicate the prevalence of the kinds of hostile and prejudiced attitudes towards blacks which the American research reveals. Such suspicions and negative images of minorities long predate the growth of any particular police concern about a 'problem' of black crime. The overwhelming weight of the evidence suggests that police prejudice is not primarily the result of any individual peculiarities but a reflection of the racism prevalent in British society and the social groups from which the police are drawn, as well as the situations in which many police-black encounters occur (themselves the product of racism within Britain). In short, the problem is structural, rather than one of individual attitudes.

Maureen Cain's study of a city force in the early 1960s found that 'immigrants, in particular the coloured immigrants....were subject to stereotyping and abuse....The characteristics attributed to "niggers" or "nigs" were that they were "in the main....pimps and layabouts, living off what we pay in taxes." '(83) There was an expectation of black violence, leading to an observed reluctance to intervene in disputes concerning them, and possibly a self-fulfilling expectation of violent encounters. 'Coloured people, even more than other "roughs", were different, separate, incomprehensible. There was, therefore, no good reason for not being violent if the occasion arose.' (84) Blacks were seen as especially likely to be offenders (although there was no evidence of disproportionate involvement in crime), they 'were by definition permanently in the area of suspicion.' (85)

John Lambert's study of Birmingham in the late 1960s was the first to concentrate on the issues of 'Crime, Police and Race Relations'. (86) It was primarily an important analysis of crime rates, and will be considered later in this context. On the basis of his observations and discussions with police officers, Lambert arrives at an understanding of their attitudes which echoes Cain's and points to future problems. 'The social system which promotes widespread prejudice, because it involves policemen as citizens in a set of attitudes which cannot but affect their attitudes as policemen, also promotes barriers to effective policing....They must be kept in their place - controlled and contained, not allowed to infect the rest of society....Ignorance and fear and resentment of the coloured immigrant place him in an unfavourable light....Denied contact with the law-abiding majority, policemen are tempted to think of the whole immigrant community in these derogatory terms....The police share commonly and widely held views about coloured immigrants and the colour problem which are detrimental to good policing and which augur badly for an improvement in the general tenor of race relations.' (87)

My study of the British police in 1973-4 found that hostile and suspicious views of blacks were frequently offered quite spontaneously in the context of interviews concerning police work in general. (88) 23% of the sample volunteered adverse comments, while 35% in the central division which included St. Paul's did so. One uniform constable commented that:

> 'The police are trying to appear unbiassed in regard to race relations. But if you asked them you'd find 90% of the force are against coloured immigrants. They'd never want to do that research and come up with that sort of finding.' (89)

Other statements revolved around the themes of supposed black violence, criminality and disreputable behaviour:

> 'On our area we have colour problems. I get people coming into the office, we had a delegation the other week. Complaining about noisy parties. On our patch if they put on a party it'll last for 3 days! And not just a couple of people. You got hundreds in there, milling around. People ring up "Can you do something?" Well, you can't expect one policeman to walk into the middle of a hundred coloured people who are anti-police and turn the radio off. You'd have a dead policeman next thing you know. So I tell people "He's only a man in uniform, he's not Superman. Take the uniform off and I'm the same as you. I've got my fears". They expect you to have BATMAN written across your chest or something! I don't like being punched, but if there's fights you've go to break it up.' (Uniform constable)

> 'St. Paul's is a terrible place, shocking. What ever job you go to, you know you're going to have trouble. You're always on the look out for a knife or a fist or something. It's a drunken Irish labourer or someone. They're always fighting, at one another's necks. You've got Hungarians, Poles. And your local layabouts that mix in with them. Prostitutes. It's a right den of iniquity.' (Uniform constable)

> 'You get ghettoes of people of a particular race or colour who are completely anti-police. Here on this division we have the St. Paul's area, which is a ghetto of multi-nations and multi-colours, and a concentration of a lot of common lodging houses. Families on the very lowest income and employment bracket. They are a cause of a lot of the crime and vice in the city. The race aspect is so bad. You get so many coloured prisoners. I very rarely see a

coloured man who is pro-police because 99 out of 100 people I'm dealing with is alleged to have committed an offence. So I don't exercise a colour bar, but I must admit that if my daughter wanted to marry a coloured man, I would most certainly object. There's this large number of immigrants coming in, the pace has increased. The number of children in families is normally quite large, and though they go to our schools, as soon as they leave school they're back in their parents' way of life. The parents are not coming round to the English way of thinking. It will take a couple of generations before the situation improves. The danger is you get people who are fluent speakers, fine leaders. They've only to get up on a soap-box and start chatting, and there's hundreds round them. You get these little bunches and there's danger.' (Uniform sergeant)

One sergeant clearly anticipated the riots to come:

'The coloured community and their laws are slightly different out there. But they still live by them over here. We get these woundings regularly. When I first went out there, I could guarantee a fight 2 or 3 nights a week. I've been stoned and all. It doesn't reach the press. But I've had occasion to duck under a car to avoid what was coming, when we started being pelted. It made us quite nervous, and we always doubled up in cars. We'd get a crowd round us when we were just making a lawful arrest of somebody who'd done a nasty wounding job.'

Simon Holdaway's mid-70s participant observation of a large city force reveals a similar pattern. 'Blacks are viewed negatively: they are usually described in derogatory terms....Of course, these terms are not derived solely from the police world; a clear connection exists between the police and the broader society.' (90) Holdaway emphasises that these attitudes are rooted in the central values of the police occupational culture. 'Control having been established as central to that culture, the truculence attributed to blacks justifies the perceived necessity for continued vigilance and the use of all the available subcultural techniques of routine policing....it also provides opportunities for challenge, police activity and therefore enjoyment'. Holdaway refers to a planned visit to a new youth club for blacks which was thought to need 'supervision'. 'The inspector said, "Right, we'll go down there tonight and turn a few of them over; if they are shouting and mucking about, we will nick a few." A sergeant who had been out of the room entered, and one of the PCs said to him, "We've got permission to beat niggers tonight, sarge; have a few tonight, sarge." A dislike and distrust of blacks is certainly evident from this episode, but even more it indicates the pleasure afforded by a scuffle or fight – by action.' (91) As Holdaway sums up his observations, the characteristics attributed to blacks are: 'their dislike of the police; their presumed disorderliness and predisposition to crime; their violence; and their exploitation of their grievances....The view is certainly a negative one; it is prejudiced and deeply rooted in the officers' assumptions about their work.' (92)

The most systematic view of police relations with ethnic minorities in any English police force is the seminally important Policy Studies Institute research on 'Police and People in London'. The PSI found pervasive prejudice amongst police officers, but comparatively little translation of this into policing practice. This parallels the findings of the Black-Reiss study for the American Presidential Law Enforcement Commission. The reasons are basically those which Friedrich spelled out clearly in a review of the American work, namely that attitudes are constrained by organisational and situational pressures – 'the expression of personal feelings is muted or deflected into different channels.' (93)

The PSI researchers sum up their results thus: 'We find from our observational research that police officers tend to be hostile to black people in general terms, and certainly indulge in much racialist talk, but often have friendly and relaxed relations with individual black people in specific instances....Although there were variations in the extent of racial prejudice and racialist talk between different groups of officers and individuals and at different times (there was an increase at the time of the 1981 riots), these things are pervasive; they are, on the whole, expected, accepted and even fashionable. Senior officers seldom try to set a different tone (though they do on occasion) and there were some cases where they initiated racialist talk and kept it going. These attitudes are, to a large extent, a reflection of those in the wider society and especially in the social groups from which police officers are drawn, though they may be magnified within the closely-knit working groups within the Force.' (94)

The PSI findings about police practices will be considered below. Their description of the police cultural view of blacks echoes earlier findings. Racialist language, hostile views and abusive terms are common amongst police, even when they treat blacks with courtesy to their faces. (95) Blacks are stereotyped as criminal – one PC said: 'How does an experienced policeman decide who to stop? Well, the one that you stop is often wearing a woolly hat, he is dark in complexion, he has thick lips and he usually has dark fuzzy hair.' (96) They are wary of cases involving Asians, which are 'likely to be regarded as "weary".' (97) Blacks are seen as naturally prone to violence, hostile to the police and white society, animalistic and stupid. (98)

A similar conclusion was drawn by a Home Office Research Unit Study of the Leeds police. 'The police culture as a whole was fairly critical and unsympathetic towards minorities, particularly West Indians. This was illustrated in the language used to describe and refer to coloured people.' The same catalogue of pejorative images occurs as in the PSI study: 'West Indians were seen as lazy, easy going and simple people. The older ones were mostly Christian and law-abiding, and the real problems for the police came from the young....They were rude and disrespectful, shouting "Babylon" at police officers in the street and refusing to comply with police requests for order or information. They gathered in large crowds very quickly if one of them was questioned by a police officer. They held noisy parties which involved illegal liquor sales and an anti-social level of noise. If stopped for any vehicle check, West Indians became excited....Asians....were great liars when suspected of any wrong-doing and would only tell the police the truth as a last resort.' (99)

(b)   Police Practices

The American research, the PSI report, and the Home Office Study reported above all stress that the link between prejudice and discriminatory or abusive behaviour is far from straightforward. Evidence about police practices comes from two sources, direct observation of police work, and the analysis of the statistical pattern of recorded outcomes of police action. The findings from these two methods are somewhat contradictory with regard to the issue of discrimination.

(i)   Statistical Evidence

Analysis of the statistical pattern of police use of their powers of stop and search, arrest, and charging, as well as of complaints against the police suggest a clear pattern of discrimination. Blacks are more likely to be stopped, searched, arrested and proceeded against, more likely to make complaints against the police, and less likely to have them sustained than whites.

(1)   Street Stops

We have seen that this is a major source of black complaints against the police. Most, but not all, of the research suggests that blacks are indeed stopped disproportionately.

A 1980 Home Office study in Moss Side, Manchester found that West Indians were not stopped, search or arrested at a rate greater than whites (10% compared to 7% - a non statistically significant difference). Young black males were stopped in the same proportion as whites, but this was high for both - about one in three males aged 16-24 had been stopped, searched or arrested in the previous year. It was only in the 35-54 age-group that West Indians were more likely to be stopped at a significantly higher level (5% compared to 1%). Most of these stops were routine car-stops. (100)

The explanation of this lack of ethnic difference in stop and search rates for young people in Moss Side may well be found in Ann Brogden's 1978/9 study of Liverpool cases. Although not able to give quantitative evidence of discrimination, Brogden's interviews with a sample of youths who had been stopped showed that this was a frequent experience for inner city young males, both black and white. Almost all her sample (black and white alike) felt that blacks were stopped more often, and cited racist verbal abuse by the police. Her argument suggests that stop and search powers are a weapon for police control of the street, which will be used to order inner-city unemployed youth both black and white. (101)

Other research suggests that stop and search powers are used disproportionately against blacks, especially young blacks. A Home Office study of stops in 4 police stations (2 Metropolitan, 2 Provincial) found that 'at all four police stations studied, annual recorded stop rates for blacks were markedly higher than those for the population as a whole. Black males, aged 16-24, were likely to be stopped particularly frequently.' (102)

The Metropolitan Police evidence to Lord Scarman on stops in Lambeth found a similar disparity, with blacks twice as likely to be stopped as whites. (103) The British Crime Survey also found in its national sample that young black males had a higher chance of being stopped than other people. (104)

The PSI study shows the most striking evidence of disparity in stop rates. 'Young people, men and West Indians are far more likely to be stopped than others, and young West Indian males are much more likely to be stopped than any other group. The differences shown are enormous....In terms of the proportions stopped, the difference between West Indians and white people is not very striking (24% for West Indians, 17% for white people); but the mean number of stops is nearly 3 times as high among West Indians as among white people, because West Indians who are stopped at all tend to be stopped repeatedly. Also, the proportion of people who have been stopped when on foot is nearly 4 times as high for West Indians as for white people. Asians are much less likely to be stopped than white people (or, of course, West Indians). Age, sex and ethnic group in combination have an overwhelming effect on the likelihood of being stopped. Taking the two extreme groups, we find that 63% of West Indian men aged 15-24 have been stopped, compared with none of the Asian women aged 45 or over....Age is a more important factor than the ethnic group, but differences between the ethnic groups remain when the comparison is restricted to men or women within a particular age group. Among men aged 15-24, the proportion stopped is 63% for West Indians, 44% for whites and 18% for Asians. Those young West Indian males who have been stopped at all over the past 12 months have been stopped 4 times on average, compared to 2½ times for whites.' (105)

The 1981 Home Office study of stops in the Metropolitan Police area found that the annual recorded stop rate in a district was significantly related to the percentage of the population which was black. Both these rates were inter-related with the recorded crime rate, i.e. high crime rate areas were those with disproportionate black populations and high stop rates. (106) The PSI study found, however, that Asians or West Indians in areas of high ethnic concentration were no more likely to be stopped than those in areas with low ethnic populations. Furthermore those stopped in low ethnic concentration areas were less likely to say they were given a reason, and were more likely to be disgruntled about it. (107) This finding can be made sense of in the light of the remarks quoted in the observational volume indicating that blacks in areas of low ethnic concentration would be more likely to be perceived as suspicious. (108)

(2)   Arrest

Arrest rates are higher for blacks than whites or Asians in all offence categories, according to the most systematic analysis, a Home Office study of the 1975 Metropolitan Police statistics. (109) There has been a lengthy, often bitter, debate about the interpretation of this. The Home Office researchers' own analysis shows that when the varying age profiles of the different ethnic groups are controlled for, blacks are mainly over-represented in 4 categories: assault, robbery, 'other violent theft', and 'other indictable offences'. (110) Asians are under-represented in all offence categories except assault, when their age structure is allowed for. (111)

Some further part of the difference is accounted for by indices of socio-economic deprivation such as rates of unemployment and home-ownership. (112) The authors conclude that part of the balance of the higher black arrest rate is the product of more offending behaviour, and buttress this with evidence about victims' identifications of the race of their attacker. An incalculable part of the disproportionate black arrest rate is a function of what they call 'extrinsic' factors i.e. greater frequenting of the streets, greater visibility, or blacks being more likely to arouse the suspicions of the police. Evidence for the significance of police stereotyping is adduced from the fact that blacks are most heavily arrested for two offences which allow the greatest scope for selective perception by police officers: 'other violent theft', and 'sus' - for which the black arrest rate was 14 or 15 times the white. But they argue it is implausible that police discrimination could account for all of the ethnic imbalance in arrests. On the hypothesis, for example, that black and white crime rates were identical and the arrest imbalance was entirely due to 'mistaken' arrests of blacks, then 76% of all black arrests would have to be

166

'mistaken'. (113)   Overall the authors conclude that the evidence suggests both that blacks are disproportionately involved in recorded street crime and that they are more liable to be picked up by the police, especially for offences giving the police extensive discretionary leeway like 'sus'. How much weight is to be given to either factor cannot be ascertained at present. (114)

Both the PSI surveys of the public and of the police show a disproportionate arrest rate for blacks compared to whites (and a fortiori Asians). (115)   This difference is confined to the 15-24 age group; the older generation of West Indians are not more likely to be arrested than whites.   The PSI analysis is similar to the Home Office's: the disproportionate black arrest rate is partly a consequence of more involvement in crime of certain kinds, especially theft from the person, (as the PSI victim identifications of offenders suggests), but partly a product of the demographic and socio-economic characteristics of the black population, and of police (and victim) stereotyping. (116)

John Lea and Jock Young, in a recent series of articles and an important book aimed at developing a new 'socialist realist' analysis of crime, have accepted the validity of the Home Office (and by implication the PSI) analysis. (117)   They explain the disproportionate black arrest rate as the consequence of two mutually reinforcing processes: 'An ethnic minority that is oppressed by racial discrimination and the denial of equal opportunities may, if the cultural conditions are there - as was the case in the West Indian much more than the Asian community - develop an even higher crime rate....But whatever the precise balance of age, discrimination etc., there was a real rise in crime among the West Indian population, and the police, in responding to it, were not responding simply to figments of their imagination.   But, in the second place, the police responded readily. Racial prejudice against black people, always present among a substantial part of the police force as in other sections of British society, was used as a specific explanatory hypothesis concerning a particular type of crime ("Street crime" or "mugging")....Thirdly, it is at this stage that the two processes reinforce each other: the increased rate of black crime and police predisposition to associate blacks with crime become part of a vicious circle.' (118)

Lea and Young have been subject to a torrent of criticism from writers, mainly associated with the Institute of Race Relations, accusing them of capitulating to 'the weight of racist logic' and of lending 'sociological credibility to police racism'. (119)   In this plethora of vituperative criticism there is no serious attempt at a rebuttal of Lea and Young's argument. Any such engagement with the issue of explaining the black arrest rate as the outcome of anything but a protean and all-pervasive racism is dismissed as 'empiricist haggling over official crime statistics'. (120)   But this sort of characterisation of all police and all aspects of policing as equally and undistinguishably racist precludes any serious analysis of how and why policing changes, and of separating out potentially positive developments within police strategy and thinking. The state, and its coercive apparatus the police, are blanketed together as a monolithic reflex of the racist logic of capital.

Against this position Lea and Young mount several powerful arguments, to which there has not been any specific response. Firstly, for many years during which (as seen in earlier sections) there was clear evidence of widespread prejudice in the police force, official arrest statistics (which probably exaggerate black involvement in crime) did not depict blacks as arrested disproportionately. This was the clear conclusion of Lambert's study of Birmingham crime statistics in the late 1960s, and of the police evidence to the House of Commons Select Committee on Race Relations in 1971-2. (121) But by the time of the 1976-7 Commons Select Committee on Race Relations and Immigration the police were claiming that the position had changed, and there was a disproportionately high rate of young black crime. As Lea and Young put it, if high black crime rates are 'simply the product of police prejudice, then to explain the change in the police position between 1971 and 1976 we have to engage in some rather dubious hypothesising. Either the police were almost entirely free of prejudice prior to 1971 and rapidly became prejudiced during the 1970s, which is rather unlikely, or their prejudice led them, in some strange way, to engage in a form of positive discrimination prior to 1971.' (122)

Apart from the implausibility of the changing black arrest pattern in the 1970s being the result of a sudden shift in police thinking, Lea and Young further rightly stress that it would be strange if the life circumstances of young blacks did not produce some increase in offences. 'The notion that increasing youth unemployment, coupled with a high young population in the black community, and the effects of massive, well-documented, racial discrimination and the denial of legitimate opportunity, did not result in a rising rate of real offences is hardly credible. If these sorts of deprivations are not crucial factors leading to increasing crime rates then what are?' (123)

All this is not to deny that 'moral panics' may be created by the practices of the police, the judicial apparatus and the media, as shown, for example, by the Centre for Contemporary Cultural Studies. Their book 'Policing the Crisis' gives a detailed account of the 'mugging' scare of 1972-3, and how it was constructed by police, judiciary and media. (124) However, there can be little doubt that during the 1970s 'mugging' i.e. robberies involving street attacks on strangers, became more prevalent and a not insignificant risk for vulnerable categories of people in some areas (although not for the population overall), and that black over-- representation in arrests for this cannot be the product exclusively of police policy or prejudice. (125)

'Policing the Crisis', for all its emphasis on the moral panic associated with 'mugging' as a symbol of increasing state and societal authoritarianism, did not deny its reality. 'The position of black labour, subordinated by the processes of capital, is deteriorating and will deteriorate more rapidly, according to its own specific logic. Crime is one perfectly predictable and quite comprehensible consequence of this process - as certain a consequence of how the structures work, however 'unintended', as the fact that night follows day....The 'so-called rising black crime rate', which presents a problem of containment and control for the system, presents a problem for black people too. It is the problem of how to prevent a sizeable section of the class from being more or less permanently criminalised....It is perfectly clear that crime, as such, contains no solution to the problem as it confronts the black worker. There are many kinds of crime which, though arising from social and economic exploitation, represent, in the last result, nothing but a symbiotic adaptation to deprivation. Crime, as such, is not a political act, especially where the vast number of the victims are people whose class position is hardly distinguishable from that of the criminals.' (126)

It seems clear that the disproportionate black arrest rate is the product of black deprivation, police stereotyping and the process by which each of these factors amplifies the other. To recognise that the police statistics have some basis in a reality of black crime is important because it underlines the point that more needs to change than just setting straight mistaken police stereotypes or prejudices. At the same time it is undeniable that the black crime statistics can be used in specific political contexts as a weapon against reform, as seemed to happen with the 1982 Met. release of figures giving the breakdown of street crimes committed by blacks and whites. This was widely seen as an attempt to 'mug' Scarman.

(3)   Charging And Prosecution

There is a body of evidence suggesting that police discrimination in arrests is augmented by their further decisions as to whether or not to charge and prosecute arrested suspects. M. Cain and S. Sadigh observed 269 cases in a South London magistrates' court during 1978/9. They found that 'West Indians....appear before the court charged with victimless crimes, as a result, that is, of pro-active policing, far more frequently than white defendants. 46.6% of black defendants were charged with motoring offences or 'public order' offences like 'sus' or obstruction, which are the product of pro-active policing, compared with 30.1% of whites'. (128) However, it should be pointed out, (although the authors do not note this) that according to their data blacks are also disproportionately charged with offences against the person (20.7% of black compared to 0.9% white defendants), while the largest single offence category with which blacks are charged is property offences (31%, although this accounts for 54.7% of all whites charged). (129) In other words blacks are also disproportionately charged for offences which do not result from pro-active policing.

The most systematic evidence of police discrimination comes from Landau's two studies of the processing of juvenile offenders by the Metropolitan Police. The first concentrated on decisions by station officers about whether to charge offenders immediately or refer them to the juvenile bureau. (130) There was no difference in the chances of black or white theft suspects being charged immediately, while blacks were slightly less likely to be charged for auto-crime. But much more significant differences were found for crimes of violence, burglary and 'public disorder' offences. Holding constant the legally relevant variables of offence type and previous criminal record, blacks were much more likely to be charged immediately rather than being referred to the juvenile bureau. Landau suggests, however, that part of this apparently 'pure' discrimination may be the consequence of interactional factors like non-co-operativeness of black suspects, which cannot be discovered from the statistical record.

Landau's later study examined the decisions of the juvenile bureau itself about whether to charge or caution those referred to it. (131) He notes that given the assumption that the earlier police decision would have screened-out the 'worst' cases it could be expected a priori that more people would be cautioned in those categories which are treated more harshly at the earlier stage i.e. there would be an inverse relation between decision-making at the two stages. In fact, this only occurs for traffic and auto offences, where blacks are more likely to be referred to the bureau, but are then more likely to be charged than cautioned. For the categories of 'crimes of violence' and 'public order' offences blacks are more likely to be treated harshly at both stages: they are less likely to be referred to the bureau, and less likely to be cautioned by it, holding constant the nature of the offence and past record. This difference cannot be accounted for by interactional factors at the second stage of bureau decision-making. But it could partly be accounted for by a lesser likelihood that cases involving blacks satisfied the legal preconditions for the cautioning process: an admission of guilt, and the consent of the victim. Furthermore, black juveniles were more likely to have those social background characteristics which lead the bureau to consider a juvenile a 'bad risk' for cautioning: being a 'latch-key' child, coming from a single-parent or disrupted family, a larger family, or having an unemployed father. The crucial determinant is thus not blackness per se, but the way that this invokes a whole set of typifications of 'bad risks' for cautioning and being a suitable case for prosecution.

(4)   Complaints Against The Police

Not surprisingly in view of the pattern of discrimination in the use of police powers, blacks are more likely to make formal complaints, but less likely to have these upheld.

Box and Russell's important study of the characteristics of complainants which made them more likely to be 'discredited' found too few complaints from blacks in its sample (4) to analyse statistically, although none was substantiated. But they anticipated that research in force areas with larger ethnic minority populations would show race to be a 'discrediting factor'. (132)

The Home Office 1981 study of 'Ethnic Minorities, Crime and Policing' in Moss Side did not clearly confirm this. (133) It found that 16% of West Indians but only 8% of whites had 'ever wished to complain', but none had used the formal complaints procedure. A much higher proportion of West Indian complaints were highly generalised, and the proportion of blacks and whites with specific personal complaints was identical.

The most comprehensive analysis is a 1981 Home Office study of complaints against the Metropolitan Police during the 1970s. (135) This showed conclusively that blacks (especially young ones) and older Asians made proportionately more complaints than whites. The proportion of complaints from blacks and Asians went up throughout the 70s, though this is largely accounted for by the increase in black population. Blacks are more likely to make serious complaints, especially of assault. Blacks and Asians were less likely to have their complaints substantiated (1.3% of complaints compared to 3.1% of white complaints substantiated in 1979). Blacks were more likely to be involved in trouble with the police at the time of the complaint : a higher proportion of them were under arrest, or had previous records, and police were more likely to allege suspect's provocation as a justification (i.e. assault or violent struggling) in the cases of black complaints of assault by the police. As less complaints of assault or of people under arrest or with previous records are substantiated, the evidence suggests that blacks are less likely to have their complaints substantiated because they have the general characteristics of 'discreditability'. This data also confirms the suspicions of the Police Complaints Board in its 1980 Triennial Review that assault allegations may not be investigated as thoroughly as less serious complaints.

The PSI study found in its survey of Londoners that West Indians said they would be less likely to make a formal complaint if they had a grievance against a police officer (79% compared with 90% of whites and 88% of Asians). (135) This suggests that the ethnic disparity in complaints rates understates the difference in grievances.

(ii)   Observational Research

There is not much observational work on the British police which touches on relations with ethnic minorities. But what there is does not confirm the clear discriminatory pattern suggested by the quantitative evidence. As with the American work, British observational studies suggest that police handling of blacks is largely to be explained by situational (where the encounter occurs, what sparked it, complainants' wishes etc.) and interactional variables (i.e. co-operativeness of citizens), rather than any observable element of discrimination.

Holdaway argues (on the basis of several years experience and research as a serving police officer) that 'the quality, the techniques of policing blacks, are essentially the same as those used to police the white population. The problem therefore is that of normal policing not one of police/race relations'. (136) He illustrates this with reference to a study of the establishment of a special crime squad to deal with a perceived rise of 'mugging' and pickpocketing' by blacks. (137) 'At every point of the arrest and questioning process, the same techniques were applicable to suspects, whether black or white'. The values involved in the policing of blacks are the basic police subcultural ones of action, control, excitement and 'keeping their figures up'. (138) But as Holdaway implies, if through mutually suspicious stereotyping and the conditions of black life black suspects are more frequently subject to 'the techniques of normal policing', the quantitative difference could make for a qualitatively different character in police-black relations. (139)

The most systematic observational evidence is that presented by the PSI study. (140) As already indicated despite discovering abusive racist rhetoric to be pervasive within the force, they did not find this translated into practice in normal encounters. 'Accompanying these officers as they went about their work we found that their relations with black and brown people were often relaxed or friendly....Even in the 6 months preceding the riots and in some of the areas where riots later broke out, most encounters between police officers and black people were fairly relaxed'. (141) The problem is that it is usually not possible to observe a 'pure' element of discrimination, over and above other aspects of the encounter. As the researchers put it: 'In most cases it would be difficult to identify aspects of police behaviour that were clearly a response to the race of the people involved'. (142) They do discuss in detail three cases where the observer felt that the police response was affected by considerations of race. 'In particular' they say 'it seems significant that some of the worst police behaviour we have observed....was towards black suspects'. (143) In one case a young black man was found on the stairs of a block of flats where a WPC had seen someone duck behind an area wall. The youth was roughly questioned and searched, and a knife found on him, for which he was charged with carrying an offensive weapon, although he claimed it was used in his work. Altogether the police behaviour observed was oppressive and irregular but the officers 'made no reference to Delroy's colour, and there is no means of knowing whether they would have treated a white young man in the same way'. (144)

An even worse case was the arrest and questioning of 3 black teenagers who very loosely fitted the description given by a mugging victim. They were interrogated roughly, abusively, threateningly, and above all, incompetently, by a series of uniform and detective officers. In the end the boys were exonerated by the victim who did not identify any of them. Far from receiving an apology they were sent away with abusive warnings, but the official record was written up as 'apologies tendered'. The observer formed the definite (but ultimately not provable) verdict that the suspects were singled out for harsh treatment because of the officers' concern about black crime and their hostility to blacks. (145)

On the other hand a more competent police inspector produced an outcome which seems to be a model of good police work in a racially sensitive situation. It involved a conflict between some black men in a lorry outside a club who were accused by a crowd of blacks from the club of taking a sound system and record box. The inspector very delicately, skilfully and firmly achieved the cooling down of the sort of tension that could lead to mass disorder if provocatively policed. In the end the sound system and records were given back, no arrests were made, racist abuse of an Asian in the crowd by the blacks on the lorry was firmly suppressed, and an attempt by the men on the lorry to unite the crowd against the police by blaming the man from the club for calling the 'pigs....they're a load of Nazis' was averted. This was a fine example of Scarman's elevation of 'the maintenance of public tranquillity' over 'law enforcement' in action. (146)

The difficulties of discerning discrimination in a welter of other processes is illustrated by another example (although the PSI report does not cite it in this context). Two officers answered a call to a house where a Nigerian man (baby-sitting for a Nigerian couple) complained of a milk bottle thrown through the window. In an adjacent garden they found five young white teenagers, two wearing NF symbols. Throughout the handling of this investigation, and a subsequent call-back to a later incident after the couple had returned home, the officers refused to take seriously the possibility of a racist element in the attack. They handled the boys more sympathetically than the complainants, never treating them as serious suspects but suggesting that the blacks might try to frame them. The officers made abusive racial remarks to each other about the complainants. Nevertheless the observer felt the main trigger for the officers' lack of sympathy with the complainants was not their manifest racial prejudice, but the 'pompous and humourless' way the babysitter had responded to the officers' opening conversational gambits. (147)

Both the statistical and the observational evidence concur in suggesting that in so far as there is apparent discrimination in the statistical pattern of use of police powers, this is not the outcome for the most part of a separable element of 'pure' police discrimination. The basic source is the character of the situations in which police-black encounters often occur, and the way the mutual backcloth of suspicion and hostility leads to a spiral of conflicting interaction. I shall now review the evidence for the last element in this, black hostility towards the police, which (like police prejudice) is both a product and cause of conflict.

(iii)   Black Attitudes

Most surveys of public opinion in the last decade have found blacks (especially young males in inner cities) to be more hostile to the police than other groups, replicating the American pattern. (148) As the PSI study gives the most detailed analysis of minority attitudes, I will concentrate on its findings. Their results show that West Indians, especially young ones, are far more critical of police conduct than white or Asian people. 'The lack of confidence in the police among young West Indians can be described as disastrous'. (149) They are far more likely to believe the police regularly engage in abuse of powers and excessive force, and that they fabricate evidence. 68% of West Indians, and 55% of Asians, but only 39% of whites feel the police do not treat all groups equally.

On the other hand, 'these hostile views by no means amount to a complete rejection of the system'. (150) West Indians are just as likely to report victimisation incidents to the police as whites. Even most young West Indians say they could co-operate with the police in various circumstances, though less so than other groups, and there is a marked reluctance to be prepared to appear in court as a witness. Although young blacks are less likely than other groups to want an increase in the number of police on partrol, only ¼ of them think there are too many police in their area. Broadly the ethnic minorities share the same view of policing priorities as whites, with a somewhat greater relative concern about racist attacks rather than street robberies compared to whites – but the majority of blacks also regard the latter as a top policing priority. The greatest gulf is not so much between blacks and whites, as between the young, and especially the older people. Young blacks are also the group that is most subject to the use of police powers. But the survey suggests that negative attitudes do not result from the handling of specific encounters, as blacks who are stopped, searched, or arrested are no more likely to say this was unreasonable or they were badly treated than white people are. The hostility may partly result from the large number of negative contacts with the police which young blacks experience, or the lower proportion of positive encounters compared with whites. But the ultimate source of hostility was not specific personal encounters with the police. It was that the police were 'the most obvious symbol and representative of an oppressive white authority'. (151) The police stood in for a society in which young blacks justifiably saw themselves as deprived and discriminated against on the grounds of their blackness.

(c)   Sources Of Police Attitudes

In the same way as black attitudes towards the police are more a reflection of their overall social position rather than the outcome of specific encounters, police attitudes are better understood as the consequence of their social background and present function than of peculiar individual personality patterns. Until recently the consensus of sociological and psychological research, here and in the US, would have confirmed this. (152) It was accepted by most researchers that, contrary to popular belief, recruits did not have particularly sadistic or authoritarian personalities. Rather they shared the values of the social groups from which they were drawn, predominantly the lower-middle and respectable working-class, which constitute the bulk of society. This is, of course, a double-edged finding, for while police recruits may not be more authoritarian than the general population, the 'normal' degree of authoritarianism is disturbing in an occupation which wields considerable power over minorities. While police officers may not be psychologically distinctive, all studies have concurred in representing a police subculture, (developed as a response to such elements of the police role as the exertion of authority in a context of potential danger), which emphasises suspiciousness, toughness, action, solidarity, and is basically conservative. (153) The conceptions of ethnic minorities which we have already outlined are a part of this.

A recent, much publicised article by Colman and Gorman (which influenced Lord Scarman) has challenged this orthodoxy. (154) They administered several psychological tests intended to assess dogmatism, conservatism and authoritarianism, as well as specific views on some controversial questions including aspects of race relations, to three samples: a group of 48 police recruits at the beginning and end of basic training; 36 probationer constables with an average of 20 months' experience; and a control group of 30 civilians supposedly matched to the police groups in socio-economic status. Their basic findings were that 'the police force attracts conservative and authoritarian personalities, that basic training has a temporarily liberalising effect, and that continued police service results in increasingly illiberal/intolerant attitudes towards coloured immigration'. (154) Their results have been subject to severe criticism on methodological grounds, but they have defended themselves on most of the points of detail. (155) Probably the most important criticism is that made by A.J.P. Butler, who has conducted similar research of his own. Butler stresses (what is already indicated in the Colman-Gorman paper) that the control groups had a higher average level of education, which could be at least part of the explanation for the more 'authoritarian' police recruit attitudes. A more substantive point made by some of Butler's own research is that his sample of police recruits did not seem to attract individuals with radically distinct value systems compared to a matched civilian control group. (156) This shows up the importance of Colman and Gorman's own caveat about their data: 'Any attempt to generalise these results to other areas of the UK or to other countries is....unsafe'. (157) Butler finds that training has little or no effect on the liberality of attitudes, but the 'reality shock' of police work is associated with an increase in prejudice, particularly against West Indians (although this declined somewhat with age). Butler also enters a welcome warning about discussions of prejudice as a simplistic blanket notion, as the views of officers towards, for example, West Indians and Asians differed, results were sensitive to the particular instruments used, and overall scores conceal important differences with regard to specific items. What Colman and Gorman's research does reveal is that (although not necessarily sharply distinctive from the population norm) the police recruits did manifest very hostile attitudes to ethnic minorities, as their quotes from the open ended responses clearly demonstrate. (158) On the question whether these views are indications of a distinctive authoritarianism it is still necessary to be agnostic. It does seem to be agreed, however, that these attitudes are accentuated with work experience, after a possible temporary liberalising effect of training. (159)

Overall, it is both necessary and sufficient to explain the police outlook on ethnic minorities (and other issues) by the police function, and the circumstances of police work, rather than peculiarities of initial individual personality. Even if, as Colman and Gorman imply, at some times and places distinctive personality types are attracted to policing, it would still be necessary to analyse the nature of police work as the determinant of the attraction.

D. Current Reforms And The Police Act

What is it about policing that tends to generate hostility between police and ethnic minorities? In order to assess the current plethora of post-Scarman initiatives, and the Police Act, it is necessary to distil some basic points from the above evidence. As previously argued, the crucial problem is not the individual character of police recruits (even if they are exceptionally authoritarian and prejudiced at the outset). If police recruits are authoritarian then they are attracted to police work because of its character rather than creating its character. If they are not especially prejudiced at the outset, then the evidence on the impact of the experience of policing suggests they become so. Either way we are forced to consider what it is in the character of police-ethnic minority interaction that generates conflict, which, of course, may be exacerbated by the effects of prior police prejudice (or minority prejudice against police).

The basic source of what often becomes a vicious cycle of spiralling conflict is the effects of societal and institutionalised racism. This forces discriminated-against ethnic minorities to acquire those characteristics upon which 'normal' policing bears down most heavily: (i) As Lambert showed, the pattern of inequalities in housing forces ethnic minorities to live in those inner-city areas which are high crime, low social amenity areas. Even if they do not have high rates of offending, a sort of psychological 'ecological fallacy' leads to negative police stereotyping. (ii) A second factor is that an immigrant population is likely to be a relatively youthful one. (iii) Inequalities in employment opportunities lead to disproportionate ethnic minority unemployment rates, and over-concentration on casual, unskilled, insecure employment. In conditions of recession all this is vastly exacerbated.

All these structural processes are likely to mean that ethnic minorities figure disproportionately in the young 'street' population which has always been the prime focus of police 'order maintenance' work. They may also become involved in specific kinds of street crime, for reasons which have already been considered. At the same time, the relative powerlessness of ethnic minorities means that the police will be less constrained and inhibited in dealing with them. In times of economic crisis and competition for jobs and other resources, the majority group (especially the white working-class) might indeed benefit from the effects of over-policing of blacks, because black stigmatisation as criminal, the acquisition of criminal records, reduces their competitiveness. (160)   For all these reasons, ethnic minorities are especially likely to become 'police property': a category of people over whom 'the dominant powers of society....leave the problems of social control....to the police'. (161)

These structural aspects of the situation of ethnic minorities provide the hard-core of conflict. But they are accentuated by cultural factors. Police prejudice, reflecting that which is prevalent in society, can exacerbate the handling of situations through verbal and other abuse etc. Culture-clash in the form of problems of communication can make even the normally uncontroversial 'service' of police work problematic. Some aspects of minority culture may be deviant from the point of view of the majority culture.   Finally, once conflicts become common, a vicious cycle develops whereby police officers and ethnic minorities approach encounters warily, with pre-existing hostility and suspiciousness, and interact in ways which lead to further tension.

The argument that police conflict with ethnic minorities is rooted in structural factors, (the consequences of the systematic racism to which minorities are subject, and the order-maintenance function of the police), might appear to hold out no hope of change. In fact, however, the American experience of the development of police-black relations since the riots suggests the reverse.   The quality of police-black relations can get better, even if the basic economic and social plight of blacks does not.   This is demonstrated by a very interesting paper by Lawrence Sherman reviewing the American experience. (162) Sherman suggests that police-black relations in American cities have improved, primarily due to changes in police behaviour. The most visible aspect is the adoption of tighter shooting policies in several cities which have successfully reduced the rate of killing of citizens, although not necessarily the proportion of blacks within the lower rates. But the overall reduction obviously means a lower absolute rate of shootings of blacks, and the statistical disparity is not immediately apparent in everyday life. More generally, observational studies suggest the police in many cities are better able to defuse conflict without the sort of behaviour that in the 60s sparked off so many of the riots. According to recent studies the statistical disparity in black over white arrest rates remains, but this (like the shooting disparity) is not as visible as the character of everyday encounter.

Sherman argues that changes in police personnel: more black police, more and better training, encouraging higher education for police - what he calls 'people' factors - were not crucial in the change (although they were recommended by all the Presidential Commissions, as by Scarman). The evidence suggests that black police officers do not behave less toughly towards blacks than white officers do. Indeed they may behave more toughly.   The Black-Reiss study found for example that black officers made more arrests than whites, patrolled more aggressively and were equally likely to use excessive force. (163)   Similar points were found by Alex's study of black patrolmen. (164)   Studies of police shootings show that black officers are twice as likely as white officers to shoot, but this is largely accounted for by their disproportionate allocation to high-crime areas. All this is not to say that more black police recruitment is not desirable, but only that as individuals black officers do not seem to behave differently in relation to use of legal powers and force. Increasing the proportion of black officers may alter the overall ethos in a department in less clearly measurable ways. For example, it may reduce the common use of racist terms. The organisation of black police unions in the US has been an important countervailing influence to the reactionary policy demands of white police unions. (165) A higher proportion of black police may reduce the internal solidarity which guards police abuse. (166) While recruiting more black police may be beneficial in these ways, the situational pressures seem to result in black officers acting in the same operational manner as white ones, which itself bolsters the argument that individual prejudice is not the major problem. The evidence on the impact of more training and higher education is similar. (167) They have no discernible consequence for the character of individual police conduct, although changing the proportion of police officers with higher education may affect the ethos of the organisation.

Sherman argues that effective changes were brought about by 'system' not 'people' changes. The crucial source of change was the rise of black political power. Between 1968 and 1980, for example, the number of black elected officials increased ten times over. Many of the internal policy changes, for example, over shootings, occurred in cities with black mayors. Internal discipline and restrictions on discretion increased, not only due to new political leadership, but because the Supreme Court expanded citizen rights to sue police departments, or police chiefs personally, for misconduct of their officers if it could be shown to result from organisational custom or practice. But the basic change, encapsulating all the separate 'people' and 'system' factors, has been 'a change in the very philosophy of police work, away from a rigidly mechanistic conception of enforcement of every law to a more malleable conception of keeping the peace'. (168)

It is this same basic shift which Lord Scarman recommends as the core of his proposals. (169) The more specific proposals of his Report do incorporate many of the features which Sherman reviews as contributing to the American change: the 'people' factors most obviously, but also tightening discipline in relation to racially prejudiced or discriminatory behaviour, increasing consultation, increasing accountability through lay station visitors, more independent investigation of serious complaints, narrowing the scope of highly discretionary powers. In the absence of the possibility of black political control as in US cities, Scarman's recommendations are the nearest it might be possible to get in terms of a clear signal to police forces of the need for reform. Certainly the Newman strategy in London, and similar initiatives elsewhere, echo many elements of Scarman's recommendations, and these are further encouraged by the current HM Chief Inspector of Constabulary, Lawrence Byford.

The new policing initiatives, and the more general philosophy of 'community policing' advocated by John Alderson, have been viewed with suspicion by many critics, who see them as an attempt to increase 'surveillance and control of communities by the police'. (170) One aspect of the criticism seems to me to be contradictory, with reference to the specific issue of police-black relations. A major complaint has been the harassment of black youth through stop and search tactics involving a large number of searches of people who are innocent of any offence. The basic source of this is the stereotyping of all blacks because of the belief (partly sustained by arrest statistics) that blacks are more likely to be involved in offending. One intended result of the new police strategy is to improve information thus allowing officers to form judgements as to what constitutes 'reasonable suspicion' on grounds more specific than race. It seems contradictory to condemn (rightly) essentially random searches, but also to condemn tactics intended to reduce random harassment by 'targetting'. Furthermore, as the new police strategy is predicated on the concern to restore police legitimacy, it does involve a genuine attempt to reduce the sorts of gross abuse which have been the source of so much bitterness (and undermining of police authority). There are certainly some signs that police-black relations are improving in areas like Brixton, and that the police are becoming more skilled at cooling-down potential confrontations. (171) The basic ground of much criticism is that the new initiatives rest on consultation and community liaison rather than democratic accountability. However, they do offer the prospect of intervening in policing at the crucial lower-levels of the organisation, which nominal political control of policy-making would leave untouched. (172)

Lea and Young, after reviewing what they see as some welcome aspects of the Newman plan, then warn that this 'is only one aspect of the post-Scarman developments in police matters. The other is the Police and Criminal Evidence Act'. (173) Clearly many aspects of the Act involve dangers of the heightened harassment of ethnic minorities, most obviously the expanded powers of stop and search and arrest. It is already clear from the evidence reviewed that these powers are used disproportionately against black people. Extending these powers in itself would enhance the likelihood that they would be used in a discriminatory way. But whether this will be the effect in practice depends on a judgement of the adequacy of the 'safeguards' introduced by the Act, and the overall context. (174) The draft code of practice on stop and search which was published on 20 July specifically states; 'Young blacks should not be stopped and searched on the basis that statistics show that they have a higher than average chance of being involved in arrests for certain types of offences'. (175) But it is not clear what sanctions, if any, will apply to this code. However, the Act will come into force in a context in which, as already suggested, Scarmania still rules in the police, and there is an over-riding concern with securing legitimacy and acceptance. The internal management and policy changes introduced by Newman (and in line with the PSI recommendations) seek to direct the use of police powers in a more finely tuned, less inaccurately discriminatory way. What is important is to ensure that this is what happens in practice. All possible opportunities must be seized to scrutinise the Act's impact on minorities, using what accountability channels are available. For example, the consultative committees introduced by the Act, and the existing powers of police authorities, should be invoked to try and collect data on the use of stop and search and arrest powers (given that the reasons will now be recorded) and monitor whether they seem to be used in a racially discriminatory way.

It is to be hoped that Sir Kenneth Newman remembers what he said in 1973 when he was just plain 'Mr' and head of the Police Community Relations Branch: 'We have to thank the West Indians for doing us a favour in asking us to think again about our authority'. (176)

NOTES

1. M. Winters and J. Hatch: 'Colour Persecution on Tyneside', Pan-Africa, Feb. 1947. Reprinted in Race and Class, Autumn 1982, pp.184-8.
2. J. Hunte: Nigger Hunting in England?, London Region of the West Indian Standing Conference, 1966.
3. Quoted in D. Humphry: Police Power and Black People, London: Panther 1972, p.13.
4. S. Fenton: 'Riots Violence and Race in American Society', Bristol University Sociology Dept., 1981. See also S. Field and P. Southgate: Public Disorder, Home Office Research Study 72, 1982, which gives a similar analysis.
5. J. A. Lee: 'Some Structural Aspects of Police Deviance in Relations with Minority Groups', in C. D. Shearing (ed.): – Organisational Police Deviance, Toronto: Butterworths, 1981, pp.49-82.
6. M. Banton: 'Policies for Police – Minority Relations' in C. Fried (ed.): Minorities Community and Identity, Berlin; Dahlem Konferenzen, 1983, pp.299-313.
7. M. Punch: Policing the Inner City, London: MacMillan, 1979.
8. P. R. Wilson: 'Police-Ethnic Relations in Australia', New Community, Summer 1974, pp.220-6; Acord (Auckland Committee Against Racism and Discrimination: A Disaster in Community Relations, Auckland, Wanganui Press, 1975.
9. J. Edmond-Smith: 'Police forces in France', New Community, Summer 1974, pp.227-233.
10. S. Fenton, op.cit., p.17.
11. These cases are discussed in detail in A. M. Platt: The Politics of Riot Commissions, New York: Collier-Macmillan, 1971. See also: D. L. Horowitz: 'Racial Violence in the U.S.' in N. Glazer and K. Young (eds.): Ethnic Pluralism and Public Policy, London: Heinemann, 1983, pp.187-211, for an excellent summary.
12. ibid., p.69.
13. J. White: 'The summer riots of 1919', in Race and Riots' 81, A New Society Social Studies Reader, p.13. (originally in New Society 13.8.81.).
14. These, together with the 1919 riots, are documented and analysed in detail in H. Joshua, T. Wallace and H. Booth: To Ride the Storm, London: Heinemann, 1983, Part 1.
15. A. H. Richmond: Colour Prejudice in Britain: A Study of West Indian Workers in Liverpool 1941-51, London: Routledge and Kegan Paul, p.103.
16. Joshua, Wallace and Booth, op.cit., p.39.
17. A. I. Waskow: From Race Riot to Sit-In: 1919 and the 1960s, New York: Doubleday Anchor, 1966, p.210.
18. Report of the National Advisory Commission on Civil Disorders, New York: Bantam, 1968, p.120.
19. ibid., p.206.
20. D. L. Horowitz: 'Racial Violence in the United States', op.cit., p.208.
21. loc.cit.

22. Major examples are: D. Humphry: Police Power and Black People, op.cit.; S. Pulle: Police-immigrant Relations in Ealing, London: Runnymede Trust 1973; Talking Blues, Birmingham, All Faiths for One Race, 1978; Blood on the Streets, Bethnal Green and Stepney Trades Council, 1978; Institute of Race Relations Evidence to Royal Commission on Criminal Procedure: Police Against Black People, London: Race and Class Pamphlet No. 6, 1979; Unofficial Committee of Enquiry: Southall 23 April 1979, London: NCCL, 1980; Final Report of the Working Party Into Community Police Relations in Lambeth; London: Lambeth Borough, 1981; P. Gordon: White Law, London: Pluto Press, 1983.

23. B. Anderton: 'Police and community: a review article', New Community, Summer 1974, p.236.

24. The Brixton Disorders 10-12 April 1981, Report of an Inquiry by the Rt.Hon.the Lord Scarman, London: HMSO, 1981, p.65.

25. P. Gordon: White Law, op.cit., p.25.

26. Scarman Report, op.cit., pp.52-3.

27. ibid., p.54.

28. ibid., p.57.

29. ibid., pp.17-28.

30. P. Gordon, op.cit., pp.38-42.

31. ibid., p.39.

32. ibid., pp.40-1.

33. The confused process of escalation into mass violence is charted in M. Kettle and L. Hodges: Uprising! London: Pan, 1982, Chap.1; and in great detail in Joshua, Wallace and Booth, op.cit., Chap.2. The latter book also gives a detailed analysis of official reactions and the ensuing riot trial.

34. For Red Lion Square see Lord Justice Scarman: The Red Lion Square Disorders of 15 June 1974 London: HMSO, 1975; T. Gilbert: Only One Died, London: K. Beauchamp, 1975; Lewisham is described from contrasting perspectives in R. Clutterbuck: Britain in Agony, London: Penguin, 1980, pp.227-32, and J. Rollo: 'The Special Patrol Group' in P. Hain (ed.): Policing the Police Vol.2, London: Calder, 1980, pp.184-6; similar instances of police protection of NF activities are catalogued in Kettle and Hodges, op.cit., pp.75-78; and the definitive account of the Southall events is the Report of the Unofficial Committee of Enquiry chaired by Professor Michael Dummett: Southall 23 April 1979, London: NCCL, 1980.

35. Kettle and Hodges, op.cit., pp.156-7.

36. Policy Studies Institute: Police and Public in London: Vol.IV : The Police in Action, London: PSI, 1983, p.161.

37. ibid., p.156.

38. PSI: Police and People in London; Vol.II : A Group of Young Black People, London: PSI, 1983, p.169.

39. Details of the police investigation and the protest march can be found in Vols.II of the study, Chap.V, and Vol.IV, pp.155-62.

40. For example, in the Institute of Race Relations evidence to the Royal Commission on Criminal Procedure, op.cit., Chap.1, Part B.

41. Home Office: Racial Attacks; November 1981.

42. ibid., p.14.

43. ibid., p.10.

44. ibid., p.12.

45. F. Klug: Racist Attacks, London: Runnymede Trust, 1982.
46. P. Gordon: White Law, op.cit., pp.56-9.
47. T. Muil: 'Triumph of Trust', Strategy '84, 13 July 1984.
48. T. Jefferson and R. Grimshaw: 'The Problem of Law
     Enforcement Policy in England and Wales: The Case of
     Community Policing and Racial Attacks' International Journal of
     the Sociology of Law, 1984, 12, pp.117-35.
49. ibid., p.128.
50. Racial Attacks, op.cit., p.17.
51. J. E. Boydstun: San Diego Field Interrogation : Final Report,
     Washington D.C.: Police Foundation, 1975, p.61.
52. R. Bogolmony: 'Street Patrol : The Decision to Stop a Citizen',
     Criminal Law Bulletin 12:5, 1976, p.571.
53. J. Piliavin and S. Briar: 'Police Encounters With Juveniles',
     American Journal of Sociology, September 1964, p.212.
54. D. Black and A. J. Reiss Jr.: Studies of Crime and Law
     Enforcement in Major Metropolitan Areas Vol.2: Field Surveys
     III, Section 1: 'Patterns of Behaviour in Police and Citizen
     Transactions', Washington D.C.: Gov. Printing Office, 1967, p.81.
55. ibid.
56. D. Black: 'The Social Organisation of Arrest', Stanford Law
     Review, June 1971, pp.1109-10.
57. R. Lundman, R. Sykes and J.P. Clark: 'Police Control of
     Juveniles', Journal of Research in Crime and Delinquency 15:1,
     1978, pp.74-91.
58. R. Sykes, J. Fox, J. P. Clark: 'A Socio-Legal Theory of Police
     Discretion', in A. Niederhoffer and A. Blumberg (eds.): The
     Ambivalent Force, 2nd ed., Hinsdale, III; Dryden Press, 1976,
     pp.177-8.
59. R. Lundman; 'Routine Police Arrest Practices: A Commonweal
     Perspective', Social Problems, October 1974, p.136.
60. L. W. Sherman; 'Causes of Police Behaviour', Journal of
     Research in Crime and Delinquency, January 1980, p.80. This is
     confirmed by a more recent multi-city study: D. Smith and C.
     Vishner: 'Street-level Justice: Situational Determinants of Police
     Arrest Decisions, Social Problems, 1981, pp.167-77.
61. A. Campbell and H. Schuman: 'Racial Attitudes in 15 American
     Cities', Supplemental Studies for the National Advisory
     Commission on Civil Disorders, Washington DC: USGPO, 1969,
     Table IV.
62. A. J. Reiss Jr.: The Police and the Public, New Haven: Yale
     University Press, 1971, p.147.
63. J. Skolnick: Justice Without Trial, New York: Wiley, 1966, p.80.
     A later study D. M. Rafsky; 'Police Race Attitudes and
     Labelling', Jnl of Police Science and Administration 1973,
     pp.65-86 found that the use of derogatory racial terms was
     related to hostile attitudes to blacks in general.
64. A.J. Reiss Jr.: 'Police Brutality', Trans-action 5, 1968, pp.10-19.
65. P. Takagi: 'A Garrison State in "Democratic" Society', Crime
     and Social Justice, Spring/Summer 1974, pp.27-33.
66. M. Meyer: 'Police Shootings at Minorities', Annals, November
     1980, pp.98-110.

67. J. Fyfe: 'Race and Extreme Police-Citizen Violence', in R. McNeely and C. Pope (eds.): Race, Crime and Criminal Justice, Beverly Hills: Sage, 1981, pp.89-108; C. Milton, et.al.: Police Use of Deadly Force, Washington D.C. : Police Foundation, 1977.

68. L. Sherman: op.cit., p.81, W.A. Geller: 'Deadly Force: What We Know' in C. J. Klockars (ed.): Thinking About Police, New York: McGraw-Hill, 1983, pp.313-31.

69. M. Halperin et.al. : The Lawless State, New York: Penguin, 1976, Chap.3. C. Perkus: COINTELPRO, New York; Monad Press, 1975, chaps.3-5; P. Chevigny; Cops and Rebels, New York; Pantheon, 1972.

70. F. K. Heussenstamm: 'Bumper Stickers and the Cops', - Trans-Action, Feb. 1971, pp.32-3.

71. W. Westley: Violence and the Police, Cambridge, Mass: MIT Press, 1970, pp.99-104.

72. J. Skolnick, op.cit., pp.81-3.

73. A. J. Reiss Jr.: The Police and the Public op.cit., p.147.

74. D. Bayley and H. Mendelsohn: Minorities and the Police, New York: Free Press, 1968, p.144.

75. R. Reiner; 'Fuzzy Thoughts: The Police and "Law and Order" Politics', Sociological Review, May 1980, pp.383-388.

76. Shoot Out in Cleveland, Report to the National Commission on the Causes and Prevention of Violence, New York: Bantam, 1969, pp.78-9.

77. R. Winslow: Crime in a Free Society, Belmont, Ca.: Dickenson Publishing, 1968, p.272.

78. U.S. Department of Justice: The Police and Public Opinion, Washington DC, 1977, p.13.

79. ibid., p.39.

80. S. Walker: The Police In America, New York: McGraw-Hill, 1983, p.203.

81. J. Baldwin: Nobody Knows my Name, New York: Dell Publishing, 1962, pp.65-7.

82. To Establish Justice, to Insure Domestic Tranquility, Final Report of the National Commission on the Causes and Prevention of Violence, New York; Bantam, 1978, p.20.

83. M. Cain: Society and the Policeman's Role, London: Routledge, 1973, P.117.

84. ibid., p.119.

85. ibid., p.118.

86. J. Lambert: Crime, Police and Race Relations, Oxford: Oxford University Press, 1970.

87. ibid., pp.183-7.

88. R. Reiner: The Blue-Coated Worker, Cambridge: Cambridge University Press, 1978, pp.225-6.

89. R. Reiner: The Blue-Coated Worker, Ph.D. Thesis, Bristol University 1976, pp.607-8.

90. S. Holdaway: Inside the British Police, Oxford : Basil Blackwell, 1983, pp.66-7.

91. ibid., pp.70-1.

92. ibid., p.70.

93. R. Friedrich: 'Racial Prejudice and Police Treatment of Blacks' in R. Baker and F. A. Meyer Jr. (eds.): Evaluating Alternative Law-Enforcement Policies, Lexington; Lexington Books, 1979, p.161.

94. PSI: Police and People in London Vol.IV, op.cit.,pp.334-5.
95. ibid., pp.111-122.
96. ibid., p.129.
97. ibid., p.131.
98. ibid., pp.114-20.
99. P. Southgate: Police Probationer Training in Race Relations, Home Office Research and Planning Unit Paper 8, 1982, p.11.
100. M. Tuck and P. Southgate: Ethnic Minorities, Crime and Policing, Home Office Research Study No.70, 1981, pp.26.27.
101. A. Brogden: '"Sus" is Dead : but what about "Sas"?', New Community Spring/Summer, 1981, pp.44-52.
102. C. Willis: The Use, Effectiveness and Impact of Police Stop and Search Powers Home Office Research and Planning Unit Paper 15, 1983, p.14. The same pattern is found in the data in S. Field and P. Southgate: Public Disorder, op.cit., pp.50-3.
103. loc.cit. Scarman's attempt to justify this police strategy by referring to the high and increasing proportion of robberies in Brixton (Para. 4.12 of his Report) has been criticised recently by L. Blom-Cooper and R. Drabble: 'Police Perception of Crime', British Journal of Criminology 1982, pp.184-7. They argue that the increasing proportion of 'robberies' matched the decreasing proportion of 'other theft and handling', implying that the rise in the robbery proportion might be the consequence of a greater propensity to define incidents as 'robbery' rather than 'theft'. J. Lea and J. Young in What is to be Done About Law and Order? London: Penguin, 1984, pp.163-4 criticise this point on the grounds that it is tautologous. If the percentage of robbery and violent theft in Brixton is higher than for the MPD as a whole, by definition other categories of crime must be lower. However, Blom-Cooper and Drabble do cite absolute figures also showing that the greater number of robberies in 1980 in Brixton was almost the same as the decline in the number of thefts. They try to explain away the higher Brixton robbery rate by figures for the age-structure of the population, showing a higher population at risk. But surely the population at risk is a relevant factor for police policy-makers to take into account when allocating resources to an area.
104. P. Southgate and P. Ekblom: Contacts Between Police and Public, Home Office Research Study No.77, 1984, p.19.

105. PSI: Police and People in London, Vol.1: A Survey of Londoners by D. J. Smith, London : PSI, pp.309-10.; the detailed data are on pp.95-101. Blacks were also disproportionately stopped according to the data from the Survey of Police Officers in Vol.III, pp.96-7.
106. C. Willis, op.cit., pp.12-13.
107. PSI, Vol.1, op.cit., pp.108-10; pp.310-1. It should be noted that not all stops would be in the person's own neighbourhood.
108. PSI, Vol.IV, op.cit., p.130.
109. P. Stevens and C. Willis: Race, Crime and Arrests, Home Office Research Unit Study No. 58, 1979, pp.15-16. See also Field and Southgate, op.cit., pp.50-3.
110. ibid., pp.18-19.

111. A Bradford study replicates this finding of a disproportionately low Asian recorded crime rate. R. Mawby and I. D. Batta : Asians and Crime, Southall : National Association for Asian Youth, 1980.
112. Stevens and Willis, op.cit., pp.19-28.
113. ibid., pp.28-34.
114. ibid., pp.41-2.
115. PSI Vol.I, pp.121-2; Vol.III, pp.96-7.
116. PSI Vol.1, pp.71-75.
117. J. Lea and J. Young: 'The Riots in Britain 1981' in D. Cowell et.al.: Policing the Riots, London: Junction Books, 1982; J. Lea and J. Young: What is to be done about law and order?, London: Penguin, 1984.
118. Lea and Young: What is to be done about law and order?, op.cit., pp.166-7.
119. For example: L. Bridges: 'Extended Views: The British Left and Law and Order', Sage Race Relations Abstracts, Feb. 1983, pp.19-26; P. Gilroy: 'The Myth of Black Criminality', in Socialist Register, London: Merlin Press, 1982, pp.47-56; P. Gilroy: 'Police and Thieves', in Centre for Contemporary Cultural Studies: The Empire Strikes Back, London: Hutchinson, 1983, pp.143-82; L. Bridges: 'Policing the Urban Wasteland', Race and Class, Autumn 1983, pp.31-48; C. Gutzmore: 'Capital, "Black Youth" and Crime', Race and Class, Autumn, 1983, pp.13-30.
120. Gilroy in Centre for Contemporary Cultural Studies, op.cit., p.146.
121. J. Lambert: Crime, Police and Race Relations, op.cit.; M. Banton: Police Community Relations, London: Collins, 1973, p.164; the Commons Select Committee is discussed in detail in Lea and Young, pp.135-8.
122. Lea and Young, ibid., p.138.
123. ibid., pp.167-8.
124. S. Hall et.al.: Policing the Crisis, London: MacMillan, 1978, Parts 1 and 2.
125. M. Pratt: Mugging as a Social Problem, London; Routledge, 1980.
126. S. Hall et.al., pp.390.1.
127. R. Reiner: 'Bobbies Take the Lobby Beat', New Society 25 March 1982, pp.469-71; J. Sim: 'Scarman : The Police Counter-Attack', Socialist Register 1982, London: Merlin, 1982, pp.57-77.
128. M. Cain and S. Sadigh: 'Racism, The Police and Community Policing: A Comment on the Scarman Report', Journal of Law and Society, Summer 1982, pp.87-8.
129. ibid., p.89.
130. S. Landau: 'Juveniles and the Police', British Journal of Criminology, January 1981, pp.27-46.
131. S. Landau and G. Nathan: 'Selecting Delinquents for Cautioning in the London Metropolitan Area', British Journal of Criminology, April 1983, pp.128-49.
132. S. Box and K. Russell: 'The Politics of Discreditability', Sociological Review 23, 1975, pp.315-46.
133. M. Tuck and P. Southgate, op.cit.
134. P. Stevens and C. Willis: Ethnic Minorities and Complaints Against the Police, Home Office Research and Planning Unit Paper 5, 1981.

135. PSI Vol.1, op.cit., pp.269-72.
136. S. Holdaway (ed.): The British Police, London: Edward Arnold, 1979, p.8.
137. D. James: 'Police-Black Relations: The Professional Solution' in S. Holdaway (ed.), op.cit., pp.81-2.
138. S. Holdaway; Inside the British Police, op.cit., pp.81-4. This distinction is similar to Banton's claim that the police exercise 'statistical' but not 'categorical discrimination' i.e. it results not from different treatment of blacks per se but the assumed greater probability that they are offenders. M. Banton; 'Categorical and Statistical Discrimination', Ethnic and Racial Studies, July 1983, pp.269-283.
139. D. James, op.cit., p.82.
140. op.cit., Vol.IV: The Police in Action, Chap. IV.
141. ibid., p.109, p.127.
142. ibid., p.137.
143. loc.cit.
144. ibid., pp.140-2.
145. ibid., pp.142-50.
146. ibid., pp.137-40.
147. ibid., pp.134-7.
148. W. Belson: The Public and the Police, London: Harper and Row, 1975; M. Tuck and P. Southgate, 1981, op.cit.; S. Jones; 'Community Policing in Devon and Cornwall; some research findings on the relationship between the public and the police', in T. Bennett (ed.); The Future of Policing, Cropwood Papers No.15, Cambridge: Institute of Criminology, 1983, pp.82-103; P. Southgate and P. Ekblom; 1984, op.cit.
149. PSI Vol.I, op.cit., p.326.
150. PSI Vol.IV, op.cit., p.332.
151. ibid., p.334.
152. J. Skolnick: Justice Without Trial, op.cit., Chap 3; R. Reiner; 'Who Are the Police?', Political Quarterly April/June 1982, pp.165-80.
153. J. Skolnick: ibid.; R. Reiner; The Blue Coated Worker, op.cit., Chaps. 9, 11; S. Holdaway; op.cit.
154. A. Colman and L. P. Gorman: 'Conservatism, Dogmatism and Authoritarianism in British Police Officers', Sociology, February 1982, pp.1-11.
155. P. A. J. Waddington: 'Conservatism, Dogmatism and Authoritarianism in British Police Officers: A Comment', Sociology, Nov. 1982, pp.591-4; and 'Rejoinder' by A. M. Colman, Sociology, August 1983, pp.388-391; A. J. P. Butler; 'Research Into Policemen's Attitudes', The Times, Oct 5th. 1981, p.13.
156. R. Cochrane and A. J. P. Butler; 'The values of police officers, recruits and civilians in England', Journal of Police Science and Administration, 8, 1980, pp.205-11; and A. J. P. Butler; 'An Examination of the influence of Training and Work Experience on the Attitudes and Perceptions of Police Constables', Mimeo., Police Staff College, Bramshill, 1982.
157. Colman and Gorman, op.cit., p.10.

158. The very disturbing flavour of these is sharply reminiscent of the notorious Hendon Police Cadet essays leaked by John Fernandes, the black lecturer who lost his job as a consequence. (P. Taylor; 'How Hendon police cadets are wooed away from racialism', Police, August 1983, pp.22-4.)

159. Waddington op.cit., suggests that the argument about socialisation into a police sub-culture is an 'over-socialised view of man' and that public views reflect the conditions of police work. But surely this is an unnecessary and futile either/or. Writers on police sub-culture (like Skolnick, who Waddington cites with approval) do not see this as a false consciousness passed on to passive recipients, but an adaptation to the circumstances of police life, which recruits do not imbibe like parrots but because it makes sense of their experiences. Socialisation is not indoctrination but the process of inculcation into this sub-culture.

160. Bruce Johnson: 'Taking Care of Labour: The Police in American Politics', Theory and Society, 1976, p.108.

161. J. A. Lee: 'Some Structural Aspects of Police Deviance in Relations with Minority Groups', op.cit., pp.53-6. The term comes from E. Cray: The Enemy in the Streets, New York: Anchor, 1972, p.11.

162. L. W. Sherman; 'After the Riots: Police and Minorities in the United States 1970-80', in N. Glazer and K. Young (eds.): Ethnic Pluralism and Public Policy,. op.cit., pp.212-35. The Horowitz article on 'Racial Violence in the U.S.' in the same volume (pp.187-211) makes similar points.

163. Sherman, op.cit., p.221.

164. N. Alex; Black in Blue, New York: Appleton, Century Crofts, 1969.

165. R. Reiner; 'Fuzzy Thoughts'. op.cit., pp.388-9.

166. J. Jacobs and J. Cohen; 'The Impact of Racial Integration on the Police', Journal of Police Science and Administration, 6;2, 1978, pp.168-83.

167. J. Jacobs and S. Magdovitz: 'At LEEP's End? A review of the Law Enforcement Education Programme', Journal of Police Science and Administration, 5:1, 1977, pp.1-18; L. Sherman: The Quality of Police Education, San Francisco; Jossey-Bass, 1978.

168. Sherman: 'After the Riots', op.cit., p.230.

169. As Sherman points out, drawing on W. Miller's comparative history Cops and Bobbies, Chicago: Chicago University Press, 1977, this amounts to a plea for a return to the traditional conception of British policing, whereas for the US it was a marked innovation.

170. P. Gordon; 'Community Policing: towards the local police state?', Critical Social Policy, Summer 1984, p.56. Similar arguments are advanced in L. Bridges and T. Bunyan; 'The Police and Criminal Evidence Bill in Context', Journal of Law and Society, Summer 1983, pp.85-107; L. Christian: Policing by Coercion, London: GLC Police Committee Support Unit; and the papers cited in note 119.

171. D. Wilson; 'Out of the Gutter', New Society, 7 June 1984, p.378.

172. S. Savage; 'Political Control or Community Liaison?', Political Quarterly, Jan-Mar 1984, pp.48-59., is a cogent argument expanding on this theme.

173. What is to be done about law and order, op.cit., p.255.

174. I have given my views on the Royal Commission's handling of these wider issues in R. Reiner: 'The Politics of Police Powers', Politics and Power 4, London: Routledge, 1981, pp.27-52.

175. 'Warnings on use of search powers against blacks', The Times, 21 July 1984, p.4.

176. Guardian, 23 October 1973.

12. REASONABLE FORCE

Michael Molyneux

How much force may I lawfully use to prevent the commission of a crime or to defend myself against attack? Every first year law student knows the short answer to that question: 'reasonable force'. Unfortunately the short answer is not very helpful when it comes to dealing with the events of real life and the judges themselves do not seem capable of giving a clear and unequivocal lead. In a recent case the Lord Chief Justice observed that 'reasonable force' raised "issues of law that have been the subject....of more learned academic articles than one would care to read in an evening". (1)

It is not the purpose of this essay to ruin anybody's evening by adding to the learned literature. It simply seeks to pose one question: where does reasonable force end and licensed violence begin? That is obviously a question that concerns us all but it must be of particular concern to police officers. The police are charged with the duty of preventing crime and in doing so they must, from time to time, use some degree of force. And today, when a large number of police officers carry guns, either on a regular basis or for particular operations, the use of force may involve the firing of a lethal weapon. It must be in their interests and ours that the law on the use of reasonable force should be clear and precise.

It is, therefore, regrettable that the massive and detailed Police and Criminal Evidence Act 1984 does not offer any guidance at all on the subject. As originally drafted the Bill expressly permitted the police to use 'reasonable force' in certain circumstances: for example to enter and search premises without a warrant (2) and to search people arrested away from a police station (3). By the time that the Bill had become an Act however these separate provisions had been replaced by a general provision in Section 117 which permits reasonable force to be used by a constable where it is necessary for the exercise of any power conferred by the Act and where there is no contrary provision requiring consent by some person other than a police officer. There is, however, no attempt in the Act to define what degree of force will amount to reasonable force when a constable exercises a power derived from the Act.

The General Law

Since there is no help to be had in the Act we must turn to the old law to discover the limits to the use of force in the prevention of crime and in self defence.

The starting point is Section 3(1) of the Criminal Law Act 1967 which provides:

> "A person may use such force as is reasonable in the circumstances in the prevention of crime, or in effecting or assisting in the lawful arrest of offenders or suspected offenders or of persons unlawfully at large".

The section is framed in very general terms and it covers all kinds of crimes from murder to motoring offences. The most obvious questions raised by the section are; how much force will be regarded as reasonable in any given circumstances and who is to decide?

The second question can be answered in the words of Lord Diplock in a case involving a soldier in Northern Ireland who had shot and killed an unarmed man:

> "What amount of force is 'reasonable in the circumstances' for the purpose of preventing crime is, in my view, always a question for the jury....never a 'point of law' for the judge". (4)

It also seems clear that the amount of force used must be appropriate to the crime that it is intended to prevent. This is not to be judged by weighing the force used against the crime on a pair of 'jeweller's scales' (5) but by the more robust standards of common sense bearing in mind that reasonable men may make mistakes in the 'agony of the moment'. Thus it could be reasonable and, therefore, lawful to kill or seriously wound in order to prevent murder if there were no other way of doing so. But would it be reasonable to kill to prevent rape? That remains a question to be decided by the jury in the light of the particular circumstances of each case.

Closely related to the right to use reasonable force in the prevention of crime under Section 3(1) of the Criminal Law Act 1967 is the old common law defence of private defence. That is the right to use reasonable force in defence of oneself or other people or even in defence of property. This defence overlaps with Section 3 since most attacks on people or property will also be crimes so that in defending myself or another I will also be trying to prevent the commission of a crime. But in so far as private defence still exists as a separate defence the standards to be applied in deciding whether the force used was reasonable are probably the same as those under Section 3 and, once again, a question for the jury and not the judge.

There remains one difficult problem. Suppose I believe that you are about to commit rape whereas, in fact, you are administering the kiss of life; suppose I think that you are a dangerous and wanted criminal whereas, in fact, you are a perfectly innocent man with a passing resemblance to the criminal; or suppose I believe that you are running out of a post office that you have just robbed carrying a shot gun when in reality you are a terrified customer running for your life and brandishing your rolled-up umbrella. In each case, if I am an ordinary member of the public, the amount of force at my disposal to stop you may not be very great and anyway you may get a chance to explain before things go too far. But if I am a police officer carrying a loaded revolver my reaction may prove fatal for you and explanations will be impossible.

How is the law to deal with mistakes of this kind? There are, it seems, two schools of thought on the subject. One holds that a defence based on Section 3 or on self-defence will only succeed if the accused person's mistaken belief about the true facts is not only an honest belief but is also based on reasonable grounds. This is sometimes described as the objective approach and it gets some support from the speech of Lord Diplock in the case referred to above about the soldier in Northern Ireland:

> "....to kill or seriously wound another person is prima facie unlawful. There may be circumstances which render the act of shooting and any killing which results from it lawful; and an honest and reasonable belief by the accused in the existence of facts which if true would have rendered his act lawful is a defence to any charge based on the shooting". (6)

The same approach seems to have been adopted by Mr Justice Croom-Johnson in his summing up in the Waldorf case. In that case two police officers, D.C.s Finch and Jardine, were charged with attempted murder and wounding with intent to cause grievous bodily harm. The facts are given below in some detail because the case has proved to be the most important single factor in the increased public and official awareness of the problems surrounding the arming of the police.

On 14 January 1983 the two detectives, together with other armed police officers, were out looking for David Martin, a dangerous criminal. Martin had been arrested in September 1982 after shooting and wounding a policeman but he had escaped from custody while awaiting trial. Finch and Jardine were part of a squad trailing a car in which Martin's former girl friend was a passenger. D.C. Finch, who knew Martin because he had helped to arrest him in September 1982, approached the car and thought that he recognised the man in the front passenger seat as Martin. In fact he was Stephen Waldorf an entirely innocent man. D.C. Finch fired six shots at Mr Waldorf and when he was lying sprawled half out of the car beat him about the head with his revolver fracturing Mr Waldorf's skull. D.C. Jardine fired four shots from his revolver at Mr Waldorf as he was lying on the ground. (A third police officer fired five shots into the back of the car but he was not charged with any offence.)

The two detectives had fired at the man they believed to be Martin because they thought he had a gun and that, even lying on the ground, he was still dangerous. At their trial the judge in his directions to the jury on the issue of self-defence said:

> "If the firing was done in an honest, genuine and <u>reasonable</u> frame of mind it is something you are entitled to do". (7) (My emphasis)

The jury found the two officers not guilty.

The alternative view of the effect of mistake is that a defence of reasonable force will succeed provided that the accused's mistake about the facts is genuine, even if it is unreasonable. In other words the accused person's state of mind is to be judged subjectively.

This view gets recent and authoritative support in the case of <u>Gladstone Williams</u>. (8) Mr Williams was travelling home on a bus when he saw a man dragging a black youth along the street and hitting him. Mr Williams jumped off the bus and asked the man what he was doing. The man said that he was a police officer, which was not true, and that he was trying to arrest the youth for mugging a woman, which was true. The man could not produce a warrant card; there was a struggle in the course of which Mr Williams punched the man in the face. He was charged with assault occasioning actual bodily harm and his defence was that he honestly believed that the youth was being assaulted. He was convicted in the crown court but on appeal the conviction was quashed. In giving the judgment in the Court of Appeal the Lord Chief Justice said:

> "The reasonableness or unreasonableness of the defendant's belief is material to the question of whether the belief was held by him at all. If the belief was in fact held, its unreasonableness, so far as guilt or innocence is concerned, is neither here nor there. It is irrelevant....Even if the jury come to the conclusion that the mistake was an unreasonable one, if the defendant may genuinely have been labouring under it, he is entitled to rely on it". (9)

The Lord Chief Justice went on to quote with approval the view of the Criminal Law Revision Committee that:

"The common law defence of self-defence should be replaced by a statutory defence providing that a person may use such force as is reasonable in the circumstances as he believes them to be in the defence of himself or any other person". (10)

The matter now seems to be in such a tangle that it can only be resolved, as a question of policy, by Parliament and there is at least some academic support for the view that the subjective approach favoured by the Criminal Law Revision Committee should be adopted. (11)

The point, however, is of more than just academic interest. It exposes a dangerous weakness in a particularly sensitive area of the law. In a civilised society the use of any force is undesirable although sometimes unavoidable. And when force is used one thing leads all too easily to another. And if it does, the answer to the question who, if anyone, is guilty of what, should not depend on conflicting dicta and decisions of the courts, but on clear and precise principles. When firearms are added to the equation it becomes, literally, a matter of life and death.

In order to assess the seriousness and extent of that problem it is necessary to consider how often the police do in fact carry and use firearms, the training that they receive in the use of guns and the law and practice concerning the issue of firearms to the police.

Guns And The Police (12)

The first difficulty in discovering the facts about the use of guns by the police is the absence of readily available national statistics. A great deal of the information on this subject is derived from written answers to questions in Parliament and from the research of individual journalists. Some figures are simply not obtainable. For example there are no national figures for the total number of firearms held by the police. The Home Office line is that this is a matter for individual Chief Constables who are not required to notify the Home Office of the firearms held by their forces. Some information is available in Chief Constables' annual reports but this is usually limited to a statement of the number of weapons bought during the year. It would be virtually impossible to collate and quantify these figures on a national basis. The probable answer is that nobody knows how many firearms are held at any one time by the police forces in England and Wales. The figures simply do not exist.

The position is much the same when it comes to the types of weapons held by the police. There is a list of 'approved weapons' issued to all police forces but even that is merely advisory and it is not available to the public. It does seem clear, however, that the weapon most favoured by the police is some type of revolver. Until 1973 the most widely used revolver was the 38 calibre Webley. Its effective range was somewhat limited and many forces changed to the Smith and Wesson. This comes in two versions, one with a short barrel firing five shots, which seems to be favoured for diplomatic protection work; the other, with a longer barrel, fires six shots and is in more general use. (Both types of Smith and Wesson seem to have been used in the Waldorf shooting). Automatic pistols such as the Walther PP (a larger version of James Bond's PPK) lost favour with the Metropolitan Police when the Walther carried by Princess Anne's bodyguard jammed after firing only one shot while he was resisting a kidnap attempt.   Revolvers are more bulky than automatics but if a revolver misfires all you have to do is to pull the trigger again and a new bullet will enter the firing chamber.

The police armoury also includes rifles and shot guns. In 1973 a Home Office working party recommended the use of the 7.62mm Self Loading Rifle (a version of the standard army model) in place of the old Lee-Enfield 303. Many police forces rejected the new rifle on the grounds that it was grossly overpowered for police work. Experiments had shown, for instance, that bullets from the army version could penetrate modern concrete buildings from end to end and that ricochets could carry for up to 1000 yards. (13)

Perhaps the most controversial weapon in the hands of the police is the sub-machine gun. In April 1984 it was disclosed that the Home Secretary had authorised the purchase by the Metropolitan Police of twelve Heckler and Koch sub-machine guns to be used for protection duties during the economic summit meeting. According to Mr Colin Greenwood, a former superintendent with the West Yorkshire police and editor of 'Gun Review', these guns are "the most expensive and sophisticated on the market". Mr Greenwood also said that he found it "horrendous that a police force should have sub-machine guns in the centre of London....We are going to have another situation where the Metropolitan Police are more dangerous than the terrorists". (14)

The parliamentary row that followed this news led to the further disclosure that as long ago as 1976 the Metropolitan Police had bought a limited number of sub-machine guns on the authority of Mr Roy Jenkins, the Home Secretary at the time, and without the knowledge of the Prime Minister of the day, Mr James Callaghan.

So much for the information, or lack of it, about the terrifying array of weaponry available to the police forces of England and Wales. We now turn to examine the number of times that guns are issued to the police and actually used by them.

The first difficulty is that some groups of police regularly carry guns as a matter of routine. These groups certainly include the Royal and Diplomatic Protection Squads and possibly, for limited periods, the Robbery Squads. In April 1984, for example, Mr James Anderton, the Chief Constable of Greater Manchester, disclosed that armed police were on regular patrol in Manchester. And in the second of two shooting incidents that took place in London, in June 1984 a suspected bank robber, carrying a replica gun, was shot in the chest and seriously wounded by a sergeant from the Diplomatic Protection Group who had been called to the bank by the unarmed police officers who were first on the scene. (15) There are no precise figures for the number of guns carried by these special squads as a matter of routine. (16)

For the issue of guns to 'ordinary' police officers there are some figures available on a more systematic basis. For the years up to and including 1982 these figures relate to 'the number of occasions on which one or more firearms were issued in connection with a particular incident involving criminals or other persons known or believed to be armed'. The figures do not include the occasions on which guns are issued to deal with dangerous animals.

The figures for the years 1980 to 1982 (with the figures for the
Metropolitan Police in brackets) are: (17)

1980	1981	1982
7275 (5968)	6149 (4983)	7952 (6035)

The first thing to notice about these figures is that they do not tell us
how many guns were issued to the police. They just give the number of
occasions 'on which one or more guns were issued'. And there is no
breakdown showing the types of weapons issued. The sheer number of
issues may come as something of a shock as well. The figures for 1982
certainly led the press to make the simple calculation that guns are issued
to the police about twenty times every day. (18) The other outstanding
feature of the statistics is the very large proportion of issues made to the
Metropolitan Police. In 1982 about three quarters of all the occasions for
issue were in London. Since these figures do not include the guns carried
by members of the Protection Groups it is, perhaps, disturbing to
contemplate the number of armed police officers abroad on the streets of
London on any given day of the week.

Some comfort may be gained from the fact that however many guns
may be issued each year to the police they are very seldom fired at
people. Figures given to the writer by the Home Office indicate that guns
were actually fired by the police in ten incidents in 1980, four incidents in
1981 and ten incidents in 1982.

All these figures, pieced together from various sources may not be
thought to give a very accurate or informative picture of the true postion.
And things are not improved by the fact that the Home Office now seems
to have changed the basis on which the figures are calculated. The
statistics supplied by the Home Office for the year 1983 relate not to the
number of occasions on which guns were issued as in previous years but to
the number of 'operations' in which guns were issued. There are still no
figures for the total number of guns issued. (19)

The figures for 1983 are: (Metropolitan Police proportion in brackets)

Number of operations:	3180 (2230)
Number of incidents in which guns were fired: (20)	3 (1)
Number of shots fired:	26 (14)

What do these figures mean? What is the difference between
'occasions' and 'operations'? If they mean much the same thing then the
number of times guns were issued to the police in 1983 shows the
dramatic fall from the previous year; from 7,952 to 3,180. That may
indeed be the case. The shooting of Stephen Waldorf took place in
January 1983 and it led to a searching examination of every aspect of the
use of guns by the police including the circulation of new Home Office
guidelines requiring, among other things, each issue of firearms to be
authorised by an officer of at least the rank of superintendent. Perhaps in
the glare of publicity following the Waldorf incident guns were only issued
half as often in 1983 as they had been in 1982. Or perhaps not. There is
no way of telling but it does raise the question of why the Home Office
has changed the basis on which the figures, such as they are, are given.

Training The Police In The Use Of Firearms

The shooting of Stephen Waldorf led to a re-thinking of the process for selecting police officers for training in the use of firearms and of the form that the training should take. In December 1983, after a police disciplinary inquiry had decided that formal disciplinary charges should not be brought against the two officers involved in the shooting, the Home Office issued a statement on the 'operational implications to be drawn from the incident'. The statement included the following passage:

> "There are further measures which need to be introduced to ensure that particular care will be taken in choosing and training officers for firearms duties, so that they can withstand the stress inherent in any armed operation. Greater emphasis will be placed on the background, temperament and personal circumstances of those applying for selection as firearms officers. There will be more and better training, which will take account of the stresses inherent in firearms operations. The continuing suitability of firearms officers will be regularly assessed". (21)

In June 1984 Sir Kenneth Newman, the Metropolitan Police Commissioner, presented his annual report for 1983 in which he outlined his plans for improving the training of police officers in the use of guns. The plan included:

> "....a much more stringent and considered selection of officers for training in the handling of firearms, with the longer term possibility of introducing psychological testing".

The report also announced plans for creating a 'mock up' of a street in which a police officer's judgement of when to fire could be tested. All this, said the report, would cost a lot of money and take a long time. (22)

It is perhaps ironic that the Commissioner's report was issued within one week of the first incident in which Metropolitan Police officers had fired their guns since the shooting of Stephen Waldorf in January 1983. On 14 June 1984 two armed detective sergeants from the Central Robbery Squad shot and wounded two armed men in a post office in North London. An internal police inquiry is being conducted into the incident and a report will be made to the Director of Public Prosecutions. (23)

About ten per cent of police officers in England and Wales are trained in the use of firearms although the figure for the Metropolitan Police is nearer twenty per cent. (24) It remains to be seen whether the new and more stringent training policies will produce any substantial change in those figures.

One thing, however, seems certain. Police officers will still be trained to shoot to kill. The main aim of police weapons training is said to be to avoid the need to fire at all through the use of superior tactics. But if shots have to be fired they should be aimed to kill. This is simply a matter of inexorable logic. Police officers are trained to use their guns only as a last resort when all other tactics have failed. In those circumstances the only safe thing to do is to aim at the largest possible target, the human torso. If a bullet from any of the standard police weapons hits that target it will probably kill. As Mr Barry Price, Deputy Chief Constable of Essex, told a coroner's jury in 1979:

"The policy cannot be to wound or maim. When the officer pulls the trigger he must know that he is going to take a life". (25)
This harsh reality has always been emphasised in police weapons training courses and it has been said that:
"more people get taken off courses for this, because they haven't really asked themselves if they could do it, than because they are potential cowboys". (26)

The Law On The Issue Of Guns To The Police

We have seen that large numbers of firearms of many different types are issued to ordinary police officers in England and Wales, every day of the week. It seems reasonable to ask – what is the legal authority for all this activity? The somewhat surprising answer is that there does not seem to be any direct legal authority at all.

In March 1983, after the Waldorf shooting, the Home Office issued 'Guidelines on the issue and use of firearms' (see Appendix A). Among other things the Guidelines cover the circumstances in which guns may be issued, they provide for the issue to be authorised by a senior officer and they require the giving of an oral warning before a gun is fired. But the Guidelines are not law.

Under Section 19 of the Firearms Act 1968:

"A person commits an offence if without lawful authority or reasonable excuse (the proof whereof lies on him) he has with him in a public place a loaded shot gun....or any other firearm (whether loaded or not) together with ammunition suitable for use in that firearm".

Under Section 54 of the same Act the police are exempt from the licensing provisions of the Act but not, it seems, from the provisions of Section 19. So what answer would an armed police officer have to a charge brought against him under Section 19 ?

According to a Q.C. engaged by the Police Federation to give an opinion on the law in the light of the Waldorf case the officer would have to fall back on the phrase 'reasonable excuse' in the section and argue that, as a trained and authorised person, he was in possession of the firearm in accordance with the Home Office guidelines. (27) This is surely a somewhat fragile basis for such a crucial legal issue.

In his 'opinion' the anonymous Q.C. goes on to emphasise that there is no special defence of 'superior orders' available to a police officer who actually fires a gun. The officer must rely, like the ordinary citizen, on the general law governing the use of reasonable force in the prevention of crime or in self-defence. That only serves to emphasise the lonely dilemma that may face the armed police officer. In the last resort, as it says in the Guidelines:

"the responsibility for the use of the firearm is an individual decision which may have to be justified in legal proceedings".

And that brings us back to where we began.

Conclusion

The arming of the police is a matter of legitimate public concern. Enough has, perhaps, been said in this short essay to demonstrate that the present position is totally unsatisfactory and that there are at least three specific ways in which the situation could and should be improved.

First the law on mistaken belief in connection with the use of reasonable force in the prevention of crime or in self-defence must be clarified. Is the test to be objective or subjective? Second, accurate national figures on the holding, issue and use of guns by the police must be produced. Without this information there can be no informed public debate. Third, the legal basis on which police carry guns must be expressly laid down. It cannot be left to unenforceable Guidelines.

The Police and Criminal Evidence Act 1984, for all the wide-ranging powers it confers on the police, conspicuously failed to tackle this basic problem. It must surely be in the interests of the police as well as the public that legislation on the subject is introduced as a matter of urgency.

How many more 'incidents' must there be before something is done?

Appendix A

GUIDELINES FOR THE POLICE ON THE ISSUE AND USE OF FIREARMS
(Reproduced with the permission of the Home Office)

Principles Governing Issue And Use

1. Firearms are to be issued only where there is reason to suppose that a police officer may have to face a person who is armed or otherwise so dangerous that he could not safely be restrained without the use of firearms; for protection purposes; or for the destruction of dangerous animals.

2. Firearms are to be used by authorised and trained police officers only as a last resort where conventional methods have been tried and failed, or must, from the nature of the circumstances obtaining, be unlikely to succeed if tried. They may be used, for example, when it is apparent that a police officer cannot achieve the lawful purpose of preventing loss, or further loss, of life by any other means.

Authority To Issue

3. Authority to issue firearms should be given by an officer of ACPO rank, save where a delay in getting in touch with an officer of ACPO rank could result in loss of life or serious injury, in which case a Chief Superintendent or Superintendent may authorise issue. In such circumstances an officer of ACPO rank should be informed as soon as possible. Special arrangements may apply where firearms are issued regularly for protection purposes, but these should be authorised by an officer of ACPO rank in the first instance.

Conditions Of Issue And Use

4. Firearms should be issued only to officers who have been trained and authorised in a particular class of weapon. Officers authorised to use firearms must attend regular refresher courses and those failing to reach the qualifying standard will lose their authorisation and must not thereafter be issued with firearms. Each authorised officer must hold an authorisation card showing the type(s) of weapon that may be issued to him. The authorisation card must be produced before a weapon is issued and must always be carried when the officer is armed. The card holder's signature in the issue register should be verified against the signature on his warrant card. The card should be issued without alteration and should have an expiry date on it.

5. Records of issue and operational use must be maintained. All occasions on which shots are fired by police officers other than to destroy dangerous animals must be thoroughly investigated by a senior officer and a full written report prepared.

Warning

6. Unless it is considered impracticable, an oral warning is to be given before a firearm is used.

Medical Assistance

7. Urgent steps are to be taken to ensure that early medical attention is provided for any casualties.

Use Of Minimum Force

8. Nothing in these guidelines affects the principle, to which section 3 of the Criminal Law Act 1967 gives effect, that only the minimum force necessary in the circumstances must be used. The degree of force justified will vary according to the circumstances of each case. Responsibility for the use of a firearm is an individual decision which may have to be justified in legal proceedings.

Briefing

9. Briefing by senior officers is of paramount importance and must include both authorised firearms officers and non-firearms personnel involved in an operation. Senior officers must stress the objective of any operation including specifically the individual responsibility of authorised firearms officers.

10. A brief summary of the most important points for an individual officer is attached. It is suggested that this summary is placed on the reverse side of each authorisation so that an officer will have it with him whenever he is armed.

AUTHORISED FIREARMS OFFICERS
GUIDELINES ON USE OF MINIMUM FORCE

The Law

Section 3 of the Criminal Law Act 1967 reads:

> "A person may use such force as is reasonable in the circumstances in the prevention of crime, or in the effecting or assisting in the lawful arrest of offenders or suspected offenders or of persons unlawfully at large".

Strict Reminder

A firearm is to be used only as a last resort. Other methods must have been tried and failed, or must - because of the circumstances - be unlikely to succeed if tried. For example, a firearm may be used when it is apparent that the police cannot achieve their lawful purpose of preventing loss, or further loss, of life by any other means. Wherever practicable, an oral warning is to be given before a firearm is used.

Individual Responsibility

The responsibility for the USE of the firearm is an INDIVIDUAL decision which may have to be justified in legal proceedings.
REMEMBER THE LAW.   REMEMBER YOUR TRAINING.

NOTES

1. R v Williams (1984) 78 Cr. App. Rep 276 at 278.

2. Clause 17(1) of the Bill.

3. Clause 29(6) of the Bill.

4. Reference under S.48A of the Criminal Appeal (Northern Ireland) Act 1968 (No. 1 of 1975) [1976] 2 ALL ER 937 at 947. The case involved a soldier serving in Northern Ireland who shot and killed a man whom he believed to be a potentially dangerous terrorist. The soldier's defence was based on S.3 of the Criminal Law (Northern Ireland) Act 1967 which is identical in wording to S.3 of the Criminal Law Act 1967 quoted in the text.

5. Reed v Wastie (1972) Times, 10 February, per Geoffrey Lane J.

6. [1976] 2 ALL ER 937 at 946. (See also note 4 above).

7. As reported in the Daily Telegraph, 19 October 1983.

8. (1984) 78 Cr. App. Rep 276.

9. Ibid. at 281.

10. Cmnd. 2659, Part 9, para 72(a).

11. See, for example, Smith and Hogan 'Criminal Law' 5th Edn. at 330

12. In writing this section I have been greatly helped by a degree dissertation 'Police Firearms - How Much do we Know?' by Oscar Rowlands, which he submitted to the University College of Wales, Aberystwyth. I would like to thank him for letting me read it.

13. Much of the information given above is drawn from 'The Arms of the Law' by Philip Jacob, Sunday Times 15 February 1976.

14. Quoted in the Times, "Sub-machine guns for the police 'horrendous'", 3 April 1984.

15. The Guardian, 'Replica weapon raider shot by police', 29 June 1984.

16. On 21 June 1984 the Times quoted Mr Wilfred Gibson, Assistant Commissioner at Scotland Yard, as saying about five hundred officers from the Special Branch were authorised to carry guns regularly on protection duties.

17. Figures supplied by the Home Office.

18. See, for example, Sunday Times 3 April 1983 and 8 April 1984.

19. It is known, for example, that on 14 January 1983, the day on which Stephen Waldorf was shot, there were twenty officers out looking for David Martin. Presumably they were all armed and they, or other officers, had been out looking for Martin on other days. Whatever the basis of calculation is that one 'issue' or several?

20. The only incident in which the Metropolitan Police fired their guns in 1983 was in the shooting of Stephen Waldorf. Three police officers fired fourteen shots between them. The other two incidents involved the Avon and Somerset police.

21. Home Office News Release 'Home Secretary: comment on Waldorf case' 23 December 1983.

22. Reported in the Daily Telegraph, 'Scotland Yard to spend millions on improving gun training', 21 June 1984.

23. At the time of writing the outcome of the inquiry is not known.

24. 'Out in the open', Sunday Times, 8 April 1984.

25. Quoted in the Times, 5 July, 1982.

26. Sergeant Keith Blyth, training instructor for the Thames Valley police, quoted in 'The Arms of the Law', Sunday Times 15 February 1976.

27. The 'opinion' of the anonymous Q.C. is reproduced in the April 1984 issue of 'Police', magazine of the Police Federation. The title of the article is: 'The loneliness of the armed police officer'.

13. DATA PROTECTION AND POLICING TECHNOLOGY

Marie Staunton

Introduction

As Aesop said of language, technology is not 'an evil in itself'. It all depends on what use is made of it. In the twentieth century, technology has not only enabled an increase in the scale and effectiveness of policing, but in some cases its introduction has fundamentally altered the relationship between the police and the citizen, and between police forces and those to whom they are accountable. This chapter will deal with an area of new technology the effect of which is not always visible - the storage, use and transfer of personal information about individuals not only in manual, but increasingly in automated systems.

In 1984 Parliament debated police information gathering and passed legislation such as the Data Protection Act and the Police and Criminal Evidence Act both of which fail to safeguard the citizen against the abuse of information technology; one police authority has refused to authorise an extensive computer system largely because of its civil liberty implications, yet another has agreed to a similar system "on the nod"; the European Court of Human Rights has remedied the failure of the domestic courts to control police use of telephone taps. (1) This chapter will examine the failure of those to whom the police are accountable - parliament, police authorities and the courts - to ensure that the civil liberties of individuals are protected against abuse of information technology. It will look forward to the changes in legislation policy and in the attitude of the courts which are necessary to ensure that the citizen's privacy is protected.

Background

The application of science to policing affects not only its scale and effectiveness, but policing methods and the relationship between the police and the community. To give some examples, the application of the technology of forensic science affected the investigation of crime. The development of 'unit beat' policing i.e. the creation of units of police officers on the beat backed up by panda cars and a collator of information at the police station, was dependent upon the introduction of panda cars and cheap transmitter radios in the 1960s. Similarly 'fire brigade' policing, an attempt to improve response time to incidents, relies increasingly on computerised command and control systems introduced in the 1980s.

Whilst theories of policing like the policies of successive Chief Constables have changed over the last 30 years, police investment in technology has steadily increased. Although the concept of fire brigade policing is now less fashionable, in July 1984 a new extensive command and control system became operational in London to allocate resources within seconds of the notification of an incident. A precursor of this is the much larger more powerful command and control system in Northern Ireland which used the street index, incident logging, information about resource availability and vehicle location, to place road blocks and intercept vehicles. Together with the extensive information held on individuals as a result of systematic information gathering since the early 1970s, this system in fact becomes a powerful method of social control.

The type of information collected on individuals, as well as its scale, has altered considerably since the first regional criminal records offices were set up in the 1950s to develop a consistent method of keeping records on convicted criminals. This is largely hard factual information, the name, date of birth, physical description, and previous convictions, which can be verified. Such information was described in the Report of the Lindop Committee (1978) as 'criminal information'. The Committee, which was set up by the government in 1976 to report on the control of computerised personal information, distinguished criminal information from 'criminal intelligence', which:

'may be speculative, suppositional, hearsay and unverified, such as notes about places frequented, known associates, suspected activities, or even just that a certain car was believed to have been involved in a certain robbery.' (2)

The 1960s saw a move towards collecting and collating criminal intelligence. The collection of information was carried out in many ways including targeting certain groups or transferring information from other data bases. For example, in the 12 months, 1972-1973, the Drug Squad increased their records of known or suspected drug traffickers from 18,000 to 250,000 by indexing names found in address books obtained through drugs raids or the use of informers. This targeting of a certain group of suspects has provided an extensive data base and the transfer of information from outside these data bases is a simpler method of amassing information. For example, information about car owners, which must be given to the Driver and Vehicle Licensing Centre, is transferred to the Police National Computer.

The Police National Computer (PNC) was set up in the early 1970s and contains what appear to be categories for criminal information and criminal intelligence. According to the Lindop Committee's report the PNC, from which information is immediately and routinely available to policemen on the beat, handles intelligence in the following instances:

"the file of stolen or suspected vehicles can include vehicles required to be kept under surveillance. The file of wanted and missing persons can include persons required to be located even if they have not been reported missing, and warrants have not been issued for their arrest." (3)

Thus one of the indexes on the PNC is headed 'stolen and suspected vehicles' and out of the 313,000 entries which it contained, a total of 41,077 entries related to vehicles of 'long-term interest' to the police, and 9,345 are 'seen and checked in noteworthy circumstances'. The latter category was used to store the vehicle numbers of suspected pickets (regardless of whether they were suspected of any crime) during the miners' dispute.

Concern about the use of 'faceless' technology, from panda cars to computers, which distances the police from the community which they serve has been criticised and contrasted with community policing developed in the mid-1970s and put into operation in areas such as Devon and Cornwall.

> 'Police should guard against the seductive nature of technological efficiency, which, if allowed too great a place in the nature of policing, may well damage or destroy the immutable essence of superior policing, namely the human side.' (4)

The two are not so separate as may appear however. Information technology is used to back up community policing initiatives. The computer can collate information gathered through neighbourhood watch schemes. With the introduction of unit beat policing came the creation of collators whose job was to sift through police notebooks and collate relevant information. The introduction of 'mini computers' in the 1980s has provided a useful tool for preparing and transmitting collator reports. A new strategy of community policing backed by computerisation in Skelmersdale in 1978 meant that logging of incidents increased threefold. These extracts from a collator record in Skelmersdale show how speculative criminal intelligence can be:

> "The Anand Vedi - a mystical meditation type set-up based in Skem - attracts seekers of the truth from some very exotic places and the latest recruit would appear to be John McGregor who hails from 121 Edinburgh Place - a part of Glasgow known as the Gorbals. McGregor, who was checked on a motorbike JYY 434D, in Connington Crescent, was apparently bound over (in the Met) for possessing explosives. His address in Skem is 13 Hardy Lane, the home of Rosalinda Jack." (5)

One would hope that the accuracy of such records would be verified before the information is computerised. However, that may not necessarily be the case. The command and control systems mentioned earlier provide a method of transferring such information between different police stations.

The Effect Of Automation

The new information technology, automation of information storage, transfer and retrieval, is merely a tool for the police, and can be a most useful one; for example, where large amounts of information have to be collated in a major enquiry. The Ripper enquiry in Yorkshire demonstrated the need for some way of categorising, retrieving and cross-referencing large amounts of information quickly and efficently, a task for which computers are ideally suited. Similarly, victims of crime would surely welcome a speedier police response to incidents. However, there is a lack of accountability about the amount of information collected, who it is collected about and how it is categorised and used in different circumstances. Any information gathering exercise, which may be justified for a major incident like the Ripper murders, forms the basis of an extensive data base on innocent individuals which is accessed as a matter of routine.

The new technology has increased information held about individuals by the police. The Police National Computer has approximately 43 million entries. Most of these are accessible to any police officer and there are about 40 PNC enquiries per year, per officer. On a local level, 39 police forces have criminal information systems which are operational or proposed, and many of these are to be linked to the Police National Computer, allowing a speedy transfer of information. The existence of the capacity to collect information increases information collection, as is shown by the Skelmersdale example. This process can affect personal privacy, as described by the New South Wales Privacy Committee's report on Special Branch Criminal Code Records issued in that Australian state in March 1978:

> "There should be more control over the decision to open a card or dossier. Once....opened, many items of information may be collected which would never of themselves have initiated a card or dossier. The extensive opening of such files leads inevitably to widespread surveillance of the subject."

The access to information, which can be obtained by local criminal information systems, leads to increased use of that information. Thus the projected Merseyside and Manchester criminal information systems would have generated between them as many enquiries as the yearly total of enquiries to the Police National Computer by all forces at the moment. This is because of their proposed expensive data bases and the ease of access to these by police officers both in the street and in the station.

The type of information stored has changed since criminal records were introduced in the 1950s and increasingly police systems combine hard factual, criminal information with speculative criminal intelligence. Some insight into this development is given by Chief Inspector Fraser of Merseyside Police, (in Modern Policing 1981), as follows:

> 'My own force, Merseyside, will implement a Crime and Criminal Information System in 1984/5. It will incorporate criminal records, criminal intelligence, crime reports, firearms and shotgun records and property. The system is expected to hold about one million entries about property, crimes and criminals....It has been estimated that there will be some 20,000 transactions daily...." (6)

Computers store information in broad categories, devoid of context. Thus in Suffolk, one of the computer categories is "suspected person". A suspected person is defined as someone who is actually involved in crime but has not yet been convicted of any office. But a person can appear on the suspected persons index, when they have been reported as being stopped three times within the County within the month. The combination of the holding of information about individuals who have not been convicted of any crime, the need to classify that information for computer purposes, and the automatic process of switching information about individuals who have been stopped three times to the suspected persons index, would therefore lead to a nightworker becoming classified as a suspected person because as such he is more likely to be out at night and thus more likely to be stopped by the police. This is apparently the case in the Metropolitan area according to the Policy Studies Institute Report.

It can be argued that the holding of information about individuals who have not been convicted of any crime, is part of "criminal intelligence" that each police officer has traditionally held in his head and that computers only enable such information which is necessary for crime prevention and detection to be shared. However, whereas the police officer acquires and keeps information in a certain context which is ever-changing, the brief summary of that information held on the computer is devoid of context. So the fact that the individual is a night-worker, that the police officers in the town are implementing a policy of, say, increasing the numbers of stops and searches, and that they can most easily make him their target, during the quiet hours when he is passing through the town, will not appear on the computer record.

The categories in which information is filed in a manual record, or held in a computerised form, can also cause concern. The subjectivity of such categories is demonstrated by the inclusion in the Stolen and Suspected Vehicles Index of 'vehicles seen in noteworthy circumstances'. There is no definition of 'noteworthy'. The process by which information could be transferred from a Neighbourhood Watch Committee to a police officer, to a collator, to a micro-computer, to a force-wide system, can act like Chinese Whispers. Clearly, it is in the interests of the police that information is sifted and inaccuracies detected where possible. However information which is partially correct can also be substantially wrong - as is shown in the following case.

This involved Jan Martin, who was due to work for Michael Barrett (ex Nationwide presenter) who had set up a film making company. A client of Mr Barrett's company stated that they would not countenance Jan Martin's employment because she was a "subversive". Through her father, who had worked at Scotland Yard, Jan Martin discovered that she was listed as a subversive on the Special Branch Computer. This was because whilst driving on the Continent she and her companion were spotted by a cafe owner who thought that her companion bore a resemblance to a member of the Baader-Meinhof gang, for whom the police were looking. He took their car number, reported their presence to the police, who reported it to Interpol, who reported it to the Special Branch. Meanwhile the two members of the Baader-Meinhof gang, with whom Jan Martin and her companion had no connection whatsoever, had already been arrested.

If inaccuracies can creep into information passed between police officers of a similar training, they are much more likely to occur when individuals from different backgrounds and with different roles approach a problem in different contexts and use different languages - for example social workers and police officers. And indeed the view taken by social workers and police officers of the purpose of, say, juvenile liaison meetings, can be different, as an example in the book Justice For Children shows. (7)

> "As a training exercise, a case conference, one of a series, was held which involved police and social workers. The participants were not told until after the session that the names used and the families discussed were fictitious. However, soon afterwards the social workers received a request from the police station for more details about one of the families who had been discussed. Clearly the information, which social workers believed to be confidential, had been passed by the police officers attending the conference through to their local collators."

It is a feature of police information systems that information flows in to the system from other sources but not out to the community - except in the rather different example of demographic data. Thus it is very difficult for an individual to check the accuracy of information held about him or her. The 'suspected person' in Suffolk could well be treated differently by the police from people not on that register, and may feel harassed but have no means of checking the reason for the police behaviour. It is only in the rare cases that inaccuracies are spotted - sometimes after the citizens whom they concern have had very distressing experiences - as in the case of Val Baker. Driving away from Plymouth in 1983, Ms. B, who was eight months pregnant, was stopped by the police. This was because, her car number, when checked through the computer, gave an address where there had been a drugs raid two years previously. In the police station she was strip-searched and detained for four hours on suspicion of carrying illegal drugs. A drugs raid did take place in 1981 - but only because police went to the wrong address. Ms. B's father had since successfully sued the police for trespass - but the wrong information had remained on computers for two years.

The effect of information technology on the right to privacy i.e. the right to a private life and correspondence as set out in Article 8 of the European Convention on Human rights, is clear. Thus while the programming of the PNC was under way in May 1972, Police Review stated that

> "Police intelligence is now forward looking, anticipating who is going to commit what, when, and where, and because it is so purposeful it is also frequently libellous....much of the information is personal details of the suspect, his family, associates, way of life, and although it may seem to trespass on the freedom of the individual it is the bread-and-butter of successful policemanship." (8)

To civil libertarians, the sacrifice of personal privacy is too high a price to pay for a policing method which has yet to be shown to be effective. Even if it were effective, it may be unacceptable just as imposing a curfew to diminish the crime rate at night would also be unacceptable in our society.

Storage of personal information, both manually and particularly in automated form, affects not only personal privacy but also freedom of association and freedom of movement. In 1984 it was revealed that devices had been installed on the M1 motorway for the purpose of detecting stolen vehicles. These devices "read" number plates, converting the registration number into a form which can be processed by a computer. The computer is periodically loaded with information from the police National Computer's "Stolen and Suspect Vehicle" Index. This allows the device to check a car against PNC information without swamping the PNC with thousands of vehicle checks. However, as we have seen, the index contains not only the numbers of stolen vehicles, but over 40,000 of long-term interest to the police, and over 9,000 'checked in suspicious circumstances'. It is, therefore, not surprising that Trade Unionists fear that this device is a means of checking and trapping the cars of activists on the way to a picket, or that prospective demonstrators are concerned that this technology, together with the new police powers in the Police and Criminal Evidence Act will be used to inhibit their freedom of movement.

The practice of taking numbers of vehicles going to and from demonstrations and checking them with the PNC, is long established - automation is likely to extend the practice. Similarly, if someone classified as a 'suspected person' on the Suffolk computer is more likely to be stopped and questioned by the police, this categorisation will affect his or her freedom of movement.

However, the very secrecy and mystique surrounding information gathering and the many misconceptions about it can be counter-productive in policing terms. The writer was present at a meeting to set up a local neighbourhood watch scheme in South London, in Spring 1984. The failure of the police to confirm or deny that information relating to named individuals, which would have been passed by the Neighbourhood Watch Committee to a police officer, would not then be transferred widely to other police officers, was one of the main reasons that the meeting decided not to adopt a Neighbourhood Watch Scheme despite the great concern of many of the individuals attending about the high burglary rate in their inner city area.

As stated above, information technology is a tool for the police and can be a most useful one - however it is not a neutral tool. The categories into which information has to be organised to be put on a computer record and the ease with which it can be cross-referenced, transferred and centralised all have an effect on policing methods. The combination of changing police methods and the use or the abuse of information technology can have serious consequences not only for privacy but also for freedom of movement and association. It is important that police information systems are subject to stringent control if civil liberties are to be preserved.

Control Of Police Information Systems

In theory, the police are accountable for this use of information technology to police authorities, parliament and the courts. They are also constrained (theoretically) by the need to operate with the consent of the public rather than by coercion. In 1984 Parliament faced the question of protecting individuals against the use and abuse of personal information, in debates on the Data Protection and the Police and Criminal Evidence Bills and the Miners' Dispute. Humberside and Merseyside Police authorities, among others decided whether to authorise an increase in computerisation of police information and intelligence. The European Court of Human Rights discussed the infringement of personal privacy, in its judgement on the case of Mr. Malone, an antique dealer whose telephone had been tapped, and the inadequacy of British law in dealing with it. It is therefore instructive to examine how successful these bodies have been in protecting personal privacy and civil liberties in this context.

Parliament

In 1984 Parliament debated and passed the Data Protection Act. The Act was described by the Home Secretary, during the second reading of the Bill in August 1983, as being for the following purpose:

> "It will reassure people in this country that when computers are used for storage and use of personal data there are special safeguards for individual privacy which are well up to international standards....to gain membership of what one might call the European Data Protection club, thus ensuring the very important commercial interests of British firms are not placed at a disadvantage in relation to firms in other European countries."

However, despite these laudable intentions the Data Protection Act is not a reassuring document for individuals concerned about the police use or abuse of information.

The Act, which is based on the principles of the European Convention on Automatic Data Processing, sets out certain principles – that information about living individuals should be collected and used fairly and lawfully, that it should be relevant, not excessive, accurate and not transferred except for the purpose for which it is collected. It also gives individuals important rights to get access to information held about them. The data protection principles are set out in schedule I of the Data Protection Act 1984:-

Personal data held by data users

1. The information to be contained in personal data shall be obtained, and personal data shall be processed, fairly and lawfully.

2. Personal data shall be held only for one or more specified and lawful purposes.

3. Personal data held for any purpose or purposes shall not be used or disclosed in any manner incompatible with that purpose or those purposes.

4. Personal data held for any purpose or purposes shall be adequate, relevant and not excessive in relation to that purpose or those purposes.

5. Personal data shall be accurate and, where necessary, kept up to date.

6. Personal data held for any purpose or purposes shall not be kept for longer than is necessary for that purpose or those purposes.

7. An individual shall be entitled –

   (a) at reasonable intervals and without undue delay or expense –

   (i) to be informed by any data user whether he holds personal data of which that individual is the subject; and

   (ii) to access to any such data held by a data user; and

   (b) where appropriate, to have such data corrected or erased.

Personal data held by data users or in respect of which services are provided by persons carrying on computer bureaux

8. Appropriate security measures shall be taken against unauthorised access to, or alteration, disclosure or destruction of, personal data and against accidental loss or destruction of personal data.

However, whatever the strength of the Act in relation to other types of information the safeguards for the individual are seriously lacking because of the exemptions allowed for information held by the police, exclusions from the Act and the difficulty of enforcement.

The Act allows for whole information systems to remain secret – those which are certified by Ministers to be 'national security systems' are exempt from all the provisions of the Act, including registration (Sec 27). However, the Act does not define 'national security' – the scope of this term depends on what the Minister certifies. Therefore Special Branch records, such as those concerning individuals such as Jan Martin, would be exempt from control or investigation to ensure their accuracy and relevance. There will be nothing to stop 'national security' information, such as that which recorded Ms Martin as a subversive, continuing to be transferred from police records to private individuals.

Although police records must be registered and are subject to the principles of accuracy and relevance in the Act, there are wide exemptions. The restrictions on the transfer of information do not apply to transfers of information to the police for the detection or prevention of crime or the apprehension or prosecution of offenders (Sec 28(3)). Thus the case of the Ealing schoolboy, reported in the Daily Telegraph, whose school record was in the possession of the police, could occur after the implementation of the Act. Schools could pass information to the police including confidential records, although they would not be obliged to do so.

Similarly, individuals will not have access to records about them which are held for the purposes set out above. Clearly it might hinder the detection of crime if those about to be brought to justice were able to look at police records and follow the police collection of information about them. However, in order to ensure that records are accurate, other countries have individuals who are specifically employed to check the accuracy of police records and to monitor their development. In Sweden for example the transfer of personal information by, say, doctors or government departments to the police must be authorised by the data protection ombudsman. In this country, however, it was only after a long struggle by the medical profession that the government agreed to regulations ensuring that sensitive medical information can only be transferred to the police with the permission of a doctor. The government has refused to implement similar regulations for the equally sensitive information held on social work records. Thus transfers are to be allowed to police systems for the prevention of crime as well as the detection of offences and the apprehension of offenders. The prevention of crime is, however, undefined – thus confidential social work information about juveniles on an estate with a high crime rate could be transferred to the police because it may be deemed to help the 'prevention' of crimes which have not yet been committed.

The mechanism set up to enforce the Act is not the powerful data protection advisory committee, recommended by the Lindop Report, which could look strategically at the whole area of technology and data protection and have the expertise to advise government, parliament, data users and data subjects and to provide an independent check on the accuracy and relevance of police data systems. The Act merely provides for one data protection registrar, with 20 staff, to deal with an estimated 400,000 registrations and to protect the interests of data subjects. (9) Thus, although police systems will have to register the type of information held and where it is obtained from and transferred to, in general terms, it is unlikely that the Data Protection Registrar will have the time and resources to check the accuracy and relevance of police systems, or even to deal effectively with individual complaints. Moreover, although it is equally important that collated records in manual form, such as those in Skelmersdale, are subject to the same principles of accuracy and relevance that now apply to automated records, they do not in fact receive the same protection. The Act fails to cover manual records. The registrar will therefore have no jurisdiction over records held in manual form.

The Act will be enforced partly by complaints to the registrar, whose limited staff and resources are set out above, and partly by individual access to the courts. However, surprisingly, an individual will not have a right of access to the courts if a record about them is transferred by the police to, say, the Secretary of their Social Club, without their permission. The Act only gives an individual a right to sue if a record is disclosed without the authorisation of the data user, that is the Police. (Sec. 23(i) (c)).

During its passage through Parliament the Bill was criticised by members on all sides of the House and some amendments were made. However those opposing the Bill suffered from a lack of information. The Data Protection Act was preceded by the report of the Lindop Committee. However, the part of that report dealing with police records is not complete - despite requests by the Committee and the Committee's attempt to involve the Home Secretary, the Metropolitan Police refused to give certain information. The Committee was placed in the unfair position of learning about the new Metropolitan Police computer from a journalist's report in the Times and being refused confirmation of that report by the Metropolitan Police. The Committee states:

> "Most of the evidence we received from the police was helpful and willingly given, but the Metropolitan Police seemed to assume that a wide exemption would be granted for police applications and that it was therefore not necessary for us to include detailed information on some of them, about which we made pressing enquiries. The observations we make on any applications are of value only to the extent that the information on which they are based is adequate; in the case of Metropolitan Police we have not been able to satisfy ourselves that this is so." (10)

Thus the parliamentary committee which was discussing the Bill was already hampered by the gaps in the Lindop Report. The lack of information was clearly of concern to the Lindop Committee, which states:

> "While we have no reason to believe that the public needs to be unduly alarmed by the general use of computers for police purposes, in relation to the Metropolitan Police we do not have enough evidence to give a firm assurance to that effect for all aspects of police practice." (11)

Thus, during the Committee Stage there was an amendment to delete the exemption in relation to information passed to the police for the prevention of crime. This was narrowly defeated, but only after two government backbenchers had voted in favour of it. Despite the concern expressed by MPs of all parties, no further information about the uses of, or controls over, police information was provided to the committee by the government - gaps in the Lindop Report were not filled.

A few amendments were made to the Act, although the main problems raised by the Lindop Committee and quoted above, were not solved. The government's first draft of the Bill allowed information to be transferred to the immigration authorities, e.g. from doctors. This was criticised as being clearly in breach of the European Convention on Automatic Data Processing, and was eventually deleted. However, many records relating to suspected illegal entrants can be held on the police computers because they relate to the prevention or detection of crime. Thus we may still face the situation of individuals being worried about consulting a doctor because their medical records could be transferred to the police. The Act was amended to give the Registrar clear duties but neither his staff nor resources were increased. Originally civil servants could certify that certain records related to National Security and were exempt from the Bill - now this must by done by a Minister of Cabinet rank or the Attorney General. (Sec 27(1)). Regulations limiting the transfer of medical information to the police are to be introduced.

The following example illustrates the failure of the Act to protect individual privacy. In 1984 an Ipswich woman was alarmed to be visited at home by police investigating the death of a newly born child. The police officer had got her name and address from the DHSS who had transferred names of all parents of newly born children to the police. The Act would do little to control such practices. The mother could complain to the Registrar that information had been transferred from the DHSS to the police. Even if the Registrar had the time to investigate he would probably conclude that the information transferred related to either the prevention or detection of crime and therefore was allowed under the Act. The Act has provisions for individuals to sue in the courts instead of going through the Registrar (Sections 22 to 25). However, in the unlikely event that the court concluded that the transfer was not exempt from the provisions of the Act, she would not be able to get any compensation. Compensation is only payable for "unauthorised" transfers - that is, unauthorised by the data user, the DHSS, not by the person to whom the information relates.

The provisions allowing transfer of confidential information to the police are permissive only; a data user would not be required to transfer that information. But as the Police and Criminal Evidence Act introduces new provisions allowing the police to obtain a warrant for evidence held on a computer relating to a serious arrestable offence the exemption under the Data Protection Act is not necessary for the detection of a serious crime. (Sec. 19(4))

The new power to search for evidence in the Police and Criminal Evidence Bill (when first introduced) was widely criticised and eventually various records such as those relating to health, social work, and journalism were wholly or partly exempted. This re-drafting did not however amend the worrying power of seizure. Under the Act a police officer who is already on the premises can seize any other item, including a computer record, which would be evidence of any offence. "Any offence" could relate to a minor matter. (Sec. 19(3) (a))

In some respects the Police and Criminal Evidence Act will generate more information gathering. During its passage through parliament, those concerned with protecting the liberties of the individual asked, and the government agreed, that provisions be inserted relating to record-keeping. Thus, in those circumstances police officers will make a detailed record of each stop and search, such records will then be available to the individual upon request. However, the government resisted all attempts to ensure that these records were destroyed after a certain period of time if they did not relate to a specific crime. The increased recording of stops and searches and details of individuals stopped during road blocks could lead to more information on police data bases and perhaps to more people appearing on a suspected persons register, such as that in Suffolk.

It was clear from the debate during the passage of both these bills that MPs from all parties were concerned about increased information gathering and police use of information. But, like members of the Lindop Committee, they were hampered in their discussions by the lack of official policy or statistics on these matters. Nevertheless the issue of personal privacy was at the heart of the House of Lords debate about an opposition amendment to the Telecommunications Bill, to ensure that the passage of information relating to the content of telephone conversations was subject to the rule of law. After strong co-ordinated opposition the government agreed to introduce a Bill to deal with this matter in the 1984/5 session of Parliament which would take into account the decision in the case of Malone then impending in the European Court of Human Rights.

The Courts

As the recent case of Mr. Malone shows, the European Courts are prepared to protect personal privacy in circumstances where the English courts are unable or unwilling to do so. The case dealt with police collection of information through telephone tapping and telephone metering.

Mr James Malone, an antiques dealer, was acquitted in 1978 of dishonest handling of stolen goods. During the trial it emerged that his telephone had been tapped and he started civil proceedings in October 1978. These were concluded before Vice Chancellor Megarry who held that Mr Malone had no remedy in English law. Although an administrative warrant procedure had been a long standing practice his Lordship observed that the matter, "cries out for legislation". Mr Malone then started proceedings under Article 8 of the European Convention on Human Rights for invasion of his private life which resulted in a ruling in his favour in August 1984. The UK was found to be in breach of Article 8 in that the process of telephone tapping and metering which constituted an invasion of privacy had not been "according to law" as interpreted under the Convention. In February 1985 details of the Government's legislative response to the judgement were announced. These included provision in legislation for continuous review of the working of the system by a Commissioner and the setting up of a Tribunal to hear complaints.

According to the minority opinion of Judge Petiti (who only dissented from the majority decision on the basis that it had not gone far enough), the Court should have prescribed what measures this government should introduce to control telephone tapping, as it was clear that telephone tapping was seen as just one method of state invasion of personal privacy.

"The danger threatening democratic society in the years 1980-1990 stems from the temptation facing public authorities to 'seeing into' the life of the citizens. In order to answer the needs of planning and tax policies the State is allowed to amplify the scale of its interferences. In its administrative systems, the State is being led to proliferate and then to computerise its personal data files. Already in several of the Member States of the Council of Europe, each citizen is entered on 200 - 400 data files. Enquiries become more numerous; telephone tapping constitutes one of the favourite means of this permanent investigation....It would be rash to believe that the number of telephone interceptions is only a few hundred per year in each country and that they are all known to the authorities." (12)

It was generally anticipated, on the basis of a previous German case (Klaus), that the European Court would find that telephone interception effected by the police within the general context of criminal investigations would be in breach of the right of privacy contained in Article 8 of the European Convention on Human Rights. It was most welcome to civil libertarians that the Court also considered and condemned the use of metering information. At present in most areas a telephone has to be metered by attaching a meter check printer device. When the new automated "system X" comes into effect throughout the country not only will the consumer have the most useful service of receiving an automatic print out of all calls made with their bill, but also the information will be readily and easily available to be transferred to the police. Thus the decision should now lead to proper control of the use of records. It is worrying that when, in 1978, Mr. Malone asked the police and Post Office to remove listening devices from his telephone he was told that they had no authority in the matter.

The clear decision of the European Court of Human Rights against the British Government together with an undertaking given by the Government at the House of Lords stage of the Telecommunications Bill have led to an undertaking to introduce a Bill to control the interception of telephone calls. Civil libertarians would argue, following Judge Petiti, that the whole question of telephone tapping has to be viewed in the context of police and state information gathering. Such information gathering, which is clearly an interference with private life, should only be allowed on a warrant issued by a judge on the basis of clear guidelines set down in an Act of Parliament. This is a system adopted in, for example, Canada and in European countries and perhaps yet another push from the Council of Europe will mean that the British Government will follow, as usual too slowly, but hopefully not too late.

The development of case law regarding privacy is one of the more hopeful signs for those wishing to bring police information gathering under parliamentary control. The Law Commission's Report on the law of Confidence (1981 Cmnd 8388) recommends a wide-ranging reform both to consolidate the existing protection for confidential relationships and extend it. This would include the concept of reasonable expectation of privacy and protection in civil law against for example, intercepting or listening devices being used in one's own home. The law of Confidence is an area which has been much neglected by lawyers concerned to protect individual privacy.

Police Authorities

Recently, police authorities have observed increased information gathering. Some of them have been asked to fund computers and software to enable the police to carry out intelligence work. Some police authorities have refused to pay for extended intelligence gathering - in others these proposals have gone through without opposition.

Police authorities outside London are made up of one-third magistrates and two-thirds elected councillors. One of the main duties of a police authority is to fund an efficient police force; they can appoint a chief constable and call for reports on policing matters. The decision of police authorities about systems is often limited - sometimes because of the lack of information before the authority and perhaps at other times because of the lack of interest by the authority members. Police authorities, without full-time officials other than the police and with no great expertise in these matters, sometimes do not realise the relevance of defending applications which they approve. Thus the police computer system of Humberside, which deals with criminal intelligence, was the subject of an application to the police authority by the Chief Constable for £400,000. According to our information it went through 'on the nod'.

In contrast Merseyside Police Authority refused to spend £4 million on what was described by the New Statesman as:

> "A powerful mainframe computer (which) would have housed all Merseyside's criminal records and provided on-line access to police stations throughout the country. Later software could have been added to enable the police to carry out intelligence work. The system would have been capable of handling up to half the current 21,000 plus enquiries being made each day on the Police National Computer in London.

> Computer sub-committee Chairman, John George alleges that the Police reneged on a commitment to allow local independent monitoring of the system to prevent abuse - while for their part the police say this function is now fulfilled by the new Data Protection Registrar, Eric Howe." (13)

As stated above it is clear from the small resources available to the registrar and from the lack of any general power to carry out enquiries (such as that given to the Equal Opportunities Commission) that such a monitoring function could not be carried out. The decision of Merseyside authority was taken at the end of 3 years discussion and investigation by the police authority's computer sub-committee during which they claim the police failed to tell them that many of the functions for which the new computer was required would eventually be offered on the Police National Computer. Merseyside is a rare example of a police authority which took note of the Lindop Committee's warnings in their report that:

> "the linking of factual personal information about an identifiable individual with speculative data about criminal activity could pose a grave threat to that individual's interests." (14)

The position of Londoners is rather more worrying. London has no police authority. This gives London MPs the advantage that they can ask the Home Secretary, as police authority for London, questions directly. However, the disadvantage is, that unlike Merseyside, there is no committee of councillors which could monitor and consider, for example, the privacy implications of computerisation.

Conclusion

According to the judgement of Judge Petiti in the Malone case:

> "The mission of the Council of Europe and of its organs is to prevent the establishment of systems and methods that would allow 'Big Brother' to become masters of the citizen's private life. For it is just as serious to be made subject to measures of interception against one's will as to be unable to stop such measures when they are illegal or unjustified, as was for example the case with Orwell's character who, within his own home, was continually surveilled by television camera without being able to switch it off." (15)

The lack of accountability of the police, in respect of their gathering and use of information, either to the Courts or the police authority, together with the lack of effective control by Parliament, have serious consequences for civil liberties. Not only personal privacy, but restrictions on freedom of movement (for example of people going to demonstrations) and of association (Special Branch at present has records of those attending lawful political meetings) are being encroached upon by default rather than by any co-ordinated policy.

It could be argued that more information gathering could lead to more effective policing and that the secrecy surrounding police information systems is necessary in the interests of detection of crime. However, the mystification of the uses to which police forces are putting the new technology, together with instances of abuses of information which come to light, can actually lead to distrust of the police.

The lack of public debate and information about police power through information technology means that there is little pressure on chief constables to justify their information-gathering methods, while the media seem to reflect no more than a vague distrust of police surveillance rather than an informed criticism. A more informed public debate could consider the following methods of providing effective control of increased police power through information technology. As the Data Protection Registrar under the Data Protection Act will be so weak, the role of overseeing the relevance and accuracy of police records could be taken more directly by Parliamentary Select Committees.

The lack of a law to protect personal privacy in this country, similar to that in existence in Sweden, Canada, USA and many Western European countries, could partly be remedied by the introduction of the Bill prepared by the Law Commission on confidentiality. This would give a remedy for individuals when information given by them in confidence has been passed on in breach of that confidence. Thus, personal information given by a patient to a doctor, by people to a teacher, would be protected from disclosure by that doctor or that teacher. The National Council for Civil Liberties has prepared a Bill to control the use of telephone tapping and surveillance devices. The Bill, which is intended to inform the debate about the Government's Bill on telephone interceptions would provide judicial control of the issue of warrants to tap telephones or to use a surveillance device.

Control over further investment in the hardware of information technology could be aided by more interventionist and informed police authorities. By having the financial control and the duty to ensure the efficiency of a police force, they should in theory be able to assess whether an increase of information gathering has actually led to any decrease in crime and whether, in any event, the disadvantages in terms of distrust of policing and invasion of civil liberties outweigh any possible advantages. The lack of conspicuous success of the Oxfordshire computerised information system should give the Home Office cause for thought before committing more resources to computerised systems.

Whereas parliamentary involvement in data protection in relation to police records, interventionist police authorities carefully scrutinising funding applications for investment in new technology, and court involvement to uphold an individual's right to privacy, will go some way to controlling police power through new technology; even if all these measures were adopted the gap between the formal law and the informal practice could still be wide. A new Privacy Act to control information transfer would have to be enforced very thoroughly ·in order to destroy the existing traditional 'Old Pals act'. This term describes the informal system under which information can be transferred by police officers to their former colleagues who are, say, working in a security firm. Adoption of a formal system of law would certainly help to set out a baseline and to create a balance between individual privacy and the interests of the detection of crime, but without effective police accountability in all aspects of policing work, its practical effect would be limited.

1984 was a year of slight progress in the formal law with the introduction of a Data Protection Act and a helpful European Court decision in the case of Malone. It is now up to doctors and patients to ensure their confidences are protected, teachers to put forward a code of practice governing the transfer of information to the police, unions to negotiate the basis on which employers will transfer information and lawyers to litigate. The problem of police use and abuse of new technology is not just one for parliament, police authorities and the courts - it is one which every civil libertarian should be aware of. Transfer of personal information to the police to solve a serious crime, such as a murder which has already been committed, is difficult to object to. However, collection by the police of speculative hearsay information from the workplace, from voluntary organisations, from housing and local authorities, social services departments, schools, and through Neighbourhood Watch schemes should be questioned by those who are the subject of, and in control of, such information.

Citizens of European states who may, according to Judge Petiti, have 200 to 400 data files compiled on them need to ensure that the content of these files is not abused; that privacy is preserved. Such an aim is not necessarily incompatible with police effectiveness and the detection of crimes which have already been committed.

NOTES

1. Judgement of the European Court of Human Rights, Malone Case, 4/1983/60/94, 2nd August 1984: also Vol.82 Series A.

2. Report of the Committee on Data Protection, December 1978, Cmnd 7341 at para 8.05.

3. Ibid at para. 23.08

4. John Alderson, Policing Freedom, p. 108.

5. The real names have been changed in this example.

6. Modern Policing, 1981, Edited by David Walls Pope and Norman L. Winer at p. 219.

7. Allison Morris, Justice for Children

8. Police Review, 5th May 1972, quoted in Political Police in Britain by Tony Bunyon

9. In the jargon of the Act, data users are those who hold information data subjects are those about whom information is held.

10. Op.cit., supra, note 2, para 8.03

11. Ibid, para 8.33

12. Op. cit., supra note 1, 2nd August 1984 at pp 36-37

13. New Statesman, 28th September, 1984, p.5.

14. Op. cit., supra, note 2 para 8.16

15. Op. cit., supra, note 12 at p. 39

14. THE POLICE AND CRIMINAL EVIDENCE ACT AND THE PRESS

John Williams

The history of the Police and Criminal Evidence Act 1984 reveals some interesting marriages of convenience brought about as a result of opposition to the Government proposals. A notable example was the joint campaign launched by the National Council for Civil Liberties and the Police Federation over the proposals in the second Bill relating to the police complaints procedure. Similarly a clause in the original Police Bill, presented to Parliament in 1982 but lost as a result of the election the following year, succeeded in bringing together the British Medical Association, the Law Society, the Church and the Press. Under this clause the police would have had the power to enter property under the authority of a warrant issued by a justice of the peace and search for, _inter alia_, documentary evidence in some way related to crime. Furthermore, these documents could be seized by the police and taken away for use in the investigation and also as possible evidence in a later trial. Their objection centred on the fact that the Bill made no distinction between non-confidential and confidential documents. As these groups regarded confidentiality as central to their relationships with clients or the public, the potential power of the police to search their files might make it more difficult for them to gain the trust of the person giving information in confidence. A powerful campaign was launched which sought special protection for those people who kept confidential records in the exercise of their duties and in the second Bill the government went some way towards meeting the criticisms. The purpose of this essay is to examine the course of the debate on this subject from the time of the first Bill to today's Police and Criminal Evidence Act. Special attention will be given to the treatment of confidential information kept by journalists and the changing attitudes of the press towards being granted special status. By mapping out the debate surrounding these provisions and considering the response of Parliament, it is possible to predict some of the problems that will arise in the operation of the Act. Initial consideration will be given to the objections put forward by the main groups opposing that early provision.

The Original Proposals

From the outset the Police and Criminal Evidence Act 1984 aimed at setting the standard and style of policing in this country for many years to come. In order to halt and reverse the rising tide of crime, the Government felt it necessary for the police to be given wide powers of investigation. Although some would argue that the Act represents a compromise between the need for effective policing and the need to protect civil liberties, it cannot be denied that the powers of the police have been considerably increased under its provisions. As a result obtaining the right balance between effective policing and the rights and freedoms of individuals in a democratic society is left to the discretion of the police through the exercise of their statutory powers rather than specifically catered for in the legislation. If, as seems likely, an imbalance arises in favour of effective policing, there is nothing that can be done in order to

219

have it redressed. This may be illustrated by the Act's treatment of confidential information. Prior to the drafting of the Bill the police had the power to enter property to search for and seize confidential information. The evidence suggests that this power had not been abused in the past. Michael Zander pointed to the fact that under the Misuse of Drugs Act 1971 the police could obtain a warrant to enter and search for evidence of drug offences (1). There was no special exemption for professional persons from its provisions, but that did not seem to have caused any special difficulties for doctors. The reason for this, argues Zander, is that the police had been sympathetic in the way in which they exercised their power. However, it is not necessarily the case that the style of policing adopted prior to the passing of the Act will survive the fundamental change in policing resulting from its enactment. Whereas professional persons had little to fear over their confidential information under the old law, the Act provides a new policing environment which does not have the same regard to the wider public interest.

The British Medical Association

Opposition to the clauses in the original Bill was centred on the need for certain groups to assure their clients or members of the public that information given would be held in confidence and would not be revealed to third parties without consent. The British Medical Association felt strongly that the original Bill threatened this relationship as it would have enabled the police to go on "fishing expeditions" through the files of a doctor; furthermore, such searches need not be limited to the files of a suspected person. The dangers were highlighted by the B.M.A. when presenting their case against the Data Protection Bill. They referred to an incident in Ipswich where police investigating the murder of a newborn boy were given information by the local D.H.S.S. about women who were pregnant at the relevant time. As a result of this information the police interviewed women mentioned on the list asking for details of the birth and the whereabouts of the child. Commenting on the decision a local D.H.S.S. spokesperson said:

> "It was decided to offer certain limited information in strict confidence to (the police). They were details of maternity benefits. I do not know how many women were involved. The information was given orally and on the basis that it would be used only for this inquiry. Confidentiality is the cornerstone of our system. Basically there is no disclosure without the client's permission. But there are occasions when the crime is so serious that we do provide information. The police are not given direct access to records." (2)

The B.M.A. criticised the handing over of the information, pointing out that what matters to patients is that information is held properly and that standards are backed by law. Once confidentiality is removed from the doctor/patient relationship, the effective practice of medicine becomes difficult - the law and the legal process should recognise this fact. An agreement between the Association of Chief Police Officers and the B.M.A. provided that there should be co-operation between the two professions, but that information should only be handed over when it is felt that there is an over-riding duty to society to release it. Routine investigation, as in the Ipswich case, does not constitute such an over-riding duty to society. The agreement in no way contemplated the police conducting a fishing expedition through all the doctor's records.

Any threat to confidentiality of the records kept by doctors could, it was argued, lead to doctors not keeping full and accurate details of their patients' medical history (3). Furthermore, it would mean that many innocent people totally unconnected with the crime would be subject to investigation by the police. Such people would be surprised to learn that they featured in an investigation as a result of information contained on their "confidential" medical records. As will be seen below, the lawyers managed to obtain total immunity for their own legally privileged material. Home Office Minister Patrick Mayhew argued that lawyers' clients "should feel able to place matters before their legal advisers so that the advice they receive shall be soundly based on all the relevant facts." A member of the B.M.A. asked whether there could be "a more eloquent description of why medical records should also be exempt" (4).

Futher concern was expressed over the use that might be made of the material whilst in the hands of the police. Assurances were given by the Government that the information would be destroyed as soon as the investigation had been completed. But this could mean it being kept for a long time if the investigations were complex or incomplete. What use would be made of the information during the period it was in police possession? Could it be used in other investigations? Could the information itself initiate a completely separate investigation into a totally unrelated crime? Who would have access to the information?

These were the arguments presented by the B.M.A. in opposition to the original proposals. After the General Election of 1983, the second Bill contained concessions made by the Government in response to the pressure put upon it during the earlier debate. The attitude of the B.M.A. changed and in November 1983 it stated that it no longer opposed the amended version because account was taken of the arguments the B.M.A. had put forward (5). The political climate had changed since the earlier Bill; the government had a large majority, the Bill had been introduced early in the lifetime of the Parliament and also the B.M.A. believed that the Data Protection Bill posed a greater threat to the confidentiality of the doctors' records. As will be suggested below, the concessions made by the Government were not as great as it first appeared and it may be that medical records still face the dangers feared by the B.M.A. in 1982.

The Law Society

The Law Society was more successful than the B.M.A. in its opposition to the original proposals. In its opposition it emphasised the importance of the confidentiality of lawyer/client communications stressing that the administration of justice depended upon clients talking freely with their legal advisers (6). During the second Bill's passage through the House of Commons the Government introduced an amendment which had the effect of completely exempting legally privileged material from the search and seizure provisions. This amendment was accepted and is now found in s.8(1) (d) of the Act. Problems may arise over the definition of legally privileged material. In cases of doubt, will the police be able to simply assert that the material is not legally privileged and therefore capable of being seized? A procedure whereby a court could make a determination of the status of material would considerably increase the value of this concession made in the Act. However, the exempting of legally privileged material is important because it conceded the point that there is some material that should escape seizure by the police altogether.

The Church Of England

The Church of England was quite vocal in its opposition to the original Bill fearing that confidences between priest and penitent might be subject to seizure. However, it is less likely that such information will be committed to paper as it is more usual for such matters to be discussed by word of mouth and no detailed record kept. Nevertheless, certain information may be committed to paper and, as such, would come within the general powers envisaged in the original Bill. By the time of the second Bill, the Church had concentrated its attention on police complaints and the issue of community policing, so the confidentiality issue ceased to be a major concern.

The Press

Thus it can be seen that opposition to the idea of the police having ready access to confidential information was partially dissipated by the amendments introduced by the Government in the second Bill. Partly this was a result of a mistaken belief that the concessions removed the dangers; partly it was a result of a realisation of the changed political climate brought about by the general election and the Government's large majority. However, the reaction of the press, the other body principally affected by this part of the legislation, to the second Bill was bizarre. Almost overnight the press changed its opinion from one which feared the potential threat that the original proposal would create to investigative journalism to one which argued that any special treatment for journalists over and above that given to the ordinary citizen was wrong in principle and should be rejected.

In February of 1983 the National Executive Committee of the National Union of Journalists decided not to oppose the clauses in the Police and Criminal Evidence Bill (the second Bill) which purported to protect confidential journalistic material. Although there were some misgivings by members of the Executive, it was felt that protection was necessary so that journalists could protect their sources of information. Paragraph 7 of the N.U.J. Code of Conduct states, "A journalist shall protect confidential sources of information." (7) By the time of the N.U.J. Annual Delegates Meeting later in the year, opposition to the Executive approach had grown. The A.D.M. passed the following motion:

"This A.D.M. believes that the Union cannot campaign against the Police Bill while accepting special privileges for journalists – a phrase that has not yet been defined and will not necessarily include all N.U.J. members. This Union has historically opposed the idea of classes of civil liberties and argued that journalists should not have better protection against the police or other state powers than is afforded to the ordinary member of the public. This A.D.M. believes the N.E.C.'s position, as stated to the Home Office in March undermines this principle."

The Case Against Special Treatment Of Journalistic Material

The N.U.J. was joined in its campaign against special treatment for journalists by other groups representing the newspaper industry. Opposition to the concessions made in the new Bill were voiced by the British Executive of the International Press Executive, the Association of Journalists, the Newspaper Society and the editors of 200 newspapers. The fear of these groups was clearly expressed by the 200 editors who said:

"We would rather be left out of the Bill. Journalists have no rights above those of ordinary citizens because journalists are ordinary citizens. We do not want special privileges conferred upon us. What is given can be taken away."

Those opposing special treatment felt that it would be difficult for journalists to do their job properly and in good conscience if they were afforded protection against search and seizure. Such a privilege would change the relationship of the press with government and change its status in society. The freedom of the press is not just a freedom for journalists and editors, it is a freedom to be enjoyed by all citizens which would be destroyed by placing journalists in a special category. Lord Hunt put it like this during the Committee stage of the Bill in the House of Lords,

"I would say that it is not too much to claim that the freedom of our press, one of our basic liberties, depends upon this exposure to search and seizure, if necessary, as a safeguard against the abuse of power of the press." (8)

Thus the press should be in no different a position vis-à-vis the police than any other citizen.

Another fear expressed was that the provisions contained in the new Bill would require the courts to formulate a definition of a "journalist". Once arrived at, the definition could be used by governments to introduce a system of registration of journalists which in turn could lead to journalists having to be licensed before they could perform their duties. This again posed a threat to the freedom of the press. Others felt that a definition of "journalist" might enable a Labour government at some future date to make journalism a closed shop. Unlike doctors, priests and social workers, journalists are not professional people. No special training is required – it is a vocation open to everybody with an ability to write. Nobody is "admitted" as a journalist, therefore nobody can be thrown out for whatever reason. However, once there is a definition, it raises all sorts of potential dangers.

A definition of a "journalist" might in itself prove to be elusive and lead to complex legal arguments. For example, should it cover a person who writes the occasional piece for the local paper? Does it include those people who write for academic periodicals? Should it be necessary for the person to earn the greater part of his income from journalism? How will people working in television and radio fit into the definition? Any legal definition would be considerably more restrictive than the natural meaning which the word currently enjoys.

On an international level, U.N.E.S.C.O. have been discussing the establishment of a new world information and communications order. Part of the proceedings involved consideration of the special status for journalists. Paragraph 50 of the Report emanating from the 1980 Conference in Belgrade states:

> "The professional independence and integrity of all those involved in the collection and dissemination of news, information and views to the public should be safeguarded. However, the Commission does not propose special privileges to protect journalists in the performance of their duties, although journalism is often a dangerous profession. Far from constituting a special category, journalists are citizens of their respective countries, entitled to the same range of human rights as other citizens....To propose additional measures would invite the dangers entailed in a licensing system since it would require somebody to stipulate who should be entitled to claim such protection." (9)

The then Minister of State at the Foreign and Commonwealth Office, Mr. Peter Blaker, fully endorsed this recommendation and recognised the dangers involved in giving journalists special status. This fact did not go unnoticed during the debate in the House of Lords (10). It is ironic that the press were now adopting the opposite argument to the one they adopted when considering the first Bill, whereas the Government was adopting an argument contrary to the one it had put forward during the U.N.E.S.C.O. Conference and in the original Bill.

The Case In Favour Of Special Treatment For Journalists

The argument in favour of special treatment emphasises the confidential nature of the relationship between journalists and their sources of information. Doctors, lawyers, priests, social workers and journalists would all find it difficult to exercise their profession if the police could have ready access to their confidential records. No distinction should be made between the type of confidence necessary for effective journalism and the type that is necessary in the exercise of those professions. The same status should be given to them all. The press has a duty to society to provide the information upon which the electorate can make their choice. Exposing confidential material to the full rigours of the s.8 search and seizure provisions would inhibit the free flow of information and pose a threat to investigative journalism which already has to endure the full burden of the Official Secrets Act 1911, in particular section 2.

Journalists are very jealous of their duty to protect their sources of information. The British Steel Case (11) and the more recent Sarah Tisdall case both illustrate that sources of information can be identified by the material handed over to the journalist. Thus it is important to ensure that such material is protected from the outset because seizure prior to any court proceedings designed to recover it would not be protected by the Contempt of Court Act. Section 10 Contempt of Court Act 1981 was designed to provide some protection for journalists by restricting the circumstances in which they may be compelled to disclose their sources of information. The section states,

> No court may require a person to disclose, nor is any person guilty of contempt for refusing to disclose, the source of information contained in a publication for which he is responsible, unless it be established to the satisfaction of the court that disclosure is necessary in the interests of justice or national security or for the prevention of disorder or crime."

Unfortunately the scope of the section, particularly in relation to the national security provision, was severely limited by the judgements of the Court of Appeal and House of Lords in Sec. of State for Defence v Guardian Newspapers (12). However for present purposes it is sufficient to note that the section does give special status to, amongst others, journalists. Furthermore, if no special status were given journalists at the investigative stage then the protection given in the Contempt of Court Act would be meaningless. For example, in the Sarah Tisdall (13) case the police could have avoided the niceties of the Act by obtaining a warrant to search the Guardian offices under the Official Secrets Act 1911. Certainly the Guardian contemplated this possibility and sought advice from their lawyers (14). It can only be assumed that this course of action was not taken because of the political repercussions that it might have caused. There is no basis for assuming that such considerations will necessarily carry any weight after the implementation of the Police Act.

When information is given to a journalist "in confidence" to whom does that confidence belong? In the case of legal privilege the confidence is that of the client and may only be waived with his or her consent. Similarly the confidence in the relationship between journalist and source belongs to the latter and may only be breached with his or her permission. It is, therefore, hardly within the power of the journalist to reject the notion of legal protection of sources. On the contrary, the journalist should be keen to ensure maximum protection for those people who at great risk to themselves provide the information upon which a free press relies.

Supporters of special status for journalists also reject the idea that it would entail the courts seeking a definition of "journalist". The Act does not refer to "journalists" but instead to "journalistic material" so the protection was being given to material rather than the person. Consequently, it was argued, the courts would not have to define "journalist". This argument does ignore the fact that a definition of "journalistic material" would probably be couched in terms of "material produced by a journalist", thus the courts would have to consider who is and who is not a journalist. This problem could be avoided by following the wording of the Contempt of Court Act. This Act avoids altogether mention of journalists or journalistic material. Instead it refers to "the source of information contained in a publication". Publication is defined by s.2(1) as including "any speech, writing, broadcast or other communication in whatever form, which is addressed to the public at large or any section of the public." It is conceded that this approach would widen considerably the scope of the protection, but if it is considered by Parliament to be the correct approach for protecting sources in court then logically it should also apply to protecting sources during the investigative process.

The end result of the debate over special status for journalists was that despite strong opposition from many parts of the press the Act included "journalistic material" in the provisions purporting to protect certain types of confidential information. It is ironic that the outcome should be that the Government included in its legislation a protection which it had originally denied to the press, whereas many elements of the press rejected the very protection which they had originally sought. The question which must now be asked is whether the provisions of the Act actually do protect such material, or are they merely a cosmetic exercise designed to destroy opposition and convince the public that the legislation is concerned with basic civil liberties?

The Provisions Of The Police And Criminal Evidence Act 1984

During the passage of the second Bill the Government made a number of concessions in response to the pressure outlined above. In cases where the police wished to have access to certain types of confidential information they had to use a procedure different from the usual search warrant found in s.8 (15). For the sake of convenience this will be referred as "the procedure". The principal difference between the s.8 warrant and the procedure is that it requires that an application for access must be made to a circuit judge rather than to a magistrate (16). Furthermore, under the procedure the police will not be seeking, at least initially, a warrant to enter and search premises, but instead an order that the material is to be made available to them within seven days (17). Such an application will normally be inter partes unlike s.8. (18) The procedure may be likened to the civil process of discovery. The need to apply to a circuit judge rather than a magistrate does little to inspire confidence that the procedure provides adequate safeguards for confidential material. During the Parliamentary debates suggestions were made that application should be made to a High Court judge, but these were rejected by the Government (19). However, there are precedents for applications for warrants being made to a High Court judge, most notably s.2 Incitement to Disaffection Act 1934 and also s.2(5) Public Order Act 1936.

Use of the procedure for the purpose of obtaining access to material held by journalists presupposes that the material being sought is "journalistic material". Such material is defined in the Act as being "material acquired or created for the purposes of journalism", a rather unhelpful provision (20). How widely the courts will interpret the word is at present speculative. Limiting it to material in the hands of those who make their living from established newspapers or periodicals is too restrictive as it might well exclude publications linked to pressure groups, academic publications and trade publications. It is here that the advantage of the word "publications" can be appreciated. The public interest requires as wide a dissemination of information as possible and the more difficult it is for the police to have access to such material the greater the safeguard.

A further gloss on the definition of "journalistic material" is that it must be in the possession of a person who "acquired or created it for the purposes of journalism" (21). Again we encounter difficulty in speculating how the courts will interpret this provision. For example, in the Sarah Tisdall case the editor of the Guardian "acquired" the Heseltine memorandum "for the purposes of journalism". If the same events took place after the Act comes into effect would he be able to insist on the use of the procedure by the police and be able to successfully resist a s.8 warrant? A literal interpretation of the section would suggest that he could, if all other requirements were satisfied. However, will the courts adopt such an interpretation or will they insist that "acquired" means "lawfully acquired"? This latter interpretation would limit the scope of the protection as much of the material that finds its way into the hands of the journalist is based on unauthorised leaks.

The unlawfulness of the acquisition could be based on the fact that the property is stolen. In such cases it is submitted that this fact should not serve to take the material outside the ambit of the procedure. The Guardian Newspaper Case recognised that the protection given by the Contempt of Court Act could serve to defeat established property rights where the sole reason for recovery was to identify the informant. There is no compelling argument as to why such reasoning should not be applied at the earlier investigating stage. More difficult is the case where the unlawfulness arises from the fact that the acquisition is a breach of the Official Secrets Act 1911.

Section 2 of the Official Secrets Act must rate as the most discredited piece of legislation in force. Political parties when not in government have pledged to repeal it. The Franks Committee (22) proposed its repeal and the jury in the recent Clive Ponting trial indicated their contempt for a piece of legislation that has more to do with covering up government ineptitude or duplicity than protecting the national interest. However, it survives and the present Government and the judiciary have shown an insatiable desire to perpetuate its most draconian effects. Any proposals for protecting the press can only be considered in the context of the repeal of the Official Secrets Act and its replacement by a Freedom of Information Act. It is salutary to note that the Heseltine memorandum at the centre of the Guardian Newspaper Case would have been freely available in America. The argument by the Ministry of Defence that the leak would threaten relations with other states because they could not trust us with secrets is therefore bogus.

It is not the purpose of this essay to consider in any detail the case for the repeal of the Official Secrets Act, such arguments have been well covered elsewhere. However, it is worthy of note that governments apply double standards in their dealing with official information. Perhaps the most blatant example of this is the principle of self-authorisation for purely political purposes. It is not unknown for ministers in charge of government departments to release what would normally be regarded as secret information if it would enable him or her to manipulate the media. Cockerell, Hennessy and Walker in their book Sources Close to the Prime Minister (23) cite what they consider to be an example of such self authorisation. In January 1981 Mrs. Thatcher invited the lobby correspondents of the Times, Guardian, Financial Times and the Daily Telegraph to a private meeting. The following day all four papers, and only those four papers, carried a story that income tax was not going to be increased in the Budget. The story was stated to have come from "high authority" and from "the heart of the Government". Of course the meeting and the story might have been a coincidence, but it seems highly likely that "budget secrets" were released to journalists through the indefensible lobby system. It is interesting to consider the likely events if the leak had been by a low ranking civil servant. The authors point out the irony of the affair because only the previous week Mrs. Thatcher had said of leaks "They should not happen....It does not make for efficient government. I think that people are very much aware of the damage they have done." (24)

The value of the safeguards in the Police Act will depend to a large extent upon the relationship between it and the Official Secrets Act. If "acquired" is interpreted as excluding material received in breach of the Official Secrets Act then the protection afforded by the Police Act to journalistic material will be of little effect. Unfortunately it is rather sanguine to expect the judiciary to favour protection of sources at the expense of official secrets given its predilection for a wide interpretation of the national interest.

Once it is established that the material is journalistic material the Act requires a distinction to be drawn between "excluded material" and "special procedure" material. The distinction is important as the means of access may differ. Excluded material is defined by s.11(1) (c) as being journalistic material held in confidence which consists of documents, or records other than documents. Thus, in addition to showing that it is journalistic material it must also be established that it is held by a person subject to an undertaking, restriction or obligation to hold it in confidence. It can only be confidential material if it has been so held since it was first created or acquired for the purposes of journalism (25). The effect of this latter provision is that it excludes material initially not given subject to confidence. For example, if a person gives a document to a journalist without any requirement of confidence it will not be excluded material if, after discovering its importance, the journalist passes it to another journalist "in confidence". Special procedure material is defined in s.14(1) (b) as being "journalistic material, other than excluded material". Bevan and Lidstone limit this to material which does not rely on the written word, such as photographs or real evidence (26). It is doubtful whether this interpretation is correct as an essential element of journalistic material which is excluded material is that it is held in confidence. Therefore special procedure material in this context must include all journalistic material which is not held subject to a confidence - in addition to material other than documents, or records not being documents, held in confidence (27). At first sight it may appear that this extension of protection to all journalistic material whether subject to confidence or not is welcome, but, as will be shown below, the effect is to actually increase the power of the police to have access compared with the pre-Act law.

If the police wish to have access to journalistic material which is either excluded material or special procedure material they can only do so in accordance with the procedure laid down in Schedule 1. The Schedule is complex and will no doubt prove to be a paradise for the legal profession. An application is made to a circuit judge for an order that the person in possession of the material should produce it to a constable for him to take away, or to give him access to it within seven days, or within such longer period as is specified. The application may be made by a constable, but under the Code of Practice it must be with the authorisation of an officer of at least the rank of superintendent. This purported safeguard is meant to emphasise the serious nature of the procedure but a failure to comply with it will not render the application or any order void, it will only give rise to the possibility of disciplinary action and may be used in any subsequent civil or criminal proceedings. Given the delicate nature of the application it would have been better if the Act had stipulated that the express authorisation of the superintendent (28) was necessary rather than making it a question of practice.

Before making an order the circuit judge must be satisfied that one of two sets of access conditions has been met. The conditions are as follows:

The First Set Of Access Conditions (29)

There are "reasonable grounds for believing" that

a. a serious arrestable offence has been committed

b. there is special procedure material on the premises

c. the special procedure material is likely to be of substantial value to the investigation in connection with which the application is made and

d. the special procedure material is likely to be relevant evidence.

In the context of the inter partes application the proof of a reasonable ground for belief is certainly fairer than under the ex parte application in s.8. However, it is inevitable that the police evidence is more likely to be accepted and much of it will be circumstantial. For example, in relation to (b) above the constable could present evidence that the journalist has been seen visiting a civil servant from the Ministry of Defence who has access to classified information. On this basis the police could argue that there were reasonable grounds for believing that secret information had been passed to the journalist. How is the journalist to deny this? Anything other than a straightforward denial is difficult as it is impossible for the journalist to prove what he has not got in his file other than by giving the police access. As in the case of search warrants issued by magistrates there is a danger that a presumption will arise that the police will not apply for an order unless it is absolutely necessary.

"Serious arrestable offence" is defined in s.116. Although the name suggests a grave offence in reality a number of fairly trivial offences fall within the definition (30). This is worrying as a number of police powers under the Act become available upon the existence of such an offence. An "arrestable offence" is a "serious arrestable offence" if it is likely to lead to one of a number of stated consequences. One of those consequences is that it will cause "serious harm to the security of the state or to public order". The courts would regard cases such as Sarah Tisdall as falling into this category. The taking of the material constituted theft, an arrestable offence. It comes within s.116 by virtue of the fact that in the Government's view, and supported by the judiciary, removal constitutes a serious harm to the security of the state. In determining whether such harm will arise the circuit judge will again rely heavily on the applicant's evidence. In such circumstances it will be argued, and probably accepted by the courts, that any breach of the Official Secrets Act entails a breach of confidence by a trusted servant of the Government. This is still the case even though the actual information is not in itself sensitive or is simply politically embarrassing. This approach will seriously limit the protection given by the procedure.

The first set of access conditions relate only to special procedure material and not excluded material. However, police access to the former material is increased compared with the position prior to the Act. Under the old law the police could only search premises for such material if the warrant was issued under the provisions of one of some forty statutes. Since the Act the court can make an order for disclosure even though such material could not have been the subject of a warrant under the old law. It can be argued that this does not matter as what is being applied for under the Act, and the inter partes nature of the application, is quite different from the procedure under a search warrant. In many cases this is correct but, as will be noted below, the Schedule does give the court the power to grant access to such material under an ex parte application for a search warrant rather than an order to disclose. Furthermore, special procedure material covers all journalistic material which is not subject to a confidence. It is ironic that a provision designed to give greater protection to journalistic material should have the effect of actually extending the number of occasions on which the police can have access.

Conditions (c) and (d) above also give rise to concern mainly because of the vagueness of the language used. Expressions such as "is likely to be of substantial value to the investigation" and "is likely to be relevant evidence" place the judge very much at the mercy of the constable making the application. Much reliance will be placed upon the officer's judgement as to the importance and weight of the material sought; it is unlikely that the constable will say that they are only of minor importance.

Once the above conditions have been proved to the judge's satisfaction the constable must then show that other methods of obtaining the material have been tried but without success, or they have not been tried because it appeared that they were bound to fail. The Act does refer to "other methods" being tried so it is incumbent upon the police to try more than one way of obtaining the material. However, no indication is given as to how hard they must try and similarly where no attempt is made to obtain the documents it is only necessary to show that it "appeared" that they were bound to fail. Presumably, this means that it appeared so to the police constable making the application. Once again this attaches great weight to the evidence of the police and gives little opportunity to the journalist to refute the assumptions upon which the application is made.

The final requirement under access conditions 1 is that making the order is in the public interest having regard to "the benefit likely to accrue to the investigation if the material is obtained; and to the circumstances under which the person in possession of the material holds it." It is a matter for speculation just how the courts will interpret this provision. Very little comfort can be taken from the recent experience of judicial regard for the confidentiality of journalistic material as it shows that judges have the same obsession with the need to protect "official secrets" as do politicians.

The Second Set Of Access Conditions (31)

The second set of access conditions is fulfilled if there are reasonable grounds for believing that there is either excluded material or special procedure material on the premises and that a search of the journalist's premises under a search warrant would have been possible under one of the forty statutes referred to above. These statutes are amended to the extent that excluded or special procedure material cannot be seized under their provisions, such material must now be obtained under the second set of access conditions.

If the circuit judge makes an order then failure to comply with it will be contempt of court and be dealt with accordingly. Where the order stipulates that the constable can take the material away then by virtue of s.22 it may be retained for use as evidence at trial or for forensic examination or investigation in connection with an offence. However, nothing may be retained where a photograph or copy would be sufficient for police purposes. The police are also under an obligation to provide the journalist with a record of the material taken, access to it under the supervision of a constable and a photograph or access to take a photograph of the material.

Access To Confidential Material By Means Of A Warrant (32)

The police may in certain circumstances be able to avoid altogether the use of the inter partes procedure outlined above. The Act enables them to do this in one of two ways by permitting the circuit judge to issue a search warrant to enter and search the journalist's premises after an ex parte application. Firstly, the judge may issue a warrant to enter and search where either set of access conditions has been met and one of the following further conditions is also fulfilled:

(a) it is not practicable to communicate with any person entitled to grant entry to the premises to which the application relates,

(b) it is practicable to communicate with a person entitled to grant entry to the premises but it is not practicable to communicate with the person entitled to grant access to the material,

(c) the material contains information which is subject to a restriction on disclosure or an obligation of secrecy contained in an Act of Parliament and it is unlikely to be disclosed if a warrant is not issued,

(d) service of the notice of the application may seriously prejudice the investigation.

Conditions (a), (b) and (d) require little comment other than to note that they are couched in the same vague language as the access conditions. This is even more crucial in this instance because the application is ex parte and the circuit judge will be relying exclusively upon the evidence supplied by the constable. Where the police are relying on (d) the Code of Practice stipulates that they must indicate why it is believed that service of notice may seriously prejudice the investigation (33). Condition (c) is of particular concern to the press as it applies to information subject to the Official Secrets Act. Wherever the police feel that the material held by the journalist comes within the Act they can avoid altogether the use of the procedure. Given the all-embracing nature of the Act and the anti libertarian interpretation given to it by the judiciary, material held by journalists will be especially vulnerable to the issue of a search warrant rather than an order to produce. Furthermore, as noted above, the first set of access conditions apply to cases where no warrant was available under the old law, in these cases a warrant will now be available. It is again rather strange that a procedure purporting to protect this type of material should end up actually increasing the scope of police powers.

231

The second method of obtaining a warrant authorising entry and search is where the circuit judge is satisfied that the second set of access conditions has been satisfied and that an order to disclose has not been complied with.

The Conduct Of The Search

The conduct of the search is dealt with by the Code of Practice accompanying the Act (34). An officer of the rank of inspector or above is to take charge of the search and he is to ensure that it is conducted with "discretion and in such a manner as to cause the least possible disruption to any business or other activities carried on in the premises." The officer in charge is to ask the person appearing to be responsible for the premises to produce the material being sought. If necessary he may also ask to see an index to the file if there is one. The officer may inspect any files which according to the index appear to contain the relevant material. More extensive searches are only possible if the person responsible for the premises refuses to produce the material sought, refuses to allow access to the index, if it appears that the index is inaccurate or incomplete or "if for any other reason the officer in charge has reasonable grounds to believe that such a search is necessary in order to find the material sought." Breaches of these provisions will not render the search unlawful nor will any evidence obtained necessarily be inadmissible; they will simply give rise to disciplinary proceedings.

One final point should be made concerning the power of the police to seize material when they are on the premises. Section 19 states that when a constable is lawfully on any premises he has the power to seize <u>anything</u> on the premises if he has reasonable ground for believing that it was obtained in consequence of the commission of an offence or if he reasonably believes that it is evidence in relation to the offence which he is investigating or any other offence. This power is only qualified to the extent that s.19(6) forbids the seizure of legally privileged material. Therefore, a constable on premises by virtue of a s.8 warrant, a warrant under any other legislation or by consent may seize excluded material or special procedure material if he or she has the requisite belief. This avoids altogether the procedure and presents a great danger to the journalist who consents to the police entering his premises. In addition it does raise the possibility of the police using the s.8 warrant as a pretext for searching his or her material.

Conclusion

Is it right that journalists should reject any special status regarding their confidential material? The N.U.J. Code of Conduct contains the following,

> "2. A journalist shall at all times defend the principle of the freedom of the Press and other media in relation to the collection of information and the expression of comment and criticism. He/she shall strive to eliminate distortion, news suppression and censorship.
> 5. A journalist shall obtain information, photographs and illustrations only by straightforward means. The use of other means

can be justified only by over-riding considerations of the public interest. The journalist is entitled to exercise a personal conscientious objection to the use of such means.
7. A journalist shall protect confidential sources of information."
(35)

The success or otherwise of a journalist in obtaining information is an important criteria for assessing his or her ability. Whereas the State is constantly seeking ways of managing news and controlling the flow of information the journalist must constantly be alert to ways in which his or her precarious position under the law can be improved. One obvious way in which this can be done is through a repeal of the Official Secrets Act and its replacement by a Freedom of Information Act. Another way is by ensuring that once information is in the hands of the journalist it is protected from seizure in all but the most extreme cases of public interest, a concept which must be clearly defined and recognise the right of the public to know what the government of the day is doing in their name. In giving such protection the law should not be seen as giving the journalist special status but instead giving special status to the public's right to know. The International Commission for the Study of Communication Problems stated,

"Freedom of the press in its widest sense represents the collective enlargement of each citizen's freedom of expression which is accepted as a human right. Democratic societies are based on the concept of sovereignty of the people, whose general will is determined by an informed public opinion. It is this right of the public to know that is the essence of media freedom of which the journalist, writer and producer are only custodians. Deprivation of this freedom diminishes all others." (36)

It is submitted that the Press is wrong in opposing in principle the idea of special protection for their confidential material from search and seizure by the police. It may be that there are those who would argue that people such as Sarah Tisdall who commit crimes should not be protected against prosecution. But against this we must balance the wider public interest. Furthermore it is salutary to recall that much of the investigation that led to the Watergate disclosures would not have been possible under our law. Investigative journalism needs the support and assistance of people such as Sarah Tisdall and consequently the press should fight for maximum protection. At one level, contempt of court, they have fought for such protection. It is inconsistent that they should reject it in an area where their information and the identity of their sources is more immediately threatened.

However, this raises the question whether the Act actually gives such material the protection that it deserves in a democratic society. The above account of the provisions of the Act indicates that it falls far short of providing adequate protection for the confidential material of journalists. In a number of areas it is found wanting. Perhaps the main criticism is that in certain respects it actually extends the power to search for material, but in addition we must also note the vagueness of the language used, the reliance that will in practice be placed upon police evidence and the current anti-press approach being adopted by the judiciary that will be responsible for interpreting the legislation. Such defects must be remedied before it can properly be said that the law protects the freedom of the press. The great danger is that the existence of the procedure will increase police awareness of the potential use of such a power whilst at the same time provide no real safeguards. In many respects the position might be worse than it was under the pre-Act law.

The law should start from the premise that such material should be protected. It should then define narrow exceptions to that general rule based on over-riding public interest rather than simply the interests of the political party that happens to form the government. Such reforms are long overdue and would certainly require a fundamental change in political and judicial attitudes. However, these factors do not in any way detract from the need to fight for a press that provides us with the information necessary to any democratic society rather than one which prostitutes itself through the lobby system whilst at the same time contemplates forfeiting information which it holds on trust for the community as a whole.

NOTES

1. Guardian 4th. February 1983.

2. Guardian 15th May 1984.

3. B.M.A. News Review, April 1983 @ pp.46-47: Times 21st March 1984.

4. Ibid p.46.

5. B.M.A. Parliamentary Unit publication 3 December 1983.

6. The Law Society - "Memorandum by the Society's Standing Committee on Criminal Law" - December 1983, p.5.

7. National Union of Journalists - "Rule Book" Appendix A.

8. Hansard Vol.454 H.L. 3rd. July 1984 Col.115.

9. Sean MacBride "Many Voices, One World" Part V @ p.264.

10. Hansard op.cit. note 8 @ Col. 114.

11. British Steel Corp. v Granada Television [1980] 3 W.L.R. 774.

12. Secretary of State for Defence v Guardian Newspapers [1984] 1 All E.R. 453 C.A., [1984] 3 All E.R. 601 H.L.

13. See Guardian March 24th. 1984.

14. Ibid @ p.4.

15. s.9.

16. Schedule 1 para 1.

17. Ibid para. 4.

18. Ibid para. 7.

19. An amendment to this effect was proposed by David Steel, David Owen, Alan Beith, Alex Carlile and others on 1st. May 1984.

20. s.13(1).

21. s.13(2).

22. "Departmental Committee on Section 2 of the Official Secrets Act 1911" - Chairperson Lord Franks.

23. "Sources Close to the Prime Minister" - @ pp. 138-39.

24. Television interview with Thatcher noted ibid. @ p.139.

25.   s.11(3).

26.   V. Bevan and K. Lidstone "A Guide to the Police and Criminal Evidence Act 1984" @ para.4.55.

27.   See Hargreave and Levenson - "A Practitioner's Guide to the Police and Criminal Evidence Act 1984" LAG. @ p.43.

28.   Code of Practice on Searches etc. para.5.11.

29.   Schedule 1 para 2.

30.   See Royal Commission on Criminal Procedure Report 1981 Cmnd.8092 paras. 3.5 - 3.9.

31.   Schedule 1 para 3.

32.   Ibid paras. 12-14.

33.   Op.cit. para.1.7.

34.   Ibid. paras. 5.11 - 5.12.

35.   Op.cit. note 7.

36.   Op.cit. note 9 @ p.233.

Paul Boateng

The view of the police officer as no more than a "Citizen in Uniform" was finally extinguished by law in 1984 with the passing of the Police and Criminal Evidence Act, and almost simultaneously in the public mind, by television. The consideration of the final stages of the Bill took place in the midst of an industrial dispute in the mining industry, characterised by the deployment of the police on an unprecedented scale, stretching their powers to the limit, whilst equally unprecedented powers were being conferred upon them by the legislature. No one witnessing the scenes at Orgreave or elsewhere in the collieries, or the style of policing that surrounded them, could be in any doubt as to the nature of the modern British Police Force or its readiness to use the powers given to it. With or without helmets and visors, and all the other paraphernalia of the force adopted in the aftermath of the inner-city disturbances of 1981, the 'Paras of the Pits' bore little or no resemblance to Dixon of Dock Green.

This was no sudden transformation. The image of the police as citizens in uniform had been crumbling steadily since the sixties. Police powers had grown in reality as the checks and constraints which might have been exercised upon them by the Court or Government, central or local, had been whittled away either consciously or by neglect. Nowhere more so than in London where the untrammelled development of police power has reached its dizziest heights. The exercise and development of police power in the capital city, unique in the absence of its own elected police authority, (a role nominally exercised by the Home Secretary), has taken place in a context in which the police have appeared accountable, quite literally, to no one but themselves and have often acted as such.

London and the Metropolitan Police Force allegedly posed considerable difficulties for the Royal Commission on Criminal Procedure, whose report preceded the Police and Criminal Evidence Act. Many of its members, in the course of taking evidence and on the basis of commissioned research, recognised the particular problems that the Met. posed in any extension of police powers. The racism of the Metropolitan Police Force and the extent of the crisis in management and discipline which bedevil it, as revealed by the Policy Studies Institute's Report (1) meant that the safeguards proposed by the Commission and enacted in an amended form in the new Act were likely to be of little effect. Abuses of police power were both more likely to occur and more likely to go effectively unchecked in the Metropolitan Police Force than elsewhere. The members of the Royal Commission, like Lord Scarman after them, failed to make any proposals which would seek to address these very real problems by tackling the issue of police accountability in London. This was, is and has been, since the formation of the Metropolitan Police, a political hot potato which Royal Commissions, High Court Judges and even very many politicians until present times have not felt inclined to take up. No such inhibitions affected the London Liberal and Radical Union which, in 1892, in its campaign for election to the London County Council (the G.L.C.'s predecessor) stated that "the London police force are the dearest police in England, they cost a 9 penny rate. The people of London have no control over them at all, they are managed by the Home Office which is not responsible to the London ratepayers. Every other great town has control of its own police. This control is exercised through a Watch Committee. London has the same right and the same need for the control of its own police, as any other great town." Very little has changed except that policing London now costs Londoners approximately 17 pence in the £ on the rates.

Outside London the position was and is different. London had seen, prior to the creation of the Met. in 1829, no less than seventeen Parliamentary Committees established to consider how to maintain law and order in the capital. Very real fears existed at the time of a police force which, at the hands of central Government, would develop on a Continental model and be used for political ends. The situation, at that time, in which law and order lay in the hands of the magistrates backed up by the army in the last event, was clearly untenable. And in the absence of a coherent or mature system of local government in the capital, it was accepted that the Home Secretary should be the police authority. This was done with reluctance, however, and with a recognition that local control would have been preferable. As a result, when local forces were set up outside London six years later in the ever growing towns and cities, Parliament gave control to the boroughs through the 1835 Municipal Corporations Act. So, from the start in the provincial urban centres, the police were made accountable to locally elected representatives. These committees, consisting solely of elected members, were granted full powers including those of appointment, suspension and dismissal of officers in their forces. The role and structure of the county boroughs, as police authorities, through their Watch Committees, was fixed in the Municipal Corporation Act of 1882. The counties, with their joint standing committees, half of whom were magistrates, were provided for in the Local Government Act 1888. Only London remained without any element of police accountability to locally elected representatives. Elsewhere the principle embodied in statute was of the police service as an integral part of local government.

The Police Act 1964, which followed the report of the Royal Commission on the Police in 1962, made no change in the position of London, even retaining the anomaly of the City of London Police Force with the common council as its police authority. The Royal Commission had stated (with no reason given whatsoever for the assertion): "We consider that these differences between control of the police in the metropolis, and elsewhere, are broadly justified by the intrinsic importance and interest of events in London which call for police attention." (para 225). The Act's effect outside London, apart from the new and larger police authorities it established, was to institutionalise the growing authority of the Chief Constable, giving him responsibility for the "direction and control of the Force", and defining the role of the police authority as the maintenance of an "adequate and efficient Force". The distinction thus created between operational matters and administrative and financial ones, the former beyond the remit of the police authority, has bedevilled the relationship between police and local government ever since. This distinction has provided for all who needed it, whether Chief Police Officers jealous of their powers, or police authorities hesitant or unwilling to test theirs, with both justification and an excuse for inaction and downright obstruction of the exercise and development of democratic control over the police.

The Police and Criminal Evidence Act might have provided an opportunity for Parliament to look again at the legal framework of policing and, if not to change the constitutional position of the police, at least to take cognisance of the need to enhance accountability as a safeguard against the extension of police powers. This would have required a Government other than one to whom an extension of the power of local authorities in any respect was an anathema, particularly when such an extension would be at the expense of the police. Not only were opportunities for fundamental reform missed, such as the police complaints system which is an integral part of any system of accountability, but where, as in the provision for statutory consultation, the issue of accountability was touched upon, not the slightest concession was made to enhance the role of local authorities. Indeed, in London, once again an exception to the pattern elsewhere, the police themselves were to be given the primary role in initiating consultation. This was not surprising, given the ethos and philosophy of the Government of the day. The Government's perception of the role of the police is exemplified by the part they have played in the miners' dispute, a role which lead even the Police Review to say that "the Police service is entitled to wonder whether it is being used to preserve law and order or to implement Government policy" (2).

The policing of the miners' dispute is worthy of study and it provides an indication of the context within which the Police and Criminal Evidence Act has become law. It was clear from the outset that the police were to play a major part in the Government's strategy in support of the National Coal Board and against the National Union of Mineworkers. To co-ordinate this strategy there was a special Cabinet Committe headed, not by the Home Secretary as in the case of the Civil Contingencies Committee in the past, but by the Prime Minister, Mrs. Thatcher, herself. This Committee, known as MISC 101, met every Monday and Wednesday morning reporting to full Cabinet on the Thursday. The Committee comprised, in addition to the Prime Minister, Lord Whitelaw, Nigel Lawson, Leon Brittan - the Home Secretary, Norman Tebbit, Peter Walker - the Energy Minister, Tom King, Nicholas Ridley, Sir Michael Havers - the Attorney General and John Stanley - representing the Armed Forces. At each meeting the different ministries provided assessments. The Department of Energy gave the daily stocks of coal from the National Coal Board and any major movements requiring police protection. The Attorney-General reported on legal developments in relation to the dispute, in which the Courts and a disturbingly compliant Judiciary played a major part. The Home Office and the Department of Energy provided intelligence reports on the Union's intentions. It is inconceivable that overall policing policies and strategies did not form a topic for deliberation at this Committee based on the information provided by the National Reporting Centre, whose role warrants close scrutiny.

The work of the Cabinet office, in preparing for the strike, was recognised by "The Economist" as follows: "Officially, the police have been keeping the peace on their own local initiative. Not in reality. All Government preparations for dealing with the miners' strike have been by word of mouth and informal. The Cabinet office has taken care to ensure there are no traceable links with the Coal Board or the police". (3)

The role of the National Reporting Centre since the inception of the strike has been described, not without cause, as pivotal to the policing of the dispute. Its functioning which John Alderson - the former Chief Constable of Devon and Cornwall - has described as "in effect a national operational centre" has done much to undermine the so-called tripartite arrangement for police accountability between a Chief Constable, his own police authority and the Home Office.

The National Reporting Centre is headed by the President of the Association of Chief Police Officers, an association of 43 Chief Constables which has no constitutional status and is accountable to no one. Concerned with the provision of mutual aid, as laid down by Section 14 of the Police Act 1964, the National Reporting Centre was established in Scotland Yard after the 1972 miners' strike, in the wake of the mass picketing of the Saltley works in Birmingham. The Centre operates around the clock with a staff which includes one of Her Majesty's Inspectors of Constabulary, who is appointed by the Home Secretary. The police and the Government persist in peddling the myth that "there are no operational directions given from this centre". (4) However, when a reporter from the Guardian was shown around the centre in March of that year, he witnessed an operational direction being given to the Midland force to monitor two bus loads of pickets until they reached the Nottinghamshire border. The admitted function of the National Reporting Centre makes a nonsense of the assertion that its role is not a political or even an operational one. The centre, in addition to meeting requests for aid, plots its disposition, collates information on arrests, and receives the daily reports of Chief Constables on the operational situation. Tactics are assessed and the daily reports from aided forces are reported to F4 Department at the Home Office, which is responsible, inter alia, for public order, terrorism, subversive activities and security liaison with MI5. This is, in turn, passed on to the Home Office and the Cabinet Office. It is hard to believe that the traffic is all one way. The miners' strike has witnessed the development of a national policing strategy by Cabinet committee and Chief Constables with a clear intention of ending the dispute on terms favourable to the Coal Board. The "back to work" drive which commenced on 15th August 1984 in Yorkshire, documented in "The Times" of that day, is a case in point...."it was planned to have a pre-arranged return to work on the first week at selected pits known only to the police and the Coal Board". The timing had been co-ordinated with ministerial speeches and "The Times" went on to refer to a "strategy of accelerating a slow drift back to work". The effect has been to create, on an ad hoc basis, a National Police Force. The conferring of wide powers on such a Force under the recent Police and Criminal Evidence Act is likely to have far-reaching consequences, not only for the nature of the Force and the public's perception of it, but for civil liberties generally.

We need not engage in hypotheses for an indication of what these powers are likely to mean in practice. The miners' dispute provided the Chief Constables with an ideal testing ground for those powers, even before the Bill had received the Royal Assent. They have been aided in this by the Government's support for "stern measures". The Home Secretary and other Government spokespersons have let no opportunity slip by for strictures on the need to counter "the violence of the pit heads", whilst the press and the media, with a few honourable exceptions, have contributed to the creation of a public mood in which the Judiciary, at every level, have exhibited a marked reluctance to impose a check on police power. The widespread deployment of road blocks, stop and search and house to house searches have all emerged as features of the policing of the dispute foreshadowing powers in the Act itself. These tactics have attracted widespread criticism in the mining communities and have embittered relationships between the police and the public. This is exacerbated by the clear identification of the police with Government policy. The use of road blocks to control the movement of pickets is an example, not only of how the dispute foreshadows the provisions of the Act, but also of the operation of the National Reporting Centre as a conduit pipe for Government-inspired policing policy on a national level. On the opening of the National Reporting Centre, Home Office officials relayed the Attorney General, Sir Michael Havers' advice on the use of road blocks. This was accepted, despite its dubious legal basis and Chief Constables have uniformly adopted the practice throughout the dispute, even stopping the cars of Kent miners at the Dartford Tunnel as they travelled North.

Police authorities have been rendered effectively powerless in the face of this National Force. The size of the operation (where as many as 8,100 police have been brought into the coal fields in any one day), has led to massively escalating costs, estimated at £120 million by mid-September 1984. (5) This has posed, even with central Government assistance, intolerable financial burdens on most police authorities, in addition to weakening police cover in their own areas by the deployment of police resources outside these areas, quite without reference to the authorities themselves. Action by the police authorities to limit the spending powers of Chief Constables provoked the threat of legal action by the Attorney General. The South Yorkshire Police Authority sought to revoke the Chief Constable's authority to spend up to £2,000 on any item and questioned the maintenance of a mounted Police Force. This provoked an outcry from the Government and the police lobby, but succeeded in forcing the Home Secretary to provide a degree of financial relief. He also, however, suggested that he would use powers in the Police and Criminal Evidence Act, presumably in the form of regulations, to check attempts by a police authority to suspend its Chief Constable. Specifically mentioning the South Yorkshire Authority, he said, "nor will we stand idly by and let left-wing police authorities undermine Police operations. South Yorkshire have tried to do that twice now. I will continue to take every action to ensure that the Chief Constable's independent position is not jeopardised. This dispute has indeed shown that Chief Constables need further protection against politically motivated acts of spite." Councillor Edward Shaw, Chair of the Association of Metropolitan Authorities Police and Fire Committee, expressed the Association's view when he said, "we are concerned that Chief Constables seem able to incur unlimited expenditure without reference to Central or Local Government or the effect on other services". (6)

No relief for the beleaguered striking mining communities was forthcoming from the activities of their police authorities. Prompted by growing concern about police tactics in the mining communities, the West Yorkshire and South Yorkshire authorities established special sub-committees to monitor police tactics and to receive complaints. They have been unable, however, to do anything to prevent the movement in or out of their areas of police forces in such numbers and using such tactics as the Chief Officers see fit. The role of local authorities in relation to police complaints is not enhanced by the Police and Criminal Evidence Act. This does not go beyond the power to refer complaints to the Police Complaints Authority in the case of complaints against senior officers and the general power to keep themselves informed of the workings of Sections 84 - 93 of the Act which are concerned with police complaints. In London, again the exception, that role is given the Commissioner. Gabrielle Cox, Chair of the Greater Manchester Police Committee, summed it up when she said, "the miners' dispute has highlighted the fact the Chief Constables can do what they like. Our responsibilities appear to be meaningless." (7)

The passing of the Police and Criminal Evidence Act imposes a fresh responsibility, however, on police authorities under section 106 of the Act, concerning arrangements for obtaining the view of the community on policing and community co-operation in crime prevention. This section seeks to give statutory force to a recommendation by Lord Scarman in his report, following the Brixton uprising of 1981. The Report argued that a "Police force which does not consult locally will fail to be efficient." (8) He recommended that a statutory liaison committee, or other appropriate consolidated machinery, be established, preferably at police division or sub-division level on every force. This report led to the establishment of a number of local consultative committees not only in London but elsewhere in England and Wales. These varied in their constitution and practices in accordance with the perceptions and attitudes prevailing in the police or other local authorities concerned and in the local police forces. The mushrooming of these committees followed the issuing, in June 1982, of Home Office circular 54/1982 which laid down certain guidelines for these arrangements.

The enactment of the new legislation does not, however, make the establishment of formal police community consultative committees a statutory requirement. Police authorities (with the exception of London) will have a discretion as to what they see as the appropriate method "for obtaining the views of the people". The Home Secretary told the Commons in March 1983 that this meant in some areas that there may be no need to have consultative committees at all as traditional informal methods of consultation might be adequate. It has been made clear that arrangements for consultation will be the subject of scrutiny by the Inspectorate of Constabulary and, under the new law, where the Secretary of State feels that arrangements are not adequate he can require the responsible person or authority to report to him and, if necessary, to review them. The Chief Inspector of the Constabulary, in his Report for 1982, commenting on the "enthusiasm" of "most forces" for more formal consultative arrangements, indicated the importance he attached to "effective dialogue" between public and police of all ranks. Just how "effective" this has been or can be, particularly in London where there is no locally elected police authority, remains to be seen. Expectations of these arrangements vary and sometimes conflict. Central and Local Government, Chief Constables, even different sections of the public, do not necessarily have a common purpose or interest in such matters. A consumer input into policing priorities, consumer education as to what the police can or cannot be expected to do, the legitimisation of police action before or after the event, consultation-based public relations exercises, the winning of more resources for crime prevention, the diversion or redirection of existing resources to this end, a forum for complaints, grievances and concerns about police action, may all exist as objectives in the minds of those who choose to participate in consultative arrangements. It is difficult enough to reach a common consensus as to what is meant by effective, let alone determine whether or not the arrangements warrant that description.

There is, manifestly, a divergence both of view and practice about those who are to be consulted and how, and in what numbers they are to be represented, and in what proportion to the elected representatives of local authorities. The Home Office and the police, particularly within London, are clearly concerned not to allow the local authority interest to predominate. The linking of such committees to local authorities, which has been the objective of a number of London Labour-controlled local authorities as a means of seeking a greater degree of accountability to Local Government structures in London, has been resisted by both the Home Office and the police. Local authorities have, in their turn, sought to establish Police/Community Liaison Committees as Council sub-committees with Councillors forming the majority of the members. A proposition which finds support from a (perhaps) unlikely source in the Conservative Political Centre's pamphlet, "Protecting the Police" (9) which recognises the potentially undemocratic nature of a floating membership and recommends a statutory requirement of at least 60% of elected local Councillors.

The effectiveness of these arrangements, however one chooses to define them and whatever the criteria to be applied, is unlikely to be clear in the relatively short passage of time since their inception and is the subject of study by the Centre for the Analysis of Social Policy of the University of Bath, whose initial survey was published in May 1984. (10) The Home Office, with its customary reticence, has as yet to publish the results of its own review and may never do so. Clearly an "effective dialogue" in Home Office terms is not assisted by the widespread dissemination of relevant data. No one should be under any illusions that such a "dialogue" is any substitute for a locally elected police authority with sufficient power to make its role more than a nominal one. In London it is not even the police authority (namely the Home Secretary) that is given responsibility under the Act for the arrangements about consultation in the Metropolis. Instead, this is conferred on the Commissioner. He is required to consult with the borough councils on these arrangements. Only after strong opposition in Parliament to this cession of the powers of the Home Secretary as police authority, to the Commissioner, was an amendment made requiring the Commissioner to take into account guidelines issued by the Home Secretary.

Events surrounding the reorganisation of the management structure of the Met. in November 1984, after the Royal Assent was given to the Police and Criminal Evidence Bill, do not augur well for the implementation of even its limited concessions to the concept of accountability. Not only were the "sweeping changes", to quote the Met's own house journal, not the subject of any consultation at all prior to the event with the local borough Consultative Committees, but at a stroke they did away with the relationship between the Committees and the local Commander. This was supposedly the lynch-pin of the whole consultative arrangement as envisaged by Scarman and reflected in the Act. This was founded on a borough basis with a supposedly accessible local figure, the Commander, responsible for policing within the borough, sitting on the Committee. This moved the Lambeth Consultative Committee, widely regarded as the jewel in Sir Kenneth Newman's crown of consultative arrangements and the first to be established, to raise its voice in protest. This was a noteworthy event in itself but futile in the absence of any means of exercising any control whatsoever over a decision of critical importance to those people who were directly affected by it. When he introduced the reorganisation, Sir Kenneth did not feel obliged to say whether he expected consultation to take place in future at divisional or area level or whether the police would be prepared for consultative groups to remain based on the boroughs.

Londoners were, once again, not considered worthy of even minimal consultation by a service to which they make a substantial financial contribution on an issue of obvious importance. The cynicism with which these arrangements are viewed by those upon whom they are imposed, both police and public alike in the capital, is therefore understandable and is likely to deepen, not diminish, with the passage of time.

Indeed, the passage of time, with the coming into effect of the new law, holds out little in the area of Local Government and accountability, but the prospect of growing alienation between police and public, and confrontation with those Local Government institutions determined to resist the onward march of police power. This is likely to be heightened where the use of powers available under the Act is linked with a marked determination on the part of the police to adopt a strategy which involves a multi-agency approach to crime. An approach characterised by police attempts to subordinate housing, planning, social services and educational policy and resources to strategies initiated by the police themselves outside of the normal democratic process.

Police accountability requires that the police be accountable to the law, to an effective and credible machinery for the investigation of complaints against the police and to effective accessible Local Government structures. The Act weakens the first of these, carries out a cosmetic reconstruction of the second and makes no real concession to the attainment of the third. The move for the reform of the relationship between Local Government and the police, and the campaigns and ad hoc institutions that have arisen at a local level to monitor police accountability, is born partly out of the failure of the first two conditions for an accountable force. The dissolution of the Met. counties and, therefore, of directly elected police authorities as part of the Government's hasty and ill-conceived reform of Local Government will deepen the current crisis of accountability. The creation of what is, in effect, a phantom national Police force capable of being conjured up and taking real and tangible form at the behest of the Executive through the agency of the Chief Constables operating outside an effective structure of local democracy, represents menace enough. Add to this the wide powers conferred on the police by the Police and Criminal Evidence Act and the inadequacy of its safeguards and all the ingredients are present for a transformation, not only of policing, but of society itself. The hallmark of a police state is no more that of a jackboot or a dark overcoat, than of a visor and truncheon. Its true characteristic is an all-pervasive police power available to the Executive within a context in which legitimacy stems not from the rule of law but the acquiescence of the Judiciary and the powerlessness of a largely quiescent public, for whom the ballot box has ceased to provide alternatives. The Police and Criminal Evidence Act was passed by virtue of a massive Parliamentary majority, despite opposition from a wide cross-section of informed opinion which was unable to marshal effective Parliamentary opposition or to mobilise any great degree of public concern. It received the Royal Assent at a time of grave social and economic crisis and in the midst of the largest and most sustained police operation that Britain has ever known. No reason exists for any complacency in the face of growing police power at such a time.

NOTES

1. Police and People in London : Policy Studies Institute, November 1983.

2. Police Review, 20th July 1984.

3. The Economist, 24th March 1984.

4. David Hall, Chief Constable for Humberside, quoted in the Guardian, 20th June, 1984.

5. The Times, 18th September 1984.

6. Local Government Review, 19th May, 1984.

7. The Guardian, 11th August 1984.

8. The Scarman Report, Cmnd. 8427, para. 5.62.

9. "Protecting The Police", by Kenneth Warren M.P. and David Trennick, November 1982.

10. "Following Scarman?" University of Bath Social Policy Papers, May 1984.

16. POLICE COMPLAINTS PROCEDURE: WHY AND FOR WHOM?

Barbara Cohen

The conduct of the police continues to be a major matter of public concern. Finding an acceptable system to deal with and respond to complaints from the public about police behaviour ought, therefore, to be a high priority for both Government and the police. But 25 years or more of inquiries, Royal Commissions, working groups, select committees and legislation have not yet produced a procedure which has public support. That this is the case stems at least in part from continuing failure by politicians, but not by the police, to appreciate fully the constitutional importance of the issues involved.

Sir Robert Mark criticised Roy Jenkins (then Home Secretary) for his failure to grasp the constitutional principles involved: 'The investigation of complaints....touches on very serious principles indeed. The operational freedom of the police from political or bureaucratic interference is essential to their acceptability and to the preservation of democracy.' (1) Mark's view, which has been uttered by other chief officers over several decades, has left the politicians very chary of any radical reform of the complaints system. In 1972 Humphry wrote, 'Almost everyone accepts that there should be some reform of the present procedure - Home Secretary, police, politicians, press - so long as any change does not upset the police. Such is police power. The neurotic fear of demoralising that body of men on whom we rely for law and order freezes the majority into accepting the status quo,' (2) yet the same words could have been written in 1984. From the perspective of a community where the well-being of individuals and groups may be seriously and permanently affected by unchecked abuse of police powers the issue is the classic one of Quis custodiet ipsos custodes?, that is, who guards the guards? If in a democratic society it is agreed to equip a select group with powers and authority beyond that held by the majority, how does the community ensure that those powers are being utilised for the benefit of the community as a whole, and what can the community do when individuals misuse their authority?

Although there is in Britain today a consensus that irresponsible and uncontrolled policing in the extreme would pose a serious threat to our society, there continues to be an unwillingness to create effective systems to prevent a possible drift to such a state of affairs. Central to this is the accountability of the police to the community for their policies, their priorities and their actions. But integrally related is the procedure by which members of the community, aggrieved by police behaviour can register a grievance and have it acted upon.

There is, of course, a third element which is part of the argument of principle, namely just and fair treatment of individual members of a police force who are the subject of complaints. There would be no gain to a democratic society if it were to introduce closed systems of investigation and adjudication, to deprive police officers of their jobs, their homes, their pensions without an opportunity to put their case forward and have it considered. That the police have for some time been regarded with suspicion, distrust and hostility by significant numbers within the ethnic minority community has been well documented both in other chapters of this book and elsewhere. It is therefore not surprising that the strongest demands for an independent system for investigating police complaints came from those groups which were working to improve police-black relations. But as they were speaking for an unpopular, often disenfranchised minority, until the riots of 1981 there was little real pressure on any government to give much credence to their views. Now in 1985, as we are about to embark on yet another scheme for the handling of police complaints, we also find ourselves at a very grave and worrying point in terms of the relationship between the police and those whom they police. We began this decade with distrust and friction between sections of the community and the police and witnessed outbreaks of violence of which this was a major contributory factor. As more people joined street level protests and demonstrations to try to bring their views to the attention of those in power, new types of police-citizen confrontation developed. The major involvement of the police in industrial disputes has created or confirmed a further area of hostility to the police. In such circumstances, the first question for those who are proposing reform or restructuring of the police complaints system must be how a system for processing complaints can be used to help create acceptable, effective forms of policing in a democratic society.

In A Fair Cop, Hewitt summarised what was needed:

"In order to meet the twin aims of preventing abuse of power and enhancing public confidence, the procedure for investigating and acting on complaints against the police from members of the public must ensure
- that each complaint is fully and rigorously investigated;
- that, where a police officer is found to have acted improperly or illegally, appropriate action follows;
- that complainants can satisfy themselves that the complaint has been properly dealt with;
- that police officers can be confident that their rights are respected within the disciplinary system; and
- that the public as a whole must be confident that the system is working fairly and effectively." (3)

Hewitt then exhorted her readers to seize the opportunity of the Government's Police Bill to implement the fully independent system she advocated. The Government remained unmoved, not only by arguments of principle, but also by illustrations of the failures of the present system. So now, two years later, we are left with growing distrust of the police and a complaints system which will not restore public confidence.

After Many Steps Still No Further Ahead

Since the 1976 Police Act there have been eight different schemes to revise or reform the police complaints procedure put forward by official bodies of some sort. The Police Complaints Board, in its first Triennial Review Report (1980) gave an early and strong indication that the scheme established by the 1976 Act needed an independent element at the investigative stage 'to provide a measure of reassurance which would be acceptable to the public at large.' (4) The Board recommended that to investigate complaints involving serious injury there should be a special force of investigative officers which would be recruited by secondment from all police forces and answerable to someone other than a police officer, possibly a lawyer. In response the Government in July 1980 set up a working party chaired by Lord Plowden (then Chairman of the Police Complaints Board) which also comprised senior police representatives. Plowden reported in March 1981, concluding that the Board's suggestion was 'impracticable and unnecessary' and recommending instead additional use of officers from outside forces to investigate serious cases. After discussions with the Police Advisory Board a working group was established under the chairmanship of Lord Belstead, then Under Secretary of State. Its members were from the police associations and associations of local authorities. The working group reported in 1982 with a less than unanimous endorsement of the Plowden approach. In 1981-82 the House of Commons Home Affairs Committee also chose to examine 'ways of improving the machinery for investigating complaints against the police.' The inner-city riots in Brixton, Toxteth, Moss Side and elsewhere, and the inquiry and report by Lord Scarman intervened in this chain of groups and committees. It is worth noting that the Belstead Working Group, set up in July 1981, did not extend its deliberations to take into account Scarman's strong recommendations for reform of the complaints procedure, and the Group's report (early 1982 but undated) lacks a single reference to Scarman or the riots.

The evidence submitted to Lord Scarman and the recommendations he made had a different starting point. The issue was not simply the complaints system and whether or how to modify it. Instead the question was much broader and, in the wake of the riots, far more urgent; how to restore public confidence in the police, especially amongst the young and members of the black community. Scarman identified 'a distrust in the procedure for investigating complaints against the police so great that many people would not even report their complaints.' This was one of the five factors which brought about the break-down in relations between the police and the community in Brixton. (5) Scarman comes down firmly in support of independent investigation of complaints as the best option. 'My own view is that if public confidence in the complaints procedure is to be achieved any solution falling short of a system of independent investigation available for all complaints (other than the frivolous) which are not withdrawn is unlikely to be successful.' (6) He also stressed the need to introduce conciliation for minor complaints. If the obstacles, which he saw as mainly practical, to a wholly independent system cannot be overcome, then, very much as second best, Scarman suggests that there could be a non-police supervisor but with direct involvement in the investigation. 'He must not be treated as an irrelevant fifth wheel on the investigation coach.' (7) Whilst he rejected the allegations that the Metropolitan Police is racist in its direction and policies, Scarman found that individual officers did on occasions display racial prejudice in their dealings with young black people. Noting the effect of such conduct Scarman recommended that racially prejudiced behaviour should be a specific disciplinary offence for which the normal penalty would be dismissal. Scarman's proposals were well canvassed by the Home Affairs Committee as they received evidence and prepared their report. The Committee expressed concern about the high percentage of complaints which are withdrawn (consistently about 50% of all complaints). 'We would observe only that the borderline between persuasion and pressure is a narrow one and may be unconsciously as well as knowingly transgressed.' (8)

Although they were presented with strong arguments in support of independent investigation from the NCCL, JUSTICE, the GLC, the Runnymede Trust and the Commissioner for Local Administration, reinforced by a surprise change of policy by the Police Federation, nevertheless the Conservative-controlled Committee remained unconvinced. The Police Federation committed themselves to independent investigation as the only acceptable approach: 'There appears to be no way in which the public, or at least those individuals who are interested in the question, will be convinced of the fairness of the system so long as the police appear to be judges in their own cause.' (9) Yet the Committee concluded: 'We are not convinced that a new and independent organisation would do a more effective job than senior police officers in investigating complaints and we are doubtful whether....the gain to the public interest would justify the extra resources involved.' (10) Instead they recommended that there should be new external safeguards which would 'command the confidence of public and police alike.' The Committee adopted more or less intact the Home Office scheme including an independent assessor or supervisor to oversee police investigation of serious complaints and conciliation of non-criminal complaints. The Committee also recommended that minor criminal offences could be dealt with by the Chief Constable under the disciplinary code rather than by referral to the Director of Public Prosecutions. They accepted the NCCL's evidence on the 'double jeopardy' rule and recommended revision of the Home Secretary's guidance to prevent further inequity.

The next document to appear in this continuing saga was the Government reply to the Fourth Report from the Home Affairs Committee. (11) Basically the Government agreed with the Home Affairs Committee where its recommendations encompassed the Government proposals which had been put to the Committee and disagreed when the Committee recommended changes in procedure based on evidence from outside bodies. In particular, the Government stated its opposition to recommendations which would introduce more openness into the procedure, and gave a fairly ambiguous response to the proposal to clarify, restrictively, the double jeopardy rule. The Government also set out its proposed new 'Three-tier Approach': (a) informal conciliation for less serious complaints, (b) investigation as at present for more substantial complaints but allegations of criminal offences no longer to be referred automatically to the DPP, and (c) investigation by a senior police officer (normally from an outside force) under the supervision of an independent assessor for the most serious complaints.

This scheme was the basis for the complaints provisions in the original Police and Criminal Evidence Bill, introduced in November 1982. Other than the proposal for conciliation of less serious complaints, the scheme appeared to satisfy few. Reactions to this part of the Bill fed the developing and unlikely alliance between the Police Federation, the Law Society and NCCL. Such an alliance led to the Government's only defeat during the Committee stage; back-bench Tories joined with the Labour and Alliance opposition to approve an amendment to enable legal representation in disciplinary proceedings where the officer faced dismissal, reduction in rank or loss of more than 3 months' pay. Unfortunately the same grouping could not get the votes on the more essential amendment to secure independent investigation of all complaints. The Police Federation spokesperson ('adviser' he calls himself) Eldon Griffiths (Conservative) opposed it and thus no effective 'deals' could be done. It was anticipated that the Government would try to take out the 'legal representation' clause but the General Election intervened.

While waiting for a second Police and Criminal Evidence Bill the Law Society and the Police Federation put their heads together and published a memorandum setting out a scheme for independent investigation of all complaints. It also included conciliation, a Police Complaints Tribunal to adjudicate and sentence for disciplinary offences, an appeal tribunal, legal representation for police officers in all matters heard by the Tribunal, and an inter-linking of the systems of internal complaints and complaints from the public. In an effort to meet objections from all sides the scheme was extremely complex and potentially incomprehensible to members of the public. But it played an invaluable role in bringing the discussion back to independent investigation.

By October 1983 the Government was ready to re-introduce its Police and Criminal Evidence Bill, after some laundering and re-tailoring to try to pre-empt those who had swung public opinion by their vociferous objections to parts of the previous Bill. So far as police complaints are concerned, not only were the provisions significantly re-drafted but the Government also published another White Paper (12) to provide background and illustration for its again revised scheme, which seemed to have taken little from the Law Society/Police Federation proposals. Of course as a Bill progresses through Parliament the Government, as well as the Opposition parties, has the opportunity to introduce amendments; the Government however has the added advantage of knowing that most, if not all, of its amendments will be approved. It is not an exaggeration to say that every clause relating to the new police complaints procedure has been substantially amended by the Government.

The Police and Criminal Evidence Act 1984 establishes a Police Complaints Authority (PCA) and abolishes the Police Complaints Board (PCB). No indication has been given as to whether the Government will appoint any of the present PCB members to the new Authority, but by creating a new body completely fresh appointments can be made. (A minimum of 8 plus a chairman). The first chairman, to be appointed by the Crown, has already been named; Sir Cecil Clothier comes to the job with the useful experience of having served for 6 years as the Parliamentary Commissioner for Administration (the Ombudsman). The Home Secretary will make the other appointments. No member can have served as a police officer anywhere in the U.K. but no such restriction applies to PCA staff. (and ex-police officers are expected to be employed). A Government amendment in the Lords removed from the Bill any restriction on the role of the PCA - should future Parliaments wish to expand its functions. However, under this legislation the PCA, other than taking on the current work of the PCB in receiving reports at the conclusion of police investigations, is given only a limited role in the supervision of some complaints investigations.

By Section 89 the PCA is required to supervise the investigation of any complaint alleging that police conduct resulted in death or serious injury to another person. However, the Home Secretary by regulations can add other types of complaints for compulsory supervision. The White Paper suggests which other 'serious' cases the PCA could decide to supervise but it would be possible without further legislation for another Home Secretary in the future to bring all investigations of complaints within the PCA's duty to supervise. This is not, however, the intent or the reality of this Act, and speeches in both the Commons and the Lords, claiming for the new scheme 'impartiality' and an independent element based on this supervisory role of the PCA were seriously misleading since only a small proportion of complaints will be affected. The police will be required to bring some complaints to the attention of the PCA. Additionally, the police will be able to notify them of any complaint, or any matter not included in a complaint, because of its gravity or exceptional circumstances. Once notified, the PCA will have discretion to supervise the investigation or not using a public interest criterion to decide. The only specific power which the Act provides for the PCA when they supervise an investigation is to approve the appointment of the officer who will conduct it; what the PCA can do to influence the course and form of the investigation is a matter for the Home Secretary's regulations (Not available at the time of writing).

If the PCA supervise an investigation they must, after reading the investigating officer's report, submit a statement to the Chief Constable indicating whether or not they were satisfied with the way the investigation was conducted and if not, why not. The complainant will receive a copy of this statement. In advance of the procedure coming to life there is a certain 'Alice in Wonderland' quality to these provisions. How does one reassure an aggrieved complainant that supervision by the PCA will have any effect at all in ensuring the fairness and thoroughness of the investigation when at the end of the day all s/he may receive is a statement that the PCA were not satisfied with the investigation? And should this be the result there is nothing in the procedure to reduce the doubt and disillusion amongst all parties: a dissatisfied, disillusioned complainant, a police officer whose name has not been cleared, and a demoralised investigative force. Lost would be the element which purportedly would increase public confidence in the handling of complaints.

The Government has not allayed the doubts which have been expressed concerning the new supervisory role of the PCA. One is the cost - effectiveness of this several-layered scheme. Under the 1984 Act some complaints will be examined four times, (by the police, by the PCA in a supervisory role by the DPP and the PCA again to consider disciplinary action) some thrice or twice, and some once or, if conciliated or withdrawn, not at all. The more the PCA takes on in terms of supervising investigations the greater the double-costing at this stage. The Government is prepared to pay for double and treble scrutiny to achieve an 'independent element', but steadfastly rejects the simpler solution of transferring all investigations to an independent body, and in doing so relies in part on arguments of cost.

A second reservation concerns the relationship of the PCA and the DPP. In the White Paper the possible points of contact were hinted at. The DPP has a duty to offer advice to investigating officers when evidence is being collected for possible criminal proceedings. In his evidence to the Home Affairs Committee (1981-82) the DPP warned that a lay supervisor other than himself was likely, on occasions, to offer advice which ran counter to that of the DPP. The Government therefore proposes that the PCA will be required to consult the DPP before giving formal directions on evidential matters, and should give advice short of a direction only if it conforms with DPP policy. If the DPP refuses consent to the making of a direction which the PCA 'as guardian of the public interest' considers important then the PCA can record this in this statement of satisfaction (or lack of it) at the end of the investigation.

Investigation Or Conciliation?

The basic procedure under the 1984 Act is very little different from that which the 1964 and 1976 Acts prescribe. When a complaint (which may be made through a third party, for example, a citizens' advice bureau or a solicitor) has been received by the appropriate chief constable, or police authority if it concerns a senior officer, the complaint is recorded. After a preliminary investigation the chief constable (or police authority) decides whether informal resolution will be suitable. If not, then an officer is appointed to investigate the complaint and to prepare a report; where appropriate the PCA will be informed. The new legislation leaves intact the investigation procedures which were laid down in the 1964 Act and the police discipline regulations, and which are to be followed whenever a complaint includes an allegation of a disciplinary offence. Until the 1984 Act complaints which fell outside the discipline regulations generally were given very short shrift by the police as they had no defined mechanism for dealing with them.

Conciliation

That the 1984 Act enables some complaints to be resolved informally is a sensible improvement; that such conciliation will be conducted by the police limits the benefit of the new procedure. Informal resolution will be considered in respect of all complaints but will be suitable only if the complainant consents and the Chief Constable is satisfied that 'the conduct complained of, even if proved, would not justify a criminal or disciplinary charge;' i.e. even if an offence is alleged it is too trivial. The initiative for conciliation must come from the police, rather than the complainant. The White Paper envisages that there will be no fixed procedure (but the Home Secretary will issue detailed guidance). The accused officer will not be required to attend any meeting with the complainant, and no apology could be tendered on his behalf for any act he denies committing.

The regulations will give the officer opportunity to comment on the allegation. The outcome of the process, whether successful or not, will be recorded in a special register to which the police authority and HM Inspectorate of Constabulary will have access. There will be no entry in the officer's personal record, and no statements made during the conciliation process will be admissible in any legal proceedings. Should conciliation fail for any reason the complaint would then be formally investigated, by an officer who has not been involved in the conciliation, and who would not be able to refer to any statements or comments made during the attempted conciliation. There is no provision for a matter to move from formal investigation to informal resolution, even though some complaints when examined more closely are likely to be considered suitable.

An effective system for conciliation of police complaints would have the potential to rectify one of the basic flaws in our complaints procedure, namely the conflicting expectations of the public and the police. The public are led to believe that their police complaint will be dealt with in a way similar to their other 'consumer' complaints, that their grievance will be acknowledged, looked into and some action taken to try to put things right. However, until the 1984 Act is in force, a complaint from a member of the public about the police, if it appears to have any substance at all, is immediately subsumed by the internal discipline procedures which are concerned with standards of conduct acceptable to the police. The great advantage of informal resolution is that complaints will not move into the discipline procedure, they will remain on the table as matters which relate to conduct which is not satisfactory to members of the public. It is therefore a serious loss that this procedure is to be in the hands of the police who cannot be expected to share perceptions with the complainant and who are more likely to try to justify police action than to accept a complaint as legitimate and well-founded.

Prosecutions Arising From Complaints

Under the present system and under the 1984 Act a certain number of complaints are referred to the DPP after investigation. The 1964 Act provides that, unless a Chief Constable is satisfied that no criminal offence has been committed, he shall send the investigation report to the DPP. It is then the duty of the DPP to decide whether or not to prosecute the officer(s) for any criminal offence.

"We never prosecute unless in our view on the evidence before us there is more chance of a conviction than of an acquittal," Sir Thomas Hetherington, the DPP told the Home Affairs Committee in 1982. He went on to acknowledge that juries are reluctant to convict police officers, as compared with other defendants, and that he takes this fact into account when he decides whether to recommend criminal proceedings.

As the following table shows clearly, very rarely does a referral to the DPP result in a decision to prosecute:

ENGLAND & WALES (Excluding the Metropolitan Police)	1978	1979	1980	1981	1982	1983
NUMBER OF CRIMINAL (NON TRAFFIC) CASES REFERRED TO DPP	2,805	3,041	2,845	2,756	2,735	2,581
PROCEEDINGS RECOMMENDED BY THE DPP (NON-TRAFFIC)	56	55	48	58	39	47

The figures for the Metropolitan police are comparable. For example, in 1982 there were 1,372 separate (non-traffic) complaints referred to the DPP and recommendation to prosecute in 8 cases only; in 1983 the figures were 725 complaints referred to the DPP and prosecutions recommended in 20 cases. (13)

It was not only the workings of the double jeopardy rule but also the inappropriateness of criminal proceedings in certain complaints which led to pressure for greater flexibility in police referrals to the DPP. The DPP himself took this view which he elaborated in an Additional Memorandum to the Home Affairs Committee. He recommended that a Deputy Chief Constable should only be required to refer cases which he believes merit criminal prosecution or which fall outside the discipline code, but not cases which he considers could more appropriately be dealt with as matters of discipline.

The Government's first scheme, in 1982, would have given chief officers of police authority to decide lesser criminal allegations themselves and to bring either criminal or disciplinary proceedings without prior referral to the

DPP. This evoked a fierce negative reaction from the Police Federation who strongly opposed increasing in any way the discretionary power of chief constables. The Federation view was that all criminal matters should be referred to the DPP who would apply his 'greater than 50%' test (which was likely to continue to result in very few prosecutions of police officers). The Federation clearly wanted part of the package to be renewed protection for its members from disciplinary action when the DPP found insufficient evidence to recommend prosecution, by some form of 'double-jeopardy' provision.

In the second Police and Criminal Evidence Bill the Government modified its line somewhat. It proposed that the chief constable's decision whenever a report suggested that a criminal offence may have been committed should be 'whether the offence indicated is too serious for him to deal with by preferring disciplinary charges' (Clause 82.) Again the Police Federation reacted strongly. For obvious reasons they opposed chief constables' discretion to prefer disciplinary charges where a criminal offence is disclosed.

> "We are not prepared to support a proposition that police officers should be deprived of their constitutional right to be tried in open court, according to the rules of evidence, and with all the rights of any other person facing a criminal charge, including legal representation, when they are accused of breaches of the criminal law". (14)

By Committee Stage in the House of Lords the Government had not only agreed to legal representation for police officers in disciplinary proceedings but had redrafted the clause to take out the 'seriousness' test. Now the chief officer of police must determine whether the investigation report dicloses that a criminal offence may have been committed and if so whether the officer concerned ought to be charged. If the offence merits prosecution then he cannot deal with it by way of discipline. There is to be a second bite at the prosecution cherry, however, in that the PCA will be able to direct a chief constable to send a report to the DPP.

The discipline regulations, which were redrafted after the 1976 Act are to be revised again to sort out more clearly who is responsible for which stages of the disciplinary procedure. It will now be the case that if the accused officer is a chief constable, deputy or assistant chief constable, the police authority will be the body to determine whether offences against discipline have been committed and to impose a punishment (see below). For all other officers this will remain with the chief constable. However, for the less serious disciplinary matters against junior officers, there can be a general down-grading so that an assistant chief constable can bring charges and a deputy chief constable can determine guilt and impose punishment (limited to reduction in rate of pay, fine, reprimand or caution).

The first major Parliamentary victory for the Opposition in relation to complaints was the surrender by the Government on the question of legal representation for police officers in disciplinary hearings (the second was the addition of 'racially discriminatory behaviour' as a disciplinary offence - see below). In the Bill as first introduced the right of legal representation was to be available only for appeals to the Home Secretary against decisions on discipline charges and on punishment. The Government argued that to allow legal representation at first instance disciplinary hearings 'would in practice be inconsistent with requiring the chief officer to be responsible at first instance for ensuring good conduct by his officers'. (15) However it was in this respect primarily that the Police Federation waged its expensive mass-media campaign. Taking full-page advertisements in the national press for several days, just as police complaints were being debated in the Commons standing committee, the Federation brought clearly to public attention the plight of the accused police officer. The publicity, which incorporated the findings of a MORI poll commissioned by the Federation, made much play of the alliance that had been formed between the Federation, the Law Society and the NCCL. On this particular issue the three bodies were unanimous although on the question of 100% state funding for legal representation, this was not the case.

Whilst all of the findings of the MORI poll concerning public attitudes towards the police and the complaints procedure (1841 adults interviewed during 16–20 Feb. '84) will have been warmly received by the Federation. most welcome must have been the response to the, perhaps too loaded, question: "Police officers accused of disciplinary offences are dealt with by their chief constables and chief officers. Do you believe that officers facing such charges should or should not have the right to be represented by a lawyer?

Yes, should	82%
No, should not	11%
No opinion	7%

Complaints against senior officers (above the rank of chief superintendent) are to be dealt with by police authorities or, in the Metropolitan Police, by the Commissioner. Conciliation will be available if no disciplinary or criminal offences are disclosed, but the complainant's consent will not be required – the police authority (or the Commissioner!) purportedly providing an 'independent outside check'. (16)

The scope for the Government to manipulate the procedure for political ends was revealed by a report in The Guardian (6 October 1984) that the Home Secretary's regulations are expected to prevent a police authority from suspending a senior officer without the approval of the (Home Secretary appointed) PCA. It was suggested that the Government had come to fear that power to suspend would be used in conflicts between police authorities and chief constables over the policing of the miners' dispute.

The Government's complacency was given a late shock when the House of Lords in its final deliberations on the Bill approved an Opposition amendment introduced by Lord Scarman which would make 'racially discriminatory behaviour' a specific disciplinary offence for police officers. Opposing the amendment the Government argued, ineffectually, that race discrimination should not be singled out (amongst all other forms of discrimination practised by the police) for disciplinary action.

In his Report on the Brixton Disorders Lord Scarman had not only recommended this new disciplinary offence but urged that it should be dealt with severely; 'While I do not go so far as to propose a fixed penalty for the offence, I do recommend that it should be understood throughout the police that the normal penalty for racially prejudiced behaviour is dismissal'. (16 a)

The precise formulation of the new disciplinary offence has been left to the Home Office draftspersons. The NCCL wrote to the Home Secretary urging that it be framed in as objective terms as possible, so that what will be under examination by the investigating officer is conduct and not attitudes. Because of the strong police resistance to 'racially discriminatory behaviour' as a disciplinary offence – the first offence which reflects a public rather than a police view of proper police conduct – the NCCL also recommended that the investigation of all complaints alleging that this offence has been committed should be supervised by the Police Complaints Authority. Senior police officers have expressed the view that such complaints will never be upheld; in view of the wide evidence of police racism the Government should ensure that this does not become a self-fulfilling prophecy.

There is considerable concern that the new multi-faceted scheme is unduly complicated and is likely to be rejected by the public, as previous schemes have been, because it is too remote and too complex. Letters received by NCCL from dissatisfied complainants under the present scheme make clear that people want to understand how their complaint will be processed and want to feel they have some control over this processing. An example is Alan Francis who wanted only an apology after he had been wrongly arrested on suspicion of possessing an offensive weapon – a tent pole and a CND flag! He got a full-scale investigation with no apology.

The scheme under the 1984 Act involves the division of complaints into a large number of categories relating to how they will be processed. A correspondingly large number of agencies or departments will or may be involved in the processing of complaints. It will be virtually impossible to advise a prospective complainant as to what would be done and by whom after s/he had submitted a complaint. For example, if a complaint alleged wrongful arrest then, depending on the circumstances and the evidence available, this could amount to the criminal offence of false imprisonment (which might or might not be referred to the DPP); it might fall into the category for mandatory notification to the Authority, it might be investigated without supervision or it might be considered so minor an infringement that it would be considered appropriate for informal resolution. Once a complaint has been made the only real control which the complainant will be able to exercise is to withdraw it.

Incidents Causing Widespread Public Concern

The Government's new scheme includes the potential for supervised investigation of matters arising from police actions, which have caused generalised concern within a community or over a wider geographical area, but which are not the subject of a formal complaint by any one aggrieved individual. How far reaching this provision will be remains to be seen.

In their recent study of police accountability, Controlling the Constable Tony Jefferson and Roger Grimshaw point out the effect of the existence of the Police Complaints Board on the willingness of successive Home Secretaries to use their powers under Section 32 of the 1964 Police Act to enquire into policing matters which had stirred grave public anxiety.

> "One of the Board's roles appears to be to supplant inquiries of the kind conducted into Red Lion Square. Since the inception of the Board, only very serious disorders, amounting to an operational

defeat for the police such as occurred only at Brixton, would appear to be the province of the public inquiry....Ironically, then, the 'gain' of an independent Police Complaints Board, albeit with its very limited powers, has apparently been compensated by a corresponding 'loss': the loss of the public inquiry other than in situations demonstrating the most extreme instances of police failure in the operational field.' (17)

The complaints procedure, as it has operated since the 1976 Act, has not filled the void when Home Secretaries have refused to institute inquiries. The PCB has not been able to provide the sort of investigation required in situations where inquiries would have been appropriate to clarify, in an open public way, roles and responsibilities of the police and others. For example, the events in Southall in April 1979 generated large numbers of police complaints by individuals who had been personally involved; the outcome was a series of one-by-one investigations processed in the normal way, with problems of identifying particular police officers, and only passing reference in the PCB Triennial Review Report for 1980.

More recently there was a massive local campaign in Hackney pressing for a public inquiry into the circumstances surrounding the death of Colin Roach in Stoke Newington Police station in January 1983. For some months the Home Secretary deflected demands for an inquiry on the basis that the inquest into Roach's death would establish the medical and circumstantial causes of his death. Although returning a verdict of suicide, the coroner's jury wrote to the Home Secretary expressing concern about the treatment of the Roach family after the death and the handling of the investigation generally. The Home Secretary decided that the criticisms implied in the jury's letter should be investigated as a police complaint. The matter was thus taken out of the public arena for a number of months, and few were surprised when the PCB concluded that they had found insufficient evidence to justify disciplinary proceedings. In view of the continuing public concern about the death, and policing in Hackney generally, after the PCB's decision NCCL and others again asked the Home Secretary to set up a public inquiry. In the reply on his behalf, his Private Secretary wrote:

> "The Home Secretary well understands the reasons that have led to requests for an enquiry and he recognises that there is a widespread feeling that the actions of police officers in Hackney over the last years have not always been above reproach....Any form of enquiry would take time to establish and time to report; a decision to set one up would in the Home Secretary's view be likely to heighten rather than reduce tension in the area; and it would certainly arouse expectations not all of which could be fulfilled. Moreover, when it had reported, the problems it had examined would remain to be dealt with...."

Another interesting example is the case of Steven Waldorf who was wrongly identified by the police and shot and beaten by them. The case, which had caused a great public outcry, was referred to the complaints procedure at the conclusion of the trial of the officers involved, all of whom were acquitted of all charges. In its Press Statement, on 22 December 1983, the PCB said that the Deputy Commissioner of the Metropolitan Police had 'decided to regard Mr. Waldorf's evidence in connection with the original enquiry into this incident as complaints against the three officers who caused his injuries alleging assault and failure to comply with force instructions on the use of firearms.' As Mr. Waldorf had never made a formal complaint he was surprised to hear from the Board and of course gravely disappointed with their conclusion that they could not recommend disciplinary action against any of the officers since the statutory double jeopardy rule (Section 11 of the 1976 Act) precluded disciplinary action after the issue of self-defence had been raised during the trial and the jury had found the officers not guilty.

If a complaint relates to operational matters or matters of 'procedure' and the conduct complained of was in accordance with instructions or directions by senior officers then the complaint will fall outside the investigative procedure altogether. An example of this is the refusal by the Thames Valley Police to investigate the large number of complaints they received from people arrested during anti-nuclear demonstrations at Upper Heyford, who objected to being compulsorily photographed. The standard letter of reply stated, 'The Deputy Chief Constable has been made aware of the contents of your letter and has decided that as they relate to matters of procedure no further investigation will be made under the terms of Section 49 of the Police Act 1964.' Thus this issue was left untouched (except that the notices regarding suspects' rights not to be photographed without consent were altered).

At the time of writing a daily front-page issue is the role of the police in the miners' dispute. The Home Secretary has solidly refused to accept the need for him to use his Section 32 powers to call for an independent inquiry. (The NCCL itself set up such an inquiry looking at the civil liberties implications of action by the police, police authorities and the criminal courts). The Home Secretary has, in various media interviews, tried to deflect criticism of police action by referring to the very few formal police complaints which have been received relating to the policing of the strike. This must raise all over again the questions of public confidence in the complaints procedure.

Instead of the frustrating experience of the complaints procedure, many people during the strike who wished to challenge police misconduct and abuse of their powers have quite wisely started civil actions against the Chief Constable for the relevant area. As those who monitor police action in London and other inner city areas have noted, there is far greater likelihood of a successful claim in the county court or the High Court – which will give the citizen some real compensation – than of a formal complaint being upheld after investigation. Of course the burden of proof in a civil court is the lesser, i.e. on the balance of probabilities. But over and above this there is mounting evidence that the complete impartiality of the court does make a difference.

Why Not The Police?

The strong and much repeated argument in support of retaining police investigation is that as a result of their training and experience the police are better fitted for this task than anyone else. Whilst there is no disagreement that the police are skilled investigators, there are convincing arguments that their identity and position as police officers, as well as their methods of investigations, make them less qualified for the investigation of public complaints against members of the police force.

The primary objection to the police investigating allegations of their own misconduct is the belief that the investigation will not be impartial. The Police Complaints Board in their 1978 Report and 1980 Triennial Report expressed concern that this may occur both in terms of the credibility given to police and non-police witnesses and the rigour with which evidence is obtained from police witnesses. Confirming such belief, and gravely disturbing if investigations are to remain in police hands, is the disclosure by the Policy Studies Institute research team of 'cover-ups' within the Metropolitan Police.

> "We were told many times that an officer who had done something wrong would always, or almost always, be backed up by other officers, even if they didn't like him. Perhaps the clearest statement on this was made by a uniform sergeant in charge of a crime squad. JG asked him whether he would 'shop' one of his mates who had committed a serious assault on a prisoner. He said, 'No, I never would. If one of the boys working for me got himself into trouble, I would get all of us together and I would literally script him out of it. I would write all the parts and if we followed them closely we couldn't be defeated. And believe me, I would do it.' JG asked if he didn't think it was wrong for police officers to get away with assaulting prisoners, especially as this would involve a conspiracy to cover up the evidence. He said, 'Oh yes, but when it was all over, I wouldn't want to work with that bloke ever again. I wouldn't want anything to do with him.' We never heard anyone contradict this point of view at the level of constable or sergeant." (18)

Unfortunately, because of the implications for members of the public of police misconduct, what might in another setting be merely workplace solidarity is, in the case of the police, a matter which undermines our law enforcement system and brings the complaints system into disrepute.

A survey conducted by Michael McConville in 1983 into the use by the police of stop and search powers in the Notting Hill area of London showed a very high rate of dissatisfaction (76% in the All Saints Road and 65% on the Holmefield Estate), but an almost total rejection of the police complaints procedure. Less than 6% of those who were dissatisfied made a complaint. 'The most common reason given for not complaining about being stop-searched was, in both areas, a lack of faith in the police complaints system.' (19)

In its evidence to the Home Affairs Committee, the Commission for Local Administration in England (the local Ombudsman) sought to bring to the Committee their experience of 8 years of operating a complaints procedure. 'Independence is vital' was the Commission's first conclusion (para 28 of the Memorandum). In 1983 less than 1% of complaints to the Commission were withdrawn compared with nearly 50% of complaints made to the police. The Police Complaints Board and MPs have queried this consistently high rate of withdrawal of police complaints but the needed research has not yet been done. Cases referred to NCCL suggest that in a significant proportion of cases there is strong pressure by the police on the complainant to withdraw. Lawyers fear that withdrawing a complaint could be used as a quid pro quo when the police try to negotiate before a complainant's criminal trial.

When a complaint is made by a concerned person who observes police misconduct from atop the 'Clapham omnibus' then, without the leverage of a prosecution, the police have been known to resort to techniques of harassment, or sexist or racist abuse to dissuade him/her from going ahead with the complaint. NCCL received a report from a teacher who on her way to work saw a man being subjected to what she considered violent and humiliating treatment by the police (trousers down, held bent over a railing). She made her complaint to the nearest police station. When, at the request of the police she called at the station, the senior officer she met was 'threatening and abusive'. Repeatedly, she was asked to withdraw her complaint and was given several explanations of the police action. She said, 'I was made to feel that I had done something wrong, that I had broken the law'.

A solicitor described similar 'criminalising' of the complainant when an investigating officer came to his office to take a statement from his client. 'He introduced his questioning as if he were cautioning a criminal suspect. Then he took out the standard criminal witness statement forms, but very grudgingly at my insistence, he used blank paper. Then he chose words carefully and was selective in what he recorded so the written version of the complainant's statement, whilst not inaccurate, read as far less convincing than it had in fact been'.

In a case in which NCCL had represented a man in a civil action which was settled out of court for £1750 none of the witnesses wanted to speak to the police. One woman, who had given a clear statement to NCCL describing an assault by the police, refused to make any statement whatsoever to the police in support of the complaint. She said that as she was black and had two sons in South London she did not want to become known to the police for any reason.

Many complaints relate to direct experience of violent, aggressive or rude conduct by the police. It is not surprising that some complainants are extremely reluctant to meet another police officer who is 'investigating' what happened. Investigating officers, under pressure to prepare reports promptly, often try to convince complainants of the urgency of their enquiries and to pressurise them into being interviewed before they have recovered from the trauma of the incident and taken legal advice. Although possibly an extreme example, the following case, referred by a Citizens' Advice Bureau makes this point. A woman complained of direct sexual advances by a police officer when he called to investigate a criminal matter. She withdrew her complaint in a highly distressed state when she was advised that a police officer (male) would need to call on her to take a statement.

The police attitude towards complainants is likely to have a significant effect on whether or not the complaint is substantiated. Research by Ken Russell published in the Sunday Times (21 March 1976) before the 1976 Act was implemented had as one of its three main conclusions that the police discriminate unfairly in appraising one or more of the personal characteristics of a complainant. Russell found that complaints were far more likely to be upheld if they had come from middle-class complainants as opposed to working-class complainants; his findings similarly showed a greater likelihood of a complaint being upheld if the complainant did not have a criminal record and was not mentally ill:

"There is no direct evidence that the discrediting is deliberate.....

the figures do give cause for concern and suggest that in a sizeable proportion of cases the police do discredit complainants by implying that for one or more of these background reasons a complainant is unreliable". (20)

The Home Office Research and Planning Unit in 1981 published the results of their study of the characteristics of complainants and the circumstances and outcomes of the complaints they make. Their data, in line with Russell's, showed that who the complainant is affects the substantiation rate of complaints fully investigated in 1979, complainants with criminal records had only 3.9% substantiated as compared with 10.0% for other complainants. (21) In the first quarter of 1979 4.6% of fully investigated complaints from white complainants were substantiated as compared to 1.5% of such complaints from black complainants and 3.6% from Asian complainants. (22) Their conclusions are cautious, however and suggest the need for more research into low substantiation of complaints of assault and complaints made by persons under arrest (which make up a substantial proportion of black complaints). They share the view of the PCB (1980 Triennial Review para 61) that 'investigations into alleged assault are not perhaps always as thorough as investigations into less serious complaints'.

Disillusion with the present police complaints system stems to a large degree from the fact that from the complainants' view it so rarely produces a result. A person makes a formal complaint and undergoes the investigation process because in nearly every case s/he feels a genuine sense of grievance about police conduct. It is true that in a good number of cases the incident was a minor one and the full brunt of a major investigation is disproportionate to the offending action, and therefore the long-overdue conciliation procedure in the 1984 Act is, with some reservations, to be welcomed. But in the majority of cases the complaint is made because a private citizen believes that one or more police officers have exceeded their lawful powers; often such police action deprives an individual of his or her liberty, right to privacy, or causes physical harm. If at the end of the investigation process the conclusion is that there was insufficient evidence to substantiate the allegations and no disciplinary action is to be recommended by the Police Complaints Board, what is the complainant meant to think? The complaints discipline system demands the criminal standard of proof – beyond reasonable doubt – which is rarely available even if equal weight is given to a single complainant's allegations and the police officer's denial. Because of the possibilities of bias (described above) there is even less likelihood that a complaint will be upheld. Does such an outcome mean that the complaint was wrong or that the incident didn't happen? Recent figures illustrate the way the system operates: (23)

	1981	1982	1983
Complaints not withdrawn	15,198	15,560	14,417
Disciplinary charge preferred	211 (1.39%)	293 (1.9%)	234 (1.6%)
Advice or warning given	1,526 (10.04%)	1,604 (10.31%)	1,346 (9.34%)

The American Experience

In arguments against non-police investigation of police complaints the spectre of failures in the United States is frequently brought to the fore. David Brown prepared for the Home Office Research and Planning Unit a study entitled "Civilian Review of Complaints against the Police: A Survey of the United States Literature" (24). Brown presents a catalogue of political controversy, allegations of bias, suspicion, lack of clarity of role, inadequate finance and staffing and in particular, continuing opposition by the police which resulted in the collapse of most schemes. For example, the Philadelphia Police Advisory Board (PAB) was set up with a flourish in 1958 by a newly elected reforming mayor, who appointed its members. It was swept away after 9 years by a Republican mayor who, with his new chief of police, was opposed to civilian review. The PAB was never integrated into the bureaucratic structure, it never had its own investigative staff, lacked funds to publicise its work and never gained solid public support. Throughout its existence it was opposed by lower grade police officers who through their union (the Fraternal Order of Police) brought two actions against the PAB which forced its activities to a halt. Yet while it functioned it did achieve redress for complainants and improvements in police practices. More recently in Detroit a civilian Board of Police Commissioners was established by the Mayor and its teams of seconded police officer and civilian investigator have operated in a less hostile environment as a result of effective negotiations with the police at the outset. The public response has been uneven however with fluctuating annual totals of complaints.

There has been little or no reference by the Government to the developments in Canada where both Ontario and Manitoba have developed procedures for police complaints which enable complainants to have complaints independently investigated if they so request.

The Double Jeopardy Rule - Justice Or Over-Protection?

In 1967 the Home Office issued guidance to the police in relation to the complaints procedure established under the 1964 Act, and this guidance remained more or less unchanged until the judgement in 1982 in R-v-Police Complaints Board ex parte Madden and ex parte Rhone. As the Home Office admit, the protection against 'double jeopardy' which has existed throughout this period was 'at the suggestion originally of two of the police staff organisations'. (25) Hewitt has recorded that the rule remains as a result of a political deal; "During the passage of the Police Bill through Parliament in 1975 and 1976, the Home Office, faced with intense opposition from the Police Federation to the creation of the new Board - came to an agreement that no police officer would be disciplined on the basis of evidence which the DPP regarded as inadequate for a criminal charge". (26)

The 1976 Act gave statutory effect for the purposes of the police disciplinary procedure to the well-settled principle in criminal law that a person is not to be prosecuted twice for the same crime. (27)

Section 11 provides:

'(1) Where a member of a police force has been acquitted or convicted of a criminal offence he shall not be liable to be charged

with any offence against discipline which is in substance the same
as the offence of which he has been acquitted or convicted.
(2)   Subsection (1) above shall not be construed as applying to a
charge in respect of an offence against discipline which consists of
having been found guilty of a criminal offence'.

The guidance which represents the Home Office agreement with the
Police Federation (Home Office Circular 15/1982) treats a decision by the
DPP not to prosecute as having the same effect as an acquittal. Para 5.14
of the Guidance (Home Office Circular No. 32/1980 and No. 15/1982)
states a principle analogous to section 11 of the 1976 Act, namely that
"where an allegation against a police officer has been the subject of a
criminal investigation and it has been decided after reference to the
Director (or otherwise) that criminal proceedings should not be taken,
there should normally be no disciplinary proceedings if the evidence
required to substantiate a disciplinary charge is the same as that required
to substantiate the criminal charge".   By section 3(8) of the 1976 Act the
Police Complaints Board was required to have regard to this guidance.

Before R-v- Police Complaints Board ex parte Madden and ex parte
Rhone the PCB acknowledge that they 'had always considered that the
obligation to have regard to the guidance meant that it could not be
disregarded'. Thus consistently the vast majority of what are considered
the most serious complaints, because they involved allegations of criminal
conduct, fell outside the police discipline system altogether; the frequent
decision by the DPP not to prosecute because of insufficient evidence
would necessarily exclude disciplinary action from consideration of the
police and the PCB.

It was the fact that more than 5,000 of the most serious complaints
(approximately 30% of all complaints dealt with by the PCB) were falling
through the net each year that led NCCL to challenge the application of
the double jeopardy rule.   In Madden and Rhone the Court held that the
PCB was wrong to consider themselves bound to follow the guidance; they
need do no more than 'have regard to' it and then must evaluate the
evidence themselves before deciding whether or not to recommend a
disciplinary charge.

The Board refused to reopen all the cases that had fallen through its
net since 1977.   The effect of the judgement on the outcome of
complaints in the following year was not significant. In only 12 cases
considered and rejected by the DPP in 1983 did the PCB recommend
disciplinary action (in 2 of these the recommendation was later withdrawn,
2 officers were found not guilty, 4 pleaded guilty and 4 results are not yet
known at the time of writing).

Two problems remain with respect to double jeopardy and the interplay
of criminal and disciplinary proceedings. First, there is not a consistent
'fit' between criminal and disciplinary offences. The Government's revised
Guidance (28) explains that some disciplinary offences under the discipline
code closely correspond to criminal offences while others do not. For
example the criminal charges of theft or corruption have elements which
distinguish them from the disciplinary charges, respectively, of 'care of
property' or 'accepting a gratuity' while the criminal charge of assault (of
whatever degree of severity) and the disciplinary charge of 'unnecessary
violence' are in substance the same. Thus after the acquittal on grounds of
self defence of charges of attempted murder and wounding with intent to
do grievous bodily harm, the officers involved in the Steven Waldorf

shooting were fully protected from disciplinary action for unnecessary violence by the statutory rule in Section 11 of the 1976 Act.

The similarity of the charges affects the possibility of disciplinary action if there is an acquittal or if no prosecution is brought. The Government although forced by Parliament to accept a new disciplinary offence of 'racially discriminatory behaviour' has otherwise failed to respond to deficiencies in the discipline code especially as highlighted by the PCB where certain types of serious misconduct cannot be easily included within an appropriate disciplinary charge. A clear example is abuse of power in connection with stop and search or search of premises. 'We are not happy that the only disciplinary offence with which an officer can be charged if he abuses his authority in such a way that his misconduct does not fit precisely into one of three categories in paragraph 8 of the Police Discipline Code is the offence of discreditable conduct....(29)

Secondly, the decision in Madden and Rhone needs to be given statutory force. It is too vital an aspect of the police complaints system to be left to administrative guidance, which could be influenced by the need of the Government of the day to appease one strong pressure group or another. There is also the risk of the judgement being over-ruled or simply ignored or minimised in practice. It is regrettable that the Government resisted an amendment to the Police and Criminal Evidence Bill which would have simply provided that a decision not to prosecute should not be regarded as an acquittal for the purposes of the double jeopardy rule.

Non-Disclosure Of Statements

On two recent occasions the Court of Appeal has conferred 'public interest' privilege on statements obtained for the purposes of investigating police complaints: Neilson -v- Laugharne (30) and Hehir -v- Commissioner of Police for the Metropolis (31). The Court feared that the prospect of disclosure was likely to inhibit both public and police co-operation and candour and prevent a full and proper investigation of complaints.

Two distinct issues arise in this connection:

a) Protection Of The Innocent

JUSTICE and other groups have pressed for the disclosure of evidence obtained during an investigation which points to the innocence of someone awaiting trial or already convicted. In Neilson Lord Justice Oliver stated, 'If public policy prevents disclosure, it prevents it in all circumstances except to establish innocence in criminal proceedings'. (32) Neither of the other Appeal judges considered this point, and whether Oliver, L.J.'s view holds true for an appeal out of time, as well as pending proceedings, have not been tested. Further, in practical terms, there is at present no mechanism to alert someone defending criminal proceedings to the availability of such evidence.

b) Inequality Before The Law

So long as investigations of complaints remain in the hands of the police the police as defendants in any civil action will, without disclosure, always be in an advantaged position. Unless a plaintiff has been advised not to co-operate with the investigation until the civil action is concluded, the police will have, protected by privilege, all of the statements supporting the complaint which they can utilise in cross examination. The police statements, however, remain inaccessible to the plaintiff/complainant.

Many complainants are not aware of the strength of their case when they make their complaint. It frequently happens that the investigation discloses police misconduct beyond that described in the complaint. If the complainant could have access to the relevant statements at discovery (or, ideally, pretrial discovery) then he or she could make an informed decision as to whether to bring, or to continue, civil proceedings. In some instances the complainant may have suffered a loss in relation to a third party as a result of police misconduct, for example, dismissal from employment after a wrongful arrest; without documentation to support the allegations against the police the complainant may not be able to establish his or her other claim.

From the accused officer's point of view, the protection given to statements restricts a possible action in defamation to the contents of the initial letter or statement of complaint only.

The Government strenuously resisted amendments which would reverse the Neilson and Hehir decisions by removing the privileged status of statements obtained for the purposes of investigating complaints. Opposition MPs pointed out the contradictions in the present position where various senior police officers, the DPP, the PCB/PCA and the police authority may see the statements but not the parties directly involved. Yet the Government persisted in its view that if there were even the possibility of disclosure at the discovery stage in civil proceedings then some witnesses, including colleagues of the police officer or friends and family of the complainant, would be unwilling to make full, frank statements during the complaint investigation.

What is already emerging, well before the new scheme is operative, is the wide areas within the provisions of the Act which can be used by the Home Secretary to control and shape the complaints procedure to his own liking or, to the liking of the strong police pressure groups whom he clearly does not want to alienate. The detailed way in which the complaints system under the 1984 Act will operate and how it will respond to and affect the interests of both the public and the police still depends on the regulations and guidance which the Home Secretary is yet to issue (or even to present in draft form for public comment). There is, in theory, the potential for a scheme which is more, rather than less, responsive to public concerns about policing.

However, to maximise the independent elements within the new scheme would mean maximising not only the cost in financial terms but also the risk of opposition by senior police officers. The close, symbiotic relationship between the Government and the police, which has been particularly highlighted during the miners' strike, suggests to this writer that the present Government would not be prepared to take such a risk at this time. Thus still longer must we wait for a Government (and the police) to acknowledge the benefits to policing which would accrue by the establishment of a complaints system which attracts public support and confidence and even longer still, it would seem, for there to be sufficient political will to implement such a system.

NOTES

1. Sir Robert Mark, In the Office of Constable, Fontana, 1979, p.213.

2. Derek Humphry, Police Power and Black People, Panther, 1972, p.170.

3. Patricia Hewitt, A Fair Cop, NCCL, 1982, p.5.

4. Police Complaints Board Triennial Review Report, 1980 HMSO Cmnd. 7966 para. 68.

5. Lord Scarman, The Scarman Report: The Brixton Disorders 10-12 April 1981 Penguin 1982 (Originally published in 1981 as Cmnd. 8427 by HMSO) para. 4.2

6. Ibid. para 7.21.

7. Ibid., para 7.23.

8. Home Affairs Committee, Fourth Report, Session 1981-82, Police Complaints Procedure, HMSO HC98-1 para. 21.

9. Memorandum submitted by the Police Federation of England and Wales, Minutes of Evidence 9 December 1981, House of Commons Home Affairs Committee, paragraph 6.

10. Home Affairs Committee, op. cit., para. 55.

11. The Government Reply to the Fourth Report from the Home Affairs Committee, Session 1981-2m HC98-1, Police Complaints Procedure, HMSO, Cmnd 8681. Oct. 1982.

12. White Paper, Police Complaints and Discipline Procedures, HMSO, October 1983, Cmnd. 9072.

13. Taken from Reports of Her Majesty's Chief Inspector of Constabulary for the years in question and Reports of the Commissioner of Police of the Metropolis for 1982 and 1983.

14. Police Federation of England and Wales, Police and Criminal Evidence Bill - OUR VIEW (undated).

15. White Paper, 1983, op. cit., para. 49.

16. Lord Elton, Hansard, 11 July 1984, col. 990.

16a. Scarman op.cit., para 5.42.

17. Tony Jefferson and Roger Grimshaw, Controlling the Constable, Frederick Muller/Cobden Trust, 1984, p.130.

18.	David J. Smith and Jeremy Gray, Police and People in London IV Police in Action Policy Studies Institute, 1983, p.71-2.

19.	Michael McConville, Search of Persons and Premises: New Data from London, Criminal Law Review [1983] p.612.

20.	As quoted by PC Harry Templeton, in Police Review, 1 September 1978.

21.	Philip Stevens and Carole Willis, Ethnic Minorities & Complaints against the Police Paper 5, Home Office Research and Planning Unit, 1981, p.13.

22.	Ibid. Table 7, p.16.

23.	Reports of the Police Complaints Board 1982 and 1983, HMSO. N.B. Nearly 50% of all complaints are withdrawn.

24.	Paper 19, 1983.

25.	Appendix B, Memorandum to Home Affairs Committee, 1981.

26.	Patricia Hewitt. The Abuse of Power, Martin Robertson, 1982, p.73.

27.	Connelly -v- DPP [1964] AC 1254.

28.	Appendix B, White Paper Oct. 1983 op. cit.

29.	Police Complaints Board Triennial Review Report 1983 HMSO. Cmnd. 8853 para 4.8.

30.	[1980] 1QB 736.

31.	[1982] WLR 715.

32.	Neilson at p.753.

Notes on Contributors

John Baxter is a Lecturer in Law at the University College of Wales, Aberystwyth. He is active in Housing Aid and Citizens' Advice work and he specialises in Constitutional, Public and Welfare Law. He is the author of several articles on these and related subjects.

Melissa Benn is a freelance journalist based in London. She has a particular interest in civil liberties and women's rights. Together with Anna Coote and Tess Gill, she is author of The Rape Controversy (N.C.C.L.).

William Bingley is Assistant Director (Legal Services) of MIND, the National Association for Mental Health, a charity concerned with improving services for mentally ill and mentally handicapped people and their families.

Paul Boateng is a solicitor and, since 1981, has been Chairman of the Police Committee of the Greater London Council. He serves, inter alia, on the Labour Party Joint Committee on Crime and Policing. In addition, he is a writer and presenter of radio programmes.

Mike Brogden is a Principal Lecturer in the Department of Social Studies at Liverpool Polytechnic. He is a well-known authority on the police and policing history and he has written a number of works on these subjects, including recently The Police: Autonomy and Consent (Academic Press, 1982).

Brian Campbell is a Senior Probation Officer based in Staffordshire. He has also been a Tutor with the Open University. He is Chairman of both the local Police Liaison Committee and the Staffordshire Youth and Community and Careers Service.

Barbara Cohen is a solicitor in private practice and former Legal Officer of the N.C.C.L. During the passage of the new legislation, she was responsible for briefing M.P.s on the proposed police complaints system. She is co-author of the N.C.C.L.'s forthcoming guide to the Police and Criminal Evidence Act 1984.

Richard de Friend is a Lecturer in Law at the University of Kent, having formerly been a Visiting Professor at the University of San Diego. His specialist academic interests are Constitutional and Administrative Law, the Sociology of Law, and Welfare Rights.

Laurence Koffman is a Lecturer in Law at the University College of Wales, Aberystwyth. His main interests are Criminal Law, Criminal Justice, Penology and civil liberties. He is the author of a number of academic articles on both the Criminal Law and its administration.

Michael Molyneux is a barrister and Principal Lecturer in Law at Ealing College of Higher Education. He is well-known to the public for his regular appearances on B.B.C. television's legal affairs programme, Out of Court.

Christopher Price is currently Pro-Assistant Director of the Polytechnic of the South Bank. He is probably better known in his former role as M.P. for Lewisham West. It was as a prospective M.P. that he became involved in the Confait Case and it was largely due to his efforts that the miscarriage of justice was discovered.

Philip Rawlings is a Lecturer in Law at the University College of Wales, Aberystwyth. He has a particular interest in Administrative and Welfare Law, as well as Legal History. He is deeply concerned about the social application of the law and he is actively involved in Housing Aid work.

Robert Reiner has taught at Bristol University since 1969, first in the Department of Sociology and now as Lecturer in the Sociology of Law. He is well established as an authority on policing and, in addition to several articles on the subject, he is the author of The Blue-Coated Worker (Cambridge Univ. Press, 1978) and The Politics of the Police (Wheatsheaf/St. Martin's, 1985).

Stephen Sedley is a successful barrister (Inner Temple) and a Q.C. He is a prominent civil libertarian and he specialises in Administrative, Employment and Public Interest Law.

Marie Staunton is a solicitor and a Legal Officer of the N.C.C.L. She has previously worked in private practice and in a Law centre. She also has experience of running hostels for addicts and alcoholics. She is responsible for the N.C.C.L.'s work on privacy and she is author of the N.C.C.L.'s guide to the Data Protection Act 1984 and co-author of the guide to the Police and Criminal Evidence Act.

Steve Uglow has taught at the University of Kent since 1973, after earlier experience as an Associate in Law at the University of California, Berkeley. He is a Lecturer in Law and has a particular interest in Criminal Law, the police and the prison system.

John Williams is a Lecturer in Law at the University College of Wales, Aberystwyth. He is Chairperson of the Mid-Wales Family Conciliation Service and he specialises in Family and International Law. He has written several academic articles on a number of legal subjects, including Criminal Law and civil liberties.

Accountability 237–244
complaints and local authorities 241
consultation in London 242–244
data protection 215–217
force independence 67
local government, miners' strike 239–241
National Reporting Centre 239–240
nature of 63
police authorities, number of, 81
policing by consent 62, 73
provincial forces 238–239
race relations 178
Watch Committees 66

Arrest 52–56
breach of the peace 54–55
damages where unlawful 52
detention for questioning 53
false imprisonment 95
general conditions 56, 141
inducement of confession 6, 56
obstruction of highway 53–54, 132
obstruction of a police officer 53–56, 155
possession of offensive weapon 97
racial distribution 166–169, 178
search after arrest 96

**Cautioning, as alternative
to prosecution,** 19–20, 105
Codes of Practice
detention and questioning 11, 27
effect of breach 43–44
entry, search & seizure 228–232
mentally ill & handicapped
persons 118
stop & search & race 178

Community Policing 72–86
communal policing 77
Community Involvement Unit 83
Community Relations Branch 74
Home Office Circular 82
race relations 171
technology, and, 203–204 ·

Complaints 246–265
American experience 262
blacks and Asians 170–171
Conciliation 252–253
disciplinary offence, of racially
discriminatory behaviour 255–256
Double-Jeopardy Rule 262–264
inequality before the law 264

legal representation for police
officers 254–255
local authorities, role of 241
Madden, Errol 263–264
Miners' Strike (1984/85) 258
new sheme 249–253
non-disclosure of statements
264–265
police investigating themselves
258–261
prosecutions arising from 253–256
Roach, Colin, death of 257
Scarman's proposals 248
Section 32 Inquiries 256–258
Southall, 1979 257
statistics 261
Waldorf, Steven, shooting of
257–258

Confait, Maxwell see Confessions
Confessions 111–117 See also
Interrogation
belief of 23, 112–113
Confait, Maxwell 13–14, 19, 27,
111–117
importance to policing 105
police evidence 23, 113–114
reliability 12

**Confidential Information (See
also Entry, Search and Seizure)**
ACPO agreement with BMA
220–221
breach of confidence 214
BMA, views on 220
Church of England, views on 222
juvenile liaison meetings 206
Law Society, views on 221–222
medical records 220–234
NUJ, Code of Conduct 232
special treatment for journalists
222–226

Data Protection 202–217
accountability 215–217
computer linkage 215
Data Protection Act 1984
208–213
European Convention, Art.8 207
Lindop Committee 203
subversives 206

Entry, Search and Seizure 219-234
access conditions 229-231
Code of Practice 228, 232
confidential material, access
  by warrant 231-232
special procedure 226-232
excluded material, 228
journalistic material 226-228
legally privileged material 221-222
NUJ Code of Conduct 232
Official Secrets Act 1911
  Sec 2 229, 231
power of seizure 232
reasonableness 50
search by consent 50
serious arrestable offence,
  relevance 229

Evidence
confessions 111-117
exclusion of unfairly obtained
  evidence 27-30
exclusionary rule 17, 114
rape victims 126

Firearms 191-200
advice by Police Federation 195
guidelines on issue 195-199
law on issue 195
statistics 191-193
training 194
use in USA 176
Waldorf, Steven, shooting of 190,
  257-258
weapons issued 191-192

Guilty Pleas and Plea Bargaining 106

Harassment by Police
call for 79
of black people 149, 153
of prostitutes 129

Independent Prosecution System:
  See Prosecution System

Industrial Deviance 144-145

Industrial Disputes (See also
  Miners' Strike 1984/85)
computerised monitoring 207
neutrality of policing 65
strikes 66-67

Interrogation (See also
  Confessions)
Code of Conduct 11, 27, 43-44,
  118
Confait, Maxwell, see confessions
"detention for questioning" 53
exclusionary rule 17
Judges' Rules 12, 17, 27-28, 50,
  114
mentally handicapped persons 115
rape victims 125-126
right of silence 13-14
tape-recording 23-26, 115
unfairly obtained evidence 27-30

Judges' Rules: See Interrogation

Juries
confession evidence 113
trial 9

Lesbians 133

Madden, Errol 14, 104, 263-264

Malone, James 213-214, 216

Media Image of Police 45-47

Mental Health
Code of Practice 118
stress among police officers 121
training of police 121

**Mentally ill and handicapped
  persons** 118-122
confessions by 111-117
power to detain 119-120
removal to place of safety 119
statistics on detention 119

Methods of Policing (See also
  **Community Policing &
  Technology**)
Community Involvement Units 83
Community Relations Branch 74
District Support Units 80
"fire brigade policing" 202
Instant Response Units 80
mutual aid 39, 63, 241
Neighbourhood Watch 81, 82
Police Support Units 63, 68, 80
policing by objectives 69
"pro-active policing" 143

Methods of Policing (Contd.)
saturation policing 79, 80, 100,
103, 153
Special Patrol Group 68, 76, 79
Tactical Firearms Units 68
targetting 82, 178, 203
"unit beat policing" 202

Miners' Strike (1984/85) 62-71,
239-241
complaints arising from 258
mutual aid 39, 63, 241
National Reporting Centre 63-64,
68, 81, 239-241
road blocks 52, 64, 240-241
women and policing 132

National Reporting Centre:
See Miners' Strike

Offences
assaulting a police officer 54-55
breach of the peace 54-55
domestic violence 127-129
mugging 74-76, 167-168
obstruction of a police
officer 15, 53-55, 101, 132, 155
obstruction of the highway
53-54, 132
offences connected with
prostitution 129
Official Secrets Act 1911, Sec 2 224-225
possession of offensive weapon 97
rape 125-127

Operation Swamp 79-80, 100, 103

Policy Studies Institute Report
Findings
police attitudes to violence 81
race relations 155, 163-165,
171, 173
stop and search 94, 99-100

Politics and the Police (See also
Rule of Law) 8, 14-16, 40-41, 83-84

Press
freedom of information, International
Commission 233
NUJ Code of Conduct, sources 232
official secrets, sources 227-228
special treatment, as to
confidentiality 222-226

use of by police in public
relations 45-47

Probation Service 140-147
inter-agency co-operation
143-144
role of social work 145

Prosecution System 18-23, 115

Prostitution 129

Public Order Equipment 68, 80

Public Protest (See also Riots)
anti-Poor Law riots 65
chartists 65
computerised monitoring 207
Greenham Common 130-131
Hunger March 1932 66
Molesworth Airbase 52
National Unemployed Workers
Movement 66

Questioning of suspects: See
Confessions and Interrogation

Race Relations 149-178
accountability 178
American research findings
157-161
arrest rates 166-169, 178
black attitudes, PSI findings 173
black women and the police
130-131
British research findings 161-175
charging and prosecution practice
169-170
community policing 177
complaints against police 170-171
disciplinary offence of racially
discriminatory behaviour 255-256
discriminatory behaviour by police
151-153
equality of treatment by police
156-157, 173
observational research of police
practice 171-173
police attitudes, 161-164,
173-176
police harassment of black people
149
police practice 164-173

Race Relations (Contd.)
Policy Studies Institute Report
 findings 151, 163-164, 171
racial attacks 154-156
recent police reforms 175-179
Scarman's findings 177
stop and search 93, 165-166,
 177-178
targetting 178

Rape 125-127

Reasonable Force 188-200
use by mistake 189-191
use in prevention of crime 188
use in self-defence 189
Waldorf, Steven, shooting of 190

**Reasonable Suspicion for Stop
 and Search** 17, 51, 93-98, 107

Reasonableness
exercise of discretion 7, 43
search and seizure 50

Riots
Bristol 1980 154
race riots 150-151
riots of 1981 75-76, 78-80,
 151, 155
Southall 1979 257
women and 1981 riots 130

Roach, Colin, death of 257

Road Blocks and Checks
Miners' Strike 1984/85 64
Molesworth Airbase 52
stopping of pickets 52

Rule of Law 38-57
authoritarianism 140-141, 144,
 168, 178
crime control taking precedence 141
Dicey, Professor A.V. 42
discretionary power 7, 42-43, 142
due process 104
equality before the law 44-49, 173, 258,
 261, 264-265
impartial law enforcement 156-157
industrial deviance 144-145
Law and Order contrasted 40-41, 142
police effectiveness 40, 62, 69, 219
police lawbreaking 9, 17, 44-45, 51

police legitimacy 63, 69, 178,
 244

Sageguards in Criminal Process
 11-31

**Scarman, Lord Scarman's Inquiry,
 (1981)** 76, 79, 177, 242-243,
248, 255-256

**Search and Seizure: See Entry,
 Search and Seizure**

Social Control
stop and search as means of
 106, 108

**Specialist Units: See Methods of
 Policing**

Stop and Search 91-110
American-practice 97
Code of Practice 178
consent to 101
discriminatory practice 98-99
due process 51
effect on public relations 15, 102
equipment for use in theft 97-98
harassment 79
local powers 92, 106-108
offensive weapons 97-98
on entry to private premises 97
police efficiency 101
race relations 93, 165-166,
 177-178
reasonable suspicion 17, 51,
 93-94, 97-98, 107
Royal Commission on Criminal
 Procedure 92, 96-97
safeguards 51, 95
Scottish practice 100
social control 108
strip searches 79-80
"war against crime" 99

Subversives 77-90
computers 206
enemy within 41, 83

SuS Law 96

Tape Recording of Interrogations
Criminal Law Revision
 Committee's view 24

Tape Recording of Interrogations (Contd.)
field trials in Britain 25, 115
Royal Commission on Criminal
 Procedure's view 24-25
Scottish experience 26

Technology
community policing 203-204
Computer Installations:
 Driver and Vehicle Licensing Centre 203
 Metropolitan Police 211
 Northern Ireland 202
 Police National Computer 203-205, 215
 provincial 205, 215-216
computerised monitoring of vehicles 207
criminal information and
 intelligence 203
Neighbourhood Watch, relationship
 to 206, 208
police authorities, response to 215
telephone tapping 213-214, 216

Telephone Tapping: See Technology

Tisdall, Sarah 44, 224-225

Waldorf, Steven, shooting of 190,
 257-258

Warrants
access to confidential information
 231-232
magistrate's warrant to search 50

Women and the Police 124-137
black women 130-131
domestic violence 127-129
Greenham Common 130-131
Lesbians 133
Miners' Strike 1984/85 132
police officers 133-134
prostitution 129
rape victims 125-127
statistics of crimes reported 136